PINCKNEY'S TREATY

America's Advantage from Europe's Distress, 1783–1800

Pinckney's Treaty

America's Advantage from Europe's
Distress, 1783–1800

by Samuel Flagg Bemis

GREENWOOD PRESS, PUBLISHERS
WESTPORT, CONNECTICUT

Library of Congress Cataloging in Publication Data

Bemis, Samuel Flagg, 1891-
    Pinckney's treaty; America's advantage from
Europe's distress, 1783-1800.

    Reprint of the ed. published by Yale University
Press, New Haven, which was issued as Y-24 of A Yale
paperbound.
    Bibliography: p.
    1. San Lorenzo Treaty, 1795. 2. United States--
Foreign relations--Spain. 3. Spain--Foreign
relations--United States. 4. Mississippi Valley--
History--To 1803. I. Title.
[E313.B44 1973]   327.73'046   73-8148
ISBN 0-8371-6954-2

© *1960 by Yale University Press, Inc.*

This edition originally published in 1960 by
Yale University Press, New Haven

Reprinted with the permission of Yale University Press

Reprinted in 1973 by Greenwood Press,
a division of Williamhouse-Regency Inc.

Library of Congress Catalogue Card Number 73-8148

ISBN 0-8371-6954-2

Printed in the United States of America

To
MY WIFE

Preface

DURING some years of study of the history of American foreign policy and diplomacy, I have increasingly marveled at its unparalleled successes in the eighteenth and nineteenth centuries. I have come to the conclusion that this good fortune is to be explained not so much by the undoubted ability of our natural statesmen (Franklin, Washington, Hamilton, Jefferson, the two Adamses, Monroe) who laid the foundations of our foreign policy in the first half-century of our independence, as it is by a fortuitous and nonrecurring geopolitical situation in the world, to which we owe not only our independence itself and the liberation of our western territories after the Revolutionary War, but also the preservation of our nation and its expanded territory during the War of 1812, and its further expansion through to the Pacific Ocean. The establishment of the Continental Republic and its preservation during the Brothers' War of 1861–1865 represents the greatest single achievement of American nationality. For better or worse, it gave us the territorial basis of our position as a world power today.

In numerous writings I have suggested that these diplomatic successes were due, most briefly put, to:

(1) Our detached and distant geographical position.
(2) America's advantage from Europe's distress.
(3) The circumstance of Canada as a hostage for Anglo-American peace after 1818; later (to use Mackenzie King's famous phrase) as a linchpin for Anglo-American solidarity.

So foolproof was our position that we were able to indulge in a great civil war without any lesion to our territory or foreign policy. What European nation could have done so? The United States could not do so in the present century.

Professor J. Fred Rippy has developed the second of the above factors in his interesting book on *America and the Strife of Europe* (Chicago, 1938), and very recently Professor C. Vann Woodward in a most thoughtful paper read to the American Historical Association on December 28, 1959, has put forth the thesis that "free security" during those centuries and indeed down to the advent of the Second World War was as important a factor in American national life as "free land" and the expanding frontier.

My own thoughts first directed themselves to America's advantage from Europe's distress when over a third of a century ago I undertook, with multiarchival research, the preparation of two successive books on the twin treaties of President George Washington's Administration: Jay's Treaty of 1794 with Great Britain, and Pinckney's Treaty of 1795 with Spain, the first two treaties negotiated [1] under our present form of government. They are essentially case histories.

I have presumed to baptize the document Pinckney's Treaty, though it is traditionally called the treaty of San Lorenzo, only because Thomas Pinckney opportunely signed it, and thus to bracket it more appositely with Jay's Treaty.

The present volume is a new edition of the second of the above-mentioned studies, a narrative expanded

1. The Consular Treaty with France was negotiated under the Confederation, but approved by the United States Senate shortly after the inauguration in 1789 of the new government of the Constitution of 1787.

from a contribution in 1926 to the Albert Shaw Lectures
on Diplomatic History at The Johns Hopkins University
and published by The Johns Hopkins Press (Baltimore,
1926, 2nd printing, 1941). I have slightly abridged the
introductory chapter, and have taken the present opportunity afforded by the Yale University Press to clean up
the all too many persistent typographical errors and
inconsistencies in the earlier prints. I have also added
references to some new publications in the same field.
Miss Helen C. Boatfield and Mrs. Marian Neal Ash
assisted me with the preparation of this present volume
for the press. I renew the numerous acknowledgments
made in general in the earlier Prefaces of 1926 and
1941, and now in particular to that distinguished scholar
of Spanish American and Latin American history, Professor Arthur P. Whitaker, who began his independent
researches in Spanish archives very shortly after I had
commenced mine.

SAMUEL FLAGG BEMIS

Yale University
April 1960

Contents

Chapter 1. Introduction: Origin of the Mississippi Question and the Boundary Dispute 1

Chapter 2. The Mississippi Question and Other Issues with Spain 37

Chapter 3. Gardoqui and Jay 60

Chapter 4. Congress and the Negotiation 81

Chapter 5. Further Negotiation, 1786–1788 91

Chapter 6. James Wilkinson and the "Spanish" Conspiracy 109

Chapter 7. Spanish Policy and the American West 126

Chapter 8. "Patience and Persuasion" 149

Chapter 9. More Patience and More Persuasion 163

Chapter 10. Godoy's Propositions for the President and Their Fate 198

Chapter 11. Jay's Treaty and Its Effect 218

Chapter 12. Pinckney's Treaty 245

Chapter 13. Conclusion 294

Appendix   I. Bibliographical Note 317

Appendix II. The Financial Debt of the United States to Spain and Its Payment; Loans and Subsidies 325

Appendix III. Pinckney's Sketches of a Treaty and Drafts of Proposed Articles 335

Appendix IV. Execution of the Spoliations Article (XXI) of the Treaty of 1795 341

Appendix V. Official Text of the Treaty of 1795 343

Index 363

Maps

Map 1. Boundary Lines Suggested by Jay, Aranda, Vergennes and Rayneval during the Peace Negotiations at Paris, August–September, 1782   33

Map 2. Indian Nations in Relation to Territory Disputed by the United States and Spain, 1783–1795   49

Map 3. Spain's Claims to Territory East of the Mississippi River and Successive Concessions Allowed in Instructions to Gardoqui, 1784–1787   67-70

Map 4. Proposed Separatist State, 1794, and Proposed Mutual Guarantees of Territory with Spain   215

KEY TO ABBREVIATIONS USED
IN FOOTNOTES

A.C.A.—Archivo Central de Alcalá. See G.D., below.

A.G.C.—Archivo General Central, Simancas, Spain. Most references to these documents are to the transcripts in the Library of Congress (L.C. trans.). References are by *legajo* (Leg.), i.e., bundle numbers.

A.G.I.—Archivo General de Indias, Seville, Spain. Most references are to Library of Congress transcripts, with citations of original archival numbers.

A.H.N.—Archivo Histórico Nacional, Madrid. References are generally to the Sección de Estado (Est.) by *legajo* (Leg.) numbers, viz.: A.H.N., Est. Leg., 3881.

A.H.R.—American Historical Review.

Arch. Aff. Étrang.—Archives of the Ministry of Foreign Affairs, Paris.

A.S.P., F.R.—American State Papers, Foreign Relations.

A.S.P., I.A.—American State Papers, Indian Affairs.

A.S.P., Com. & Navig.—American State Papers, Commerce and Navigation.

Despatches—Department of State, Despatches from United State Ministers abroad. Usually listed by countries, viz.: Despatches, Great Britain.

Dip. Corres.—Diplomatic Correspondence of the United States, 1783–1789, 7 vols. (Washington, 1833–34).

Domestic Letters—Department of State, Domestic Letters.

Est.—Sección de Estado (section).

Expdte.—*Expediente* (*dossier*) within a *legajo*.

G.D.—Gardoqui Despatches in the Durrett Collection of the University of Chicago Library, being transcripts of originals formerly in the Archivo Central de Alcalá (A.C.A.), of which original section (Est.) and bundle (Leg.) numbers are also cited, but which are now in the Archivo Histórico Nacional in Madrid.

Hague and Spain—Department of State, Despatches of Wm. Short from The Hague and Spain.

Instructions—Department of State, Instructions to United States Ministers abroad.

L.C.—Library of Congress.

L.C. trans.—Library of Congress transcripts.

Leg.—*Legajo* (bundle).

Spanish Legation—Papers of the Spanish Legation at Washington (also at Philadelphia previously) in the Departamento de Estado, i.e., Department of State building, Madrid.

Wharton—*Revolutionary Diplomatic Correspondence of the United States,* Francis Wharton, editor, 6 vols. (Washington, 1889).

CHAPTER 1

Introduction: Origin of the Mississippi Question and the Boundary Dispute

I

"I say no, no, no, my cousin is losing altogether too much; I do not want him to lose anything in addition for my sake, and would to Heaven that I could do yet more for him."

So said Charles III of Spain on the thirteenth day of November, 1762, when the French Ambassador at Madrid thrust into his hands the deed for the vast province of Louisiana, insofar as it extended to the west of the Mississippi, with the added "island" of New Orleans, on the east side of the river near its mouth. The Spanish monarch knew full well, as he voiced these generous sentiments, that his royal kinsman, Louis XV of France, was anxious to get rid of Louisiana, that he had offered it in vain, during the recent peace negotiations in Paris, to the enemy as an equivalent for relinquishment of Havana, which had been captured by Great Britain from Spain toward the close of the Seven Years' War. But Great Britain had preferred Spanish Florida to the vast, unknown, and certainly unprofitable colony of Louisiana. Both of the Bourbon allies, France and Spain, had to acquiesce. Great Britain took Spanish Florida and released Cuba, and thus, having also secured Louisiana to the east of the river, became master of all North America on that

side of the Mississippi, with the sole exception of that
marshy lowland, south of the Iberville, where the city
of New Orleans now stands.[1] For the moment Florida
was preferable for British purposes. Louisiana, as that
territory to the west of the river is to be called from
now on, could wait. Because France retained the
"island" of New Orleans, the Mississippi still flowed
to the sea through two hundred miles of French territory on both banks. This fact is the beginning of the
Mississippi Question.

Why did the King of France feel obliged to compen-
sate his royal cousin for territorial losses sustained by
that ruler during the Seven Years' War? Because by
the terms of the Third Family Compact of 1761 and
the ancillary military alliance of 1762, the two kings
had agreed to share all their territorial profits and
losses as a result of the war which Spain had entered
so unwisely at the last moment. There remained nothing but losses for them to share. To induce Spain
despite her losses to make the quick peace so necessary
to France, Choiseul, the French Minister, offered the
compensation of Louisiana, a land of great potential
value. To persuade Louis XV to make the sacrifice, he
represented the province as it seemed then to be, a
colonial white elephant.

Misgovernment and neglect had made it a pauper
province. It had cost the King of France every year far
more than it brought in directly or indirectly to the
French crown or nation. So Louis XV believed himself
to be palming it off on his royal relative and ally. With
some misgivings the chivalrous King of Spain accepted

1. A. I. Aiton, "The Diplomacy of the Louisiana Cession," *A. H. R.*,
XXXVI, 701–720, has thrown new light on the text of the article by
W. R. Shepherd, "The Cession of Louisiana to Spain," *Pol. Sci. Quar.*,
XIX, 438–458.

it. It was better to have it as a bulwark and buffer to New Spain than to leave it, ultimately to fall or to be traded into the hands of the British. Such aggressive neighbors might mean the loss of Mexico itself and the eventual downfall of all Spain's colonial empire in America.[2]

When Louis XV thus transferred Louisiana on to his kinsman and ally it was saddled with a servitude which a few days previously had been written into the preliminary articles of the Peace of Paris. Because France had been left the "island" of New Orleans and thereby the control of both banks of the Mississippi, south of the Iberville, it had been necessary for Great Britain, which now held the vast domains along the whole east bank above, to secure navigation rights through French territory to the sea. Article VII of the definitive Anglo-French treaty stipulated:

It being well understood that the navigation of the Mississippi River shall be free equally to the subjects of Great Britain and to those of France, throughout all its length and breadth, from its source to the sea, and particularly that part of it which is between the above-said island of New Orleans and the right bank of this river, as well as entrance and exit by its mouth; it is further stipulated that the vessels belonging to the subjects of either nation cannot be stopped, visited, or subjected to the payment of any tax whatever.[3]

Because Louisiana, nothing being mentioned in the treaty to the contrary, would by the law of nations go to the new owner, Spain, burdened with all the obligations as well as loaded with all the advantages—if indeed it had any of the latter, in the politics of those days—it changed sovereignty with this servitude still

2. Ibid.
3. Martens, *Recueil des traités*, I, 39.

in force. Spain did not deny this. The servitude continued unchallenged until the outbreak of hostilities
between that country and Great Britain in 1779, when
war naturally canceled all treaties between the two
countries and with it the right of British subjects to
navigate the lower reaches of the Mississippi. Until
then Spain, we repeat, did not deny the right of British
subjects to sail in and out of the river from the Gulf
of Mexico, but she did her best to vitiate that right,
after 1769, by refusing to allow those ships to moor on
shore, or to permit a British officer or sailor to set foot
on Spanish soil.[4] We shall see that this possibility of
frustrating the right of navigation introduces a new
complication into the Mississippi Question.

For the purpose of our study we may dismiss the
Question of the Mississippi for a few pages, while we
turn to the boundaries of Florida. They will play an
important part in the diplomatic history which will be
the subject of this monograph.

For nearly two hundred years following the discovery of North America Spain and France had been
rivals on that continent. In the dynastic wars of the
sixteenth and seventeenth centuries Spain would not
recognize the legal right of France to possess colonies
or territory in the New World, which was claimed
exclusively by His Catholic Majesty—except for a
portion of South America now comprising Brazil—
under title of the papal demarcation bulls of 1493.
Nevertheless Francis I and subsequent kings of France
made grants to their subjects which completely ignored
the exclusive title of Spain. In the region of Florida

4. Vera Lee Brown, "Anglo-Spanish Relations in America in the
Closing Years of the Colonial Era," *Hispanic American Historical
Review*, V, 370.

and Carolina rival colonial expeditions of Frenchmen and Spaniards came into murderous conflict. Spain succeeded in colonizing and holding Florida, indefinitely bounded, while French pathfinders came down the Mississippi from the Great Lakes and laid claim to the interior valley of the continent on both sides of the river.

During the War of the Spanish Succession Spain and France became allies, and there was established that traditional connection so fatal to the former during the eighteenth and nineteenth centuries. The Treaty of Utrecht, 1713, contained a mutual recognition by France and Spain of each other's colonial possessions in North America but with no agreed boundary between them. The eastern and western boundaries of French Louisiana between 1713 and 1763—it then extended on both sides of the Mississippi—remained a matter of minor diplomatic contention while those two powers, through most of that period, stood jointly facing Great Britain in the wars of the eighteenth century. Precisely what was the boundary between Louisiana and New Spain, and between Louisiana and Florida, was never officially determined. After the Peace of Paris of 1763 all territory to the east of the Mississippi, except the "island" of New Orleans, having become British, the old Franco-Spanish boundary question between Louisiana and Florida of course disappeared, to be revived a little later for the benefit of American diplomacy after the independence of the United States.

For his own purposes of administration, the King of Great Britain, by the Proclamation of October 7, 1763, declared the boundary line between Georgia and Florida, and at the same time divided the latter province into two new provinces, East and West Florida. The northern boundary of East Florida by that proclamation coincided with the line between the present American states of Florida and Georgia, that is, the St. Mary's River to its source and from there due west to the Apalachicola, which now became the boundary between the two Floridas. The northern boundary of West Florida was made the line of 31° north latitude. On the west were the Mississippi and the Iberville, which bounded the still Spanish "island" of New Orleans and controlled the outlet of the Father of Waters to the sea.

The Proclamation of October 7, 1763, also set off as an Indian reserve the territory to the west of the watershed between the Mississippi Basin and the Atlantic-flowing streams.[5]

A further adjustment of British colonial boundaries to the east of the Mississippi must not escape our attention. In order to include some straggling settlements on the lower Mississippi, east bank, in what was known as the Natchez district, the Crown by another proclamation in 1774 moved the northern boundary of the recently created province of West Florida yet farther north to the latitude of the mouth of the Yazoo River where it flows into the Mississippi at the present city of Vicksburg. Thenceforth the northern boundary of West Florida was approximately 32° 30′ from the Mississippi east to the Chattahoochee; the eastern boundary of the province followed the Chattahoochee-Apalachicola watercourse southward to the Gulf of Mexico. It is important to bear these British boundaries in mind when we come to the reconquest of Florida by Spain in the War of the American Revolution.

5. C. W. Alvord, *The Mississippi Valley in British Politics*, passim.

II

The American Revolution immediately raised new problems for diplomacy in both the Old and the New World, and in some of these the Question of the Mississippi assumed increasing significance. The problems which will concern us here relate to the efforts of France and the United States to bring Spain into the war against Great Britain, if possible as the ally of the United States; the policy of Spain toward the United States following her actual intervention, in 1779, as the ally of France alone; and those issues pertaining to the Mississippi and the western and southern boundary of the United States which arose during the peace settlement at Paris in 1782, when it was the effort of French diplomacy to reconcile the diverging interests of Louis XVI's two separate allies.

The outbreak of hostilities between the American colonies and the mother country presented the opportunity for which many astute Frenchmen had been waiting ever since the humiliating Peace of Paris—of splitting apart the British Empire and of raising the power of France in the European scale proportionately to the abasement of Britain. The political religiosity of French public opinion toward the end of the eighteenth century beheld in American republican institutions the avatar of its own dreams and made it possible for French statesmen to direct their King and nation into the war against Great Britain as the ally of the United States with an enthusiastic popular support behind them.[6] But at first, while the chances of ultimate success of the United States were so uncertain, the Count de Vergennes, able French Minister for For-

6. B. Faÿ, *L'Esprit révolutionnaire en France et aux États-Unis à la fin du XVIII siècle*, 1–105.

eign Affairs after 1774, maintained a policy of watchful
waiting, meanwhile furnishing (together with Spain)
to the rebels secret aid in money and munitions to keep
the war going in North America. After the capitulation of Saratoga in October, 1777, it was apparent that
he might have to choose between recognition of the
independence of the United States and a consequent
treaty of alliance, with an excellent chance of winning
the war, and witnessing the Americans, thanks to the
prestige of the victory over Burgoyne's army, make an
acceptable peace within the British Empire. Vergennes
hastened to choose the former.[7] France became the
ally of the United States, and thanks to French intervention American independence was ultimately secured.

When the decision was made to recognize the United
States, Vergennes thought, or certainly desired, that
Spain would follow the French lead, but he did not
wait for official Spanish approval for this new step.

In 1776 Spain, then under the administration of
Grimaldi as Minister for Foreign Affairs, had been
willing to consider intervening, with French alliance,
in the war against Great Britain, because circumstances
had then presented an opportunity to conquer Portugal, Britain's traditional ally, with whom a serious
territorial dispute had evolved in South America. But
at that time Vergennes was not sure enough of the
chances of the United States for success against British
armies to dare to intervene, nor did he wish by the
Spanish acquisition of Portugal and Portuguese colonies to raise the power and prestige of Spain higher
than that of France. By December of 1777 the Portuguese-Spanish issue had been settled and Spain was

7. S. F. Bemis, "British Secret Service and the French-American
Alliance," *A. H. R.,* XXIX, 474–496.

under the guidance of a new Foreign Minister, the able Count of Floridablanca, who was anxious above all things not to serve as a catspaw for French diplomacy. He refused to be wholly convinced by Vergennes' impressive arguments that it was indispensably necessary for Spain to join with France in a preventive war against Great Britain because of the danger to Spanish and French American islands and continental colonies, a conquest of which might conceivably serve to occupy British military forces after an Anglo-American reconciliation; nor was he willing to go to war solely on the theory that any kind of serious damage to the British Empire would redound sufficiently to the advantage of Spain to pay for the trouble of the war.

France therefore, to the intense chagrin of her family ally, precipitately entered the war alone. The affair called for a speedy decision at the close of 1777, and the opportunity appealed to Vergennes as too good to pass by. In the Franco-American alliance of February 6, 1778, a separate and secret article provided for the future adhesion of Spain, with the privilege of proposing other conditions analogous to the principal aim of the alliance and conformable to the rules of equality, reciprocity, and friendship.[8]

From almost the first the Congress of the United States had been desirous of securing recognition from Spain of American independence, together with a treaty of friendship, commerce, and alliance, and had empowered its commissioners to the French Court to

8. See E. S. Corwin, *French Policy and the American Alliance*, 120–172; P. C. Phillips, *The West in the Diplomacy of the American Revolution*, 69–90; J. F. Yela Utrilla, *España ante la independencia de los Estados Unidos*, I, 242–343; H. Doniol, *Histoire de la participation de la France à l'établissement des États-Unis*, III, 1–87. Hereinafter these works will be cited by the author's name only.

open negotiations to that end. In 1777 Arthur Lee, one
of the three commissioners in Paris, had been sent by
his colleagues, Benjamin Franklin and Silas Deane,
on a mission to Madrid. For this purpose, Lee bore a
letter of introduction from the Count de Aranda,
Spanish Ambassador in Paris; but at Floridablanca's
direction he was met at Burgos by the Minister Grimaldi, then just retired from the Council, who persuaded the American emissary to return to Paris, after
giving him promises of financial assistance for the
revolted colonies, promises which were soon fulfilled.[9]
Congress already, on January 1, 1777, had appointed
Franklin as commissioner to Spain to negotiate a treaty
of friendship, leaving the direction of the negotiation
to Franklin's own discretion. Arthur Lee's recent experience and the advice of the Spanish Ambassador
determined Franklin not to leave Paris, for it was certain that he would not be received by the Spanish
Court. Spain already had furnished a million livres to
put with another million with which the King of
France was keeping alive the flames of rebellion in
America.[10] But even Grimaldi, an Italian by origin
and francophil in all his conceptions of foreign policy,
had hesitated about recognizing the independence of
the United States. For an absolute monarchy with
American colonies of her own thus to set a premium
on insurrection was a dangerous precedent from which
both he and his greater successor Floridablanca shrank
with utmost abhorrence. For this reason the Spanish
Council of State in 1776 had strongly advised against
such recognition.[11]

9. Yela, I, 161–181.
10. Yela, I, 99.
11. Yela, I, 143–157.

III

Don José de Moñino y Redondo, Count of Florida-blanca, succeeded Grimaldi as Foreign Minister of Spain on February 19, 1777. He remained in that position for the next fifteen years, during which time he exercised a supreme influence on the formation of Spanish foreign policy and the administration of affairs of state. He was born in Murcia in 1728 of middle-class parents, his father an army officer, who spared no pains to secure for his son an adequate education. Trained to the law by a university course, and by severe study as well, buttressed by his own rigorous self-discipline and honest ambition, he attracted as a young man the favor of influential patrons who opened to him a future in public service. After notable work as an advocate he was appointed to the judicial office of the Council of Castile, where he played a prominent part in the expulsion of the Jesuits. Himself of proud but humble origin, he was a constant enemy of privilege, ecclesiastical or lay, until the French Revolution frightened him, like his English contemporary Burke, into the sentiments of reaction. From 1772 to 1777 he served as Spanish Ambassador to the Holy See, where he won distinction and acquired insight into the international politics of his generation. He returned to Madrid in February, 1777, to exchange places with Grimaldi. Floridablanca's administration soon proved to be one of the most able and enlightened that Spain had experienced for many years, particularly in the reform of domestic abuses and the encouragement of the country's economic and educational progress. Unlike the Genoese Grimaldi, Floridablanca was a "Spaniard of Spaniards." An ascetic figure throughout his long life, his force of character, dignity, and ability raised him to the high-water mark of Spanish statesmanship during the eighteenth century. He was the Spanish counterpart of his English rival, the younger Pitt.

Floridablanca's logical mind had already conceived a foreign policy: speedy and cordial reconciliation with Portugal looking forward, by means of a dynastic marriage, to the achievement of a Spanish protectorate over that kingdom; and the emancipation of Spain from the guiding reins of French diplomacy. As a loyal ally of France, Spain must have an equal if not a directing voice in the Family Compact.[12] From the moment of his accession to office he also had a cleancut American policy. He agreed that it was desirable to keep the Anglo-American war going as long as possible, if only to weaken Great Britain, not to mention the colonies too. For this purpose Spain and France should keep flowing the stream of secret subsidies and military supplies to the American rebels.

He did not accept Aranda's eager advice to recognize the independence of the United States and to make a treaty of alliance with them which should include a mutual guaranty of territory. Aranda considered that, whether the American colonies should win their independence or not, Spain's possessions in North America were in the future certain to be endangered by the neighborhood of the aggressive Anglo-American settlements, that the wisest way to prevent this was by a treaty with the United States which, in return for Spain's entrance into the war, should guarantee Spain's contiguous colonial possessions. He urged this notwithstanding the danger, for the future, to Spain's sover-

12. The best biographical sketch of Floridablanca is A. Ferrer del Rio's biographical introduction to his *Obras originales del Conde de Floridablanca* (Madrid, 1887).

eignty over her own American colonies, in encouraging revolution. The independence of the American colonies from Great Britain, Aranda believed, was bound to happen eventually. The day would come, too, when Spain would likewise lose her colonies on the American continents. He would postpone that evil day by securing a guaranty from the new republic in North America.

Floridablanca believed, on the other hand, that without recognizing American independence, and perhaps without fighting a war with Great Britain, Spain could best secure her own interests by mediation between Great Britain and her revolted colonies, on the basis of establishing their independence *de facto* but not *de jure* by means of a long-time truce during which the colonies were to be placed under the joint protection of Spain' and France. In case the British Government should reject the mediation, the two Bourbon allies ought to be prepared for a joint war against that power and a jointly negotiated peace. In such a war it would not be enough for Spain to see the British Empire crippled by division—her own far-flung colonies made an adventure against British sea-power a greater risk to her than to France, and there must therefore be proportionately greater compensations in sight. Floridablanca specified his objectives: conquest of the British islands in America, or at least complete freedom to share in the Newfoundland fisheries; restoration to Spain of Gibraltar, Minorca, the Floridas, and clearance of the British from their settlements on the Honduran and Mosquito coasts of Central America, where they had got a dangerous vaguely-bounded lodgment by the terms of the Peace of Paris.[13]

13. Yela, I, 182–192.

After France, without waiting fully to consult Spain, had committed herself to the American cause, Floridablanca held aloof and persisted in his policy of mediation. A formal offer was made in 1779 to Great Britain and France of a truce on the basis of *uti possidetis* in America, which would have left the British in possession of Long Island, New York City, Georgia, and the Carolinas, as well as the northern frontier posts along the Great Lakes. By the terms of the mediation offer the truce was to be guaranteed by the two Bourbon monarchs. Fortunately for the United States the North Ministry rejected it, and thereby threw away an excellent chance to break up either the Franco-American alliance or the Bourbon Family Compact. The two family allies had anticipated the British refusal of mediation by signing (April 12, 1779) the secret Convention of Aranjuez, wherein they agreed to fight a common war and make a common peace against Great Britain, which peace *must* include the restoration to Spain of Gibraltar, and *if possible* other specified objectives: Minorca, the Floridas, Jamaica, and the fisheries.[14]

In this convention Spain carefully refrained from any recognition of the independence of the United States. Her policy toward the revolted American colonies had already been mapped out by Floridablanca, as we have seen. Meanwhile that minister had sent to Philadelphia an unaccredited official observer to gather on the spot first-hand information about the American Revolution, and the demands of the United States, for the guidance of Spanish policy.[15]

---

14. Corwin, 149–195; Phillips, 69–108; Yela, I, 305–371; Doniol, III, 742–798.

15. Yela, I, 385–388.

IV

Until the close of the year 1778 those who were
responsible for Spanish policy do not seem to have considered very seriously if at all the Question of the
Mississippi or the future boundary of the United States
on the south and west. Such questions naturally did not
arise so long as Great Britain and Spain remained at
peace. Floridablanca weighed well the advantages
which would redound to Spain from a conquest of the
British Floridas by placing the Gulf of Mexico under
a Spanish seal, and Spanish colonial administrators had
shown some nervousness lest the United States might
capture and retain some portions of the Floridas. Even
though this might cause some concern, much as Floridablanca professed to fear the possibility of an Anglo-
American reconciliation followed by an attack on
Spanish colonies, much as he distrusted American
independence as a future menace to Spain's American
possessions, the Mississippi navigation and the future
boundaries of the United States were not primary questions in his mind when war against Great Britain began. The Spanish Governor at New Orleans had, under
orders, given military succor to the American expedition under Willing which came down the Ohio and
attacked British settlements in West Florida. Floridablanca himself had stated to the French Ambassador at
Madrid in March, 1778, that the Mississippi constituted
a "boundary sufficiently definite and visible" between
the possessions of Spain and the United States.[16]

According to Professor Corwin,[17] the views finally
adopted by Spain in regard to the Mississippi Question

16. Corwin, 240.
17. Ibid., 243.

and the western and southern boundary originated in the brain of a Spanish official observer, Juan de Miralles, who reached Philadelphia in July, 1778. We do not know the nature of his first instructions.[18] Presumably they enjoined him merely to gather and send in information. On December 30, 1778, he wrote to Josef de Galvez, Minister of the Indies, in Madrid:

> Having arranged to confer in my house and in that of the French Minister with the new President of Congress [John Jay] and various members of it, I have explored (and the said plenipotentiary conspired to the same end) the idea which they hold as to the territory which the Americans have taken from the English in the interior of the Province of Louisiana, Illinois, etc., and on Florida in case they make conquest of it. In regard to the first we discovered, that it is that of encouraging, by means of a company already established, the settlement and cultivation of that vast and fertile country, promising that there will be 20,000 souls there inside of four years, and more than five thousand ready to bear arms; and that the population will increase proportionately in the future.
>
> That the right which they have acquired from the English by conquest would give them the facility of exporting their produce by the Mississippi River which flows into the Gulf of Mexico; and as to Florida [they intend] to make another province out of it and add it to the rest of the confederation.

To such ideas Miralles says he replied, supported by the officially accredited French Minister to the United States, Gérard. Miralles stated that, so far as Florida was concerned, it having been a former Spanish province the King of Spain would not be pleased to see it pass into the possession of other nations. Such states, with Florida in their possession, could never flatter themselves that they would enjoy perfect quiet and harmony with Spain. Therefore it was Spanish opinion

18. Yela's searches in the Spanish archives did not turn them up. See Yela, I, 387, note 1.

that the preparations for the conquest of Florida might
go ahead. In case Spain should change her system of
neutrality, Spanish naval cooperation might be available from Havana—the Floridas, of course, ultimately
to go to Spain. Miralles suggested that the United States
in that case would be indemnified for their military
expenses. These suggestions, it is needless to say, never
bore fruit.[19]

As to the project of settling the interior of "the
province of Louisiana"—this meant, of course, the old
Northwest Territory, much of which was once French
Louisiana before 1763—it was "our opinion"—i.e.,
the opinion of Gérard, the French Minister, and of
Miralles—that the isolation of that country and its
facility of communicating with the sea by the St. Lawrence and the Mississippi eventually would make it
economically and politically independent of the eastern
states; before that happened it would be better to sell
it to Spain for a good sum, money badly needed by the
struggling states.

> All these reflections and various others to the same end which
> followed so attracted the attention of the said President and
> Members that they found them very just and well founded and
> agreed that they would represent and explain them, with their
> support, to the Congress in full, in order that the mode in which
> propositions might be made to Spain might be considered.
> So far this is what we have been able to do for the present, we
> shall see what will result. . . .[20]

Miralles and Gérard found that some members of
Congress from the northern and eastern states, like
Gouverneur Morris, of New York—who wanted to

19. Corwin, 252.
20. Miralles to J. de Galvez, Phila., Dec. 30, 1778, A. G. I., Indiferente
General, 146/3/11 (L. C. trans.).

limit the confederacy particularly on the south and
west and who was convinced that the more virtuous
and sagacious qualities of human character were not
abundant beyond the mountains, whence hordes of
new citizens might eventually arise to throw the old
states and their leaders out of political power—were
willing to set bounds to the western lands and to yield
Spain everything she could have wished in that quarter.[21]

Congress had been requested by the Count de Vergennes, through Gérard, to formulate peace terms and
to appoint a plenipotentiary to represent the United
States in case the Spanish mediation should result in a
peace conference. These terms were at first drawn up
by a committee headed by Gouverneur Morris. The
Spanish mediation not being accepted by Great Britain,
no peace negotiations followed; but Congress debated
several months over the formulation of the terms, and
the discussion was still going on long after Spain actually entered the war (June, 1779). The cause of this
protracted debate on peace terms was the question
whether to demand as a *sine qua non* of any peace a
share in the inshore Newfoundland fisheries. As committees brought forth reports, and as separate articles
of instructions were debated, the Mississippi Question
and the boundaries were discussed in great detail, and
Congress gradually came to affirm and to take a more
decided stand on both.

On these last two matters, the committee of which
Gouverneur Morris was chairman took a precise and
positive stand in its original report. It recommended
as the southern and western boundaries of the United
States: "southerly by the boundary settled between

21. Corwin, 249.

Georgia and East and West Florida; and westerly by
the River Mississippi." [22] As if to make it unmistakably
clear the Congress considered these boundaries between
Georgia and the Floridas according to the definition of
the old Carolina charter of 1663. This article of the
report was soon modified by the committee of the whole
to read: "The middle of the River Mississippi from
its source to that part of the said river which lies in
the latitude 31 degrees north from the equator, then
by a line drawn due east to the river Apalachicola or
Catahouche, thence to the junction thereof with the
Flint river, then in a strait line to the head of St. Mary's
River, and thence by a line along the middle of St.
Mary's River to the Atlantic Ocean. . . ." [23] There
was no further debate on this, and the article in these
words was soon ratified by Congress, March 19, 1779.[24]
Thus at the outset the United States laid positive claim
to all the territory east of the Mississippi and north of
31° north latitude. Great Britain must agree to these
terms as a *sine qua non* and evacuate all its military
forces out of that territory.

Decision in regard to the navigation of the Mississippi was not so quickly reached. The committee
reported originally, February 23, 1779:

That the navigation of the River Mississippi, as low down as
the southern boundary of the United States, be acknowledged and
ratified absolutely free to the subjects of the United States.

That free commerce be allowed to the subjects of the United
States with some port or ports below the southern boundary of
the said states, on the River Mississippi, except for such articles
as may be particularly enumerated.

22. *Journals of the Continental Congress*, XIII, 241, Feb. 23, 1779.
23. Ibid., 329, March 17, 1779.
24. Ibid., 248.

Congress in committee of the whole modified this to read:

That the navigation of the River Mississippi be acknowledged and ratified absolutely free to the subjects of the United States.

This left it ambiguous, whether the "free" navigation of the "River Mississippi" meant to the sea, or merely down to the southern boundary of the United States. It might be interpreted either way. As consideration of the article proceeded, efforts were made to insert again the qualification which would limit that navigation to the southern boundaries of the United States,[25] but these failed. Gérard, the French Minister at Philadelphia, urged Congress to offer proper terms to His Catholic Majesty, in order to reconcile him perfectly to the American interest, and not to upset his mediation plans.[26] But Congress evolved more and more positive ideas about the navigation of the Mississippi, especially after it became known that the mediation had failed and that Spain had declared war on Great Britain. It then became a question of what terms to offer Spain to accede to the Franco-American alliance, and of appointing a minister from Congress to seek recognition and alliance at the Court of Madrid.

The debate finally turned on the instructions to be given to such an envoy. Congress favored an offensive and defensive alliance of all three powers, which should obtain for the United States not only its boundaries now already formulated for the west and south, but also Canada, Nova Scotia, and Bermuda. An amendment to include the Floridas in the proposed article was passed, August 5; then one to add: "and the free

25. Ibid., 369.
26. Ibid., XIV, 835, July 14, 1779.

navigation of the Mississippi." [27] Later, it was proposed
that a subsidy be secured from Spain,[28] and that in
return for this the United States give to Spain a free
hand, and even cooperate with the military forces of
His Catholic Majesty, for the conquest of the Floridas,
guaranteeing them forever to Spain. Then it was proposed to trade the Floridas, which were still in the
hands of Great Britain, to Spain, for *either* the navigation of the Mississippi, *or* a subsidy.[29] Although the
fact had been rumored ever since the beginning of
August it was formally announced to Congress by the
new French Minister Luzerne on September 7, 1779,
that Spain had declared war on Great Britain.[30]

On September 10, 1779, John Dickinson, of Delaware, introduced an entirely new motion, which eventually was rejected, the purpose of which was, in any
treaty negotiations with Spain, to get Canada, Nova
Scotia, the Bermuda Islands, free navigation of the
Mississippi River "to the sea," *and* a subsidy. In return
for all this the United States would agree to furnish to
the Spanish navy what ships' masts it could spare from
its own uses. If Spain should insist on the Floridas for
herself and the exclusive navigation of the Mississippi
below 31°, the plenipotentiary of the United States
might yield and guarantee both to the King of Spain,
who in his turn should guarantee to the United States,
Canada, Nova Scotia, Bermuda, and the Newfoundland fisheries. It was also desirable that the United
States should enjoy free commerce and have a free port
on the Mississippi below 31°.

27. Ibid., XIV, 926.
28. Ibid., 937, Aug. 7, 1779.
29. Ibid., XV, 1047, Sept. 11, 1779.
30. Wharton, III, 310.

As finally adopted, on September 27, 1779, the instructions to John Jay, who was elected as the new plenipotentiary to Spain, provided that:

1. In case the King of Spain acceded to the Franco-American alliance, he should not by any term in that alliance be precluded from securing to himself the Floridas: "On the contrary, if he shall obtain the Floridas from Great Britain, these United States will guaranty the same to his catholick majesty: provided always the United States shall enjoy the free navigation of the Mississippi into and from the sea."

2. Treaties of alliance and of amity and commerce with Spain should be negotiated.

3. If possible, "some convenient port or ports below the thirty-first degree of north latitude, on the Mississippi River, for all merchant vessels, goods, wares and merchandizes belonging to the inhabitants of these states" should be procured.

4. A subsidy, or at least a loan of five million dollars at not more than six per cent interest should be solicited.[31]

Such were the terms which the struggling United States, eager to get Spain into the war in alliance with itself, laid down to that great power!

V

John Jay will play a large part in the diplomacy which is to be the subject of the main narrative of this volume.

At the time he was appointed plenipotentiary to Spain, Jay enjoyed the prestige of having recently finished a term as President of the Continental Congress. He came from an old New York family of mixed French

31. *Journals of the Continental Congress,* XV, 1118, Sept. 27, 1779.

and Dutch ancestry. The well-to-do circumstances of his parents afforded him a comfortable youth and an education at King's College, of which he took full advantage. His first public office was of a semi-diplomatic character, that of Secretary to the Royal Commission which settled the New York-New Jersey colonial boundary dispute. It was presumably his experience at this time which gave him a taste for international law and a persuasion of the efficacy of mixed commissions as a means of settling arbitrable disputes. He had completed his reading for the law and had been admitted to practice before the New York bar when the Revolution began and shut up the courts. Jay early identified himself with the mercantile wing of the colonial protest. He became a member of the original Committee of Fifty-one on British Grievances, in New York. Though one of the most conservative of all the Fathers and one of the last to be convinced of the desirability of complete separation from the British Empire, when the step was taken he threw his whole soul and energy into the winning of independence.

No American public servant was ever more jealous of that independence. Jay was early elected to the Continental Congress, for the convocation of which he worked diligently. He drafted the Constitution of the State of New York and was appointed Chief Justice of that state. He also held the rank of colonel in the New York militia. In 1779 he resigned the Chief Justiceship of New York, as well as the Presidency of Congress, in order to repair his depleted personal resources. This intention was frustrated by the new diplomatic appointment.

Jay had married in 1774 "the beautiful Sarah Livingston," of the prominent New Jersey family of that name, a woman of extraordinary charm and attraction, who exercised an uncommon influence over him throughout his career, an influence which was not without its diplomatic significance. Of deep piety and unbreakable religious faith of a strong Protestant persuasion, unbending in his patriotism, endeavoring always to keep an even political balance, possessed of a judicial temperament, fond of good society, with strong and affectionate attachment for domestic life, Jay was a young statesman of spotless personal reputation and strict integrity. But he had a certain personal vanity which was evident to his acquaintances, a ponderous way of pronouncement on men and measures, and a rather over-confident appreciation of his own merit. "Mr. Jay's weak spot is Mr. Jay," said a close student of him at this period.[32]

Jay arrived in Spain January 27, 1780, bringing with him William Carmichael, who had just served a term as delegate to Congress from Maryland, and who had already had some experience in a secretarial capacity to the American Commission at Paris. Jay remained in Spain, as the unrecognized diplomatic agent of the United States, until May, 1782. The story of his mission there has been fully told. Throughout his sojourn, Floridablanca was studiously careful not to take any step which would be a recognition of American independence. Jay tried in vain to get a subsidy, even to obtain a loan for $5,000,000. He attempted without success to get a treaty of alliance. Floridablanca fre-

32. S. F. Bemis, *Jay's Treaty*, 203–205. See also my sketch of John Jay as Secretary for Foreign Affairs in Volume I of the Knopf series, *The American Secretaries of State and Their Diplomacy*, 10 vols. (New York, 1927–1929), reprinted in 5 vols. (New York, Pageant Book Co., 1958).

quently met him informally, but would give no more than the courtesy which that statesman could so abundantly display. Floridablanca was determined not to recognize American independence.[33] When pressed to assist him with money enough to pay drafts which Congress had drawn on Jay in anticipation of a loan, Floridablanca granted upwards of $150,000 to take up these drafts, but he carefully refrained from entering into any contract which would imply a recognition of independence.[34]

When Jay reached Spain, Miralles' reports on the instructions of Congress to that agent had not yet arrived,[35] but Floridablanca had heard of their general nature through France, and had made up his mind never to relinquish the exclusive navigation of the Mississippi. The Spanish campaign which resulted in the occupation of the British Floridas was already under way, and there was little likelihood that Spain would accept the American principle of 31° as the northern boundary of West Florida. Jay soon found that his instructions on the Mississippi Question would be a bar to any treaty. He apprised Congress of this and of all the details of his mission, and Congress responded in the dark days of the war against Great Britain, on February 15, 1781, by altering his instructions on the Mississippi Question, permitting him, in return for a Spanish alliance, to recede from his former instructions,

33. Corwin, 318–329. So cautious was Floridablanca on this point that he refused to receive Gérard, who was returning with Jay via Spain to France, as the French Minister to the United States, except as a distinguished subject of Louis XVI. Yela, I, 421.

34. For summary of Spanish subsidies and loans to the United States, see Appendix II at the end of this volume.

35. Yela, I, 415.

so far as they insist upon the free navigation of that part of the Mississippi River which lies below the 31st degree of north latitude and on a free port or ports below the same, provided such cession shall be unalterably insisted upon by Spain, and provided that the free navigation of the said river above the said degree of north latitude shall be acknowledged and guaranteed by his Catholic Majesty to the citizens of the United States in common with his own subjects.[36]

Jay did not approve of these instructions. He thought them more adapted to negotiations with Spain before she entered the war against Great Britain than to the existing circumstances in which that power was a co-belligerent with the United States and France. "The cession of this navigation [to Spain]," he wrote to Congress, "will, in my opinion, render a future war with Spain unavoidable, and I shall look upon my subscribing to the one as fixing the certainty of the other." [37] Nevertheless, he carried out his instructions. "For whatever might have been or may be my private sentiments," he declared, "they shall never in mere questions of policy influence me to deviate from those

36. Wharton, IV, 257.

37. "Had Spain been at peace with our enemies, and offered to acknowledge, guaranty, and fight for our independence, provided we would yield them this point (as once seemed the case), I should for my own part have no more hesitation about it now than I had then. But Spain being now at war with Great Britain, to gain her own objects, she doubtless will prosecute it full as vigorously as if she fought for her own objects. There was and is little reason to suppose that such a cession would render her exertions more vigorous or her aids to us much more liberal. The effect which an alliance between Spain and America would have on Britain and other nations would certainly be in our favor, but whether more so than the free navigation of the Mississippi is less certain. The cession of this navigation will, in my opinion, render a future war with Spain unavoidable, and I shall look upon my subscribing to the one as fixing the certainty of the other." Wharton, IV, 743.

of Congress." [38] He submitted formal propositions for a treaty of amity and alliance to Floridablanca on September 22, 1781, which contained the following articles:

VI. The United States shall relinquish to his Catholic majesty, and in future forbear to use, or attempt to use, the navigation of the river Mississippi from the thirty-first degree of north latitude —that is, from the point where it leaves the United States—down to the ocean.

VII. That his Catholic majesty shall guaranty to the United States all their respective territories.

VIII. That the United States shall guaranty to his Catholic majesty all his dominions in America. [39]

Jay explained that these were to be considered as the most essential articles of a treaty; subordinate ones could be worked out; and he concluded the subject

38. Ibid., 744.

39. The first five articles of the proposal read as follows:

"I. There shall forever subsist an inviolable and universal peace and friendship between his Catholic majesty and the United States and the subjects and citizens of both.

"II. That every privilege, exemption and favor with respect to commerce, navigation, and personal rights which now are, or hereafter may be granted by either to any the most favored nation, be also granted by them to each other.

"III. That they mutually extend to the vessels, merchants, and inhabitants of each other all that protection which is usual and proper between friendly and allied nations.

"IV. That the vessels, merchants or other subjects of his Catholic majesty and the United States shall not resort to or be permitted (except in cases which humanity allows to distress) to enter into any of those ports or dominions of the other from which the most favored nation shall be excluded.

"V. That the following commerce be prohibited and declared contraband between the subjects of his Catholic ajesty and the United States, viz: All such as his Catholic majesty may think proper to specify."

The articles were accompanied with "remarks" by Jay in elucidation of them. See Wharton, IV, 760.

with a *general offer and propositions* to make and
admit all such articles as in the course of the negotiations should appear conducive to the great objects of
the proposed treaty.

The issue was now put squarely before Floridablanca.
Had that statesman been willing to accept an American
alliance and consequent recognition of American independence, the propositions of Jay could not have been
better.[40] They offered to Spain the possibility of getting
everything she could desire, particularly when they admitted the principle of further negotiation on other
points, the boundary of West Florida, for example.
They made it necessary to choose between a frank
recognition of American independence and an alliance
which would have secured from the future republic a
guaranty of Spain's adjacent colonial possessions, as well
as recognition of Spain's exclusive control of the river.
This was the step already urged in vain by Aranda. Had
Floridablanca accepted the offer, the reader might have
been spared the pains of reading this book, for the
issues which give occasion to the following chapters
presumably would never have been presented. But
that Minister, still unwilling to recognize the independence of the revolted colonies, preferred to pursue the
war against Great Britain without an American alliance, and to leave the Question of the Mississippi, and
the Florida boundary, to the future.

With adequate caution Jay had made his offer contingent upon Spain's acceptance of it; if Spain should
not accept the offer, the United States would reserve
all its rights to the navigation of the Mississippi.[41]

40. Yela, I, 445.
41. "Mr. Jay thinks it his duty frankly to confess that the difficulty
of reconciling this measure to the feelings of their constituents has

Floridablanca refused to do more than *discuss* the proposed treaty through an undersecretary. A few months
later, Jay, disgusted with the policy of the Spanish
Court and now suspicious of all things European, received a letter from Franklin asking that he repair to
Paris to assist in the peace negotiations with Great
Britain, for which Jay also held a commission from
Congress. With real relief he shook the dust of Spain
from his feet and set out for France. Congress fully
ratified the condition which Jay had attached to his
offer in regard to the navigation of the Mississippi.[42]

VI

Jay's departure was attributed by Floridablanca to
pique at lack of success in getting more money out of
Spain. "His two chief points," he commented to Aran-

appeared to Congress in a serious light and they now expect to do it
only by placing in the opposite scale the gratitude due to his Catholic
majesty, and the great and various advantages which the United States
will derive from the acknowledgment and generous support of their
independence by the Spanish monarchy at a time when the vicissitudes,
dangers, and difficulties of a distressing war with a powerful, obstinate,
and vindictive nation render the friendship and avowed protection
of his Catholic majesty in a very particular manner interesting to
them. The offer of this proposition, therefore, being dictated by these
expectations and this combination of circumstances, must necessarily be
limited by the duration of them, and consequently that if the acceptance
of it should, together with the proposed alliance, be postponed to a
general peace, the United States will cease to consider themselves bound
by any propositions or offers which he may now make in their behalf.
   "Nor can Mr. Jay omit mentioning the hope and expectations of
Congress that his majesty's generosity and greatness of mind will
prompt him to alleviate so much as possible the disadvantages to
which this proposition subjects the United States, by either granting
them a free port, under certain restrictions, in the vicinity, or by such
other marks of his liberality and justice as may give him additional
claims to the affection and attachment of the United States." Wharton,
IV, 761.
   42. Wharton, V, 380.

da, "were: Spain, recognize our independence; Spain, give us more money." [43] Unwilling to let the American business go entirely, because of the importance to Spain of the Question of the Mississippi in the approaching peace negotiations at Paris, the Spanish Foreign Minister authorized Aranda to *discuss* matters with Jay in Paris, but not to agree to anything before referring it to Madrid.[44] After an exchange of amenities, in which Aranda was elaborately careful to act as a private gentleman rather than a Spanish diplomatist, a conference between the two took place on August 3, 1782. Aranda produced a French edition of Mitchell's Map of North America of 1755, and suggested to Jay the necessity of fixing a boundary between Spanish possessions and the United States in the West. Desirous of eliciting an expression of the western boundary views of the American peace plenipotentiaries, Aranda asked Jay to indicate the boundary. Jay drew his finger along the Mississippi from the source south to 31° north latitude, thence east along that degree to the Chattahoochee, and thence along the undisputed boundary of East Florida to the sea. Aranda replied that this was impossible for Spain. He insisted that the boundary should be some line considerably to the east of the Mississippi and parallel to it. Jay asked him where, and the Ambassador, or rather the distinguished Spanish nobleman in his capacity as a private gentleman, promised to work out a line on the map and send it to Jay.

When Jay received the map, a few days later, it contained a red line, which according to his description ran "from a lake near the confines of Georgia, but

43. Yela, II, 365.
44. Yela, I, 459.

east of the Flint River, to the Confluence of the Kana-
wha River with the Ohio, thence around the western
shores of Lake Erie and Huron, and thence round Lake
Michigan to Lake Superior." [45] Jay took the map so
marked to Vergennes, and in a conference at which
Franklin was also present the two American commissioners protested at the extravagance of the Spanish
claim. Vergennes, records Jay, was "very cautious and
reserved; but Mr. de Rayneval, who was present,
thought we claimed more than we had a right to."

Aranda on his part now appealed to Vergennes to
intervene in Spain's interest with the United States for
the settlement of the western boundary. Vergennes
showed himself disposed to reason with the Americans,
and himself suggested, for the territory north of the
Ohio, a compromise line to be drawn a little farther to
the west, but still distant from the Mississippi—the line
of the Wabash River—or, in case Jay would not listen
to reason, the possibility of settling the question by
setting up some sort of neutral Indian state between
the United States and the Mississippi. He referred
Aranda to Rayneval, his chief assistant, as one familiar

45. Aranda's description, which we have followed in plotting the
line on Map 1 accompanying the text, was as follows: "En la parte de
línea de confrontación fui a tomar expresamente la punta de los Lagos,
a empezar del *Superior* y la seguida marginal de parte de ellos hasta
la punta del Erié u Oswego, como posiciones que no podian dejar a
sus espaldas nada disputable, y con la mira de que poniendo la España
en ciertos puntos un presidio, estuviesse a la vista de su confrontante,
e hiciesse lo que quisiesse de permitir, o no tráfico con establicimiento.
Vine después a caer al confluente del rio gran Conhaway con el Obío
[sic], para ir a buscar el recodo más entrante de la Carolina meridional,
a fin de continuar la demarcación como visual a un lago, en la tierra
de los Apalaches, o George River, pero sin llegar a él, sino marcando
sólo el cabo de la línea como indicante a caer azia allí; dejándola sin
correr al acercarse de los limites de Georgia y Florida, hasta saber quales
fuessen los verdaderos." Yela, II, 356.

with these territories. Rayneval and Aranda collabo-
rated and worked out a line satisfactory to the Spanish
Ambassador, which limited the claims of Spain to the
region south of the Ohio.[46] With Vergennes' countenance it was presented to Jay as the "personal ideas"
of Rayneval for a means of settling the issue between
Spain and the United States.

The memoir proposed this territorial settlement for
the West, reinforced with Rayneval's historical arguments: a boundary was to be drawn from the "eastern
angle of the Gulf of Mexico" to Fort Toulouse on the
upper Alabama River, thence by various water routes to
the southeast tributary of the present Tennessee River,
the Hiawassee (then known as Euphrasee), down that
stream to the Tennessee (Cherokee) itself and following
the Tennessee to the Pelisippi (presumably the Sequat-
chie on a modern map), up the Pelisippi to its source,
from which a "right line" was to be drawn to the
Cumberland River; from there the proposed division
line followed the Cumberland into the Ohio River.
The Indians to the west and south of that line were
to be free and under the protection of Spain: those
to the east to be free and under the protection of
the United States, or the United States to make such
arrangements with them as it might see fit. The Indian
trade was to be free to both parties. North of the Ohio
it was agreed that Spain had no pretensions; the fate
of this territory was to be regulated by the Court of
London. "As to the course and navigation of the Mississippi," read the Rayneval memoir, "they follow with
the property, and they will belong, therefore, to the

46. See my study of *The Rayneval Memoranda of 1782* (Worcester,
American Antiquarian Society, 1938), reprinted from *Proceedings of
the American Antiquarian Society*, April 1937.

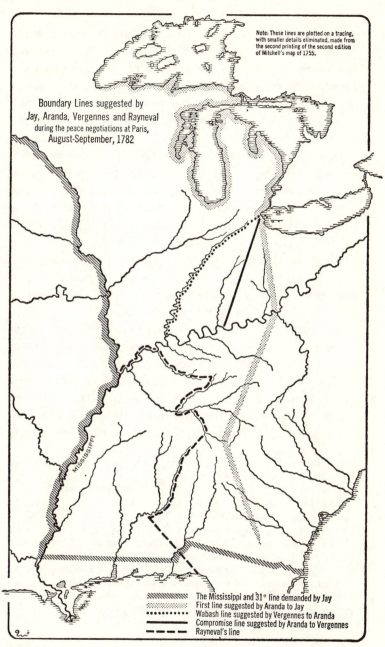

Note: These lines are plotted on a tracing, with smaller details eliminated, made from the second printing of the second edition of Mitchell's map of 1755.

Boundary Lines suggested by
Jay, Aranda, Vergennes and Rayneval
during the peace negotiations at Paris,
August-September, 1782

MISSISSIPPI

|||||||||||| The Mississippi and 31° line demanded by Jay
.... First line suggested by Aranda to Jay
•••••••••••• Wabash line suggested by Vergennes to Aranda
Compromise line suggested by Aranda to Vergennes
– – – – – Rayneval's line

MAP 1

nation to which the two banks belong. If then, by the future treaty of peace, Spain preserves West Florida, she alone will be the proprietor of the course of the Mississippi from the thirty-first degree of latitude to the mouth of this river. Whatever may be the case with that part which is beyond this point to the north, the United States of America can have no pretentions to it, not being masters of either border of this river." [47]

As is well known, or at least ought to be well known to every American schoolboy, the commissioners of the United States refused to listen to such a curtailment of the territory claimed by their sovereign. It was a device erected at the instance of Spain for the purpose of shutting the new republic off from any contact with the Mississippi. We must take pains to point out, in this instance, that Vergennes never put this forth as the official proposal of France. He was not disappointed when the American commissioners, in their own negotiations with Great Britain, obtained from that country the western and southern boundary which Congress had instructed them to secure. The treaty of peace between Great Britain and the United States stipulated further, "The navigation of the Mississippi from its source to the ocean, shall forever remain free and open to the

47. Wharton, VI, 27. Map 1 accompanying the above text illustrates the several lines. The Vergennes line and Aranda's compromise line were drawn north of the Ohio only. Jay's line for the northern boundary of East Florida follows a line drawn on a copy of Mitchell's Map in the New York Historical Society's collection, on which the St. Mary's River has been drawn in. Mitchell's Map of 1755 did not have the St. Mary's River on it. Note also that Mitchell's Map places the junction of the Flint and Apalachicola north of 31°, whereas it really is south of it. Again note that the negotiators were using a French edition of Mitchell, somewhat different from the English. This has been taken into account on the revised Map 1 accompanying our text. See *Hisp. Am. Hist. Rev.*, VII, No. 3 (Aug., 1927), 386–389.

subjects of Great Britain and the citizens of the United States."

The same day on which the treaty was finally signed as definitive, September 3, 1783, Spain and Great Britain also made peace, by the terms of which the two Floridas, conquered by Spanish troops, were ceded to Spain, without any mention of their boundaries.

The peace settlement of 1783 thus closed without Spanish recognition of the independence of the United States, without a settlement of the Mississippi Question, and without an agreement on the Spanish-American boundary in the southwest. It will be the purpose of the following chapters to trace the history of these principal issues between the two countries, and of other issues subordinate to them.[48]

48. The policy of France in regard to Spain and the United States during the war and the peace settlement has been made the subject of a great deal of careful investigation. See on that subject particularly the monographs of P. C. Phillips, *The West in the Diplomacy of the American Revolution* (1913), and E. S. Corwin, *French Policy and the American Alliance* (1916). Both of these are based upon careful perusal of Doniol's documentary *Histoire de la participation de la France dans l'établissement des États-Unis,* and other European and American archival collections. The Spanish publication of J. F. Yela Utrilla, *España ante la independencia de los Estados Unidos* (2d ed., 1925), completely supersedes the less adequate study of Manuel Conrotte, *La intervención de España en la independencia de los Estados Unidos de la América del Norte* (Madrid, 1920). Yela throws much new light on the details of Franco-Spanish and Spanish-American relations, after a study of Spanish archives, acting in this respect as a sort of Spanish documentary supplement to Doniol and Wharton, but he does not, in my opinion, require us to alter the conclusions of Corwin and Phillips, which might be summarized as follows: At the beginning of the Franco-American alliance, Vergennes did not dispute, but on the contrary supported, the United States' claim to the Mississippi boundary and to the free navigation of that river to the sea. The exigencies of European diplomacy, however, arising from the desirability (1) of getting Spain into the war as France's ally and if possible as also the ally of the United States, (2) of keeping Spain in the war after she

went in, (3) of holding the two French allies together against Great Britain during the peace negotiations, caused Vergennes to intercede openly with the United States on behalf of Spain's claims in the American West and for the Newfoundland fisheries. At no time did he push these claims to the extent of insisting on them; in fact, during the peace negotiations, he never put forward the Spanish claims as a formal French proposal. His problem was that of reconciling two French allies whose interests were in opposition. My *Diplomacy of the American Revolution* (New York, 1935) reviews these problems and other details.

CHAPTER 2

The Mississippi Question and Other Issues with Spain

Spain had entered the war against England for the sake of safely humbling her ancient heretic enemy at a time when she felt sure of winning certain incidental and valuable advantages for herself: the recovery of Gibraltar and Minorca, which would make the Mediterranean a Bourbon lake; and Florida, to round out the coastline of His Catholic Majesty in the Americas and keep the Gulf of Mexico a Spanish sea, sealed to foreign settlers, log-cutters, and traders. The principal design of the Bourbon allies, the abasement of England, seemed accomplished to a great degree by the peace treaties, even though Gibraltar was not retaken. This mammoth rock and the British navy, redeemed by Rodney's victory over De Grasse in the Caribbean, continued to threaten French and Spanish ascendancy in the Mediterranean. But Spain secured her one great conquest, the Floridas. She also succeeded in so limiting the Campeche log-cutting concession—a menace to her colonial domains in America—as to place it apparently in a fair way of extinction. Her victory in the war of the American Revolution shed on her some of the effulgence of old-time greatness. The continental coastline of Spanish America now stretched unbroken[1]

1. The Anglo-Spanish treaty of peace had carefully and narrowly restricted the boundaries of British wood-cutting settlements in Honduras and placed them under Spanish sovereignty.

and for the most part unchallenged from the southern boundary of Georgia around Florida and along the Gulf and Isthmus to circumscribe South America and reach up the Pacific Coast of the northern continent until it met the vaguely bounded claims of Russia on the foggy shores of chill Alaska. With the British Empire split apart and British forces apparently spent, Jamaica and the islands saved to that power in the Caribbean had lost some of their immediate menace for Spain in future wars.

But a new menace, greater than ever came from Great Britain, to the security of Spain's colonial Empire, had lifted its head beyond the agitated Atlantic —the American idea of independence and of republican government. The diplomatists of His Catholic Majesty were haunted by the vision of material power which an independent American republic might develop, a new power conscious of its own strength and of its possibilities for expansion at the expense of Spanish dominions. A premonition of this had caused the Spanish Court to be consistently unfriendly to American independence during the war and steadily zealous for the limitation of American territorial expansion, a zeal abundantly displayed in the peace negotiations of 1782–1783. Spain, ally of France and associate of the United States in the contest against Great Britain, showed to the world her true colors by steadfastly refusing to recognize officially an American envoy at Madrid. Not until George III was forced by France and the United States to recognize American independence in the definitive treaty of 1783 did Charles III somewhat grudgingly do so by accepting an American diplomatic agent at his court.[2]

2. Wharton, VI, 663–667.

Spain had preferred that her action should not result in the complete independence of the United States. In complete independence she saw danger to her own future. Whether authentic or not, the oft-quoted reflection, attributed to Aranda, after the signature of the treaty of 1783 suggests the world-changing events that were to follow the war of the American Revolution:

This federal republic is born a pigmy. A day will come when it will be a giant, even a colossus, formidable in these countries. Liberty of conscience, the facility for establishing a new population on immense lands, as well as the advantages of the new government, will draw thither farmers and artizans from all the nations. In a few years we shall watch with grief the tyrannical existence of this same colossus.[3]

So far as the United States is concerned, particularly so far as the subsequent expansion of the United States territorially from Atlantic to Pacific is concerned, the great service which Spain rendered to this republic during the American Revolution was the conquest of the Floridas which placed herself, instead of the strong military and naval power Great Britain, in possession of that strategic territory. Had Great Britain been able to repossess the Floridas in 1782, as John Jay singly and secretly suggested to the British peace negotiators at Paris in that year,[4] in the hope of luring

3. Quoted by Fiske, *Critical Period,* 19.
In a less quoted passage he stated, anent American independence: "We must imagine that sooner or later in [Spanish] America there will occur revolutions like those of the English colonies, and that it is most important that it be bound to the island capitals of Cuba and Puerto Rico, which by virtue of their firm establishments will come to be the only worthwhile possessions and thereupon will serve to bridle the continent and be a military base in case of necessity." Aranda to Floridablanca, Paris, Oct. 4, 1782. Conrotte, *La intervención de España en la independencia de los Estados Unidos,* 166.
4. Channing, *Hist. U. S.,* III, 384.

British troops away from the United States into a
Florida campaign against Spain, it is interesting indeed to speculate on the future hopelessness of American territorial expansion to the south or even to the
west. Great Britain in West Florida after 1783 might
have meant Great Britain in New Orleans later, not
only in New Orleans but in all Louisiana. It is likely
in that event that American territory would never have
crossed the Mississippi. By taking the Floridas from
Great Britain, Spain profoundly influenced the future
of the United States.[5]

Between Spain and the United States, whose territories were now contiguous from the source of the Mississippi to the mouth of the St. Mary's, there sprang
from the fact of American independence immediate
issues of vital importance for the latter nation, though
seemingly of secondary moment in the world-wide range
of Spanish colonial and foreign policy. One was the
future commercial arrangements to be established between that monarchy, including her colonial dominions, and the new trading republic which was so eagerly
seeking free and open navigation and commerce with all
the ports and peoples of the world. Another was the
question of the exact boundary between West Florida
and the American Southwest. Accompanying this were
two further issues of even greater gravity, the navigation of the Mississippi River and the relations of
Spain and the United States respectively with the Indian
tribes in and adjacent to the disputed territory. The
problems which the American Confederation faced in

5. In discussing the preliminary articles of peace in Congress,
March 22, 1783, Mercer of Virginia, reflecting on the secret article,
"observed that it was unwise to prefer Great Britain to Spain as our
neighbor in West Florida." Wharton, VI, 330, quoting Madison's
Debates.

its Spanish policy in the Southwest were not unlike those confronted in dealing with Great Britain on the northwestern frontier. A sinister political and geographical symmetry placed the hinterlands of the United States between two great sovereign millstones that threatened to grind out the life of the weak Confederation.

The southwestern boundary controversy, with its accompanying issues of Mississippi navigation and Indian affairs, was fruitage of the inconsistencies of the Anglo-American and the Anglo-Spanish definitive treaties of peace. It will be remembered that the preliminaries of peace between the United States and Great Britain stipulated that the northern boundary of the Floridas should be the thirty-first parallel of latitude from the Mississippi to the junction of the Chattahoochee and Flint,[6] thence to the source of the St. Mary's River and down that stream to the Atlantic Ocean. A secret article added that in the event Great Britain should recover the Floridas from Spain before the conclusion of peace, their northern boundary should be the latitude of the mouth of the Yazoo River (then close above the present city of Vicksburg). This secret article, itself a confession that Great Britain was not then in possession of the Floridas, never came into effect, because in the definitive treaty with Spain, Great Britain ceded both Floridas with no mention of their boundaries; therefore it was not repeated in the definitive Anglo-American treaty of the same day. Spain at the time was in military possession of West Florida. She broadly defined her boundaries by actual conquest and occupation, and her definition was not by any line granted to the United States by Great Britain, a power

6. Where they unite to form the Apalachicola.

not then holding the property it presumed to cede away. Spain had an unanswerable argument in the latest definition of the boundaries of West Florida as a British colony.

The impartial student must admit that abundant unimpeachable evidence proves that the northern boundary of West Florida under British dominion from 1764 until the Spanish conquest had been the latitude of the mouth of the Yazoo River[7] from the Mississippi to the Chattahoochee. Since Great Britain ceded the province to Spain without mention of boundaries simultaneously with the signing of the definitive peace with the United States, Spain was perfectly justified in contending that the boundaries of West Florida as taken over by her were exactly what they had been under British dominion, and that nothing in the treaty between the United States and Great Britain could change those boundaries without Spain's consent. Spain also had the immensely great advantage of being actually in possession of the territory. The United States in fact had no more just claim to territory south of the line of the Yazoo than it did to the territory of Quebec north of the 45° boundary of New York and Vermont. The easiest way for an American to appreciate how Spain felt about this boundary question is to imagine Great Britain agreeing with some third power, simultaneously with the going into effect of the Anglo-American treaty of peace, that the boundary of the

7. This line has been variously referred to as 32° 28' and 32° 30'. Actually the old channel of the mouth of the Yazoo was located about 32° 25' to 32° 26'. In 1878 the channel was at 32° 21.5'. The present, artificial, channel of the mouth of the Yazoo at Vicksburg is at 32° 20'. See Mississippi River Commission, Charts No. 47 and No. 48 (Scale 1:20,000, 1878–80), Vicksburg Quadrangle, *U. S. Geological Survey* (1918 ed.). We shall refer to the line henceforth as the line of the Yazoo.

United States, say in the region of Maine, should be different from what had been fixed in the treaty between Great Britain and the United States. Naturally the Government of the United States in such a case would pay no attention to Great Britain's treaty with a third party.

But Spain claimed more than the line of the Yazoo. We have seen that Floridablanca and Aranda vainly had endeavored through France in the peace negotiations of 1782–1783 to cut off the Southwest from American sovereignty and to place it under a Spanish Indian protectorate. These maneuvers were based on arguments deduced from alleged conquest of the territory of what Spain considered a common enemy, that is, British territory on the left bank of the Mississippi above the British province of West Florida, as far north as the Ohio River, and even as far as the Great Lakes. The claims of this nature were not altogether abandoned, at least to the south of the Ohio, after the peace treaties had been ratified. They were to furnish the resources of Spanish diplomacy with good trading equivalents to use in any negotiations with the United States.

As to the Mississippi Question, Spain with good reason contended that her conquest of the Floridas placed a bar of inviolable Spanish territory across the lower Mississippi over which could leap no foreign claims based on cessions to the United States by an enemy already dispossessed of the territory. Further, Spain could argue with weight that her reconquest of the Floridas thoroughly canceled the navigation servitude which had been placed on the lower reaches of the river by the treaty of 1763.[8]

8. See memorandum for Gardoqui's instructions as to boundaries, San Ildefonso, July 25, 1784, A. C. A., Est. Leg., 3457, G. D., V, 205–213.

It is difficult to find a respectable legal argument to demolish the Spanish contention. International law at that time admitted no rights of riparian states downstream below their own boundaries. Spain never maintained, for example, that she could navigate the Tagus through Portugal to the sea. The closure of the Scheldt by the Netherlands was a standing illustration of what international practice allowed to the power controlling the mouth of a great navigable river. If we grant, as I think we must acknowledge, that the United States without the consent of Spain could derive no right to the use of the river through Spanish territory by virtue of the Anglo-American peace treaty, then the plain fact of the matter is that citizens of the United States had no more legal right to the navigation of the lower Mississippi than they did to that of the lower St. Lawrence. It is not surprising that Spain was determined that no foreign craft should go up or down the Mississippi through her dominions without her consent. To her it made no difference what various foreign powers might presume to agree upon concerning matters within her exclusive domestic jurisdiction, so long as she was able to defend her soil and waters from such alien intervention. The year after the peace settlement of 1783 the Governor of Louisiana was instructed to proclaim that, until the boundaries of Louisiana and the Floridas should be settled, Americans would not be allowed to navigate the Mississippi within Spanish territory.[9]

It was the plenipotentiaries of the United States who put into the treaty of independence the Florida bound-

---

9. J. Galvez to the Governor ad interim of Louisiana, Aranjuez, June 26, 1784. Louis Houck, *Spanish Regime in Missouri*, I, 237; *Dip. Corres.*, I, 136. A copy of this proclamation was officially transmitted to Congress by Rendon, the Spanish observer at New York.

ary and navigation stipulations.[10] On this treaty, principally, rested American claims against Spain. Though the claim to navigation was not altogether precisely defined or argued in full until the beginning of negotiations with Spain in 1785, it was based on the conception that the transfer of territory from Great Britain had carried with it full sovereign rights as they had existed under the British Crown, that one of these was the right to navigate all the way down the river to the sea exactly as British subjects had been entitled to do before the American Revolution. That West Florida, a portion of former British territory below the United States boundary, had reverted by conquest to Spanish dominion did not, in the American way of looking at it, cancel or lessen the servitude which the treaty of 1763 had placed on the lower river in favor of an up-stream riparian state. In this contention was at least an arguable if not a juridically formidable claim. But there was a weightier, if a less juridical argument.

Since the Revolution a great change had taken place

10. As one reads the despatches relating to the negotiation of the peace treaty between the United States and Great Britain one is impressed by the paucity of reference to the Florida boundary and the navigation of the Mississippi. These appear to have been granted without debate. It cost Great Britain nothing to cede away something she no longer possessed; but if there were a deliberate purpose thereby to create a dispute between the United States and Spain it does not appear in the despatches. It would not necessarily have been revealed. The secret article in the Anglo-American preliminaries was due to John Jay's secret suggestion to Oswald. Jay hoped in this way possibly to lure away to a Florida campaign the British garrisons from the Atlantic ports occupied in the United States. Channing, *Hist. U. S.*, III, 384. Livingston in his notable letter of March 18, 1783, to the President of Congress, denounced the secret Florida article of the preliminaries of peace as "calculated to sow the seeds of distrust and jealousy between the United States and their allies [*sic*]." Wharton, VI, 314.

in the American West, which in 1784 comprised the basin drained by the lower Ohio and Tennessee rivers. During the few years before the Declaration of Independence the "long-hunters" and forest pathfinders of the Virginia and Carolina frontiers had penetrated through the Appalachian watergaps to the rich territory of Kentucky and Tennessee. The war only slightly checked this advance. After the close of hostilities settlers poured into the new lands with greater volume than ever. Now more than academic argument was brought to bear on the free navigation of the Mississippi. To the aggressive "men of the western waters," as they delighted to call themselves, the river was the only practicable route by which they might trade profitably with the outside world. Their whole future prosperity hung on its unrestricted use. To them it was of paramount and vital interest—more important before the day of railroads and bonded transit than was the Danzig "corridor" to Poland later, or the Rhine to Germany. Rendon,[11] the Spanish observer at Philadelphia, commented to his principals on the increasing political importance of the West and the unlikelihood of the Congress yielding in its demand for the unrestricted navigation of the river. It was a grave issue, he informed his superiors, as was also that of the disputed southwestern boundary of the United States, and Congress was showing its determination by instructing its plenipotentiaries at Paris to negotiate with Spain for a settlement of these questions.[12]

The Indians of the Southwest constituted another issue of fundamental importance. Spain, by denying American jurisdiction over all the territory south of

11. Successor to Miralles.

12. Rendon to Josef de Galvez, Aug. 31, 1783, Oct. 12, 1784, A. G. I., 87/1/7 (L. C. trans.).

the Ohio and Tennessee and, roughly, west of a line between the headwaters of the Tennessee and Flint rivers, assumed a perfect freedom to traffic and negotiate politically with tribes in that region, which were principally the Cherokee, Choctaw, Chickasaw, and Creek. As British traders and agents were circulating freely on American soil among the Indians north of the Ohio, monopolizing the fur trade and keeping them under political tutelage while furnishing munitions useful for hostilities against the Government of the United States, so Spanish agents and traders were working amongst the tribes of the Southwest—but with more justification. Spain, at any rate, had a strong claim to dominion over a part of that territory.

To set forth the Indian question we shall have to carry our narrative a little ahead of the diplomatic negotiations presently to be described. The peace treaty between Great Britain and the United States made no more mention of the Indians of the Southwest than it did of those of the Northwest. The silence of the treaty as to the Indians within the stipulated boundaries of the United States was acknowledgment of their inclusion under American sovereignty, so far as European powers and principles were concerned. It served as a denial of the right of any other power to interfere with tribes within acknowledged American boundaries. The Indians considered naturally that they still owned their loosely bounded tribal lands and hunting grounds and that they had the political capacity to negotiate or to make war with any government or people. With this notion Congress compromised to the extent of recognizing their simple property rights to lands and their right to make treaties with the United States alone.[13] Ac-

13. See *18th Ann. Rept. Bureau Am. Ethnology,* Pt. I, 640.

cordingly peace commissioners were sent forth, at the
close of the war, to adjust all questions with the southwestern tribes, similarly to the negotiations that were
being attempted at the same time with the tribes north
of the Ohio.

These efforts were not wholly successful. The negotiations were frequently interrupted by hostilities caused
by the aggressions now on the part of the Indians and
now on the part of lawless white settlers, but eventually
treaties were made with such constitutional organs of
the tribes as could be got hold of. The first attempt
was with the Creek in 1785. Here Congress was fore-
stalled by the state of Georgia, immediately alarmed
by any federal negotiations with Indians within her
boundaries which she regarded as extending west to
the Mississippi and south to the treaty line of 31°
north latitude. While federal commissioners were waiting to meet a delegation of Creek, agents of Georgia
signed a treaty with a few irresponsible representatives
of that tribe, November 12, 1785, by which were ceded
lands in the southwestern part of the present state
limits.[14] Another Georgia treaty with the Creek was
signed the following year. These unsatisfactory state
treaties, something possible only before the adoption
of the federal Constitution of 1787, remained the sole
settlement with the Creek until the treaty of New
York was ratified by the United States Senate in 1790.
No cessions of lands were made within this territory,
disputed between the United States and Spain, but all
Creek Indians dwelling within Georgia were made
"members" of that state, thus of course including some
Indians within the area disputed with Spain. The real

14. *A.S.P., I.A.*, I, 15–17. A previous treaty had been signed between
Georgia and the Creek in 1783. Ibid., 55.

leaders of the Creek repudiated these treaties with Georgia as having been made by two young Indians without authority. Until the establishment of the new federal government of the Constitution, relations with the Creek therefore rested in a state' of imperfect and precarious peace.

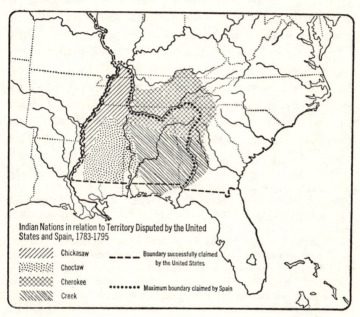

Indian Nations in relation to Territory Disputed by the United States and Spain, 1783-1795

///// Chickasaw
::::: Choctaw
XXXXX Cherokee
\\\\\ Creek

- - - - Boundary successfully claimed
by the United States

•••••• Maximum boundary claimed by Spain

MAP 2

With the other three tribes of the Southwest nominal peace settlements were easily made, despite the protest of Georgia that such treaties encroached upon her sovereignty.[15] In November, 1785, a treaty was signed

15. See resolutions of the General Assembly of the state of Georgia, Feb. 11, 1786, *A. S. P., I. A.*, I, 17. North Carolina also protested against the right of the United States Government to make treaties with Indian tribes within the state.

with the Cherokee at Hopewell, and in January, 1786, with the Chickasaw and Choctaw, at the same place, by which those three tribes acknowledged themselves under the protection of the United States *and of no other sovereign whatsoever,* agreed to accept and to protect American traders within their limits, to the regulation of their trade by Congress, and to give information of any hostile designs being set on foot against the Government of the United States. They acknowledged loosely defined boundaries for their hunting grounds. These boundaries in all three treaties, we observe, were drawn in the territory claimed by Spain. The southern boundary of the Choctaw lands was stipulated as the line of 31°, "being the southern boundary of the United States of America." [16] The

16. See our Map. 2, p. 49. Kappler, *Indian Treaties*, 8–16.

The confused and incomplete nature of these boundaries can be seen from the terminology of the treaties.

The Cherokee treaty of Nov. 28, 1785, signed at Hopewell stipulated the boundaries of that tribe: "Beginning at the mouth of Duck river, on the Tennessee; thence running north-east to the ridge dividing the waters running into Cumberland from those running into the Tennessee; thence eastwardly along the said ridge to a north-east line to be run, which shall strike the river Cumberland forty miles above Nashville; thence along the said line to the river; thence up the said river to the ford where the Kentucky road crosses the river; thence to Campbell's line, near Cumberland gap; thence to the mouth of Claud's Creek on Holstein; thence to the Chimney-top mountain; thence to Camp-creek, near the mouth of Big Limestone, on Nolichuckey; thence a southerly course six miles to a mountain; thence south to the North Carolina line; thence to the South-Carolina Indian boundary, and along the same south-west over the top of the Oconee mountain till it shall strike Tugaloo river; thence a direct line to the top of the Currohee mountain; thence to the head of the south fork of Oconee river."

The Choctaw treaty of January 3, 1786, ran a boundary for their hunting grounds as follows: "Beginning at a point on the thirty-first degree of north latitude, where the Eastern boundary of the Natches district shall touch the same; thence along the said thirty-first degree of north latitude, being the southern boundary of the United States of

boundaries described in these Choctaw and Chickasaw treaties of Hopewell, of January 3 and 10, 1786, were never actually surveyed. They do not appear ever to have been plotted on any map. Their description is so uncertain that parts of the described lines can be indicated only approximately on the map which accompanies this text; the significant thing is that both of these tribal boundaries were described in such a way as to serve as an assertion of American sovereignty within

America, until it shall strike the eastern boundary of the lands on which the Indians of the said nation did live and hunt on the twenty-ninth of November of the year one thousand seven hundred and eighty-two, while they were under the protection of the King of Great-Britain; thence northerly along the said eastern boundary, until it shall meet the northern boundary of the said lands; thence westerly along the said northern boundary, until it shall meet the western boundary thereof; thence southerly along the same to the beginning; saving and reserving for the establishment of trading posts, three tracts or parcels of land of six miles square each, at such places as the United [States] in Congress assembled shall think proper; which posts, and the lands annexed to them, shall be to the use and under the government of the United States of America."

The Chickasaw treaty of January 10, 1786, ran their boundary as follows: "Beginning on the ridge that divides the waters running into the Cumberland, from those running into the Tennessee, at a point in a line to be run north-east, which shall strike the Tennessee at the mouth of Duck River; thence running westerly along the said ridge, till it shall strike the Ohio; thence down the southern banks thereof to the Mississippi; thence down the same, to the Choctaw line or Natches district; thence along the said line, or the line of the district easterly as far as the Chickasaws claimed, and lived and hunted on the twenty-ninth of November, one thousand seven hundred and eighty-two. Thence the said boundary,. eastwardly, shall be the lands allotted to the Choctaws and Cherokees to live and hunt on, and the lands at present in possession of the Creeks; saving and reserving for the establishment of a trading post, a tract or parcel of land to be laid out at the lower port of the Muscle shoals, at the mouth of the Ocochappo, in a circle, the diameter of which shall be five miles on the . . . . . . [original treaty omits name of the river] river, which post, and the lands annexed thereto, shall be to the use and under the government of the United States of America."

that disputed region. The Cherokee boundary was for
the most part within the present states of Kentucky
and Tennessee and well outside the limits claimed by
Spain to the south of the Tennessee River. This boundary line, though of intimate concern to the American
settlers living within that region, allotted to the Cherokee, was not run until 1797. It is to be noted, however,
that such of the Cherokee country as extended to the
south of the Tennessee was also within the area then
disputed by the United States and Spain.[17]

17. For delineation of boundary line of Cherokee treaty (Hopewell)
of Nov. 28, 1785, see *18th Ann. Rept. Am. Bureau of Ethnology*, Pt. II,
Plate 54.

For description of the boundary line, never surveyed, of the Chickasaw
treaty (Hopewell) of Jan. 10, 1786, see terms of the treaty, and *18th
Ann. Rept. Am. Bureau Ethnology*, Pt. II, Plates 1 and 36, where
territorial claims made later by the Chickasaw on the basis of this
treaty are indicated in part.

For description of the boundary line of Choctaw treaty (Hopewell)
of Jan. 3, 1786, see terms of treaty as quoted in preceding note. The
last treaty between the King of Great Britain and the Choctaw was
that of May 26, 1777. It defined the boundary between their hunting
grounds and the British settlements in West Florida. This boundary is
indicated on a manuscript map made, *circa* 1776, by the mapmaker
Joseph Purcell, for John Stuart, then Indian Agent for Great Britain
for the Southern Department, who explains in his official correspondence
that the boundary on the map is that followed in the later treaty of
1777. This map was photographed by Professor John C. Parish in the
Colonial Office, London. See his "John Stuart and the Cartography of
the Indian Boundary Line," in *The Persistence of the Westward Movement and Other Essays* (Berkeley and Los Angeles, 1943), 143–44. With
the assistance of this map, the eastern and southern boundaries of the
Choctaw as last fixed under British dominion can be traced. The
western boundary of the Choctaw is that of the "District of Natchez"
and the southern boundary was in 1777 approximately but not precisely the line of 31°. The line of 31° was introduced in the treaty
between the United States and the Choctaw in 1786 obviously for the
purpose of strengthening the American claim to that boundary. No
eastern or northern boundary was made between Choctaw and British
settlements. On this Stuart map are traced in color lines of boundary
dividing the Cherokee, Creek, Choctaw, and Chickasaw from each

Vague and unsatisfactory as the new Indian boundaries were, full of possibilities of much murderous warfare with the Kentucky and Tennessee settlers, the
treaties did serve to put all the tribes north of the disputed boundary line of 31° and south of the Ohio
definitely under the protection and sovereignty of the
United States.

The several Indian treaties, including those of the
state of Georgia with the Creek, and other sovereign
acts of Georgia[18] within the disputed territory, served
to raise a clear-cut issue between the United States and
Spain, for a few months previously the Spanish Governors of Louisiana and West Florida had made similar treaties with three out of four of these self-same
Indian tribes by which they placed themselves under
the protection of the King of Spain and allied themselves with him for the defense of his provinces. Before
the United States treaty agents had arrived on the
frontier, the disputes between the Georgians and Creek
already had impelled the gifted leader of that tribe,

other. These lines are described by Stuart as claimed by the several
tribes and "settled for the Indian's by His Majesty's Superintendent."
In Map 2, I have followed Stuart's lines as the last and most authorita-
tive definition of the hunting grounds of the several tribes as of
November 29, 1782, as referred to in the language of the Choctaw
treaty of Hopewell, and of the limits of the Chickasaw mentioned in
the Chickasaw treaty of Hopewell. The eastern boundary of the
Natchez District and the southern boundary of the Choctaw hunting
grounds in the treaty of 1777 are laid down in detail on the Purcell
Map in A. B. Hulbert's Crown collection of Maps, Series III, Map 56,
Plate 120. It should be observed that the Indian boundary lines on the
map accompanying this text are political; they do not correspond to
the precise ethnography of the region.

18. In 1785, upon petition of American inhabitants living in the
Natchez District, Georgia established Bourbon County on the east bank
of the Mississippi between the Yazoo and the 31° north latitude.
A.S.P., Public Lands, I, 100. For documents on Bourbon County and
Spanish interests, edited by E. C. Burnett, see *A.H.R.*, XV, 66–111.

the half-breed chieftain, Alexander McGillivray, to appeal for support to the Spanish Governors. They listened to him eagerly. Creek, Chickasaw, and Choctaw signed treaties at Pensacola and Mobile in the summer of 1784 by which they formally accepted Spanish alliance, made peace among themselves, agreed to admit no white man within their villages or lands without a Spanish passport, and promised to receive and protect Spanish traders, who were to furnish them with necessary goods at reasonable prices. To the Spanish guaranty of Creek possessions was appended a proviso: "that these are comprehended within the line and boundaries of His Catholic Majesty our sovereign." The Choctaw and Creek had agreed to defend if necessary with their lives and property the provinces of Louisiana and West Florida, and to take military orders from the governors for the execution of that pledge.[19] The Spanish treaties, unlike the American treaties, did not define boundaries, except for the proviso just quoted in the Creek treaty. Aside from the stipulation excluding all whites without Spanish passports from all the Creek territory (part of which was within undisputed boundaries of the United States) these treaties did not directly violate the uncontroverted rights of the United States.[20] The fact that both governments were endeavoring to control the vacillating Indian

19. The treaties are summarized by Jane Berry, "Indian Policy of Spain in the Southwest, 1783–1795," Miss. Vall. Hist. Rev., III, 464, who cites what are apparently transcripts of the treaties in the Mississippi Provincial Archives (Spanish Dominion, 2:181). The Choctaw treaty, in Spanish text, is printed by Manuel Serrano y Sanz, España y los Indios Cherokis y Chactas en la segunda mitad del siglo XVIII (Madrid, 1916), 82–85.

20. Berry, op. cit.

tribes illustrates the importance of these savages in the diplomacy of the time. To Spain they were a protective buffer against the restless American frontiersman. To the United States they were a means of dominating the disputed territory and making good American dominion over lands within the boundaries laid down in the treaty of the United States with Great Britain.

In the winter of 1784–1785, when Diego de Gardoqui arrived at Cuba on his way to Philadelphia, empowered to negotiate a boundary settlement with the United States, news of this mission had soon spread to the Indian country of the neighboring continent. The three treaty tribes, and with them the Cherokee, immediately protested, through McGillivray as their spokesman, to the Spanish colonial authorities in Louisiana and Florida, that the treaty between Great Britain and the United States—a settlement in which they had no part —could not in any way cede away their lands to the United States. They appealed to the King now to make good his treaties recently signed with them, and to support and protect their pretensions in any settlement which might be reached between Spain and that republic. They asked to be protected from encroachments on their lands both from the side of Georgia and along the Mississippi and Cumberland rivers.[21]

To make his representations more impressive McGillivray stressed the activities on foot by the emissaries of Congress to win over the Indians—this was before the treaties with the American commissioners had been signed—and their offers of an unrestricted

21. The Spanish text of McGillivray's letters of July 10 and 24, 1784, is printed by Serrano y Sanz, op. cit., 21–24.

and profitable trade. The strategic time had come, he suggested, to alienate the several tribes for good and all from American interests:

> At present the memory of past injuries, and the great fear which exists among them of being deprived of their hunting grounds (the greatest injury which an Indian can conceive) makes it a favorable occasion to effect a complete separation of these nations from the Americans and to establish among them an interest or affection for the Spanish nation, which would not be easily dissolved and for which they ardently long; but if the Indians are not attracted by the usual supplies from this place [Pensacola], necessity will compel them to accept the friendship of the American states, through which medium they will receive the supply of all their usual needs, to the exclusion of any other power on the continent.[22]

To supply the Indians with the trading goods promised at the time of the Pensacola treaties, a firm of English traders, William Panton and Company, had been licensed by Spain to import upon payment of duties a cargo of goods from London. English-made goods were all that these Indians had known for a long time. The foreign-trading prohibitions of the Spanish colonial system made it impossible for Spanish traders to supply the native demands. The tribes, at the suggestion of McGillivray, who became Panton's partner, now asked that further license be extended to Panton for the importation, with lowered duties, of English goods, and the abolition of export duties on peltries. The answer by the Spanish Court to this request was to continue license to the house of Panton, Leslie and Company to supply the Indian trade,[23] and to grant

22. Serrano y Sanz, op. cit., 24.
23. Serrano y Sanz, op. cit., 25; Gayarré, *History of Louisiana*, Vol. III, *The Spanish Domination* (hereafter cited as Gayarré), 162. For documents summing up the activities of Panton, see "License of

secret military supplies to the Creek for use against the Americans.[24]

The natives were not satisfied with the Panton trade. A falling market for raw furs and rising prices of goods for the Indian trade[25] made the English firm unable to compete successfully with Yankee traders from over the mountains or across the Georgia rivers. Nor were Spanish agents able to prevent three of the tribes from entering into the above-mentioned treaties with the United States, even though the Indians later were induced to declare to the Spanish Governor that they repudiated those treaties.[26] Governor Miró, who ruled Louisiana at New Orleans, feared that war between the United States and the Creek might wipe out the latter and destroy their value as a protection to West Florida. He dealt out munitions to them too cautiously and too parsimoniously to suit McGillivray.

William Panton, of Pensacola, to import merchandize into Pensacola for Indian trade, and to export from thence products of the Province," and associated documents. The license was continued even after Spain and England went to war. Its history is described in a letter of the Governor, Gayoso de Lemos, Feb. 7, 1799. See L. M. Pérez, *Guide to the Materials for American History in Cuban Archives*, 91. Dr. J. F. Jameson had these documents copied from the Havana archives for Dr. A. P. Whitaker. I was kindly permitted to inspect them. A large mass of Panton's correspondence with the governors of Louisiana, and with McGillivray, and informants in the Indian country, is preserved in the Library of Congress, "Cuban Transcripts." This valuable material, which presents the history of his operations, 1785–1818, is alluded to in item 375, p. 91, Pérez's *Guide*.

24. Supporting documents abundantly establishing this are used by Miss Berry, op. cit. My own examination of contemporary Spanish colonial documents yields nothing to add to the particular subject covered by this excellent paper, unless to suggest that it was not trade rivalry per se that caused Miró nervousness concerning Yankee traders, but rather the influence which these traders had in alienating the Indians from Spanish influence.

25. Serrano y Sanz, op. cit., 31.

26. Ibid., 40.

As the allegiance of the Indians to Spain wavered in response to overtures from agents and traders from the United States, Governor Miró anxiously watched his chief defense against the restless men of the western waters weakening under his eyes. To protect his provinces he was forced to fall back on his feeble forts and their thin Spanish garrisons. He began to contemplate means of bringing them up to more adequate strength.[27]

The remaining principal matter to be settled between the two countries was the regulation of commerce. John Jay's treaty proposals to Spain in 1781 had suggested reciprocal most-favored-nation trading privileges. During the Revolution American ships were admitted at European ports of Spain practically on that basis.[28] To support hostilities against the common enemy, they had been permitted to trade in Havana and New Orleans. Such entrance to these ports was a special privilege, advantageous to Spain only because of war conditions. Shortly after the re-establishment of peace it was abruptly proclaimed at an end, not without considerable hardship to American merchants who had established themselves in those localities.[29] Trade between Spain proper and the United States continued

27. Miró's correspondence with his immediate superior, the Captain-General of Cuba, is a continual reiteration of the weakness of his garrisons, and a never-ending and unsuccessful plea for reinforcement from Cuba or Spain. See Despatches of Spanish Governors of Louisiana, 1766–1791, a series of photostats made by the Carnegie Institution from various *legajos* in the Papeles de Cuba, at Seville. For efforts to hold the affections and allegiance of the Indians, see Serrano y Sanz, op. cit., 28–42.

28. In the case of Spain, most-favored-nation privileges were superior to privileges enjoyed by Spanish nationals themselves, because Spain in past treaties, particularly with Great Britain, had given foreign subjects particular commercial privileges. See J. Becker, *Historia de las relaciones exteriores de España durante el siglo XIX*, I, 1–21.

29. Rendon to Galvez, No. 87, Phila., Aug., 31, Sept. 30, 1783. A. G. I., 87/1/7 (L. C. trans.).

on the sufferance of Spanish municipal decrees, without legal certainty, but apparently without particular discrimination. In the absence of any treaty, Spanish vessels visited the several American states on what amounted in practice to a most-favored-nation basis, but of course also without treaty protection. Spain was no more willing or likely to open her colonial ports in times of peace to American vessels than she had been when those craft had flown the British flag, or to foreign ships of any kind, which were legally excluded, except for special license, from all her vast American dominions. In September, 1784, the American commissioners stationed at Paris to negotiate treaties of commerce with European nations exhibited to the Count de Aranda their full powers for a treaty of commerce and friendship. That Ambassador answered that it was not the custom of Spain to negotiate such matters on the soil of a third party. He asked if one of the commission could not be sent to Madrid for that purpose. The commissioners asserted that they were already engaged in so many important negotiations that they could not yet spare one of their members. Politely they asked that for this particular occasion the King of Spain make an exception to his general rule.[30]

This overture to Aranda was professed to be the immediate occasion for the beginning of the important but unsuccessful negotiations carried on between Spain and the United States in New York from 1785 to 1789, negotiations in which these several questions of river navigation, boundaries, Indian affairs, and commerce played a vital part.[31] We are now in a position to review them.

30. *Dip. Corres.* II, 202, 209–211; Yela, I, 481.
31. See Whitaker, *Spanish-American Frontier*, 229, note 13.

CHAPTER 3

Gardoqui and Jay

I

It was in October, 1784, that Floridablanca instructed Aranda to inform the American commissioners plenipotentiary at Paris that a special plenipotentiary of Charles III would be sent to the United States to reside near Congress with the title of *encargado de negocios,* furnished with full powers to treat not only of commercial relations but also of the Question of the Mississippi and the boundary issue, subjects inseparably connected with any treaty settlement that would be acceptable to Spain.[1] From memoranda preserved on the subject of instructions for the Spanish representative who was to be sent to the United States, dated as early as July, 1784, it is evident that the mission had already been decided on, and that Don Diego de Gardoqui had been selected for that appointment.[2]

Concerning the personal biography of Diego de Gardoqui too little is known. He was a son of Joseph de Gardoqui, of Bilbao, whose firm, Gardoqui and Sons, had been the chief go-between through which the Spanish Court furnished secret military stores to the American insurrectionists in the earlier years of the

1. For correspondence between the commissioners and Aranda, in Sept. 1784, see *Dip. Corres.,* II, 202, 209–11. Aranda's report on the subject to Floridablanca and the latter's reply to him are printed by Conrotte, op. cit., 266–270.

2. Memorandum on Gardoqui's instructions as to boundaries, San Ildefonso, July 25, 1784, A. C. A., Est. Leg., 3457, G. D., V, 205–213.

Revolution. Don Diego had separated himself from the business connections of the family house and embarked upon a government career. During the period of the American Revolution he served in subordinate capacity in the Ministry of Finance, at Madrid, and made of himself a ready instrument through which Spanish subsidies could be disguised as private commerce in contraband from Bilbao. He was the person through whom unofficial contact was preserved by the Spanish Foreign Office with the American agents in Spain, particularly Jay. In this office he early familiarized himself with all phases of the American problem from its very beginning. Service later in England as consul thoroughly acquainted him with the English language.[3] Gardoqui's experience during the four years of his mission in the United States, from 1785–1789, equipped him with a more accurate understanding of that country than was possessed by any other man in Spain. On his return to Spain in 1790, he became Minister of Finance and the monarchy's chief adviser and negotiator in questions pertaining to the United States from then until after the negotiation of the treaty of 1795. During the same time he was the ablest and most active minister in the Spanish Council of State, which was not made up of lazy men.[4]

The study which he made of John Jay in Madrid

3. The Spanish designation, *encargado de negocios,* implied to the Continental Congress a slightly different status than that of *chargé,* and raised a question of precedence. See *Dip. Corres.,* VI, 65–89; Monroe to Jefferson, N. Y., July 15, 1785, Jefferson Papers, Library of Congress. For some interesting notes on Gardoqui's personal appearance, together with a portrait, see C. W. Bowen, *History of the Centennial Celebration of the Inauguration of George Washington,* 32.

4. Gardoqui's reports and recommendations as recorded in the Minutes of the Junta de Estado in the Archivo Histórico Nacional, Madrid, occupy much more space than those of any other minister.

during the Revolution enabled Gardoqui to make certain suggestions for incorporation into his instructions:

The American, Jay [he observed to Floridablanca], who is generally considered to possess talent and capacity enough to cover in great part a weakness natural to him, appears (by a consistent behavior) to be a very self-centered man (*es hombre muy interesado*), which passion his wife augments, because, in addition to considering herself meritoriously and being rather vain, she likes to be catered to (*gusta que la obsequien*), and even more to receive presents. This woman, whom he loves blindly, dominates him and nothing is done without her consent, so that her opinion prevails, though her husband at first may disagree: from which I infer that a little management in dealing with her and a few timely gifts will secure the friendship of both, because I have reason to believe that they proceed resolved to make a fortune. He is not the only one in his country who has the same weakness (*flanco*), for there are many poor persons (*muchos necesitados*) among the governing body, and I believe a skilful hand which knows how to take advantage of favorable opportunities, and how to give dinners and above all to entertain with good wine, may profit without appearing to pursue them.

He added that Jay's influence would control the votes of six or seven states in Congress, because the northern states depended for the most part upon three or four articles of commerce, the principal consumption of which was in Spain.[5]

Gardoqui's instructions were drawn up after consultation between Floridablanca and Josef de Galvez, Minister for the Indies, a sagacious and veteran administrator of long and varied experience in the management of Spain's colonial possessions, whose nephew, Bernardo de Galvez, conqueror of Florida, was then Captain-General of Cuba and Louisiana. The elder Galvez recommended that Gardoqui be enabled to carry out his proposal to regale members of Congress and

5. A. C. A., Est. Leg., 3420, G. D., V, 17.

individuals of importance in the United States; that the boundary line of East Florida in the Anglo-American peace treaty should be acceptable to Spain, but under no circumstances the line of 31° north latitude for West Florida: that Spain should not relinquish her right to the exclusive navigation of the Mississippi where it ran between Spanish banks. Spain's claim to the east bank of the river, he thought, could be bounded by the Apalachicola River[6] and a line extending from its source to the Tennessee River, thence down that to the Ohio and thence along that river to the Mississippi. But on that point the King's passion for a peaceable and friendly settlement with the United States might allow special concessions. Gardoqui was to be referred to further instructions from Bernardo de Galvez, upon arrival at Havana, as to acceptable maximum and minimum boundary lines. Commerce with Spanish colonies, prohibited to European nations, could not be allowed to the United States, but Spain would be glad to agree to reciprocal most-favored-nation privileges, which would include liberal treatment at Spanish peninsular ports,[7] a trade esteemed valuable to the eastern states of the American Confederation, particularly because it paid plenteously in hard cash. For such a treaty Gardoqui should be given full powers. In case it was necessary, in order to secure a recognition of Spanish interests in the matter of the exclusive navigation of the Mississippi and the boundary of West Florida, the agent might offer a treaty of alliance to

6. Known above its junction with the Flint as the Chattahoochee.
7. See Memorandum on Gardoqui's instructions as to boundaries, San Ildefonso, July 25, 1784, A. C. A., Est. Leg., 3457, G. D., V, 205–213; and Memorandum for Gardoqui's instructions, unsigned and undated, apparently (by interior evidence) by Josef de Galvez, A. C. A., Est. Leg., 3420, G. D., V, 186.

guarantee the remaining territory of the United States.

The actual instructions followed precisely these suggestions. As a basis for the proposed alliance they referred to Articles VII and VIII of the treaty draft proposed by Jay in Madrid, September 22, 1781, which stipulated a mutual guaranty of possessions in North America. Article VI of that proposed treaty was now interpreted to Gardoqui as conceding to Spain "exclusive navigation" of the river from the limits of American territory to the sea. It was not at this time recalled that Jay's carefully worded offer of 1781 was not an absolute relinquishment, but was conditional upon Spanish acceptance of the proposed alliance then and there during the war.[8]

At Havana, Bernardo de Galvez, long familiar with the frontier affairs of Louisiana, drew up instructions for Gardoqui's governance as to the West Florida boundary.[9] The claim to territory north of the Ohio was not mentioned. After elucidating the familiar Spanish claims to West Florida above 31°, Galvez stated that during the war a Spanish officer, Capt. Baltazar de Villiers, had crossed the river from the Spanish post at Arkansas and had taken formal possession of the east bank of the Mississippi as far north as the Ohio.

> I must say to you that the Court is firmly resolved in its desire to have the line begin at least at the Cherokee [i.e., the Tennessee], without admitting contradiction, for the effective fulfilment of which we should not listen to solicitations directed against

8. The instructions, dated San Lorenzo, Oct. 2, 1784, are printed in Conrotte, op. cit., 270–276. For proposed Articles of 1781, see ante, p. 27.

9. "General Galvez and Don Diego de Gardoqui, envoy for the United States, arrived here a few days ago." Oliver Pollock to John Jay, Havana, Feb. 10, 1785, *Dip. Corres.*, VI, 71. This suggests that the two arrived from Spain on the same ship.

such an irrefragible position [*irrefragable sistema*], and that whatever the Americans may allege against it must be considered ill-founded and unjust, and any claim and any act to realize it as an insult. In this conception the least condescension on our part would be so uncalled for (*fuera del caso*) that it would appear as weakness, and would bring irreparable prejudice and weakness to the King's sovereignty and rights.

I firmly believe that the Americans, aware of the weakness of their case, will agree to the evidence of our right, but if they should be so unreasonable as to reply in threatening terms, you will take them down by your knowledge that we have no cause to fear them because we have a sufficient number of veteran troops in the provinces, a trained and well disciplined militia, and friendship with many Indian natives who are disaffected toward the Americans, as well as sufficient experience in wilderness warfare, a familiarity (*conocimiento*) which they perhaps think exclusive to themselves.

The above document reads as if for exhibition. A separate instruction stipulated, after marshaling arguments, that if the boundary of the Ohio and Cherokee rivers could not be secured, strong efforts should be made for the line of 35° north latitude east from the Mississippi until it should meet either the Cherokee, the Euphrasia, or the Flint,[10] from which river it should

10. "Hasta encontrar bien sea el rio Cheraqui, el Euphrasee, o el Flint y desde el continuar por el medio de sus aguas del mismo modo que está especificado hasta la boca del rio Santa María en el Oceano Atlantico." The Euphrasia River appears on Faden's Maps of the United States, of 1783 and 1785; also on Sayer and Bennett's Map of 1783 as "Uphase R." In the Archivo Histórico Nacional at Madrid is the southwestern quarter of Buell's *Map of North America* of 1783 (New Haven). Gardoqui's No. 13 of July 25, 1785 (A. C. A., Est. Leg., 3886, G. D., VI, 52) covered the conveyance to Madrid of two copies of this map which was used in formulating the above instructions (G. D., III, 249). The above-mentioned boundary line is traced on this map, but leaves the Tennessee at "Stoney River." I cannot identify Stoney River with any contemporary name, so far as a study of the maps in the Library of Congress would help. It is probably Chickamauga Creek. The line as described in Gardoqui's instructions (that is, by the

follow the line to the St. Mary's and thence to the Atlantic. As a last resort, he might accept a line east from the mouth of the Yazoo River, provided that lands possessed by the treaty Indians be included within the line.[11] It is noteworthy that Spain after 1783 made no claim to territory north of the Ohio, nor any allusion to the Spanish expedition to Fort St. Joseph, Illinois, during the American Revolution.

II

Gardoqui presented himself at New York, where he found Congress in session, in July, 1785. He brought a commission empowering him, as *encargado de negocios* plenipotentiary, to treat with a properly authorized person for a settlement of commercial intercourse and boundaries between the two countries, and in regard to other points "conducive to the enjoyment of these important and beneficial objects."[12] This full power did not permit him to yield the navigation of the Mississippi.

Congress received him ceremoniously.[13] It commis-

Euphrasia) follows the present Hiawassee (the next stream above Stoney River on Buell's Map) which had been known previously as the "Euphrasee." See Jedidiah Morse, *American Gazetteer* (Boston, 1797), under "Euphrasee," and Bradley's map therein published.

11. Instructions to Gardoqui as to boundary with the United States, Havana, April 28, 1785, A. C. A., Est. Leg., 3891, G. D., III, 238. A monthly packet service was established between Havana and New York, to care for Gardoqui's despatches and keep communication regular between him and Spanish colonial officials at Havana and on the mainland.

12. *Dip. Corres.*, VI, 66.

13. The etiquette observed on the occasion of Gardoqui's reception was as follows: he was conducted by the Secretary for Foreign Affairs to the Congress Chamber and announced, the President and Members of Congress keeping their seats and remaining covered. His commission and letters of credence were then delivered to the Secretary of Congress,

MAP 3

Maps Illustrating Spain's Claims to Territory East of the Mississippi River and Successive Concessions Allowed in Instructions to Gardoqui, 1784–1787

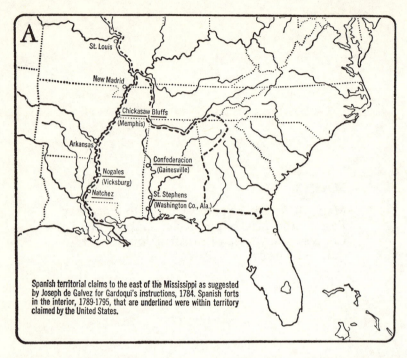

A

Spanish territorial claims to the east of the Mississippi as suggested by Joseph de Galvez for Gardoqui's instructions, 1784. Spanish forts in the interior, 1789-1795, that are underlined were within territory claimed by the United States.

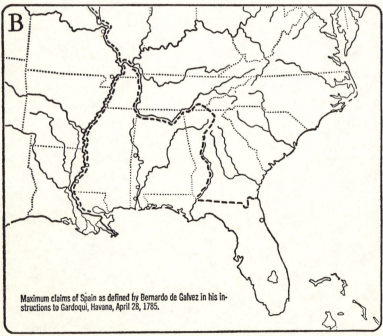

B

Maximum claims of Spain as defined by Bernardo de Galvez in his instructions to Gardoqui, Havana, April 28, 1785.

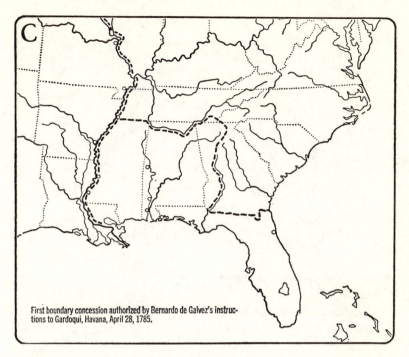

First boundary concession authorized by Bernardo de Galvez's instructions to Gardoqui, Havana, April 28, 1785.

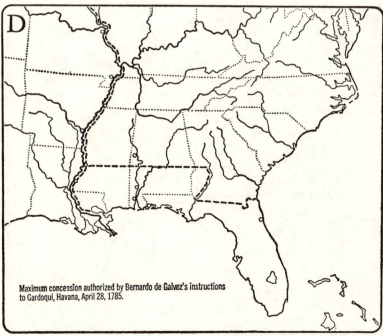

Maximum concession authorized by Bernardo de Galvez's instructions to Gardoqui, Havana, April 28, 1785.

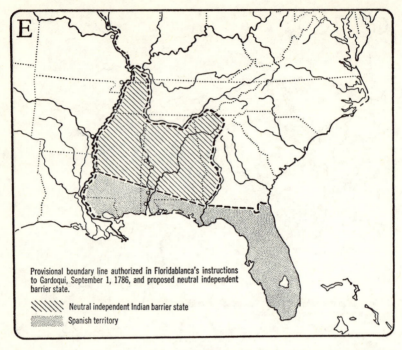

E

Provisional boundary line authorized in Floridablanca's instructions
to Gardoqui, September 1, 1786, and proposed neutral independent
barrier state.

Neutral independent Indian barrier state

Spanish territory

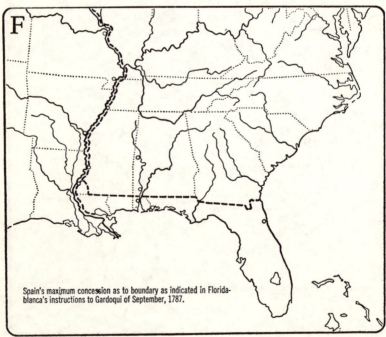

F

Spain's maximum concession as to boundary as indicated in Floridablanca's instructions to Gardoqui of September, 1787.

sioned John Jay, Secretary for Foreign Affairs, to treat with him on the subjects covered by his full powers. Jay was specifically enjoined in any treaty to stipulate the right of the United States "to their territorial bounds and the free navigation of the Mississippi, from the source to the ocean as established in the treaties with Great Britain," and not to conclude anything until he had previously communicated it to Congress and received the approbation of that body.[14]

Full powers and commissions duly exchanged, the two plenipotentiaries entered a long series of oral negotiations which consumed the autumn and winter of 1785. In the first conference Jay insisted on the American claim to the navigation of the Mississippi and the boundary of 31° as stipulated by the treaty of peace and independence. He requested entrance for American commerce into the Spanish American colonies, and also hinted at the desirability of receiving privilege to cut dye woods in Honduras, which the English colonies used to enjoy before the Revolution (a point soon dropped). Gardoqui replied that it was impossible to grant either the navigation of the Mississippi or commercial privileges in the colonial provinces, but that there would be less difficulty in reaching a boundary settlement.[15] As a matter of fact, Jay had in his files a

---

who read a translation made from copies previously left with Jay for the President of Congress. Gardoqui then briefly spoke acknowledging his cordial sentiments, after which he awaited a formal reply of the Congress through its Secretary for Foreign Affairs. Ibid., 81; Monroe to Jefferson, July 15, 1785, Jefferson Papers, Library of Congress.

14. Resolution of July 20, 1785, *Dip. Corres.*, VI, 102.

15. Gardoqui to Conde de Galvez, Viceroy of New Spain, N. Y., Aug. 23, 1785, A. C. A., Est. Leg., 3891, G. D., III, 304.

In the first conferences with Gardoqui, Jay made much of an admission by Floridablanca to Lafayette, during the latter's visit to Madrid in February, 1783, of the right of the United States to the

copy of a letter from Floridablanca to Gardoqui, dated
October 24, 1784, directing the latter to confer with
Bernardo de Galvez as to "how far it may be proper to
modify the same [boundary] as regulated by the instructions of July 29, 1784." [16] He was therefore fairly
certain that the Spaniards would make some concessions on this point if pressed.

From the first the Spanish envoy was impressed with
the difficulty of securing the consent of Congress to
any exclusion from the Mississippi. If the matter
rested with Jay alone, he believed that a settlement
between Spain and the United States would be easy.
Gardoqui's expense accounts have numerous items for
entertainment of the Jays as well as influential members of Congress. Mrs. Jay he cultivated from the first.
Within a few months after he arrived at New York

---

navigation of the Mississippi and the boundary line of 31 degrees north
latitude. This occurred in an exchange of letters in which Floridablanca stated: "You have perfectly well understood whatever I have had
the honor to communicate to you, with respect to our disposition
towards the United States. I shall only add that, although it is his
Majesty's intention to abide for the present by the limits, established
by the treaty of the 30th of November, 1782, between the English and
the Americans, the King intends to inform himself particularly
whether it can be in any ways inconvenient or prejudicial to settle
that affair amicably with the United States."

It is enough to quote the passage to show that it was not an admission. Floridablanca answered Gardoqui's despatch relative to this
point by saying that the correspondence between him and Lafayette
"proved nothing." Floridablanca to Gardoqui, El Pardo, Jan. 28, 1786,
A. C. A., Est. Leg., 3886, G. D., VI, 145. See also *Dip. Corres.*, VI, 186.
Nevertheless, the contemporary correspondence of the French diplomatic
representative at Madrid indicates that he understood from Floridablanca that Spain was prepared to recognize the boundary of 31°.
See Montmorin to Vergennes, Madrid, Feb. 19, 1783, Archives des
Affaires Etrangères, Correspondance Politique, Espagne, Vol. 610, folio
253–257. I am indebted to Dr. Waldo G. Leland for transcripts of this
and other material from the same archives.

16. Papers of the Continental Congress, MSS., L. C., Vol. 97, p. 17.

he felt at home in Jay's house. Jay asked him for a
license to import from Spain a Spanish stallion. Gardoqui promptly responded with the gift outright of a
splendid animal sent by Charles III himself, and Jay
secured permission from Congress to accept the gift.[17]
But the majority of the state delegations in Congress
were then set against conceding the Mississippi, and
Gardoqui soon realized that back of Jay's genial friendship there stood a wall of public opinion which the
Secretary dared not openly oppose. That opinion supported the new West.

Fifty thousand people already had their homes in
the western country, wrote Gardoqui to Bernardo de
Galvez—now Viceroy of Mexico—most of them trans-
formed overnight by the increased value of their cheaply
acquired lands from beggars to comfortable "peasants."
The future prosperity of these settlers depended on
the river. Congress, he thought, would not dare to take
that from them. Even if it should, the western inhabitants, hundreds of miles distant from the seat of government, would take matters into their own hands.
Nevertheless, he found that "men of judgment" in
Congress were persuaded that free navigation was not
a really desirable object, because if secured it would
serve to attract the population away from where it was
most needed—in the eastern states. But these same
eastern men of judgment feared that if such a right
should be abandoned expressly by treaty the indignation
of the West would be so powerful as to split apart the
Confederation. He cited the efforts, already being made
to prevent such a happening, by the states of Maryland,

17. Gardoqui to Floridablanca, Confidential No. 3, N. Y., Aug. 23,
1785. For the stallion, see Gardoqui to Floridablanca, N. Y., June 30,
1785, A. C. A., Est. Leg., 3902, G. D., V, 335, 345; Floridablanca to
Gardoqui, San Lorenzo, Oct. 28, 1785, ibid.; and *Dip. Corres.*, VI, 141.

Virginia, and Pennsylvania, to improve their own rivers, particularly the Potomac, in such a way as to make the nearer western lands more inviting to emigrants and to bind by interest the frontier communities more closely to the Atlantic seaboard.

"I leave it to the superior talent of Your Excellency," added the *encargado*, "to infer how well it would be for us to avoid the vexations of such a naturally robust people, trained to war and accustomed to the last degree of greatest hardships, as was duly proven when England lost the flower of her troops at the hands of a few naked colonists without military discipline." Every inhabitant of the West was a potential soldier, he commented; the appearance of a military leader of impressive personality easily might result in the descent of a veritable army of frontiersmen on the Spanish provinces in some such ill-founded hope as that of capturing silver treasure. "The well known perspicacity of Your Excellency will note that though in their present state they may not be very dreadful neighbors, nevertheless it appears to be well for us to watch out (*precavernos*) and stand well with them in order to avoid their joining with any other power whose aid would make them very respectable." [18]

The prudent tone of this despatch contrasts notice-

18. Gardoqui to Conde de Galvez, Viceroy of New Spain, N. Y., Aug. 3, 1785, A. C. A., Est. Leg., 3891, G. D., III, 304. A copy of the same was forwarded to Floridablanca. Gardoqui concluded the despatch by quoting a letter of Washington, recently communicated to him by the French chargé: "Irrespective of the justice or not of the prohibition of the Court of Spain," it stated, "it will not be easy to constrain that class of people into depriving themselves of the enjoyment of their natural utilities. It is earnestly to be hoped that Mr. Gardoqui reach such an understanding with Congress as will avoid the threatened danger and be mutually advantageous to both countries."

ably with the ostentatious allusions, in Gardoqui's own instructions, to Spain's military strength in Louisiana.

As a means of absorbing some of this American feeling on the Mississippi Question, Gardoqui proposed to Floridablanca not a portentous exhibition of the military defenses of Louisiana which his first instructions had suggested, but special tariff privileges reciprocally for Spanish and American goods and ships in Spain proper and in the United States, even at the risk of Spain thereby incurring the obligation to extend the same privileges to European nations possessing most-favored-nation rights. Should this not be approved, he suggested a treaty of commerce and boundary which should not mention the Mississippi, letting it rest uncompromisingly in the condition of having been formally denied to everybody.[19]

The two plenipotentiaries continued their conversations throughout the winter of 1785–1786. We have the record preserved in detail in the Spanish envoy's numerous despatches. The latter assiduously obeyed repeated orders from Floridablanca to regale Jay and other influential men who might be induced to favor Spain's claims. He continued to be most attentive to Mrs. Jay. "Notwithstanding my age," he wrote his chief, "I am acting the gallant and accompanying Madame to the official entertainments and dances, because she likes it and I will do everything which appears to me for the King's best interest." [20] He began to derive some satisfaction from talks with prominent persons whose

19. Gardoqui to Floridablanca, Confidential No. 3, N. Y., Aug. 23, 1785, ibid., Leg., 3895, G. D., IV, 14–28.

20. Gardoqui to Floridablanca, Confidential No. 7, N. Y., Feb. 1, 1786, A. C. A., Est. Leg., 3895, G. D., IV, 52–72.

eastern industrial interests might be injured by the
drain of cheap labor in emigrations to the West. One
of these was Governor Clinton, of New York. He also
got comfort from the fact that Congress seemed really
anxious to restrain, pending the negotiations, the irresponsible Georgian frontiersmen and other westerners
from aggressive action in the disputed territory, or
from attempting to force the navigation of the river.

To Gardoqui, at this time, it was a matter of alarm
that the Kentucky District of Virginia was petitioning
for a separation from the parent commonwealth and
admission into the Union as a new, fourteenth state.
As a new state, or perhaps more as an independent
power, they would be more difficult to restrain in their
efforts to get down the river; he therefore thought it
well to tie up the Confederation to a definite exclusion
before the petitions of the Kentucky people were
granted.[21] The potential menace to Spanish provinces
of these western settlements, especially when denied
the use of the great river, was the subject of frequent
despatches to Floridablanca, and eventually of the suggestion that the demand of the American West for the
use of the Mississippi would have to be met by Spain
with some arrangement similar to that by which Den-
mark regulated, by toll charges, the traffic of the
Sounds.[22]

Neither gifts nor attentions, reflections nor arguments seemed as yet potent enough to drive Jay from
his stand as to the Mississippi and the southwestern

21. Gardoqui to Floridablanca, No. 65, N. Y., Mar. 13, 1786, A. C. A.,
Est. Leg., 3891A, G. D., III, 20. See also Floridablanca's reply of Sept.
1, ibid., agreeing with that idea.

22. Same to same, Confidential No. 9, April 16, 1786, A. C. A., Est.
Leg., 3895, G. D., II, 86–95.

boundary.[23] After many conversations, the two agreed to work out the draft of a treaty of commerce which should exhibit the reciprocal advantages of such an instrument, particularly to the states which might thus be induced to accept the cloture of the river. "We are working it out while the new Congress is being formed," wrote Gardoqui, "so that when we see a favorable moment, that Minister [Jay] will present it and ask for a resolution whether that matter should be acceded to, without which I have declared I can proceed no farther." Really he had little hope that Congress would assent without some valuable equivalent.[24] In agreeing to present the matter to Congress, Jay had not yet accepted Gardoqui's claims, as the latter's despatches show, though he then had in mind the recommendations which the following summer he made to that sovereign body.

III

The negotiators had now agreed, after several confidential conferences, on heads for a proposed treaty covering points other than the still unsettled issues of the Mississippi Question and the boundary. These in-

23. In February, 1786, Gardoqui reported that in addition to his attentions to the Jays he had made use of the reflections, which Floridablanca meanwhile had furnished to him, to stress the importance of the successful Spanish mediation between the United States and Morocco, which demonstrated the value of Spanish friendship in the Mediterranean, and was a reason for concessions; because, unrestrained, the Barbary corsairs could drive American commerce out of that sea. He also emphasized the disadvantage to the eastern states of diverting western trade to the Mississippi. Gardoqui to Floridablanca, Confidential Despatch No. 7, N. Y., Feb. 1, 1786, A. C. A., Est. Leg., 3895, G. D., IV, 52–72.

24. Same to same, Confidential No. 6, N. Y., Nov. 21, 1785, A. C. A., Est. Leg., 3895, G. D., IV, 33.

cluded a treaty of commerce and alliance for thirty years, in which Spain accepted commercial reciprocity between the United States and the peninsular domains of the Kingdom as well as the Canary Islands, the merchants of each party to be given the treatment of nationals[25] within the domains of the other in matters of duties. It included reciprocal permission to introduce all the *bona fide* manufactures and products of either party (except tobacco) into the (stipulated) domains of the other, with tariffs to be based on principle of reciprocity according to a scale to be worked out in a separate convention. Each party was to guarantee the other's territory in America as it should be determined by the treaty, against attack by a third party.[26] "In consideration of the fact that the United States has no mines of gold and silver to supply the demands of a circulating medium," His Catholic Majesty agreed to purchase every year, for cash specie, a quantity of hard wood for building purposes, providing it be equal in quality and price to that which might be obtained elsewhere. Finally Spain agreed to mediate between the United States and Great Britain for the recovery of the American posts on the northern frontier, and "will see that they get justice, by force of arms if otherwise it cannot be promptly secured." [27]

25. See note 28, p. 58 ante.

26. As to the article of mutual territorial guaranty, as first worded by Gardoqui it included all the possessions of Spain in Europe and America. Jay objected that the United States ought not to commit itself to such obligations, so difficult to fulfil because of the distance involved. Gardoqui replied that it was just as difficult for Spain to fulfil hers for the same reason. They finally agreed to leave out Spain proper, but to include under the guaranty the territories of the King of Spain in both Americas as they should exist after agreement between the United States and Spain in regard to the disputed boundary. Gardoqui to Floridablanca, Confidential No. 7, N. Y., Feb. 1, 1786, G. D., IV, 64.

27. Ibid.

Such were the contingent articles to which Jay agreed, and which Gardoqui recommended to his court for acceptance provided the United States would relinquish specifically its claims to the navigation of the Mississippi, and make some compromise in regard to the Florida boundary.[28] It was a notable proposal for an entangling alliance. The article of mutual guaranty specifically stated that neither party, in case of an attack on its dominions in America by a third power, should make peace until the territory of the other, attacked and invaded, should be restored. Spain still denied the one great object for which the West pleaded, while these initialed articles bound the United States to fight for the restoration of any portion of the far-flung colonial domains of the Spanish Empire in North and South America, and set up at the same time a self-denying ordinance against any future expansion at the expense of contiguous Spanish territory. This obviously was the chief value of the arrangement to Spain. The commercial articles were carefully designed to offer powerful inducements to the commerce of the eastern states, and when made public the articles further would have displayed to the country at large a possible means of expelling British garrisons from the northern posts.

Let us now see how the Continental Congress received these articles insofar as they were revealed to it. Jay, we must remember, presided over no separate executive department which had any power of initi-

28. Gardoqui was empowered in 1786 to make some concessions from the line of the Yazoo laid down in the instructions of the Conde de Galvez. Floridablanca to Gardoqui, El Pardo, Jan. 28, 1786, A. C. A., Est. Leg., 3886, G. D., VI, 145. This instruction says that "some but no great modification" of his original instructions as to boundaries might be allowable.

ating a negotiation and presenting a finished product to a branch of the legislative body for approval, as is the case with the Secretary of State acting under the President according to our present constitution. Congress itself was the sole executive and the Secretary for Foreign Affairs was its clerk. This negotiation had been initiated by Congress itself. Jay was the instrument of this executive body and bound by instructions which had positively forbidden him to recognize any right of Spain to close the navigation of the lower Mississippi to American citizens or to possess a square inch of territory north of the line of 31° north latitude along the boundary of West Florida.

CHAPTER 4

Congress and the Negotiation·

I

The proposed alliance, described in the preceding chapter, an alliance which was contingent upon a settlement of the Question of the Mississippi and the disputed boundary, was not published, nor has it ever been until now. The articles were digested as a summary of the confidential interviews of the two negotiators, not divulged to anybody. As far as Gardoqui was concerned, he had made it clear that they had to be referred back to Spain for final sanction. So far as Jay was concerned, he had not failed to have it understood that they must secure the approval of Congress. This, we know, would depend in great part upon the larger issues still left unsettled, concerning which Congress in the beginning had expressly prohibited Jay from making any concession whatsoever. Jay in his negotiations in Spain during the American Revolution had recorded himself as a staunch opponent of any yielding of the navigation of the Mississippi to the sea,[1] even when Congress, pressed by the hardships of war and desirous of Spain's alliance, had voted, upon Madison's motion, to yield the navigation in return for a satisfactory treaty of alliance.

We have seen that Gardoqui's own instructions of 1784 were equally fixed on these two important issues: he was forbidden to recognize any American right to

1. Wharton, IV, 629, 741; Pellew, *John Jay*, 138.

navigate the Mississippi where it ran between Spanish banks, and he was allowed to make concessions as to the boundary only, provided the United States accepted the Spanish position in regard to the navigation of the river. To support his claim Gardoqui now had the precedent which Congress had set by offering, in 1781, to accept the Spanish cloture of the Mississippi in return for a treaty of alliance during the Revolution, albeit that offer straightway had been withdrawn prudently by Jay upon Spain's refusal to accept it.

The initialed articles, as they were intended to do, served to give to Jay, with whom and with whose family Gardoqui was now on most intimate and friendly terms, a glimpse of advantages which might be secured if only he would relinquish the claims to the river. Jay and Gardoqui now awaited an opportune moment to submit to Congress the Question of the Mississippi.[2] The Spanish envoy, nervously watching the growth of the Kentucky settlements, protested to Jay every appearance of hostility from that quarter against Louisiana. Jay's answers, approved by Congress, satisfied him that the United States Government was sincere in its professions to discourage every such movement pending the settlement of a treaty. Gardoqui, we repeat, was at that time anxious to get a treaty pact through before the turbulent West should get beyond control of Congress.

The opportune time to present the subject came in May, 1786, when Congress had finally reached a quorum and assembled in full. On the 23d of that month Gardoqui, with little hope that it would have much effect on Congress,[3] drew up a note to Jay, summarizing

2. Gardoqui to Floridablanca, No. 73, N. Y., April 16, 1786, A. C. A., Est. Leg., 3886, G. D., II, 64.

3. Gardoqui to Floridablanca, No. 81, N. Y., June 18, 1786, A. C. A., Est. Leg., 3886, G. D., II, 82.

the case for Spain. Jay was asked to inform Congress that "the King will not permit any nation to navigate between the two banks belonging to His Majesty, from the extent of his conquests made by his royal arms over the English in East and West Florida, according to the dominion formerly held by the English and the jurisdiction exercised by the commandant of Pensacola, on which it depended, *as well as the countries to the East of the Mississippi, of which formal possession was taken by Captain Don Baltazar de Villiers,* commandant of the post at Arkansas, for his Majesty on the 22nd of November, 1780." [4] Having laid down this condition, Gardoqui elaborated the advantages which the United States had already enjoyed because of the "good and generous disposition" of the King: fruitful intercession with the Barbary States, and forbearance to request till now the payment of the principal of the debts contracted by the United States both in Spain and her colonies during the Revolution, not to mention interest thereon. By not yielding the navigation of the river, the United States would run the risk of losing the trade with Spain, the only commerce which brought to America a cash balance. That trade depended on the good will of the Spanish King, whose subjects stood in no necessity of getting their fish, grain, flour, and rice from America, nor anything else; a royal regulation could easily exclude them without loss to Spain, particularly when that nation had no appreciable market in the United States. In consideration that nothing be said of the difficulties of navigation and boundaries, and without alluding to the details of his arrangement with Jay, the Spanish agent stated that he believed that His Majesty would consent to guarantee to the United

4. Italics inserted.

States their rights and dominions as they should be left by the new treaty, and he further promised to pray the King "that the satisfaction of the debts due from the United States to Spain, may be with such relaxation as may be convenient to them." [5]

If there was little hope that Congress would yield on the point of the Mississippi and repeal the instructions which limited the American negotiator, Jay had already conceived a means of circumventing those limitations. In the spring of 1786 he explained to James Monroe, then a Virginia delegate in Congress, the status of the negotiation, without mentioning the feature of the proposed alliance. He emphasized the unyielding Spanish position on the Mississippi Question. He suggested that the United States, without giving up principle, might *forbear*[6] to use the river within exclusively Spanish limits during the term of the treaty—twenty-five or thirty years. Monroe listened without comment as Jay explained that such a proposal would probably not be acceptable to Congress if presented. He therefore wished Congress to appoint a committee to control him in the negotiation, in lieu of his former instructions. Monroe ended the conversation by significantly reminding Jay that Virginia had specifically instructed her delegates in such a way as to make impossible any such maneuver.[7]

5. *Dip. Corres.*, VI, 151. May 25 is the date here given for the note. The original MS. in Papers of the Continental Congress is dated May 23. For explanation of these debts, see Appendix II at end of this volume.

6. For previous use of this word by Jay, see his proposed Article in 1781, Chapter 1, above.

7. James Monroe to Patrick Henry, N. Y., Aug. 12, 1786, *Writings of James Monroe* (S. M. Hamilton, ed.), I, 144–151. Quoted by Mc-Laughlin *et al.*, in *Source Problems in United States History*. The editors of this book have made, for college students, an interesting

Jay made the same proposal to Congress May 29, 1786,[8] following the receipt of Gardoqui's memoir of the 23d.

The communication from the Secretary for Foreign Affairs immediately precipitated the most serious issue that agitated the Continental Congress during its five years of peacetime history. A debate followed, behind closed doors, which united the southern states as a bloc in resistance to the equally undivided position of the seven states from north of Mason and Dixon's line. Could seven states—a bare majority of the thirteen—repeal diplomatic instructions when a vote of nine was necessary to ratify any treaty? The seven northern states, in favor of accepting the Spanish offer, declared yes. The five southern members of the Confederation (Delaware being absent) denied it. Previously warned by Jay's imprudent approach to Monroe, they were horrified at the idea of bartering away the navigation of their great river for commercial privileges for the benefit of the eastern states which were already jealous of the rising population of the West and apprehensive of a shift of the future center of political gravity away from New England and New York.[9] "This is one of

little source problem out of the conflict between eastern and western states over the Mississippi navigation.

8. *Dip. Corres.*, VI, 158.

9. Rufus King, delegate from Massachusetts, wrote to Jonathan Jackson, a former delegate from that state, a long letter, Sept. 3, 1786, arguing in favor of the proposed treaty: "If, therefore, our disputes with Spain are not settled, we shall be obliged wholly *to give up* [italics inserted] the Western Settlers or join *them* in an issue of Force with the Catholic King: the latter we are in no condition to think of, the former would be impolitic for many reasons, and cannot with safety be *now* admitted, although very few men who have examined the subject will refuse their assent to the opinion that every Citizen of the Atlantic States, who emigrates to the westward of the Allegany is a total loss to our Confederacy.

the most extraordinary transactions I have ever known," wrote Monroe to Patrick Henry, "a minister negotiating expressly for the purpose of defeating the object of his instructions, and by a long train of intrigue and management seducing the representatives of the states to concur in it." [10]

At the height of the debate Jay was summoned. He appeared before Congress on the third of August, 1786, exhibited Gardoqui's note of the 23d of May, and explained the negotiation. He presented the articles agreed upon as a basis for a treaty of commerce, saying nothing of the terms of the proposed alliance.[11] Then he followed with as able an argument as could be made for temporarily relinquishing the navigation of the Mississippi. Spain positively had refused to yield on that point. The United States was not prepared to go to war for it. He believed in the right, he said, was not prepared to relinquish it in principle, but asked how, under the circumstances, it could be enforced. He formally recommended that for the term of the proposed treaty—twenty-five or thirty years—the United States *forbear* to use the river, by this word implying the continuing existence of the right with a self-denial of its usufruct for a comparatively short period. After that, Jay believed the West would have filled up with a population sufficiently formidable to persuade Spain not to try any longer to deny the right. As to the Florida

---

"Nature has severed the two countries by a vast and extensive chain of mountains, interest and convenience will keep them separate, and the feeble policy of our disjointed Government will not be able to unite them. For this reason I have ever been opposed to encouragements of western emigrants." *Mass. Hist. Soc. Proceedings*, XLIX, 88.

10. Monroe to Henry, Aug. 12, 1786, supra.

11. For articles divulged by Jay, see *A. S. P., F. R.*, I, 249.

boundary he believed it better "to yield a few acres than to part in ill-humor." [12]

II

The southern states held their vast appanages of land on the western waters. They were inhabited by rapidly increasing thousands of settlers who were impelled by the atmosphere of frontier conditions to seek redress of grievances through direct action and to be impatient of control from remote seats of authority.[13] To states with such constituencies the Jay proposal appeared rank political heresy. This strong sectional minority, more than enough to block any two-thirds vote, rallied feverishly to the defense of the Mississippi. Charles Pinckney,[14] of South Carolina, delivered a crushing reply to Jay, entirely conclusive from the

12. *Dip. Corres.*, VI, 165.

13. If Congress were sitting at Fort Pitt instead of at New York, Madison wrote a year afterward to the Governor of Virginia, two votes could not be found for the surrender of the Mississippi. N. Y., April 16, 1787, Madison Papers, Library of Congress, Accession 1081.

14. *A. H. R.*, X, 817–827. See also *Writings of George Washington* (Ford ed.), XI, 174, 463. The speech was privately printed at the time. See Charles Pinckney to [Charles Lester?], Charleston, July 8, 1801, Carnegie Institution Transcripts. Monroe and Grayson had at the moment faltered before the weight of northern opinion and proposed a compromise by which American citizens would be allowed to export goods out by the Mississippi under a small toll charge at New Orleans, but not to import goods except through ports of the United States. "It is manifest here that Jay and his party in Congress are determined to pursue this business as far as possible, either as the means of throwing the western people and territory without the Govt. of the U. S. and keeping the weight of population and Govt. here [New York], or of dismembering the Govt. itself, for the purpose of a separate Confederacy." Monroe to Madison, N. Y., Aug. 14, 1786, *Writings of Monroe*, I, 151. A resolution to that effect was defeated, Aug. 29, 1786, by the same vote of 7 to 5. *Secret Journals of Congress*, IV, 108.

viewpoint of the South and West, and to the reader today. As one reads over the mass of contemporary sources in which the unrecorded debates of the Congress are reflected, and as one envisages the question from the point of vantage of the twentieth-century historian enlightened by the confidential correspondence of Gardoqui, one can easily understand that the future of the territorial expansion of this country was being protected by the vehement protests of the southern state delegations. To keep open the Question of the Mississippi was to lead to the Spanish treaty of 1795, from thence by the adventitious assistance of Toussaint l'Ouverture and Napoleon Bonaparte to the Louisiana procurement, to Florida, to the Pacific. We can see today that the claim so ardently championed by the southern states was big with no less a matter than the future territorial basis of the United States as a world power fronting on two oceans.

Neither Jay nor any other honest man then could lift the veil of time to see this continental vista. There is no doubt that he and Gardoqui concerted these articles with a view to appeal to the peculiar advantages and sectional jealousies of the eastern states, hoping that they would be attractive enough to secure a ratification of the treaty, abandoning the Mississippi, notwithstanding the clamors of the West and South. There is also no doubt that Jay thought he was acting for the best interests of his country in postponing for twenty-five years the ultimate issue with Spain. He could not anticipate the remarkable results of the Philadelphia Convention of the next year and the resurrection of American nationality by President Washington's new government. Nor could he, nor any man then living, foresee that a European cataclysm would soon engross and exhaust the military energies of those powers whose possessions gripped our hinterlands and encroached upon our actual territory. How could he know that the United States was to have during the next generation, thanks to the distress of the old world during the wars of the French Revolution and Napoleon, an unexampled opportunity to secure its territorial integrity and to expand at the expense of its European colonial neighbors to the Pacific Ocean?

To all this Jay was perforce blind. Instead, he saw the United States rushing into political anarchy. Great Britain was watching from the north eagerly anticipating the breakup of the American Union. Spain was stirring up the Indians in the south and claiming our south-western territory to the Ohio. There was no army worth the name. No navy at all. The Government could not enforce its existing treaty obligations with foreign powers. Small wonder that a man less susceptible to personal flattery and attention than the uxorious Jay should have considered the realities of the situation sufficient to argue for a temporary *forbearance* of using a right to navigate the river. Even General Washington was of this opinion.

The Mississippi Question monopolized the attention of Congress throughout the whole summer of 1786 and finally ended with a strictly sectional vote of seven to five in favor of repealing Jay's original instructions.[15] The five minority delegations maintained that this was unconstitutional and let it be understood by both Jay and Gardoqui and by Congress that they would never ratify any treaty signed under the instructions thus

15. For the various resolutions, motions, and divisions in Congress during the debate, see *Secret Journals of Congress*, IV, 42–132. The Delaware delegation was absent.

amended without the concurring vote of nine states. The staunch attitude of the southern states saved the Mississippi but at the expense of a serious constitutional issue. The movement for the Philadelphia Convention was already under way and the question whether a bare majority of states could sanction a treaty cast an ominous shadow over the approaching deliberations for a more perfect union. The southern states, alarmed by the determination of their western constituents and the depreciating effect which such a treaty as that proposed by Jay would have on their backlands, began to suspect the movement for a new constitution as simply another means by which the eastern anti-Mississippi men meant to lift Jay's instructions.[16] Monroe even smelled a plot of Jay's supporters to force the issue with the South in order to split the Union into two confederacies.[17]

16. Gardoqui to Floridablanca, Confidential No. 18, N. Y., Dec. 5, 1787, A. G. C., Est. Leg., 3895, G. D., IV, 301–315. Madison wrote to Jefferson, March 19, 1787: "But although it appears that the intended sacrifice of the Mississippi will not be made, the consequences of the intention and the attempt are likely to prove serious" in the coming federal convention at Philadelphia. *Writings of Madison* (Hunt ed.), II, 328. See also letters of Timothy Bloodworth to the Governor of North Carolina, Sept. 4, 29, Dec. 16, 1786, Carnegie Institution Transcripts.

17. Monroe to Madison, Aug. 14, Sept. 3, 1786, *Writings of Monroe*, I, 151, 160.

CHAPTER 5

Further Negotiation, 1786–1788

I

Congress by a bare majority and a strictly sectional vote, North versus South, had voted to rescind Jay's instructions of August 25, 1785,[1] in regard to the navigation of the Mississippi and the southern boundary. Jay was at liberty now to go ahead with Gardoqui and complete the treaty. But under the Articles of Confederation any treaty which the Secretary for Foreign Affairs might sign had to receive the votes of two-thirds of the thirteen states, five of which had placed themselves already on record against any change in the instructions, as well as opposed to the principle that a change in his instructions could be voted by less than a two-thirds majority. On October 6, 1786, Jay informed Gardoqui, in answer to his note of the 23rd of May, that "in consequence of some recents acts [of Congress] I find myself more in capacity than I was, to make and receive propositions relative to certain matters in difference between our two countries." [2]

Gardoqui knew well enough that even though seven states had voted to change Jay's instructions, it required nine to ratify any treaty that the Secretary and he might sign. He had also observed that five states had land claims in the territory disputed by Spain, that many individual members of Congress owned military

1. *Dip. Corres.*, VI, 102.
2. *Dip. Corres.*, VI, 196.

land grants there. On the main issue, he concluded, there was not the slightest hope that Congress in a treaty would modify its original position.[3] Some members of Congress, feeling this, went so far as to broach to him the idea of a treaty which would remain silent on the Mississippi navigation. To anything like this, which would leave the American claim alive, he would not now consent.[4] He began to discern a panicky fear in Congress that, if the navigation should be given up, all the new establishments on the western waters would group together as an independent state and seek the protection of Great Britain and her assistance to get them the thing they most wanted. To support this he quoted testimony, confidentially given him by James White, at that time a delegate to Congress from North Carolina, as well as a letter written to Henry Lee, of Virginia, by George Washington, to the effect that much management would be required to restrain the restless and turbulent spirits of Kentucky whose action was more to be feared by the United States than anything Spain could do.

From this conversation with James White, which took place under conditions of strictest secrecy at Gardoqui's house in New York, on August 26, 1786,[5] there developed a few months later a complete change in Spanish policy. It will be more convenient to refer to this on a later page. Meanwhile, with his apprehensive

3. Gardoqui to Floridablanca, No. 90, N. Y., June 18, 1786, A. C. A., Est. Leg., 3886, G. D., II, 95–101. He wrote Floridablanca, Aug. 6, that although the several states were divided north and south, he could not find out much about the secret debates. Ibid., 223.

4. Same to same, Confidential No. 11, N. Y., July 4, 1786, A. C. A., Est. Leg., 3895, G. D., IV, 117.

5. Gardoqui to Floridablanca, Confidential No. 12, Sept. 8, 1786, G. D., IV, 134.

eye on Kentucky, and keeping in touch with White, Gardoqui continued his negotiation with Jay. Whilst he awaited new instructions as to the articles already initialed with the American Secretary, Gardoqui persuaded Jay to agree secretly to the following formula for the Mississippi:

It is expressly stipulated and concluded that His Catholic Majesty and the United States are freely and in common and without any interruption from each other to use and navigate the said river from its source down to the southern boundary of the said states, and that the United States will faithfully observe that limitation and not navigate or use the said river below, or further down, than the said boundary in any part of its course therefrom through His Majesty's countries to the mouth of the river.[6]

In return for this Gardoqui accepted Jay's proposition that the boundary of West Florida be referred to a joint commission, provided Congress would agree to that, of which Jay admitted he was not certain. The Spaniard prided himself, as well he might, on having reduced Jay to this article, but he was careful to state to Floridablanca that the Secretary had no hopes of Congress agreeing to these terms and that Jay had refused to sign anything without the consent of nine

6. The above formula was preceded by this paragraph: "And *to the end* that this treaty may the more effectually provide for the continuance of the perfect harmony which at present happily subsists between His Catholic Majesty and the United States; and that all differences and questions which might otherwise arise respecting the navigation of the River Mississippi may be avoided and obviated by an amicable stipulation on the subject; as His Catholic Majesty's system of government and policy prohibits all foreign trade, intercourse and commerce within his territories, and as the United States are desirous as far as possible to meet the wishes of his Majesty and to evince the sense they entertain of his friendly dispositions towards them, and of the recent proofs he has been pleased to give them of it;
"It is expressly stipulated and concluded, etc. . . ."

states.[7] Gardoqui apparently was satisfied with this formula as a satisfactory recognition by the United States of Spain's exclusive right. Jay, who wrote it out in his own hand, relied on it as being a carefully worded *forbearance* to use a right which would revive at the expiration of the term of the treaty, in twenty-five years.[8] The conclusion of neither man was stated in clear language, not because either was unable to make himself unmistakably clear, but obviously because neither would accept an unambiguous definition of the other. The only hope for the success of Gardoqui's mission now lay in the possibility of inducing nine states to ratify a treaty which should close the Mississippi by this formula. To do this required two southern states in addition to the seven northern ones which already, in the test votes on the repeal of Jay's instructions, had recorded themselves in favor of it. The Spaniard therefore set to work on influential personalities and members of Congress from Virginia and North Carolina. Col. Henry Lee, a member of Congress from Virginia, had expressed himself in favor of the proposals of Jay to Congress. Gardoqui had purposely cultivated an intimacy with him. He gave him on several occasions money to the total of $5,000 as a "loan," which apparently was never paid, though Spanish representatives several years later tried to put pressure on Lee by asking for its payment.

7. Gardoqui to Floridablanca, Confidential No. 13, N. Y., Oct. 28, 1786, A. C. A., Est. Leg., 3895, G. D., IV, 160–178. In this despatch, amongst many other animadversions, Gardoqui states that the "principal men" believe that no one in Congress would have dared to propose the cession of the navigation of the Mississippi, but he relied on the sagacity of a group of men from the northern states to prevail.

8. *Dip. Corres.*, VI, 173, 199. Compare this with the phraseology of Article VI of the draft proposed by Jay at Madrid in 1781, ante, p. 27.

Lee used his influence in Virginia in favor of the proposed treaty, and was dropped from the Virginia delegation to Congress for so doing.[9] He wrote several letters to Washington, favoring the cloture of the river in language already familiar and acceptable to the proprietor of Mount Vernon, who from the first had believed, as Jay did, in temporarily yielding the navigation of the river until the western settlements were strong enough successfully to demand it from Spain; meanwhile he advocated "cementing" them to the union by so improving the navigation of the Potomac River as to make communication with them easier from the eastern states.[10] Richard Henry Lee, the uncle of Col. Henry Lee and recently the President of Congress, also was an intimate, though evidently not a tool, of Gardoqui. He had much similar correspondence with Washington and others. At first Richard Henry Lee had believed Spain would consent to the navigation if the United States were firm enough,[11] but he changed his mind after his contact with the Spanish *encargado*. Gardoqui himself had several visits with Washington during the Philadelphia Convention and some correspondence with him about the proposed treaty.[12]

9. *Writings of Washington* (Ford ed.), XI, 88; Gardoqui to Floridablanca, No. 153 [N. Y.], Dec. 31, 1786, A. C. A., Est. Leg., 3895.

10. *Writings of Washington* (Ford ed.), X, 487–507.

11. Ballagh, *Life and Letters of Richard Henry Lee,* II, 382, 426, 448, 488. In Gardoqui's No. 222, of Dec. 6, 1787, he mentions "the Ex-President, Lee, and his nephew of the same name, who came to Congress at my instance to favor our cause."

12. For evidence of Colonel Henry Lee receiving money from Gardoqui, and R. H. Lee's intimacy with Gardoqui, who considered both of them valuable as approaches to Washington and in moulding in Virginia a sentiment favorable to Spain, see Gardoqui's confidential despatches Nos. 14, 16, 17, 18, of Nov. 29, 1786, May 12, July 6, and Dec. 5, 1787, and his expense account for 1786–1787, A. C. A., Est. Leg., 3895, G. D., II, 332, IV, 181, 213, 301. The correspondence be-

At Gardoqui's behest the King of Spain sent a gift to Washington in 1786 of a jackass to be used for breeding mules on the General's Virginia plantation. It is needless to record that neither the importunities of the Lees nor this curious personal gift of the King had the slightest effect in fixing Washington's opinion on the question of the Mississippi. His mind had been made up on that subject before Gardoqui's arrival in the United States. In the autumn of 1784 Washington made a visit to the upper waters of the Ohio to inspect lands which had been granted to him and his fellow officers as bounty for services during the French and Indian war. He thus had an opportunity again to ob-

---

tween the Lees and Washington can easily be consulted in the *Writings of Washington* (Ford ed.) XI, 42, 43, 79, and in Sparks's edition of *Letters to Washington,* IV, 137, 174, 180. See also Gardoqui's regular despatch No. 222, of Dec. 6, 1787, A. C. A., Est. Leg., 3886, G. D., VI, 389. In 1795 the Spanish diplomatic agent in Philadelphia, Jaudenes, who had been attached to Gardoqui's staff, sent the Spanish consul for Virginia and Kentucky on a secret mission to stir up insurrection in Kentucky. En route he was to sound out the sentiment of leaders in Virginia. He was instructed at this time to try to collect the loan which Gardoqui had made to Henry Lee, who since then had served a term as governor of the state. Jaudenes to Alcudia, No. 297, Phila., July 29, 1795, enclosing Jaudenes's instructions to Argote, the consul. I have not been able to discover the results of Argote's mission from anything in the papers of Jaudenes or Yrujo, his successor. See A. H. N., Est. Leg., 3896.

In December, 1786, Gardoqui learned of Washington's interest in breeding mules for plantation work. Since he had specific instructions to cultivate the General along with other influential American personages, he let it be known to Floridablanca that Washington, through Lafayette, was trying to secure some Spanish jacks. But the Spanish Government had already been apprised of this, and there was at that very time at Mount Vernon a jackass, appropriately named "Royal Gift," which had arrived as a special gift from the King of Spain. Two others were procured by Lafayette from Malta, one of which bore the name "Knight of Malta." I am much indebted to Dr. J. C. Fitzpatrick for information about Washington's dealings with jackasses.

serve at first hand the interlocking water systems of the upper courses of the Potomac and Ohio rivers. His observations convinced him that it was a favorable time to attach the trade of the new western settlements to Virginia by joining the headwaters of these two rivers by means of a canal. This, he believed, would have a favorable effect in uniting the two sections politically. Under date of October 4, 1784, he recorded his conclusions at length in his diary, the gist of which is summed up in these paragraphs:

A combination of circumstances makes the present conjuncture more favorable than any other to fix the trade of the Western Country to our Markets. The jealous and untoward disposition of the Spaniards on one side, and the private views of some individuals coinciding with the policy of the Court of G. Britain on the other, to retain the Posts of Oswego, Niagara, Detroit, &ca. (which tho' done under the letter of the treaty is certainly an infraction of the Spirit of it, and injurious to the Union) may be improved to the greatest advantage by this State [Virginia] if she would open her arms, and embrace the means which are necessary to establish it. The way is plain, and the expence, comparitively speaking deserves not a thought, so great would be the prize. The Western Inhabitants would do their part toward accomplishing it, weak as they now are, they would, I am persuaded, meet us half way rather than be *driven* into the arms of, or be in any wise dependent upon, foreigners; the consequence of which would be, a separation, or a War.

"The way to avoid both, happily for us, is easy, and dictated by our clearest interest. It is to open a wide door, and make a smooth way for the produce of that Country to pass to our Markets before the trade may get into another channel—this, in my judgment, would dry up the other Sources; or if any part should flow down the Mississippi, from the Falls of the Ohio, in Vessels which may be built—fitted for the Sea—and sold with their Cargoes, the proceeds I have no manner of doubt, will return this way; and that it is better to prevent an evil than to rectify a mistake none can deny—commercial connections of all others, are most difficult to dissolve—if we wanted proof of this, look to the avidity with which we are renewing, after a *total* suspension of Eight years, our corrispondence with Great Britain:—So, if we are supine, and suffer without a struggle the Settlers of the Western Country to form commercial connections with the Spaniards, Britons, or with any of the States in the Union[13] we shall find it a difficult matter to dissolve them altho' a better communication should thereafter be presented to them—time only could effect it; such is the force of habit!

Washington had a vision of the time when river boats could be propelled by mechanical means against the current of the western rivers. When this should come, a canal connection with the upper Ohio would be of still greater advantage. The age of steamboat navigation on the Mississippi was then, in fact, only thirty years in the future; but it was not steam power that Washington anticipated:

> Rumseys[14] discovery of working Boats against stream, by mechanical powers principally, may not only be considered as a fortunate invention for these States in general but as one of those circumstances which have combined to render the present epoche favorable above all others for securing (if we are disposed to avail ourselves of them) a large portion of the produce of the Western Settlements, and of the Fur and Peltry of the Lakes, also —the importation of which alone, if there were no political considerations in the way, is immense.[15]

13. Indicating Washington's interest in diverting this western traffic to his own state of Virginia.

14. Superintendent of construction of the Potomac Navigation Company, 1785.

15. *Diaries of George Washington* (J. C. Fitzpatrick, ed.), II, 327–328.

In this connection the following of Gardoqui's despatches is interesting: "By accident I met a person named John Fitch, native of these States, a man of good judgment, a proprietor and resident in the new establishment of Kentucky, with whom I succeeded in having an extended conversation about those establishments, concerning which I will give Your Excellency an account on a more suitable occasion." Gardoqui to Floridablanca, N. Y., No. 19, September 3, 1785, A. C. A.,

For Henry Lee to "borrow" money from Gardoqui, under such circumstances as we have recited, was of course unpardonable; but if he got it on the strength of his alleged ability to influence Washington to recommend the cloture of the Mississippi, he was getting it almost under false pretences! Everybody who knew Washington at all well, as the Virginia Lees certainly did know him, was aware of his opinions on the Mississippi. The Spaniard might have saved his money and had the same results. As everybody knows, and knew then, it was Washington's interest in this scheme of connecting the headwaters of the Ohio and Potomac which had led to the incorporation in 1785 of the Potomac Navigation Company, of which he himself was President.[16] It was the attempts of the Company to secure from Maryland and Virginia an agreement for the control of the use of the Potomac, which, we remember, led to the Annapolis Convention of 1786 and by a well known chapter of political events to the Philadelphia Convention of 1787 and the framing and adoption of the Constitution of the United States.

Through the influence of the Lees the Spanish *encargado* tried to undo the instructions of the Virginia Assembly to its delegates in Congress to maintain inviolate the right to navigate the Mississippi. He even importuned Washington, unsuccessfully it is needless to say, to help him in this.[17] In his home in New York City, the most pretentious house which he could rent

Est. Leg., 3891A. In his No. 30 of Oct. 21, 1785 (ibid.) Gardoqui, speaking of the attractive fertility of Kentucky lands, explained that Fitch had invented a boat with a fixed wheel propelled by horsepower to climb against the current; and that Fitch had promised to send him information about Kentucky.

16. Cora Bacon-Foster, *The Potomac Route to the West.*

17. Sparks's *Letters to Washington*, IV, 187 (N. Y., Oct. 29, 1787).

there—the historic Kennedy House at No. 1 Broad-way[18]—Gardoqui assembled about his luxurious hearth-stone Virginia and North Carolina delegates to Congress and tried to argue them out of their convictions on the Mississippi Question. Neither the lavish hospitality of the zealous Gardoqui, nor the already fashioned opinion[19] of Washington, nor the recommendations of Jay, nor royal gifts of stallions and jackasses[20] could make conquest of the logic with which the geography of North America had convinced the majority of southern delegates that the rapidly increasing population of their backlands demanded for their economic salvation the control of the Mississippi River and its outlet to the sea.

III

By the spring of 1787 Jay had advanced no further in his negotiations than the formula above mentioned. Congress was rapidly melting away. On the fourth of April of that year, however, enough states were present to call for a report by Jay on the state of the Spanish negotiation.[21] Jay stated that as the result of conferences during the winter he had not been able to secure

18. For Gardoqui's residence see: Gardoqui to Floridablanca, N. Y., June 30, 1785, A. C. A., Est. Leg., 3902, G. D., V, 355; M. L. Booth, *Hist. City N. Y.*, 589; J. G. Wilson, *Memorial Hist. N. Y.*, III, 105. For Gardoqui's arguments with the Virginia delegates, see *The Papers of James Madison* (H. D. Gilpin, ed.), II, 599.

19. Sept. 17, 1786, Washington in a letter to Rochambeau had said: "With respect to the Spaniards I do not think the navigation is an object of great importance to us *at present*; and when the banks of the Ohio and the fertile plains of the western country get thickly inhabited, the people will embrace the advantages which nature offers them in spite of all opposition." W. C. Ford, *The United States and Spain in 1790*, 10.

20. Note 12, above.

21. *Dip. Corres.*, VI, 199.

any recognition of the right of the United States to navigate the river other than that which might be inferred from a forbearance to use it for the period of duration of a proposed treaty. "As to limits," Jay stated, "I have reason from him [Gardoqui] to believe that, notwithstanding the extent of their claims, he would in case all other matters were satisfactorily adjusted, so far recede as to give up all the territories not comprehended within the Floridas, as ascertained by our secret and separate articles with Great Britain, of which I early perceived he was well informed." [22] This, of course, meant the line of the Yazoo, disguised under the expedient of referring the boundary of West Florida to a joint commission, as accepted in principle between Jay and Gardoqui.

Jay recommended that Congress, during the residence of the "sincerely-disposed" Gardoqui, do something to fix a stable plan of policy with Spain. Congress replied by adopting a resolution presented by Madison to send to Madrid the plenipotentiary of the United States at the Court of France to secure for the United States the navigation of the Mississippi and a satisfactory settlement of the southern boundary. It was a maneuver intended to take the negotiation out of the hands of Jay and put it into those of Jefferson, then in Paris. The proposed resolution requested Jay to draft proper instructions to be given to such a plenipotentiary. He

22. It has been an accepted belief among American historians (see for example the rhetorical passage in Fiske, *Critical Period,* 209) that Spain knew of the secret article of the American preliminaries of peace with Great Britain which accepted the line of the Yazoo River as the boundary of Florida in case it should remain English. This statement of Jay to Congress is the only indication of this which I have found in consulting the Spanish sources of the subject. I have found no instance in which such knowledge was discussed or made use of by Spanish diplomatists.

succeeded in convincing Congress that this step was useless and ill-advised, that the King of Spain would not
treat at Madrid on what he refused through his personal
representative in America, and that his opinion of the
candor of the United States would be greatly diminished by the measure in question. On May 9, 1787,
Jay asked Congress in vain for express instructions on
the Spanish negotiation.[23]

Congress, though it lived on a year more, was by now
nearly defunct. The movement for the Philadelphia
Convention and the organization of a more perfect
union under a new constitution was already under way.
All political interest was absorbed by that approaching
experiment and the legislation of the expiring Congress
on the Northwest Ordinance. The enactment of that
law, and the settlement which flowed into the Ohio
Valley with it, only increased the nervousness with
which Gardoqui had been watching the teeming restless West. He gave up hope of being able to negotiate
anything with the Congress, even if he could secure in
favor of Spain's policy the impossible number of nine
state delegations. Instability of the Congress and uncertainty of the political situation made it almost impossible to do anything. He asked for a leave of absence to
return to Spain pending the establishment of a stable
government. During the rest of his stay in America,
which was prolonged two years, he had no further
regular diplomatic conversations with John Jay.[24]

Meanwhile the proposed articles on which Jay and
Gardoqui had agreed in principle in the summer of

23. *Dip. Corres.,* VI, 199, 228, 233; Madison to Jefferson, April 23,
1787, *Writings of Madison* (Hunt ed.), II, 357.

24. On April 18, 1788, he wrote that it was a year since he had had
conference with Jay. To Floridablanca, A. C. A., Est. Leg., 3886, G. D.,
VI, 206.

1786, pending an adjustment of the real issues of the Mississippi and of boundaries, articles which Gardoqui had forwarded to his court for approval and which Jay in part, but only in part, had explained to Congress, reached Madrid. The principal members of the Council of State who had to deal with American and colonial affairs, deliberated on them. Floridablanca replied to Gardoqui by transmitting the draft of an acceptable treaty. Because of the cessation of negotiations with Jay, due to the condition of Congress, this draft never actually entered into discussion. It nevertheless shows what the Spanish Government wanted. A "provisional" treaty in sixteen articles, it purported to be drawn up from three sources: Gardoqui's former instructions and his conferences with Jay, new concessions which the King was willing to make for the sake of peace and accommodation, and certain articles which Jay several years before had proposed to Floridablanca during the bootless negotiations of 1781 at Madrid. There was also what was really a wholly new proposal, which reminds one of Rayneval's notorious proposition at the peace negotiations at Paris in 1782.

The draft included commercial articles with most-favored-nation privileges together with a particular reciprocity to be separately agreed upon; a mutual guaranty of the American territory of each party's dominions; purchase by Spain at world market price in hard cash of naval stores annually in the United States; cancellation of debts owed by the American Congress to the Spanish Government or individuals on account of supplies furnished during the recent common war against Great Britain. Such articles had been suggested already by Gardoqui's conversations and agreements with Jay. Article twelve stipulated that in consequence

of the mutual guaranty of territory, the contracting parties, pending the determination of the Florida boundary
by a joint commission and separate convention, should
recognize the northern boundary of the province of
West Florida as a line to be drawn [diagonally] from
the confluence of the Yazoo and Mississippi rivers to the
junction of the Flint and Chattahoochee. Article thirteen declared: "Since a part of the lands comprehended
within the said line may be occupied by certain Indian
nations, it is not to be understood that it is the intention of His Majesty to dispossess them, nor to expel
them from where they have been living, but to shelter
them under his dominion and protection."

Article fourteen introduces the new idea. There was
to be created a neutral independent Indian barrier
territory bounded by West Florida (as fixed by article
thirteen) and the Mississippi on the south and west, and
on the north and east by a line which ascended the
Ohio River from the Mississippi, thence up the Tennessee River to the "Euphrasia" or Hiawassee of contemporary maps, up this stream to its source (which
lies in the height of land near the junction of the
present four states of Tennessee, Georgia, South Carolina, and Virginia) and thence striking south across to
the source of the Flint River and down that watercourse to its union with the Apalachicola, the eastern-
most extremity of the northern boundary of West Florida.[25] This was very nearly the territory which Rayneval
had suggested to Jay at Paris, five years before, might

25. Spain's maximum and minimum boundary claims, and the proposed neutral Indian barrier state, 1785–1786, are indicated on an
official Spanish map. A. H. N., Est. Leg., 3890 *bis*, No. 16. A photograph of the Spanish map was reproduced opposite p. 118 of the
original edition (1926) of this work. These claims are similar to those
indicated on Map 3E, p. 70 of the present edition.

become Indian territory under Spanish protection. It was now provided that neither Americans nor Spanish were to establish settlements within this area, which was to belong to the Chickasaw, Choctaw, and Creek Indians, under the protection of both governments. In case of frontier hostilities either party might be permitted to pursue native forces across the Indian frontier. Article fifteen stipulated: "As the Yazoo River serves as the limit of Spanish land possessions, as does the Ohio for American navigation of the Mississippi, so that it will not be legal for Americans, or for any other foreign nation to go up or down that river between the sea and the Ohio, at least until this point shall be settled in some other way by separate convention. . . ." Gardoqui was allowed to yield ground on this article alone, if necessary, but only to the extent of accepting the mouth of the Yazoo as the lowest limit for American navigation.[26]

These new instructions reached New York in the latter part of November, 1786, after the discussions had been renewed with Jay and the Jay formula for the Mississippi agreed upon, and while Gardoqui was trying in vain to win over the southern delegates. Immediately he perceived that to couple the idea of an Indian buffer territory with a modification of the Mississippi formula, recently won from Jay and the chief object of his negotiation, would ruin the already meager chances for the success of the treaty. He and Jay were then waiting for the new Congress to assemble, to see how best it might be dealt with. Their conferences had been entirely confidential for fear that an opposition might rise up to defeat them in Congress. For such a

26. "Plan of a Treaty with the Americans," A. C. A., Est. Leg., 3886, G. D., VI, 165.

proposition as that advanced by Floridablanca to become public would have left the proposed treaty without any support.[27]

The new project was never even presented to Jay, if we are to judge by Gardoqui's despatches. He was quick to point out to Floridablanca that the buffer Indian territory would include land already settled by some American citizens or granted to others by military warrants. There was no chance that the proposed new Florida boundary would be acceptable in case the United States should be deprived of the intervening buffer lands, nor that a provisional treaty without a time limit would be agreed to. Gardoqui himself was persuaded that the existing Indian tribes on those lands would act as a sufficient buffer without being mentioned in any treaty—so strong was the influence of their hostility that American surveyors had not yet dared to

27. Gardoqui to Floridablanca, Confidential No. 14, N. Y., Nov. 29, 1786. Cited supra.

Regarding the secrecy with which Jay and Gardoqui had their conferences, Madison wrote to Governor Randolph of Virginia, from New York, March 17, 1787: ". . . the negotiations with Spain are carried on, if they go on at all, entirely behind the curtain. The business now has been put into such a form that it rests wholly with Jay how far he will proceed with Gardoqui, and how far he will communicate with Congress. The instructed states [i.e., instructed to vote against any relinquishment of the Mississippi] are hence under some embarrassment. They cannot demand information of right, they are unwilling by asking it of favor to risk a refusal, and they cannot resort to the present Congress with any hope of success. Should Congress become pretty full, and Pennsylvania follow North Carolina, Virginia and New Jersey in giving instructions, the case may be altered." *Papers of James Madison* (Gilpin ed.), II, 622.

Two days later he wrote to Jefferson: "The Spanish project sleeps. A perusal of the attempt of seven States to make a new treaty, by repealing an essential condition of the old, satisfied me that Mr. Jay's caution would revolt at so irregular a transaction. . . ." *Writings of Madison* (Hunt ed.), II, 328.

run the boundary lines determined by the recent treaties of Congress with those tribes. He asked permission
to relinquish this point in order to secure the more
important object of the occlusion of the river, against
which a party of great vigor was already forming in
Congress despite his efforts to prevent it.[28]

This request was late in reaching Spain. Not until
the following September, 1787, were the proposed articles revised in Madrid. The Indian barrier was then
definitely given up. Spanish protection over the Indians
north of the boundary line was relinquished. The
American claim to the line of 31° as fixed in the Anglo-
American treaty of peace was admitted in part—that is,
the boundary of West Florida should be that parallel
of 31° north latitude from the Apalachicola west to the
Amité River. That river was then to become the eastern boundary of a corridor of Spanish territory which
was to extend north along the east bank of the Mississippi to give Spain possession of that bank of the river
north so as to include the Natchez district, and to insure communications between it and New Orleans. For
the Mississippi the following article was proposed,
which corresponded to Jay's idea of forbearance: "The
United States will not navigate the Mississippi below
its riparian possessions and will forego all claims to
navigate it where it flows between two Spanish banks,
until this question be taken up and examined by some
particular convention."

Such a treaty should last ten years, and be continued
thereafter indefinitely until denounced by one party
with six months' notice. In no case should any treaty
be signed by Gardoqui until the full development of

28. Gardoqui to Floridablanca, Confidential No. 14, supra.

the Kentucky separatist movement and the results of
the Philadelphia Convention—concerning which Gardoqui had prophesied probable failure—should be
known.[29]

To this instruction, the utmost limit of Spanish concession, Gardoqui replied, in the spring of 1788, that
while the latest draft might have been acceptable at the
beginning of his mission in the United States, there was
not the least chance of securing it now.[30]

This mention of the Kentucky situation makes it
necessary now to turn to a subject which was responsible for a complete change of Spanish policy toward the
United States. In the beginning of the year 1788, as
a result of the approaches of James White, above alluded to, and of similar overtures from other western
separatist intriguers to the Spanish colonial authorities
at New Orleans, Spain had abandoned the policy of
attempting to hold in the dissatisfied western frontiersmen by any treaty with the feeble Continental Congress. She now turned definitely to clandestine negotiations with the West itself.

29. New plan of treaty for Gardoqui, Sept., 1787, A. C. A., Est. Leg.,
3886, G. D., VI, 180–192. See also Floridablanca to Gardoqui, S.
Ildefonso, Sept. 5, 1787, A. C. A., Est. Leg., 3895, G. D., IV, 242.
Printed in part by Serrano y Sanz, *El Brigadier Jaime Wilkinson y
sus Tratos con España,* 14–16.

30. Confidential No. 19, N. Y., April 18, 1788, A. C. A., Est. Leg.,
3895, G. D., IV, 246.

CHAPTER 6

James Wilkinson and the "Spanish" Conspiracy

I

What Thomas Marshall Green in 1891 entitled in his book *The Spanish Conspiracy* was really a conspiracy initiated by American frontiersmen to which Spanish colonial officials in New Orleans readily lent themselves. Arthur P. Whitaker made that clear in his work on *The Spanish-American Frontier,* and more recently two Spanish scholars, J. Navarro and F. Solano Costa, who did not know of Whitaker's work until after they first went to press, make a great point of the fact that Americans rather than Spaniards made the first approaches.[1]

In the months following the Anglo-American treaty of peace of 1783, a flood of frontier settlers broke through the gateways of the Appalachian Mountains or swept down the Ohio River to take up the rich limestone and bluegrass lands of Kentucky and Tennessee. On its tide it bore many a former soldier setting forth to take up a military land warrant and many an ambitious and adventurous army officer whose copious energies were seeking expression in the business of earning a livelihood and in the prospect of leadership in the development of a new country. Some of these men felt

1. J. Navarro y F. Solano Costa, *¿Conspiración Española?* (Zaragoza, 1949).

no overweening loyalty to the imperfect union of the states which had succeeded the military victories against the British. Many a Wilkinson, Morgan, Steuben, Lee, Brown, White, was willing to travel outside the orbit of patriotic loyalty to the United States, provided the path led toward personal emolument and fame. To a few individuals like these the dissatisfaction of the frontiersmen of the western waters, loyal and true to the American flag as most of those settlers were, offered a fruitful field. The game became even more inviting when the gullibility of the Spanish officials at New Orleans, plagued with nightmares of an American invasion, was revealed.

Among the men who thus floated into the western country in 1784 was James Wilkinson. Only twenty-six years old, he was already deep-schooled with experience which had sharpened his powers for intrigue. Companion of Benedict Arnold and Aaron Burr before Montreal in the winter of 1775, conjurer of self-heroics during the Saratoga campaign when he served on Gates's staff, dilatory bearer to Congress of the British capitulation, participant in the so-called Conway Cabal—this was the Wilkinson who emerged from the war with a brevet brigadier generalship, a faculty for discerning the meaner motives of human nature, a smooth-quilled vocabulary, a not unimpressive personality—judging from corroborative witnesses to his own generally untrustworthy account of himself, for he was a thorough liar—and an unfaltering conviction of his own importance and qualities of leadership.

When this impecunious young man settled near Lexington, Kentucky, in 1784 with his growing family he was not long in perceiving a situation most favorable for the adaptation of his peculiar genius. The Spanish

proclamation closing the river[2] came up from New
Orleans a few months after Wilkinson's arrival in Kentucky and filled with dismay the hearts of those immigrants who were counting on recouping their initial
hardships of pioneer life out of the proceeds of their
first surplus crops. The population of the Kentucky
District was already fifty thousand, equal to if not more
than all Spanish Louisiana.[3] The state of Virginia had
been unable to extend to that frontier region the advantages of government, in the shape of adequate courts
of law and the quick and equitable administration of
justice, for the settlement of tangled land titles; nor
were the settlers satisfied with the unequal incidence of
taxation and their meager protection against Indian
wars. They were confronted with the familiar grievances of a new embryo state which had been launched
too far ahead of the more slowly advancing tide of
effective representative government. With typical western impatience at distant agencies of authority they
had already met in 1784 in the first informal convention
to consider their grievances—foremost on this occasion
the urgent necessity of military protection against a
threatened Indian invasion. This informal meeting of
militiamen was the first[4] of a dozen conventions of the

2. Instructions to Governor *ad interim* of New Orleans, by Josef de
Galvez, Aranjuez, June 26, 1784, printed in L. Houck, *The Spanish
Regime in Missouri*, I, 237; *Secret Journals of Congress*, III, 517.

3. Filson, the surveyor, estimated the population of Kentucky in
1783 at 30,000. Winsor, *Westward Movement*, 331. A census of all
Spanish colonists in Louisiana, including east of the Mississippi, in
1788 gave approximately 45,000 whites. Gayarré, 215. See Louis Pelzer,
in *Miss. Vall. Hist. Assoc. Proc.*, VI, 112–114. Gardoqui reported the
population of the western country of the United States in 1785 at
50,000.

4. My reference to the conventions by ordinal numbers starts with
the militiamen's informal convention as the first.

citizenry of Kentucky between 1784 and 1792 in which separate statehood took shape.

The militiamen's convention had been summoned before the Spanish cloture of the Mississippi was announced. As soon as that edict was known, as it was in 1785, we should expect Kentucky conventions to reflect seriously upon this new, spectacular grievance.

The militiamen's convention of November, 1784, found itself without ways and means for providing and supplying any military expedition. It therefore referred this question to a second convention, to be elected, to consider the matter. The second convention, the delegates to which had a more representative character, met at Danville the following month, December, 1784. Its principal action was the passage of a resolution to petition the General Assembly of Virginia for a separation of the district from the parent state. Before the petition was sent across the mountains it was referred to a third convention, to be chosen at the regular Virginia state elections in April, 1785, to decide on the expediency of such a resolution and petition. The third convention of twenty-five delegates from Fayette, Jefferson, and Nelson counties, now elected for the specific purpose of deciding this question, duly assembled in May, 1785, and declared in favor of a separation from Virginia by constitutional methods and an admission into the union of the United States as a separate and equal state. It prepared a petition to that end to the Virginia Assembly. It also ordered that an address to the people of the district, explanatory of the step taken, be drafted. The inveterate convention habit of the Kentuckians resulted in both address and petition being referred for final action to a fourth convention, which was elected in July and assembled in August, 1785.

II

Thus far, states Green in his shrewd work *The Spanish Conspiracy,* there is no evidence of any ulterior motive, beyond that of separate statehood in the American Union as a solution for Kentucky's unsatisfactory political status. But the address to the people had been penned by James Wilkinson, a spectator not a member of the May, 1785, convention, and a man who had a purpose of his own. It was written in an inflammatory tone as if calculated to inspire a deeper sense of injury than had yet been entertained by the delegates or their constituents. Wilkinson was an influential member of the following fourth convention, in August. Instead of approving and forwarding to the Virginia Assembly the May petition, the August convention adopted a new petition written by Wilkinson in a more rhetorical style. This made appeal for the passage of an act "declaring and acknowledging the independence of the District of Kentucky," under the "persuasion" that the independent and sovereign state thus created would be admitted into the Union upon the recommendation of the parent state. After this another exaggerated address to the people was concocted, also by Wilkinson. The petition itself was carried to Virginia by two of his friends, George Muter and Harry Innes.

Now the plot appears. The "independence of Kentucky," as requested by the petition actually sent to the Assembly, unlike the first petition now rejected, did not make that independence contingent upon admission into the Union as a fourteenth state. It was the purpose of the conspirators under Wilkinson's inspiration to secure the separation of the state under general expectation that it would continue to be a part of the United States and straightway admitted into the Union as a state. By construing such separation into absolute sovereignty and warping public sentiment away from the Union, Wilkinson hoped to detach Kentucky altogether from the United States. He would be the chief personage and leader of an absolutely independent western state. Public opinion in the West, already stirred by normal frontier grievances, would be incited by working on the universal indignation against the recently announced Spanish cloture of the Mississippi. The addresses of the convention to the people of Kentucky were written by Wilkinson to stir them to demand what the feeble American Confederation, undoubtedly dominated in part by the jealous interests of eastern seaboard states, could not secure. Failing to protect their interests this way they would, he hoped, be induced to declare their absolute independence and secure the coveted navigation by their own efforts, according to a plan which was already more or less definite in Wilkinson's treacherous brain and selfish heart.

The response of the Virginia Assembly to the petition of the Kentucky District did not fit into his project. An act passed January 6, 1786, provided for the separation of Kentucky into another state of the Confederation. It also fixed for still another, but now a regular and legally assembled, *fifth* convention of delegates at Danville on the first Monday in September, 1786, to determine whether it should be the will of the people that the District be erected into an independent state on the terms defined in the act of the state of Virginia. In case they should so determine, the authority of Virginia was to cease at a set date, not earlier than September 1, 1787, *provided* Congress by June of the same year had consented to the admission of Kentucky into the Union at the agreed time.

In pursuance of the said act this fifth (but the first provided by Virginia law) Kentucky convention met in September, 1786. It did not reach a quorum until January, 1787. Apprised of this continued lack of quorum and apparently considering that the convention would not be able to function in time to fulfil the terms of the act of January 6, 1786, the Virginia Assembly passed a second act, January 10, 1787, submitting the subject of separate statehood to another (sixth) convention to meet at Danville in September of that year. The date limit for separation and admission by Congress was now advanced to 1789.

Meanwhile the fifth Kentucky convention had actually reached a quorum and acted on separation according to the terms of the Virginia act of 1786, only soon to find that act already superseded and another convention called. The fifth convention therefore accomplished nothing constructive. Rather the contrary. The idle delegates, waiting from September, 1786, to January, 1787, for a quorum, presented an ideal medium for intriguers like Wilkinson. He had appealed for election to the fifth convention on the platform of immediate separation, regardless of the action of Virginia, and by an electoral trick had managed to get his seat. At this very time, as if designed to assist Wilkinson's maneuvers, news reached Kentucky of Jay's proposal to Congress to forbear the use of the river for twenty-five years in return for special commercial privileges in Spanish ports. This naturally aroused the indignation of honest men in that region. It furnished ideal fuel to feed the flames already kindled by Wilkinson and his group, which now included John Brown, Harry Innes, Benjamin Sebastian, and George Muter, the last, however, soon to dissociate himself from the cabal. They played

upon the indignation of the delegates and the people
by displaying Jay's proposal and the vote of Congress
on it as a demonstration of the hostility of the eastern
states to vital western interests. Nevertheless, the convention adjourned without action, albeit in some
irritation, and awaited the new convention which had
been called by the act of Virginia for the following
September.

In vain the conspirators tried to frustrate the action
of the anticipated September convention. Muter, Innes,
Brown, and Sebastian issued an inflammatory circular
reciting the Jay proposals and their ominous implica-
tions for western happiness. Very carefully they kept
out of sight the prompt protest which the Virginia
Assembly had made to Congress on that subject. They
called for an irregular convention to assemble in May,
three months before the one provided by the Virginia
law. This, they proposed, was to consider the Jay-Gardoqui negotiation *"and to adopt such other measures
as may be conducive to our happiness."* On this latitu-
dinous phrase hung the hopes of the conspirators. They
did succeed in calling their irregular convention at
Danville, but by that time the real facts about the action of Congress were pretty generally known in the
West, including the opposition of the five southern
states to Jay's proposal, as well as the loyal protests of
their own state of Virginia. Realizing that their desires
had been completely anticipated and provided for by
the Virginia Assembly's act of January 10, 1787, the
irregular convention refused to be excited by the ap-
paritions displayed in the inflammatory addresses of
the conspirators. It adjourned peaceably without action. The regularly called convention assembled in

September. Wilkinson was then at New Orleans. Brown did not attend.[5]

Eased of the presence of these persons, the convention unanimously accepted separate statehood within the Union on the terms of the Virginia act. Except in the minds of the Wilkinson group there had been no intention to do otherwise. At this time, as if to fit in perfectly with the designs of the conspirators, there occurred at Natchez the seizure of a Kentucky boat and the confiscation of its cargo for violating the Spanish order closing the Mississippi. Immediately this became known, the states of North Carolina and Virginia protested to Congress and demanded protection of their navigation right.[6] Before this could be done, irresponsible western leaders had taken redress into their own hands. George Rogers Clark, now degenerated into an inebriate sloth only occasionally roused for the commission of some lawless act, led a raid of frontiersmen on the property of a Spanish storekeeper at Vincennes, in Illinois, and captured and destroyed a boatload of his goods there. General Thomas Green, inspired by the deed, wrote a letter from his new home at Lexington, Kentucky, extolling Clark's actions and prophesying a descent on Natchez and New Orleans by an army to be recruited and led by Clark. The letter was intercepted by the Spanish and presented by Gardoqui to Jay with other threatening letters. Congress immediately passed resolutions condemning these irresponsible acts.[7] Gardoqui was satisfied that this expressed a genuine effort

5. The above account of the Kentucky conventions is based on T. M. Green, *The Spanish Conspiracy*, and Gayarré, *Spanish Domination*.

6. *Dip. Corres.*, VI, 203.

7. *Dip. Corres.*, VI, 199–262.

to preserve friendly relations during his negotiations with Jay. But the misplaced zeal of Clark and the ominous mutterings of hot-headed westerners had served to stimulate the plottings of Wilkinson.

III

All this excitement, if not actually created by him, was grist to Wilkinson's mill. His plans began to take broader scope and to reveal themselves more tangibly. Presumably while the 1786 convention had been awaiting a quorum, he had applied to his acquaintance, John Marshall, in Virginia—the later Chief Justice of the Republic—to secure for him from Governor Patrick Henry a passport to proceed to New Orleans. The Governor refused on the ground that none was necessary to travel through American territory and that he had no power to grant one good for Spanish dominions.[8] Later in the year, Wilkinson, without giving his name, applied unsuccessfully to Gardoqui through the person of General Steuben for a passport to descend the river.[9]

Undaunted by the lack of passport, Wilkinson continued with his plans. He loaded some flatboats with a cargo of Kentucky tobacco and other products. Pro-

8. John Marshall to James Wilkinson, Richmond, Jan. 5, 1787. *A. H. R.*, XII, 347.

9. Serrano y Sanz, *El Brigadier Jaime Wilkinson*, 20. See also Gayarré, 210, 247. Steuben, embittered at lack of attention shown to him by the United States Government, was at this time applying for a Spanish land grant where, as a vassal of the King of Spain, he hoped to found a frontier military colony for the protection of Louisiana. He was even considering a trip to Madrid. He died before his plan could be developed. For correspondence about Steuben, see Gardoqui to Floridablanca, April 18, 1788, Confidential No. 18, A. C. A., Est. Leg., 3895, G. D., IV, 301–315, 346; same to same, No. 282, April 18, 1788, ibid., Leg., 3895, G. D., I, 142.

tected only by his own nerve and the plausibility of his stratagems he set out for New Orleans. His ready wit somehow got him by the Spanish outposts. He actually floated down to New Orleans before his cargo was seized and himself brought before the Spanish Governor, Esteban Miró, and the Intendant for Louisiana, Don Martin de Navarro.[10]

Whether Wilkinson's plan of operations had already been carefully worked out when, while agitating the theme of Kentucky independence, he first began to think of a trip to New Orleans, or whether in the presence of the Spanish authorities it waxed more luxuriant than originally conceived, is impossible to say. It is certain that he was no whit daunted by his detention. Soon Miró and Navarro were treating him with unusual consideration for one who had broken the laws of the King of Spain. Well might they do so. The artful frontiersman had opened up to their view a new possibility for the defense of Louisiana.

Ever since the American treaty of peace the Spanish authorities of Louisiana had nervously watched the northern frontier. A few feeble forts, widely separated, and garrisoned by a total of 500 men, defended the expansive province.[11] It had been the policy of the Spanish to rely for supplementary defense upon Indian alliances until the country could be filled up by immigration from the United States of a sufficient body of settlers from which, once naturalized, a suitable militia could be recruited. This policy gave only the weakest of military and potential defense. It was also most ex-

10. For Wilkinson's contacts with Spanish commanding officers at St. Louis and Natchez and his arrival at New Orleans see A. P. Whitaker, "James Wilkinson's First Descent to New Orleans," *Hispanic Am. Hist. Rev.*, VIII, 82–97.

11. Miró to Espeleta, Aug. 27, Oct. 25, 1787. See note 16 below.

pensive.[12] The affections of the Indians were unstable and capricious. Today they loved one, tomorrow they loved someone else. They negotiated as frequently with Congress as with Spain, and without any regard to obligations of their previous treaties with the latter power.[13] Any reliance on a militia recruited out of American immigrants was a delusion and a sham. Meanwhile the lower Ohio Valley was filling with a great and restless population of potential fighting men. Overt acts like that of Clark at Vincennes and intercepted letters indicated that these men were not to be stemmed by any paper cloture of the river. Though Gardoqui had assured the colonial governors that Congress did not sponsor or sanction such threats or aggressions while the negotiations were under way with Spain, he was not certain that sincere and well-intended resolutions of disapprobation by that body could restrain the western citizens—even if his treaty should actually be accepted by the United States.[14] He constantly had counseled the colonial authorities to keep the province vigilantly and adequately prepared.[15]

Their vigilance was constant but their defenses were never adequate. The despatches of Miró and Navarro and their successors are a long lament on the weakness of their situation and the increasing strength of the American settlements in the Kentucky and Cumberland regions.[16] Of what avail five hundred Spanish troops

12. Sums spent on presents to the Indians, 1779–1787 inclusive, amounted to approximately $300,000. Gayarré, 192.

13. Serrano y Sanz, *España y los Indios Cherokis y Chactas*, 25–42.

14. Gardoqui to Floridablanca, May 12, 1787, A. C. A., Est. Leg., 3886, G. D., VI, 193.

15. Gardoqui to Zespedes, N. Y., April 26, 1787, A. C. A., Est. Leg., 3891, G. D., I, 62.

16. See Despatches of the Spanish Governors of Louisiana, 1766–1791. This consists of a collection of photographs of the Governors'

against a population of fifty thousand restless Kentuckians, schooled in frontier impertinence and backwoods
rifle-fire?

Wilkinson now came down the river from out of this
tornado country in the summer of 1787 and made the
stimulating proposition that these potential enemies
be converted into actual friends, allies, and defenders—
he to be the instrument of conversion. After sketching
forth his project to the fascinated Spaniards, he swore,
as proof of his good faith and "honor," an oath of
allegiance to the King of Spain. Then, at their request
and fortunately for the historian, he wrote down his
ideas.

He began with a recital of the grievances of the westerners and an assertion that there was a strong tendency
to separate themselves from the eastern states. Independence once achieved these people would do anything to secure the navigation of the Mississippi which
the Congress had been unable to get for them. If they
could not obtain it from Spain they would appeal to
Great Britain, whose reward would be the possession
of Louisiana itself, to be acquired by the assistance of
these same westerners. Spain could frustrate any such
event. By a partial indulgence and an accommodating
deportment she might attach the western settlements
and make them subservient to her own interests. This

despatches during the years indicated, made for the Carnegie Institution of Washington, from the Papeles de Cuba at Seville. Ten sets
of these photographs were distributed to representative libraries in
the United States. One set is in the Library of Congress, another, for
example, in Harvard University. See, particularly, Miró to Troncoso,
June 11, 1785 (mentions that Louisiana was garrisoned with "only
the first battalion of the Louisiana regiment under my command"
from which he was drawing 101 men to reinforce Natchez), and Oct.
7, 1785; Miró to Espeleta, Aug. 27, Oct. 25, Dec. 20, 1787; Jan. 10, 28,
Feb. 20, Sept. 16, 1788.

was a policy better calculated than those hostile re-
straints and rigorous exactions which might throw the
men of the western waters into the arms of Great
Britain, to the danger of Louisiana and Mexico itself.

The picture painted, Wilkinson counseled his new
fellow-countrymen not to grant to the United States
the navigation of the Mississippi. He applauded Gardoqui's firm stand on that head. He pointed out that
the failure to secure the navigation was the wedge of
separation between the eastern states and the new western communities. If that navigation should be granted
it would remove the issue between east and west and
destroy forever any power which Spain could have over
the western country. The wise policy of prohibition
should continue generally, but with relaxations in particular instances to influential individuals, like himself
and his friends, who could exhibit to the Kentucky
people at large the advantages which might be secured
by Spanish favors. After Kentucky had secured her
independence, Wilkinson averred, she undoubtedly
would send agents to treat with Spain. These overtures
once made by the Kentuckians, Spain "would have
the game in her own hands," without compromising
herself; for "if any part of the United States should
violate the federal pact or the laws of the Union, to
obtain this blessing [that is, the navigation of the
Mississippi], it must be the violators and not the Spanish Court, who stand answerable to Congress." This
sentence is adequate testimony to the turpitude of
Wilkinson's intentions.

As an alternate policy to be adopted only in case
the first plan should not succeed, Wilkinson proposed
that a fortified post and trading station should be

erected at L'Anse à la Graisse (New Madrid), and that strenuous efforts be made to attract emigration to Louisiana from Kentucky and the West. In promoting this he stated that he could be of service.

He professed to represent the leading characters of Kentucky, who were anxious to know whether Spain "would be willing to open a negotiation for our admission *to her protection as subjects,* with certain privileges in religious and political matters, consonant to the Genius and necessary to the happiness of the present generation. These privileges would have been specifically defined, and I should have borne a written commission, had not Kentucky (though on the eve of declaring herself a free and independent state) still appertained and continued subordinate to the commonwealth of Virginia." As soon as such an independent government should be organized, Wilkinson promised it would make a formal application to Spain on the subject. He offered his services to foster this. He begged orders from his new superiors. He proposed to return to Kentucky via Philadelphia and to establish a confidential observer at the seat of the American Government. He himself would be Governor Miró's confidential informant in Kentucky.

In taking his secret oath of Spanish allegiance, Wilkinson had recorded that whoever would impute a different motive to human conduct than that of self-interest "either deceives himself or endeavors to deceive others." In return for all this service to Spain he sought permission for himself to send an agent the following year to New Orleans with a cargo of $60,000-worth of Kentucky produce. The goods were to be sold on his account and the proceeds held, credited to him, as a pledge for his good conduct "until the issue of our plans is known, or I have fixed my residence in Louisiana."

Captivated by the possibilities opened up by Wilkinson's alluring paragraphs and persuasive manner, and convinced of his good faith by the oath of allegiance and offer to leave money in Spanish hands, Miró and Navarro granted him permission to send from Kentucky a $30,000-consignment of tobacco, negroes, cattle, swine, and apples, the proceeds to be deposited in the Spanish treasury until the King's pleasure was known. They promised to recommend his proposals to the King, who, they were persuaded, would heed the reasons for his memorial. This they encouraged him to make known to the "prominent men and other inhabitants of Kentucky for their satisfaction and hope." Miró, in a confidential despatch of September 25, 1787, forwarded the memorial to Madrid with his and the Intendant Navarro's endorsement. The more he reflected on it, the more Miró was pleased with the project. "The delivering up of Kentucky into his Majesty's hands," he wrote on January 6, 1788, "which is the main object to which Wilkinson has promised to devote himself entirely, would forever constitute this province a rampart for the protection of Spain. . . . The western people would no longer have any inducement to emigrate, if they were put in possession of a free trade with us. This is the reason why this privilege should be granted only to a few individuals having influence among them, as suggested in Wilkinson's memorial." [17]

17. Wilkinson's Memorial in Spanish translation was discovered in Madrid by Professor W. R. Shepherd. He printed a synopsis of it, and other documents which I have quoted anent Wilkinson's sojourn in 1787 at New Orleans, in *A. H. R.*, IX, 490–506. The English original of Wilkinson's Memorial has been found in the archives of the

Louisiana Historical Society, also Miró and Navarro's "Despatch No. 13" of Sept. 7, 1787; and is described by Gilbert Pemberton, *La. Hist. Soc. Pub.*, IX, 45–54. See also Serrano y Sanz, *El Brigadier Jaime Wilkinson y sus Tratos con España*, 17–21; and de Villars, Commissaire à la Louisiane aux Géneral et Intendant de St. Domingue, La Nouvelle Orleans, Feb. 26, 1788, Archives Nationales, Colonies, Paris; and "Rapport au Comte de Luzerné, Ministre de la Marine, au sujet du Passage du Mississippi, projeté par le Général Wilkinson, March 27, 1788." Transcripts of these last two documents are in the Library of Congress. Gayarré, 198, et seq., prints copious extracts from the above cited Spanish documents, of which he secured transcripts for preparing his *History of Louisiana*.

CHAPTER 7

Spanish Policy and the American West

I

The idea of separating the western settlements from the United States may not have been original with Wilkinson. It had already been proposed by James White, of the Tennessee settlements, to Gardoqui in New York a year before Wilkinson's visit to New Orleans.[1] That White was not a fellow conspirator of Wilkinson, though nevertheless he may have known in the summer of 1786 of a Kentucky separatist movement similar to his own project, is suggested by his begging Gardoqui at that time to remember, in the future, that he, White, had been the first to propose this sort of thing. Gardoqui had reported White's project to Spain without committing himself to its support. He does not appear to have looked upon western separation as a solution for Spain's American problem until after he received Floridablanca's instructions accompanying the treaty project of September 7, 1787. Rather he was still seeking by a treaty to secure a recognition by Congress of Spain's exclusive navigation of the Mississippi, hoping without much confidence that Congress would then restrain the disappointed and turbulent western citizens. The rest he would leave to the Spanish defenses of Louisiana.

Floridablanca's instructions of September 7, 1787,

1. See above, pp. 92–93.

presenting Spain's last treaty terms, were written in Madrid while Wilkinson was composing his notorious memorial in New Orleans. They forbade Gardoqui, as we have noticed, to conclude anything with the United States until he should have known the outcome of the movement for the new Constitution, of the projects of James White, and also of a colonization scheme of Wouves d'Argès. The latter, introduced to the Spanish Court by Aranda, was a French adventurer who had secured the sanction of Floridablanca for a colonization project for the settlement of Louisiana by emigrants from the United States. Wouves d'Argès had been authorized to offer to prospective emigrants from the Kentucky and Cumberland districts free importation for two years of slaves, livestock, and farming implements; importation of other American products for sale in Louisiana on payment of twenty-five per cent duty; and free (but not public) practice of their religion.[2] He was guided by Gardoqui at New York and Miró at New Orleans.[3]

"You will see by the new plan of treaty," wrote Floridablanca in a private letter to the *encargado* on this occasion, "how we have adopted the article of Mississippi navigation agreed upon between yourself and Mr. Jay. And throughout all my present despatches you will realize that bearing in mind the conversations which the delegate James White had with you, we are announcing concessions and facilities which may help give body to the idea of attaching Kentucky and the other new settlements to us. In effect there will be no difficulty in opening the commerce of New Orleans to

2. Gayarré, 197.
3. See Whitaker, *Spanish-American Frontier*, 78–79, for d'Argès.

them, conformable to the instructions which the Chevalier Wouves bears, if they attach themselves to Spanish protection." [4]

The proposition of Wilkinson therefore fitted in perfectly with what Floridablanca had already constructed out of Gardoqui's contact with applicants for land grants to colonize Louisiana and with James White's plans for western intrigue.

It was reinforced further by a memoir by Navarro on the defenses of Louisiana, which after vividly depicting the danger to Spanish-American frontiers from the United States proposed as the best protection the stratagem of dividing the Union, and that without loss of time. "Grant," he urged, "every sort of commercial privileges to the masses in the western region and shower pensions on their leaders." [5] The possibility of luring the western settlers away from American allegiance, with the help of a few leaders of supposed influence like White and Wilkinson, who for their own profit were willing to conspire such plots, henceforth appealed to Floridablanca as a more effective means of keeping the United States away from the Mississippi River and the frontiers of Spanish provinces than any treaty with the impotent Continental Congress. The idea of a treaty was abandoned. Although he had just received from Gardoqui a copy of the United States Constitution—for the ratification of which the *encargado* was not very hopeful—with assurances of George Washington that he would use all his influence for a "good treaty" to settle Spanish-American difficulties, Floridablanca wrote, May 24, 1788:

4. [Floridablanca] to Gardoqui, Confidential, San Ildefonso, Sept. 5, 1787, A. C. A., Est. Leg., 3895, G. D., IV, 242. James White was at this time a delegate to Congress from North Carolina.
5. Gayarré, 217.

Our idea is to attract the inhabitants of the Ohio and Mississippi region to our devotion, either by the alliance or by their placing themselves under the protection of the King, or by union with their dominions under pacts which assure their liberty, granting them the export of their products to New Orleans, and the providing themselves at that place with goods they need from other countries. But as the commerce of Louisiana is now under discussion [*esta disponiendo del commercio de la Luisiana*] no more detailed instructions can be given you until that matter is decided.[6]

Gardoqui was enjoined to remain in America to cultivate the Kentuckians and observe the development of the new government of the United States.

Receipt of Wilkinson's memorial undoubtedly fortified the Spanish Ministry in this new policy. After the Council of State had deliberated on the general matter of encouraging immigrants into Louisiana, it decided November 20, 1788—and here it followed Wilkinson's own hint—that it could not consider receiving the inhabitants of Kentucky under the King's protection until they had first made themselves and their country independent of the United States. Those people should be encouraged by holding out the prospect in that event of receiving such protection. Meanwhile the second of Wilkinson's projects should be adopted, the alternate one of attracting immigrants from that region by easy conditions of entry[7] into Louisiana and promises of the

6. A. C. A., Est. Leg., 3895, G. D., IV, 296.

7. "That property of every kind, cattle and produce, and even marketable commodities, brought from Kentucky and the Ohio country by families or individuals who may come to settle in the territory of that province, are to be exempt from all duties and imposts upon their first entry, without reference to the duty of 25 per cent. levied upon the produce of Kentucky; but they shall be subject later to the payment of the usual duties as established, upon exportation.

"That henceforth a duty of 15 per cent., instead of 25 per cent. as imposed by previous order, shall be levied upon the inhabitants

private, but not public, enjoyment of their religion. Miró was to be instructed to reconcile the conflicting interests of Wilkinson and d'Argès, and to wean the latter from the idea of bringing in immigrants. To Wilkinson should be held forth the "hope" of remuneration while he was being sounded guardedly to find out what his real desires actually were. Natives of Kentucky generally were allowed to export their produce by the Mississippi to New Orleans upon payment of 15 per cent tariff duty instead of the 25 per cent hitherto charged, and to re-export the same upon payment of the regular export tax. Even more favorable conditions might be granted at the discretion of the Governor to prominent Kentuckians whose attachment to Spain was desirable. The shelving of d'Argès' project in favor of Wilkinson's more expansive operations arose from Miró's fear that d'Argès would interfere and even frustrate Wilkinson, who had already complained about his rival.[8]

The separatist conspiracy was now left to work itself out. Wilkinson returned to Kentucky and in due time sent an agent, one Isaac Dunn, down the river with the second consignment of trading goods. Dunn delivered despatches to Miró. He took back eighteen thousand

---

of Kentucky who elect to remain there and ship produce by the Mississippi to New Orleans, this produce being subject later to the payment of the regular export duties in case it is re-shipped elsewhere; and that the governor of the province is authorized at his discretion to make any reduction he pleases of this 15 per cent. for the benefit of prominent persons who request this favor, so as to preserve the attachment of those already well inclined toward our government, and similarly to dispose the remaining ones, it being understood that they are to be favored in all possible ways under the actual circumstances, and that they will continue to be favored whenever more opportune conditions appear." *A. H. R.*, VIII, 749–750.

8. Gayarré, 199.

dollars' worth of eatables and drygoods, to be sold in Kentucky by Wilkinson at fair prices, as a means of persuading the inhabitants of the economic advantages of a future commerce dependent upon their adoption of Wilkinson's ideas.[9]

For the next several years it appears that most of the Mississippi River trade with New Orleans from Kentucky was carried on in the name or under the influence of Wilkinson, who obtained Spanish passports for numerous Kentucky exporters. The result of this outlet for western surplus crops was an appreciable increase in land values, and a rise in tobacco prices from $2.00 to $9.50 per hundredweight, thanks to the annual purchases which the Spanish colonial government made. According to Pelzer's study, "Economic Factors in the Acquisition of Louisiana," the annual exports of flour alone from the western waters under this informal licensing to particularly favored exporters amounted to from ten to fifteen thousand barrels.[10] Despite this outlet, the tariff duties, the uncertain status of the Spanish regulations, and the loss of time due to these regulations kept up the demand of the westerners for the free navigation of the river to the sea.

II

After the Kentucky convention of September, 1787, had accepted the terms of the Virginia act of January 10 of that year, it prepared and despatched to Congress a petition requesting admission into the Union of the new state now about to be erected. The Kentucky members of the Virginia Assembly were requested to try to have one of their own number appointed as a

9. Gayarré, 278; Shepherd, *A. H. R.*, IX, 503.
10. *Miss. Vall. Hist. Assoc. Proc.*, VI, 117.

delegate to Congress to represent their interests. As a result John Brown, of Frankfort, was elected. He presented the petition of Virginia, on behalf of Kentucky, on July 3, 1788. The old Continental Congress was then on the point of yielding to the new government of the Constitution, which on June 21, by the action of New Hampshire, had been ratified by the required number of states.

Brown was a hand-picked man, elected through Wilkinson's influence.[11] His real purpose in New York seems to have been to spy on the Congress rather than faithfully to represent in that body the people of Kentucky. He speedily got in touch with Gardoqui, who zealously cultivated him and guardedly gave him assurances to the extent authorized by Floridablanca. He told Brown that so long as Kentucky remained a part of the Union, Spain would never grant the free navigation of the Mississippi; but the people of that district had a remedy in their own hands, "inasmuch as if separated they would afford excuse for regarding them as an interior district without maritime designs, and perhaps we could devise some plans for adjusting the markets so much needed in our own possessions." [12]

Congress soon disposed of the Kentucky petition. A committee of the thirteen states had reported on it, but news of the final adoption of the Constitution by the required number of state conventions resulted in deferring Kentucky statehood, as well as the Spanish negotiations and all other business of importance, to the consideration of the new Government. This was the

11. Gayarré, 241.

12. Gardoqui to Floridablanca, Confidential No. 20, N. Y., July 25, 1788, A. C. A., Est. Leg., 3895, G. D., IV, 315; same to same, No. 279, N. Y., July 25, 1788, ibid., Leg., 3891, G. D., III, 31. Part of the latter is printed in Green, op. cit., 160.

only reason for postponement of positive action. There was not evident in the committee or in the final vote of Congress any hostility to the proposed new state.

This postponement of Kentucky statehood, so easily explained by unavoidable difficulties, offered an issue to the promoters of the "Spanish" conspiracy in that district. John Brown was careful not to send back to his constituents a true explanation of the postponement of statehood. He represented it as due to the jealousy of eastern members.[13] He wrote artfully to different correspondents, and with various degrees of positiveness, that under existing circumstances absolute independence was the only recourse for Kentucky.[14] At the

13. Green, op. cit., 154–156.

14. To Madison, advocate of Kentucky statehood, but staunch upholder of the Mississippi navigation and zealous advocate of the new Constitution, he wrote, June 7, 1788: "I fear the contracted Policy of the present Congress will be productive of Consequences ruinous to the Tranquillity of that promising Country; or to the importance and dignity of the United States; and perhaps to both—My disappointment in this Business has in a great measure prevented those exertions which I intended to remove the Objections of the delegates from that Country to the New Constitution." *Doc. Hist. Const.*, IV, 685.

To Archibald Stuart, member of the Virginia Convention then deliberating on the ratification of the federal Constitution, June 25: "The Eastern States are opposed to the measure lest another vote should be added to the Southern States. Others are opposed lest it should Embarrass the new government. Kentucky must and will be independent." Stuart Papers, Va. Hist. Soc. (Carnegie Inst. Transcripts).

To Jefferson, who had expressed to Brown his desire to see the bonds of union between the West and the East grow tighter and advised against pushing the right to navigate the Mississippi to extremity as long as it could be tolerably dispensed with (Jefferson, *Works* [Federal ed.], V, 397), Brown wrote, Aug. 10: "During my residence in that Country [Kentucky] it was my constant care to cultivate that Idea" [of union]! He went on to explain that the rejection by Congress of Kentucky's petition, and the revelation of the Jay-Gardoqui negotiations had now convinced the West against any union with the United States, even in the "New Confederacy." Yet he hoped that

same time he told Gardoqui that he had sent home word as to the action of Congress on the petition, that in the very same month a convention would meet and declare an independent state. He himself would leave for Kentucky on the first of August, 1788, and arrive in time to assist in the consummation of that event, according to his understanding with Gardoqui, whom he thanked profusely in the name of "the whole country, which would be eternally grateful." "This is," wrote the Spaniard to Floridablanca, "another point of departure for this prickly business, concerning which I believe that now more than ever it is well for us to take time, in order to let it develop without the resentment of others." [15]

Wilkinson by now had returned from New Orleans to Kentucky. He wrote Miró enthusiastically (May 15, 1788) that before the district could be constitutionally incorporated within the Union as a separate state, a convention would meet and declare it to be wholly sovereign and independent, that Congress then would have to recognize it as such. At a proper time before the meeting of this convention he proposed to reveal to select persons "as much of our great scheme as shall appear opportune" for the purpose of swinging Kentucky from separate statehood to absolute independence.[16]

Miró exulted. "This affair proceeds more rapidly than I presumed," he wrote to Madrid, November 3,

threatened Indian hostilities would cause Kentucky to "see the impropriety of breaking off from the Union at this time & that it may still be in the power of Congress to conciliate their minds & secure their attachment to the Confederacy." *Doc. Hist. Const.*, V, 9.

15. Gardoqui's No. 279, N. Y., July 25, 1788, A. C. A., Leg., 3891A, G. D., III, 31.

16. Gayarré, 208.

"and some considerable impetus is given to it by the answer of Congress to the application of Kentucky to be admitted into the Union as a separate state." [17]

The several threads of the Wilkinson plot seemed ready to be spun together.

When Kentucky in a convention of September, 1787, had voted in favor of separate statehood according to the terms of the Virginia act of January 10, 1787, it had provided that another (ninth) convention be elected to meet in July, 1788, for the drawing up of a proposed state constitution. This was the convention to which Wilkinson had referred in his letter to Miró. It was in session in Danville in July, 1788. Brown forwarded to it from New York the disappointing decision of Congress on the petition of the Kentucky district. He also despatched secretly to his confidants there Gardoqui's assurances as to what Spain could do for Kentucky in case it separated from the United States. Wilkinson himself was a member of this convention. Exploiting Brown's explanation of the motive of Congress in deferring Kentucky statehood, he caused to be put before the convention a proposal to continue with the framing of a constitution regardless of the fact that postponement by Congress of the subject had annulled the act of Virginia, which had provided for admission by Congress prior to July 4, 1788. Now that Kentucky statehood had been left suspended, Wilkinson proposed that the convention submit to the people of Kentucky a constitution "with such advice relative thereto as the emergency suggests." The proposal, an effort to set up an independent government, was defeated. He did get adopted a decision to call yet another convention to sit in Danville the following November, 1788, to continue

17. Gayarré, 221.

until January, 1790, with full powers to provide for separate statehood in the United States, "or to do and accomplish whatsoever, on a consideration of the state of the district, may, in their judgment, promote its interests." The straddled position of this resolution was of course designed to capture the votes of those who were opposed to separation from the Union and at the same time to give the conspirators leeway under the last loose clause.[18]

By now the intrigue was too public to succeed. John Brown's information to the conspirators had been passed about in the (July, 1788) convention and Wilkinson's intrigues had been so openly insinuated into so many ears that it was pretty well known that a small group of men was endeavoring, under guise of a movement for independence following disappointment in statehood, to deliver Kentucky over to Spain. Thomas Marshall, who had seen Brown's letters, disclosed what he knew to President Washington, in a notable letter dated February 12, 1789.[19] The people of Kentucky, ardently desiring separate statehood within the Union and the navigation of the Mississippi as American citizens, did not want a Spanish or any other alliance, to say nothing of protection under, or allegiance to, the King of Spain. Men now stood as candidates for election squarely on a pro-union platform. The proposals and intrigues of Wilkinson and his associates faltered before the ominous silence with which the majority of the delegates to the November (1788) convention received them. The delegates adjourned after framing a respectful address to Congress expressing their desire for statehood and the opening of the Mississippi. Ken-

18. Green, op. cit., 182–196.
19. Ibid., 240.

tucky, aside from the Wilkinson coterie, preferred to trust the new Constitution rather than the vague allurements of Spanish representations and the twisted tongues of a few self-interested intriguers.[20]

III

Brown's principals in Kentucky, as Gardoqui had said, presented only another point of departure for the prickly business first presented to him by James White.

In what is now eastern Tennessee had grown up another settlement, distinct from the Kentucky District, in part settled before Kentucky, on the upper waters of the Tennessee River within the region claimed by the most expansive pretensions of Spain. This territory had been ceded by North Carolina to Congress in 1784, but under such conditions that the cession was not actually consummated until 1790. In the interim the settlers in the region lying between the Holston, the Cumberland, and the southern spurs of the Appalachian system found themselves confronted by the same frontier grievances which impelled the Kentucky people to seek separate statehood. Apparently abandoned by both North Carolina and Congress, so far as effective protection and law and order were concerned, they organized an abortive government of their own, comprising Washington, Greene, and Sullivan counties, under the name of the "state" of Franklin, with the veteran pioneer, John Sevier, as Governor. They, too, applied to Congress for admission as a fourteenth state. North Carolina refused to recognize them and suppressed the "state" of Franklin by force, in 1788.[21] Disappointed and discouraged, John Sevier,.

20. Ibid., 220, 226.
21. G. H. Alden, "State of Franklin," *A. H. R.*, VIII, 271–289.

leader of the Holston settlements, thought of Spain as a means of saving the cause of Franklin. So did James Robertson, leader of the band of about 4,000 settlers who had established themselves in isolated communities farther to the west, centering at Nashville, in the bend of the Cumberland River, where they had their similar troubles and an anxiety equal to that of Kentucky to share in the commerce of the Mississippi and to secure proper protection from the hostile Indians, whose lands they coveted. At Nashville, James White had settled on a military land grant. It was the Cumberland group which White had represented to Gardoqui while Wilkinson was memorializing the Spanish authorities at New Orleans with a similar but unconnected project. In April, 1788, "our Don Jaime," as Gardoqui refers to White, had returned from the Cumberland country by way of Franklin, where he had sounded the dissatisfied leaders of that defunct "government." He arrived at New York as Gardoqui received Floridablanca's instructions to negotiate with the westerners on the basis of the directions to Wouves d'Argès, i.e., to promise treaty relations with them after they should have secured their independence from the United States. Gardoqui immediately sent him back to Tennessee. "The King claims that territory by the late conquest," wrote the *encargado* to Floridablanca, "and I propose to do the rest by sending Don Jaime there. . . ." Gardoqui referred White and "this complicated and dangerous mission" to the Louisiana authorities who could "most happily and with the least risk conclude this most important business. . . . The moment cannot be better, nor could we have fixed it better, in view of the variety of opinions and treachery against the new government, which if not ratified may end in confusion or, better, in two confederacies." [22]

White's connections seemed to Gardoqui, who then had not yet heard of Wilkinson and was only now just making his acquaintance with John Brown, to offer the best chance for success.[23] He gave White letters to the chief men of the Franklin and Cumberland districts with (presumably oral) instructions to assure them that if they wished to put themselves under Spain and to favor her interests, they would be protected in their civil and political government, in the form and manner most agreeable to them, on the following conditions: first, that it should be absolutely necessary, in order to hold office or to own land, to take an oath of allegiance to the King of Spain, to support him against all enemies on all occasions; secondly, that the inhabitants renounce all submission or allegiance whatever to any other sovereign or power.[24]

White's personal interests seem adequately explained by Gardoqui's despatch describing his use of the man:

It appearing to me very regular to pay his expenses for such a journey as this, I agreed to give him what he asked which was the moderate sum of three hundred dollars which I shall charge up in the confidential despatch that I gave you [Floridablanca]. . . . Perhaps I deceive myself but it appears to me that we have more to hope from him than from the other [Brown] who set out

22. Gardoqui's Confidential Nos. 18 and 19, of April 18, 1788, A. C. A., Est. Leg., 3895, G. D., IV, 246, 301.

23. Gardoqui's Confidential No. 20 of July 25, 1788, A. C. A., Est. Leg., 3895, G. D., IV, 315, and Despatch No. 279 of same date. Ibid., Leg., 3891A, G. D., III, 31.

24. White's confidential statement to Miró, April 18, 1789, quoted from Gayarré transcripts by Archibald Henderson, "The Spanish Conspiracy in Tennessee," *Tenn. Hist. Mag.*, III, 232. See also Gayarré, 259.

[for the West]. Recently Don Jaime told me naively that his views are those of working for our interests and his *own,* for he hopes by way of recompense to establish himself advantageously among us.[25]

IV

In the summer of 1788 when White[26] reached the West, North Carolina was in convention assembled debating the new Constitution of the United States, which was rejected on August 1. The defunct state of Franklin seemed now hopelessly out of the Union and hopelessly misgoverned by the parent state. Sevier in October, 1788, was actually arrested for treason to North Carolina, but he soon got out of custody, thanks to the assistance of his hard-riding pioneer friends from the Holston. It is perhaps not surprising that he listened to White's overture, proposed to Gardoqui an alliance and commercial connection with Spain, and asked for a Spanish loan of money and for military assistance to carry out his ideas.[27] He sent his son, James Sevier, to New York with letters to this effect, and conveyed similar assurances by White to Governor Miró at New Orleans.

James Robertson, leader of the Cumberland settlers since 1784, had been covertly communicating with Miró through McGillivray, the Indian ally of Spain. The

25. Gardoqui's Confidential No. 19, N. Y., April 18, 1788, A. C. A., Est. Leg., 3895, G. D., IV, 246.

26. White resigned his position in the U. S. Indian Service in 1787. Virginia delegates to the Governor of Virginia, N. Y., Dec. 11, 1787, Carnegie Institution Transcripts. See A. P. Whitaker, "The Muscle Shoals Speculation, 1783–1789," *Miss. Vall. Hist. Rev.,* XIII, 378.

27. John Sevier to Gardoqui, Sept. 12, 1788, G. D., I, 311–315. The letter, in English facsimile of copy from the Spanish Archives, not of the original Sevier letter, and the Spanish translation of same is printed by Henderson, op. cit.

Cumberland settlement was in 1788 as much a political
orphan as the Franklin people—for it also lay along
North Carolina's western waters—and had no protection
either from state or federal government. It was here
that White's property was located. He had doubtless
been in touch with Robertson for several years on the
Spanish business. Robertson and his associate, Anthony
Bledsoe, in 1788, sent messages to Miró declaring their
willingness to become Spanish subjects. They stated
that both Kentucky and Cumberland were determined
to free themselves from their dependence on Congress,
"because that body cannot protect either their property
or favor their commerce." Miró cautiously sent back
a vague answer. In November, 1788, James Robertson
was delegate to the North Carolina legislature that
erected the three western counties into a new political
district which, at Robertson's motion, received the
name of Miró. Writing confidentially from the "District
of Miró" in fulsome terms to the Spanish Governor
after whom it was named, Robertson continued his
appeals to Spain. This overture, to which Miró responded too tardily for success, ceased, when North
Carolina, aware of it, hastened to put an end to it by
ceding over the district to the United States as a part
of the common federal domain.[28] During 1788 and
1789 Robertson was appealing now to Miró, now to
McGillivray. "The constant factor was Robertson's

28. Dr. A. P. Whitaker suggests that Robertson was appealing to
McGillivray for an alliance with a new southwestern state which the
Tennesseeans at this time imagined might be set up through plottings
between the Creek chieftain and the white adventurer, William
Augustus Bowles. See his article on "Spanish Intrigue in the Old
Southwest," in *Miss. Vall. Hist. Rev.*, XII, 154–178, 409–412 (docu-
ments). For Bowles, see Gayarré, 314–320, and a short sketch by
Elisha P. Douglass, "The Adventurer Bowles," *Wm. and Mary Quart.*,
3rd. Series, VI (1949), 3–23.

desire to placate McGillivray and thus avert from Cumberland the hostility of the Creeks." [29] In 1789 White at Gardoqui's demand made a journey to Havana and New Orleans in the interests of this intrigue, which he cherished as the product of his own genius, and carried messages from Governor Miró back to the Cumberland country. It has been very plausibly argued that these intrigues of the Cumberland leaders, who included particularly James Robertson and Daniel Smith, were purposely concocted and subtly exhibited as a "bogey" designed by them "to serve simultaneously as a threat and a promise. As a threat to reluctant North Carolina, it would secure a cession of the state's western territory to Congress. As a promise to Spain, it would obtain from the Spanish governor of Louisiana commercial concessions and, above all, relief from Indian attacks." [30]

The political organization of the Tennessee country and of the Southwest ended the whole affair. After the Southwestern Territory was created in 1790, Robertson and Sevier became unswervingly loyal citizens of the United States, and soon afterward able leaders of the new state of Tennessee.[31] Sevier's connection with

29. Ibid. James White's peregrinations and contacts with Spanish officials and western separatists are discussed in detail by Dr. Whitaker from information in the correspondence of Spanish authorities in New Orleans and Havana, in "The Muscle Shoals Speculation, 1783–1789," op. cit., 365; and the same author depicts from Spanish archival sources the career of "Alexander McGillivray, 1789–1793," in North Carolina Hist. Rev., V, 181–204, 289–310.

30. Ibid. For D. Smith's conviction that McGillivray incited the Cherokee to war against the frontiers of Georgia and North Carolina, see Diaries of George Washington (Fitzpatrick ed.), IV, 81.

31. For a summary of the Robertson intrigue, based on Gardoqui's Despatches and Gayarré, see Henderson, op. cit. With it should be studied the later researches of Whitaker. See also Roosevelt, Winning of the West, III, 152–202.

Gardoqui, and the Louisiana Spanish officials, ceased promptly after he had been pardoned by North Carolina for his alleged treason and had accepted a seat in the Assembly of that state and the rank of brigadier general. His own intrigues may also have been designed in part to have an alternate possibility (in case of failure with Spain) of alarming North Carolina into action for the better governance of her isolated western settlements.[32] Like so many of these western intrigues, Aaron Burr's later famous one for instance, it is impossible to unravel its precise character at this date without more explicit information. The very nature of an intrigue of this kind is to leave as little documentary evidence as possible.

As to Wilkinson's plot, there is plenty of documentary evidence in the Spanish archives to reveal its true nature. Without the slightest doubt it was an attempt to detach Kentucky and as much additional United States territory as possible from the Union and bring

32. Dr. Whitaker's conjecture is that Sevier's whole trafficking with the Spanish was studiously exhibited to the authorities of North Carolina in order to alarm them into giving better terms to the western political faction which Sevier represented, as well as to get Spanish intervention to prevent the southern Indians from attacking the Tennessee settlers. "Between the sympathetic administration of Governor Blount [made Governor of the new Southwestern Territory in 1790] and the more acceptable policy of the new federal government disaffection gradually died out in the Holston settlements." "It is impossible to say," continues Dr. Whitaker, after a careful study of the relevant Spanish sources in Seville, as well as the North Carolina state records, "to what extent Sevier's letter of September 12 [1788, to Gardoqui] represented the sentiment of his community or even of his faction. James White informed Miró that many of the notables of Franklin were in accord with Sevier, but only Sevier committed himself to pen and paper." Whitaker, "Spanish Intrigue," op. cit., 161, 163. The reader is referred to Dr. Whitaker's volume *The Spanish-American Frontier,* for this and other incidents of frontier diplomacy.

it over to Spanish sovereignty. That man's conspiracy
with Harry Innes, Benjamin Sebastian, Caleb Wallace,
Isaac Dunn, John Brown, and others still harbored
this project hopefully. Despite the failure to swing the
convention of November, 1788, in favor of separation,
Wilkinson continued to receive trade concessions at
New Orleans and to act as a secret Spanish informant
in Kentucky. In 1792 he accepted a pension of $2,000
a year from Spain, after having recommended his
fellow-conspirators and likely converts for a graded
scale of pensions.[33] Wilkinson and Brown remained in
communication with Gardoqui, working over their
plans for Kentucky, until the Spanish envoy's departure from Philadelphia in October, 1789.

V

The widespread indignation of the West at the Jay-
Gardoqui negotiation, the opposition of their delegates
to the federal Constitution, and the universal smell of
intrigue had a chastening effect on the eastern and
northern states. Support for the Jay proposals, which
had been so solid in the North, began to weaken as the
determined demeanor of the West and its opposition
to the Constitution was observed. It is doubtful whether
at any time after the summer of 1787 a majority of
the states again could have been marshaled in favor
of the occlusion of the Mississippi.

In September of 1788 the delegates of North Carolina presented a resolution to Congress, which began
by reciting that many citizens of the United States who
possessed lands on the western waters were uneasy
after having heard a report that Congress was disposed

33. Shepherd in *A. H. R.*, IX, 748; Green, op. cit., 318–358; Serrano
y Sanz, *El Brigadier Jaime Wilkinson*, 18–38.

to treat with Spain for the surrender of the navigation
of the Mississippi. In order to quiet the minds of these
people the delegates of North Carolina proposed that
Congress resolve "that the United States have a clear,
absolute and unalienable claim to the free navigation
of the River Mississippi, which claim is not only supported by the express stipulation of treaties, but by the
great law of nature." The proposed resolution was
referred to Jay for report. In a statement made for
the benefit of Congress, on September 16, 1788, he said
that records of Congress would show that never for
once had he denied that right, that accordingly such a
rumor was not warranted by any of his negotiations;
but that it would be expedient for Congress to rescind
the orders of secrecy, under which the negotiation
between that body and Gardoqui had been conducted,
to the extent that the delegates from North Carolina
and other delegates might contradict the rumor in the
most explicit and positive terms. Then Jay went on
with a statement which shows how the political situation, caused by southern opposition to his proposed
treaty, and the relation of that opposition to the recent
ratification of the Constitution had influenced him:

Whether it would be wise in the United States to consent, in
consideration of equivalent advantages, to any and what modifications of the use of that right, is a question on which his [the
Foreign Secretary's] opinion, communicated to Congress in writing, is well known. The modifications *then* contemplated appeared to him at that time advisable; but he confesses that
circumstances and discontents have since interposed to render it
more questionable than it then appeared to be. How far the
resolution proposed by North Carolina, which declares the right
to be unalienable, as well as absolute, would tend to exclude all
modifications, however temporary and adapted to present circum·
stances and convenience, merits consideration, nor is it clear to

him that such exclusion would be a measure, which however supported by right would also be warranted by good policy. *Whether that right be unalienable or not, does not depend on the nature of the title, but on the extent of the powers constitutionally vested in government.* How far the present or ensuing government may be restrained or authorized in these respects, is a question of too great magnitude to be decided without deliberate and mature investigation. He knows the prejudices and opinions prevailing in the western country respecting whatever may concern that navigation; and he knows also that groundless though not unnatural jealousies are also entertained of him respecting it; but as personal considerations ought not to influence his publick conduct, he thinks it his duty to report in plain terms, that any resolution calculated to exclude the possibility of such modifications, as without impairing the right, might be advantageous to the United States, and satisfactory to the citizens, would not in his opinion be wise. Whether such modifications would be formed he will not attempt to conjecture. Certain it is that the probability of it will become greater and increase as the population of those countries advances, and as the respectability of the United States rises in the estimation of Spain and other foreign nations.

He therefore thinks it best to let these negotiations pass over in their present state to the new government, who will undoubtedly be tenacious of the publick rights, and may be enabled, by *circumstances not yet developed,* to terminate these negotiations with Spain in a manner perfectly consistent with the rights in question and with the interests and wishes of their constituents.[34]

The language of this report to Congress was really a *volte face* on Jay's part. The discontents in the West so alarmed him as a threat to the new federal government—the movement for the Constitution and its consummation was to him, as to most thinking men, the *summum desideratum* of the times—that he changed his mind again on the Mississippi Question. He came back to the view he had held during the negotiations in

34. Italics, except those occurring in the last paragraph, inserted.

Madrid, that the right to navigate the Mississippi ought never to be given up under any guise.

With the position of the Secretary for Foreign Affairs modified, it is not surprising that the expiring Continental Congress that same day:

Resolved, That the said report [that is to say, the said rumor], not being founded in fact, the delegates be at liberty to communicate all such circumstances as may be necessary to contradict the same, and to remove misconceptions.

Resolved, That the free navigation of the River Mississippi is a clear and essential right of the United States, and that the same ought to be considered and supported as such.

Resolved, That no further progress be made in the negotiations with Spain, by the secretary for foreign affairs; but that the subject to which they related be referred to the federal government, which is to assemble in March next.[35]

Though the Constitution had been definitely adopted and the new government actually installed by the time Gardoqui sailed from New York in October, 1789, he left America convinced of the impolicy of a treaty with the United States and persuaded that the possibilities of western separatism and the notorious jealousies of the eastern states presented the combination best suited to the purposes of Spanish diplomacy. His five years' experience with the Continental Congress formed an essential background for Spanish-American relations when President Washington took up anew the vexing issues with Spain. It will now be our task to examine

35. Secret Journals of Congress, IV, 447–448. "Congress has agreed to some resolutions in favor of the Mississippi which were well calculated to appease the discontents of our western brethren. They are grounded on a remonstrance from North Carolina on that subject." Madison to Edmund Randolph, N. Y., Sept. 24, 1788, Madison Papers, Library of Congress, Accession 1081 (11) 44. See also Madison's letters to Jefferson of August 23, Sept. 21, 1788, Writings of Madison (Hunt ed.), VI, 253, 262.

how the new federal government was to cope with this problem of international relations, and how a cycle of unforeseen European political disturbances was to present to the United States peculiar advantages in diplomacy—in short, how Europe's distress was to become America's advantage.

CHAPTER 8

"Patience and Persuasion"

I

When Diego de Gardoqui left America in 1789 there seemed to exist not the slightest reason why one of the greatest and oldest monarchies in the world should grant to the feeblest sovereign state in existence demands which were supported by nothing more formidable than reliance on highly disputable interpretations of treaties, mooted principles of ill-defined international law, and very vulnerable deductions from vaguely described natural rights. Still less to a government strained by sectional interests and containing conspiracy within its own household. Upon the successful assertion by the United States of its claims to the Florida boundary and the free navigation of the Mississippi depended, what then no man could foresee, the future territorial expansion of this nation to its physical basis as a world power today. It will be the task of this chapter to describe a part of the peculiar procession of events by which American diplomacy was to find its great good fortune in the necessities and embarrassments of European nations arrayed against each other as bitter belligerents or distrustful allies.

Nothing was done toward resuming the suspended Spanish negotiations until the arrival of Thomas Jefferson to take up the newly-created office of Secretary of State. Jefferson in 1790 was ripe with six years of experience at the Court of Versailles, focal point of old-

world diplomacy. Though much of the Virginian's
time had been spent closeted with a coterie of philo-
sophical radicals intellectually and actually on the eve
of the French Revolution, he had not failed to measure
the sensitive European balance of power.[1] Repeated
diplomatic crises in Europe had suggested to him that
on general principles a war might be expected in Europe at almost any time, inevitably very soon.

It became Jefferson's settled conviction that sooner
or later Europe's quarrels would be sure to be America's advantage. An implicit trust in this, rather than
in military preparedness—though at this time Jefferson
recommended a navy as a protective force not capable
of civil tyranny—was to be characteristic of his long
career in handling the foreign relations of the United
States. It was to the imminent likelihood of some war
in Europe in which Spain might be seriously jeop-
ardized at home that Jefferson looked, on becoming
Secretary of State, for the solution of issues with that
monarchy.[2] Out of future chapters of circumstances,
the precise description of which he could not foresee,
but to the general character of which he confidently
trusted, he awaited the opportune moment when the
United States, a nation of no appreciable organized

1. See my sketch of Jefferson as Secretary of State in Vol. II of the
Knopf series on *The American Secretaries of State and Their Diplomacy,*
10 vols. (New York, 1927–1929). See also Jefferson, *Works* (Federal
ed.), IV, 372, and *Writings* (Ford ed.), V, 23; also *Dip. Corres.*, III, 311,
400–446.

2. In 1788 he had written to his friend John Brown, whose real connection with the "Spanish" conspiracy was unknown to him, counseling
the western citizens to moderation in their demands for the Mississippi.
"I should think it proper for the Western country to defer pushing
their right to that navigation to extremity as long as they can do
without it tolerably. . . . A time of peace will not be the surest for
obtaining this object. Those therefore who have influence in the new
country would act wisely to endeavor to keep things quiet until the
western parts of Europe shall be engaged in war." *Writings*, V, 17.

military or naval power, could by a threat of potential strength and by astute diplomacy force from Spain, harassed by troubles in Europe, the navigation of the Mississippi and the southern boundary line of 31°. More than this, Jefferson expected that later generations of his countrymen would take, piece by piece, at other opportune moments, the whole of Spain's dominions in North America.[3] That could wait. It was this menace, indeed, which had already stiffened Spain to resist any first concession on her frontiers.

A persuasion of this kind may seem to the reader of today an artless and childlike policy for a diplomat of the eighteenth century, but after reflecting on the expansion of the United States during the remainder of Jefferson's long life one cannot but feel that his confidence was abundantly warranted. Faith like this happened to be well placed because of the wars of the French Revolution, the vast scope or even the proximate arrival of which no man could have foretold six months before France's declaration of war on England in 1793.

II

The very European contingency so expectantly anticipated by Jefferson loomed on the horizon soon after he became Secretary of State—before he had taken up the suspended Spanish-American negotiation. On the distant northwest coast of America, in Nootka Sound, Spanish naval officers, on order, had seized a British trading ship for violation of Spain's alleged exclusive sovereignty over that region. News of the seizure reached London early in 1790. The young Prime Minister, the "God-given" William Pitt, son of the redoubtable Lord Chatham, resolved to make of this seizure a question of

3. *Writings,* V, 23.

power between reviving Britain and Spain, which now saw her ancient family ally, France, paralyzed by revolution.[4] News of the Nootka Crisis was known in New York in July, 1790. Though Washington and Jefferson dreaded British encirclement by a conquest of Louisiana in such a war as seemed about to occur, the Secretary of State thought the moment appropriate to approach Spain, not as the reader might imagine with any feelings of mutual concern against British aggression, but with demands for the navigation of the Mississippi and the recognition of the southern boundary. Not only the free use of that river, but also a port at its mouth, where American sea and river vessels could anchor and exchange their cargoes, was desired. "The right to use a thing comprehends a right to the means necessary to its use, and without which it would be useless." [5] Jefferson's interpretation of our Mississippi treaty claims was much looser than his construction of the Constitution of the United States!

Jefferson had been pondering the Spanish business almost from his first day in office.[6] Following news of Nootka, he first despatched to Madrid Colonel David Humphreys, intimate and former aide of General Washington, to lay the facts of the Mississippi case freshly before William Carmichael, our chargé there since 1784, and to deliver to him a memoir reiterating the already familiar American arguments to which

4. For summary of this affair, see my *Jay's Treaty*, 52–78.

5. To Carmichael, N. Y., Aug. 2, 1790, *Writings*, V, 216.

6. On March 24, 1790, Jefferson, who had taken up the duties of Secretary of State on Feb. 22, suggested to the President that it might be advisable to direct Carmichael to sound the Spanish Ministry on the Mississippi Question, the boundary, and the possibility of a treaty of commerce. *Diaries of George Washington*, IV, 108.

was now appended the characteristically Jeffersonian one of natural rights.[7]

> We press these matters warmly and firmly [Carmichael was instructed], under this idea, that the war between Spain and Great Britain will be begun before you receive this; and such a moment must not be lost. But should an accommodation take place, we retain, indeed, the same object and the same resolutions unalterably; but your discretion will suggest, that in that event, they must be pressed more softly, and that *patience and persuasion*[8] must temper your conferences, till either of these may prevail, or some other circumstance turn up, which may enable us to use some other means for the attainment of an object which we are determined, in the end, to obtain at every risk.

France was invoked to assist the favorable turn of events. Jefferson sent the same memoir, and a copy of the instructions to Carmichael, to William Short, the chargé whom he had left behind at Paris, to be communicated to Lafayette, whose assistance was relied on in matters which interested both the United States and France.

> He and you will consider how far the contents of these papers may be communicated to the Count de Montmorin [Vergennes' successor at the Foreign Office], and his influence be asked with the court of Madrid. France will be called into the war, as an ally, and not on any pretence of the quarrel being in any degree her own. She may reasonably require then, that Spain should do everything which depends on her, to lessen the number of her enemies. She cannot doubt that we shall be of that number, if

7. Humphreys was also charged with the delivery of papers to Gouverneur Morris, then supposed to be in London in connection with his informal mission there for President Washington, and with overtures in Lisbon for the opening of diplomatic relations between the United States and Portugal. F. L. Humphreys, *Life of David Humphreys*, II, 1–80.

8. Italics inserted.

she does not yield our right to the common use of the Mississippi, and the means of using and securing it.[9]

France, her power in international affairs already crippled for the time being by the Revolution, could not come forth wholeheartedly as Spain's ally. The Nootka Crisis shattered the Family Compact. Spain could not trust to effective French support. She accepted Pitt's ultimatum. Compensation was paid for the fur-trading ships seized at Nootka Sound, the vessels themselves restored and British subjects admitted henceforth to trade and to establish themselves on the northwest coast of North America above the districts already colonized by Spain. The Pope's Bull and the Portuguese-Spanish Treaty of Tordesillas which had divided the new world in Columbus's age, now lost for all time even the shadow of hoary authority. This was a diplomatic achievement of the first order for England. Its chief significance here is that the golden opportunity of European distress and American advantage, so ardently expected by Jefferson, vanished from his immediate view.[10]

III

The Nootka affair passed peacefully. Nothing remained but to keep American claims in Madrid gently alive until another opportunity should chance to fall

9. To Short, N. Y., Aug. 10, 1790, *Writings*, V, 218.

10. While the crisis was still imminent the Spanish Ambassador at Paris was unusually attentive to Short. He spoke of the interest which both countries had in being better acquainted and always united, that Spain, in contrast to England, had no desire to extend her possessions, that it would really be to her advantage to get rid of some of them provided they did not fall into the hands of enemies. Short to Jefferson, No. 44, Paris, Oct. 21, 1790, Despatches, France, I, 335. Such hints and sentiments disappeared as soon as peace was certain. Short did not even show Jefferson's communication to Lafayette.

more perfectly out of the unquiet European sky. Meanwhile "patience and persuasion."

During the year 1791 this appears to have been patience on the part of the United States, persuasion by France. Jefferson's next move was to try to get France to induce Spain to yield what American arguments had hitherto failed to secure. He made use of an incident which happened as far back as 1787, when an American citizen, one Joseph St. Marie, had been arrested on the left bank of the Mississippi in latitude 34° 40', with his trading goods, by a Spanish official. The Secretary of State instructed Carmichael to take this as an occasion to present again the American claims, "in the most friendly terms but with that earnestness and perseverance which the complexion of the wrong demands." A copy of these instructions was sent to Short in Paris to be exhibited to Montmorin, with a request for France's "efficacious interference" in favor of the United States at the Court of Madrid. Lafayette's good offices also were invoked again.[11]

Lafayette advised the United States to proceed at once, without stopping for negotiation, to wrest the disputed territory from Spain and to incorporate it into the Union. So did Montmorin. Let the western inhabitants, whose restlessness Jefferson was always exhibiting, act for themselves, go down the river, and take New Orleans. Vital as were American needs for the navigation of that river, he thought there was no other way to impress Spain. Nevertheless, if Short would put his request into writing, Montmorin agreed to transmit it to the Court of Madrid.[12]

11. To Short, N. Y., March 12, 1791, *Writings*, V, 298.
12. Short to Jefferson, No. 67, Paris, June 6, 1791, Despatches, France, II, 170.

Jefferson, whom doubtless Montmorin had correctly measured during the Virginian's onetime sojourn in Paris, had no intention of going to war to get what he wanted from Spain. "We are not inattentive to the interests of your navigation," he wrote at this time to Harry Innes, John Brown's friend, whom Jefferson did not know as one of the Spanish conspirators. "Nothing *short of actual rupture* is omitted. The nail will be driven as far as it will go *peaceably,* and farther the moment that circumstances become favorable." [13] By this Jefferson meant the moment that the United States might be neutral during a European war in which Spain should be involved.

The French Revolution was by now anathema to Spain. Nootka had revealed the hollowness of the Family Compact. No longer was anything good to be expected out of France. The Spanish Court dreaded the spread of revolutionary doctrine across the Pyrenees. It placed the frontier under a military *cordon sanitaire,* heavily guarded. Before and after the flight to Varennes Louis XVI and Marie Antoinette were intriguing with the King of Spain, through the Spanish Ambassador at Paris, to overthrow the Constitution which the captive King had publicly sworn to obey.[14] Even the royalist Montmorin, who perforce had adapted himself to the new regime, could not be trusted with Spanish interests. The two governments were drifting rapidly apart. Spain was sure to shrink from any discussion with the United States of its interests under the good offices of increasingly republican France.

13. March 7, 1791, *Writings,* V, 294. (Italics inserted.)
14. A. Mousset, *Un témoin ignoré de la révolution, le comte de Fernan Nuñez,* 199–273. This volume consists of the publication, in French translation, of the more significant despatches of the Spanish Ambassador at Paris, 1787–1793.

IV

To return to the Mississippi Question. After referring to the St. Marie case and the difficulty of restraining the turbulent impatience of the West, Short declared that the United States was confronted with the alternative of seeing its western citizens separate and take with them half the territory of the nation, or of supporting their just claims against Spain. No choice but the latter was possible, and Short appealed to French friendship to support at Madrid the representations of the American agent there to secure the free navigation of the Mississippi and, near its mouth, a port under American jurisdiction.[15]

This note made a great stir when transmitted by Montmorin to the Spanish Government and actually supported by the French chargé at Madrid. Carmichael already had opened as portentously as was possible, without support of any kind, discussion of the claims of the United States.[16] He had met with no ready response. The new American note from Montmorin was referred immediately to Gardoqui. He found it disturbing. "In October of '89 when I left that country it was very far from setting forth in writing the pretenses it now makes," he stated to Floridablanca. The change in tone he ascribed to the incapacity of France as Spain's family ally and to a possible rapprochement between the United States and Great Britain, which seemed likely now that a British Minister was known to have been sent to America for the first time.

15. Short to Montmorin, Paris, June 1, 1791, Despatches, France, II, 170. See p. 153 above.

16. Carmichael to [Floridablanca, or Gardoqui?], Madrid, Aug. 8, 1791, A. H. N., Est. Leg., 3890, Expdte. 1.

Actually neither of these factors was responsible for the attitude of the United States in 1791. Any increased resolution which Gardoqui may have discerned in the United States Government was due to two other factors which that Minister, with all his transatlantic experience, did not quite evaluate. One was that the northern states had been convinced, after it had become apparent that the Jay-Gardoqui negotiation of 1786 had nearly defeated ratification of the federal Constitution, that to relinquish or even to *forbear* to use the navigation of the Mississippi was dangerous to the future union of East and West. The other was the increased national power of the new Constitution, expressed in the Administration of President Washington. Already it had been felt abroad and had begun to command the respect of foreign powers. There was not at this time, particularly while Jefferson remained Secretary of State, any likelihood of such a rapprochement, although Great Britain had just decided to send a minister to the United States in order to stave off tariff discriminations against her trade.

There was not, as Gardoqui feared, really the slightest danger of an Anglo-American combination against Spanish possessions, such as Alexander Hamilton suggested to President Washington as a means of opening the Mississippi. This possibility was the constant nightmare of Spain's officials familiar with North America, for it would embolden the people of the United States to take the offensive against Louisiana. "The first rifleshot [of any hostilities by the United States] I would regard as the beginning of our disasters in America," declared Gardoqui. Supposing that England was the clue to this new overture, then the best thing to be done by Spain, he thought, was "to get as much as we can out of a bad business," to temporize with the United States and undertake some diversion which might hold up any joint action by the two English-speaking nations; for example, England might be diverted by holding out to her the exchange of the Floridas for Gibraltar. Let a reply be made directly to the United States instead of to France, advised Gardoqui, to the effect that as soon as that republic should send to Spain a proper person the King hoped that direct negotiations might result in a treaty satisfactory to both parties. He added that for the American negotiation His Majesty should appoint a Spanish subject (presumably like himself) thoroughly familiar with the United States and its party divisions, including the disinclination of the Atlantic states to see granted the free navigation of the Mississippi, for fear of draining population away from the East. He emphasized the political division in America by quoting a letter of June 18, 1786, written by General Washington to Gardoqui's one-time informant, Henry Lee, speaking against free navigation and advocating the opening and improvement of the Potomac to foster better communication with the West.[17]

Finally I would say, Sir [Gardoqui concluded], it would be possible to get the utmost advantage from the cession of that navigation, if the thing were undertaken skillfully; to resist it in our present state is impossible, but we ought not to neglect to put that invaluable bulwark [Louisiana] immediately in a respectable situation. According to information from America they hope that England will deliver the posts the cession of which was stipulated but which England retained despite the treaty. If this is so, we may be too late, and cursed be the day when any hostility is committed in that part of the globe, for those seas will be inundated with privateers fitted out by all nations, which will end by introducing revolution into the possessions of the King.

17. *Writings of Washington* (Ford ed.), XI, 41.

Floridablanca endorsed the memorandum: "All that which is set forth in this opinion is borne in mind. Never will the English listen to an exchange of the Floridas." Since the treaty of 1783 he had discussed repeatedly with England the project of taking Gibraltar in exchange for something. No agreement had been possible.[18]

The Court accepted Gardoqui's advice. Jaudenes and Viar, the young attachés[19] whom Gardoqui had left to represent Spanish interests at Philadelphia after his own departure, informed the Secretary of State in December, 1791, that Spain would be glad to resume the suspended negotiation at Madrid.[20] They reported that Jefferson welcomed this news with indescribable satisfaction. He explained that the American overture had been made through France instead of directly to Spain because of the difficulty in securing prompt correspondence from Carmichael from whom only one letter had been received in two years. He spoke of the difficult task of keeping Kentucky quiet, of his fear that the people there could not be restrained if the federal gov-

18. Gardoqui to Floridablanca, Madrid, Aug. 22, 1791, "Dictamen que dió Don Diego de Gardoqui del papel de D. Augustin de Urtovise, sobre la libre navegacion del Misispipi y otros asuntos." A. H. N., Est. Leg., 3889 bis, Expdte., No. 4. Urtovise was the French chargé at Madrid. See also in this same expediente, Gardoqui to Floridablanca, Sept. 7 & 9, 1791. Great Britain might have accepted the Floridas for Gibraltar, if accompanied by an offensive and defensive alliance with Spain. This would have meant, of course, the disruption of the Bourbon Family Alliance before the Nootka Crisis destroyed it. Conversations on this took place very secretly at various times between 1783 and 1786. See A. G. C., Leg., 2617, moderno (L. C. trans.).

19. These men technically had no diplomatic rank. They are however referred to in the Spanish documents as chargés (encargados).

20. Carmichael was also informed at Madrid, but no word of this ever reached Jefferson from him. Carmichael to Floridablanca, No. 7, 1791, A. H. N., Est. Leg., 3889 bis, Expdte., No. 4.

ernment did not get for them their desired navigation. He assured Jaudenes that "if the King should come to it [i.e., a recognition of that navigation] the United States not only would not desire an inch of territory which actually belonged to His Majesty, but that rather they would end by becoming guarantors of the integrity of all his possessions in America" (*sino que antes bien le saldrán garántes por la conservación de todas sus posesiones en América*). Jefferson did not doubt that the President would send immediately the proper powers to Carmichael. He asked if the latter would be acceptable for such a negotiation. On this point Jaudenes did not commit himself, having no instructions. Later, recollecting that Floridablanca had once expressed to Gardoqui, several years before, dissatisfaction with Carmichael as a representative of the United States, he suggested to Senator Butler, of South Carolina, whose intimacy he had cultivated, that someone other than Carmichael was probably desired.[21]

As a result of the Spanish statement President Washington adopted Jefferson's recommendation to send William Short, former chargé at Paris and recently appointed minister resident at The Hague, to Madrid, to act with Carmichael, the regular chargé there, as a

21. Jaudenes and Viar to Floridablanca, No. 61, Phila., Dec. 18, 1791, A. H. N., Est. Leg., 3894. *Writings*, V, 403, 404. See also letters exchanged between Jefferson and Jaudenes and Viar, Jan. 25, 26 and 27, in ibid., 431 and 432, and State Dept., Notes, Spain, I (for Jaudenes and Viar's note of Jan. 25). There is also in the Archivo Histórico Nacional at Madrid a memorandum by Carmichael dated Nov. 7, 1791, which repeats the substance of a conversation with Floridablanca at the latter's request. It attests that Floridablanca had indicated his intention of sending a plenipotentiary to America to adjust matters with the United States upon the basis of the free navigation of the Mississippi and the boundary as fixed by the treaty between the United States and Great Britain. A. H. N., Est. Leg., 3890.

joint commissioner plenipotentiary for the purpose of negotiating a treaty of boundaries and navigation. Short arrived in Madrid armed with joint powers and with a lengthy state paper in which Jefferson, the future leader of the crystallizing Republican-Democratic Party in American politics, marshaled all his subtle skill and ingenious arguments to support the claims of the United States and to display them in such a way as to demonstrate to voters on the western waters the assiduity of the Secretary of State personally, as well as of the federal government generally, in supporting their one most vital interest.[22]

22. "Report on Negotiations with Spain," March 18, 1792, *Writings*, V, 461–481. See note by the editor, P. L. Ford, p. 461.

CHAPTER 9

More Patience and More Persuasion

I

When Floridablanca in September, 1791, decided to invite an American negotiation at Madrid, the decision was dictated by fear that the despatch of a British minister to the United States and the rumored decision of Great Britain to evacuate the northern frontier posts betokened a rapprochement between those two Governments. Between that time and Short's arrival in Madrid, eighteen months elapsed. A year and a half in 1791–1792 meant staggering transformations in the politics of Europe, changes utterly beyond the comprehension of even Thomas Jefferson and his trust in European instability. The flight of Louis XVI to Varennes occurred just after Short presented his note to Montmorin. The capture and return to Paris of the King, his sham adherence to the Constitution of 1791, the Declaration of Pilnitz, the invasion of France by the allied monarchs of Austria and Prussia, the Manifesto of the Duke of Brunswick, the Jacobin revolution, the Terror of August and September, 1792, the proclamation of the Republic, French occupation of the Austrian Netherlands, the trial and execution of the King —all this cycle of cataclysmic events had intervened while the despatches and instructions of American diplomatists were being buffeted slowly to and fro across the Atlantic Ocean. As Louis XVI's head dropped from the guillotine a thrill of horror and genuine dread electrified the monarchs of continental Europe. But the French in Belgium and at the mouth of the Scheldt were an even more effective alarm to England than the decapitation of his royal cousin was to Charles IV of Spain.

William Short, concerning whom we shall have much to say from now on, was a young Virginian who had left the United States with Jefferson in 1783 to complete his education by travel in Europe and study in France. Then but twenty-four years of age he was already a man of much perspicacity and great promise. A graduate of William and Mary College he was one of the charter members of Phi Beta Kappa, of which society he had been president for three years. In 1783 before leaving for France he served with credit a term as a member of the Virginia Executive Council. Jefferson was early attracted to him because of his "peculiar talent for prying into facts." He describes him at that time as young, with little experience in business, but well prepared for it. The friendship which developed between these two men was an important feature of Short's life as long as Jefferson lived. Short was fortunate to begin his career as a protégé of Jefferson. In 1705 he became his private secretary. At Jefferson's departure from Paris, Short remained in charge of the legation, and in 1789 upon Jefferson's recommendation was nominated by Washington, and confirmed as chargé d'affaires of the United States to the Court of France, the first nomination, incidentally, to be made to the Senate of the United States.

Short perceived the fact that the new nation would require presumably in the future the services of trained diplomats, that there were at the time few such avail-

able in America who did not already occupy higher sta-
tions in public employ, and he embarked consciously
on that profession as a career. It was his ambition to
secure ultimately the appointment of minister to France
as successor to Jefferson, after the latter became Secretary of State. Instead, Gouverneur Morris was appointed, despite the fact that Lafayette had strongly
recommended Short to the President, and preferred
him to Morris.[1] The young diplomat then fixed his
eyes on the London legation, which required an incum-
bent in 1791, only to see Thomas Pinckney, a man without actual experience, receive that important post.
Short's friend Jefferson, though Secretary of State, had
no decisive influence in making either of these appointments, both of which were Washington's own acts.
Short did, however, get the station at The Hague,
where he served as minister resident during 1792. In
this capacity he negotiated with great ability the complicated business of the several loans from Dutch bankers by the United States for the purpose of taking up
arrears of the revolutionary debts to France and Spain.

Meanwhile from Paris and The Hague this young
man with the capacity for prying into facts had observed the tremendous political events which accompanied the outbreak of the French Revolution, and
from which he had a rare opportunity of measuring the
European balance of power. It was his experience of
this nature as well as Jefferson's friendship which led
the Secretary of State to recommend him as a well-
qualified person to be joined with Carmichael, the regular chargé at Madrid, in the joint commission plenipotentiary for this important negotiation, relying on
Carmichael and his long experience in Spain to supply

1. Lafayette, *Mémoires*, I, 385.

the local information and firsthand knowledge of Spanish policies and personalities.[2]

William Carmichael who also has already appeared in our narrative, and whom it will be necessary from now on to notice considerably more, was a son of a Scotch emigrant to Queen Anne County, Maryland. A fortunate legacy from a rich Maryland relative enabled Carmichael to go to England for his education, where he found himself upon the outbreak of the Revolutionary War. In England he came into touch with the radical politicians of the day and also made the acquaintance of a number of companions who certainly did not improve his personal morals, though they furnished acquaintances who later proved of value as recruits for sea-captains and sailors necessary to American agents in France in running guns and munitions through the British navy to the revolted colonies. Carmichael explained to Congress in November, 1776, that he was on his way home from London via Paris in that year with despatches from Arthur Lee, when illness detained him in France. There he made the acquaintance of the American commissioners to the French Court and served them in the function of fitting out munition ships and other clandestine military help destined for America. During this part of his life the history of Carmichael is not very clear, but it seems certain that he was a good deal in contact with British spies in Paris who had at least hopes of converting him to their own profession. These contacts are suspicious,

2. There is no adequate biography of Short. The above information is based on the Short Papers in the Library of Congress, and Jefferson's *Writings*. See also Lafayette's *Mémoires*, I, 385, and the *Dictionary of Am. Biography*. See also George Green Shackelford, "William Short: Diplomat in Revolutionary France, 1785–1793." *Am. Phil. Soc. Proc.*, Vol. 102 (1958), 596–611.

but there is no evidence that the agents were actually successful. Carmichael cultivated Franklin's friendship, won his confidence, and served in a secretarial capacity to the commission. In December, 1777, he returned to Maryland, and was soon thereafter elected as a delegate to the Continental Congress, in which he served one term. When John Jay left for Spain, Carmichael accompanied him as secretary. He served in this office throughout Jay's mission to that country, and upon the latter's departure for Paris in 1782, Carmichael remained in Madrid as *locum tenens* in charge of American interests. In 1784 he was recognized by Charles III as chargé d'affaires of the United States. He held this office until his removal in 1794.

Carmichael's mission to Spain is a dark and not a very important chapter in the history of American diplomacy. His despatches were very rare. Jay and later Jefferson complained of this. Only sixteen official communications from Carmichael appear in the authentic and very complete publication of the diplomatic correspondence of the United States from 1783 to 1789, yet the man was otherwise a busy correspondent and during this time wrote many letters to American representatives at other European capitals. His own explanation was that his despatches were intercepted, and that he relied on Jefferson, during the latter's ministership in Paris, to relay to Jay, then Secretary for Foreign Affairs of Congress, his private letters as substitutes for official despatches that could not get safely through. But Jefferson, after becoming Secretary of State, found Carmichael an inactive correspondent. Jefferson received between August 6, 1789, and January 24, 1791, only two despatches from him, despite frequent solicitations to be more assiduous. Jefferson had been on the point of dismissing him, but believed that he would be useful to the joint commission because of his familiarity with the Spanish Court and Spanish affairs. Carmichael was at this time in very poor health, which appears to have been brought on by his irregular and intemperate habits. He was not particularly *persona grata* to the Spanish Court, though no formal complaint had ever been made about him.[3] These were the two representatives of the United States upon whom the Government was to rely for the negotiation of the Mississippi Question and cognate matters during the next two or three years. Neither one of them had been in his own land since 1783.

Short reached Madrid on the very day when France, in anticipation of hostilities from Great Britain, declared war against that power, February 1, 1793.[4] On March 7, France similarly declared war on Spain, which was answered, March 23, by a counter-declaration against France. Within a few weeks the two maritime

3. Carmichael is another interesting personality about whom practically no biographical information exists. He seems to have been a very young man in 1776, though I have not been able to ascertain the date of his birth. For his early career, see my articles in *A. H. R.*, XXIX, 474–494, on "British Secret Service and the French-American Alliance," and on "The United States and Lafayette," in *D. A. R. Magazine*, LVIII, 341–350; 405–414; 481–489. See also a scrap book in the library of the Maryland Historical Society, entitled "History of Queen Anne County," p. 34, which contains a clipping from the *Centerville Observer*, of March 15, 1887, with brief mention of Carmichael's early career. Also see S. G. Coe, *The Mission of William Carmichael to Spain* (Baltimore, 1928). There are many Carmichael letters in the Jefferson Papers in the Library of Congress. See F. L. Humphreys, *Life of David Humphreys*, II, 147. See also Jefferson's *Writings*, V, 297, 302, 314, 344, 441–449, 456. For Carmichael's intemperate habits, see despatches Nos. 17 and 21 of David Humphreys, Despatches, Lisbon, III.

4. Short to T. Pinckney, Aranjuez, Feb. 26, 1793, Short Papers, XXIII, 4006.

monarchies, traditional enemies since 1585, negotiated
an alliance against the French Republic. They agreed
on May 25, 1793, to take all means in their power to
reestablish the public tranquillity and the security of
their common interests; to damage in all possible ways
the commerce of France and to reduce that power to
just conditions of peace; to endeavor to unite all neutrals "on this occasion of common concern to all civil-
ized nations" in refusing protection to French commerce, directly or indirectly, on the high seas; and,
most important for our present study, "their Britannic
and Most Catholic Majesties reciprocally agree not to
lay down their arms (unless by common agreement)
without having obtained restitution of all the estates,
territories, cities or places which belonged to the one
or to the other before the beginning of the war, and of
which the enemy may have taken possession during the
course of hostilities." [5] Spain for a few months became
heart and soul a member of the First Coalition of allied
monarchs against revolutionary France.

Thus when Short arrived in Spain, any alarm which
the rulers of that monarchy may have once felt for the
immediate safety of Louisiana had vanished. Far from
fearing any Anglo-American combination, Spain herself was rapidly, though reluctantly,[6] slipping into the

5. Cantillo, *Tratados,* etc., 547.

6. "Spain would, I think, have remained neutre, if the Court could
have been fully convinced that France would not finally have forced
them into war—but it being morally impossible to have this conviction
—and the Cabinet of St. James finding the war inevitable for them
and pressing the decision of this Court by various arguments which
will suggest themselves to you, it has been deemed better probably
to enter into the war at present, *comme de soi même,* than to be forced
in hereafter." Short to Gouverneur Morris, Aranjuez, Feb. 18, 1793,
Short Papers, XXII, 3994. "As to general European politics, there seems
to me an impossibility of peace between this country and France, and

embrace of Great Britain. The European war anticipated by Jefferson, instead of placing Great Britain
and Spain on opposite sides, had reversed the traditional balance of power and made allies of them. Now
neither had the other to fear in North America. To
outside observers their alliance suggested mutual support in all quarters of the globe. Together controlling
the sea, there appeared no danger either from their
common enemy or from uneasy neutrals to any of the
colonial dominions of either ally. As long as this new
alliance rested on an unshaken foundation Spain paid
little attention to the United States.

While Europe was undergoing this kaleidoscopic
history, a spectacular change had taken place in the
personnel of the Spanish Ministry. It was now under
the guidance of the court adventurer, Manuel de Godoy, whose princely parts and comely person had won
the amours of the dissolute Queen Luisa and had raised
him over the ruin in succession of the able and patriotic Ministers for Foreign Affairs, Floridablanca and
Aranda, and had given him the title of Duke of Alcudia. Not that the youthful Godoy—he came into power
in his twenty-fifth year—was without some pretence to
ability. Short later reported that the diplomatic corps

yet many people even at the fountain-head express hopes of it—they
consult more their wishes than their reason probably—for most of
them wish for peace—the King from sentiment, it is thought, is ardent
for war and certainly imposes as yet silence on those who are against
it—this conflict may produce half-way measures. The French Minister
left Madrid three days ago—he was forbidden by the minister here to
come to this place, the present residence of the Court. Until the death
of the King he was admitted to conference—from that time it ceased,
and without that atrocious and impolitic act this country would not
have been the aggressor. What will be the conduct of Great Britain
toward neutral vessels going to France?" Short to Thomas Pinckney,
Aranjuez, Feb. 26, 1793, ibid., XXIII, 4006.

acknowledged a new spirit of regularity and despatch in the Foreign Office after Alcudia had ensconced himself there.[7] The multitudinous marginalia on his despatches attest his industry though not his moral stamina, maturity, nor the judgment necessary in a statesman of the first or even of the second rank.

Godoy, after much delay and leisurely punctilio,[8] deputed the negotiations with the United States to the Minister of Finance in the reorganized Council of State. This was none other than Diego de Gardoqui, the former chargé at New York, who certainly knew as much about the Mississippi as either of the American envoys, and had been in America much more recently than they. His time monopolized by the tremendous business contingent upon the prosecution of the war, Gardoqui was willing to give them appointments only on Saturdays. It was soon evident that he now ridiculed both of the American claims, for which eighteen months before, under much different circumstances, he had advised respect. The commissioners were courteously received, but there was always a pretext for putting them off. On one excuse after another interviews were postponed. Answers to their written notes met delays beyond all justification. A reply was sure to open some technical avenue of elusion. Week

7. Short to Sec. of State, No. 137, Madrid, Jan. 4, 1794, Hague and Spain, I, 146. On Godoy and the Spanish Court in general see, in addition to the classic description in Henry Adams, *History of the United States in the Administrations of Jefferson and Madison*, I, 334–351: *Memoirs of Don Manuel de Godo·* and *The Intrigues of the Queen of Spain with the Prince of Peace and Others*, by "A Spanish Nobleman," (London, 1808); H. Baumgarten, *Geschichte Spaniens zur Zeit der Französischen Revolution* (Berlin, 1861), 419 et seq.

8. Carmichael and Short to Sec. of State, Aranjuez, Feb. 19, 1793, Short Papers, XXIII, 3998. The original is missing from the State Department, and is not in *A. S. P., F. R.*

after week, month after month, to the hearty indignation of Short, upon whom in Carmichael's physical
incapacity fell the great burden of the negotiation, the
American plenipotentiaries were put off. Yet they
lingered on in Spain, hoping that news in America of
the outbreak of the European war and the signature of
the Anglo-Spanish alliance would cause them to receive altered instructions more adaptable to the new
situation. From Madrid to the Escorial, to Aranjuez,
to San Ildefonso and La Granja and back to the Pardo
and the capital, through the dust of Castile, they weari-
ly pursued the peripatetic and leisurely Spanish Court.[9]

When despatches did finally arrive from Philadelphia
announcing Washington's proclamation of neutrality
they brought no new nor positive instructions. Instead,
a special messenger appeared from Philadelphia bringing directions to present a fresh and weighty issue
arising out of Spain's interference with the Indian
tribes of the Southwest. We must now leave the Madrid
negotiations at a standstill, in order to examine the rise
of this issue.

II

The rout of the Spanish conspirators in the Kentucky convention of November, 1788, marked the col-
lapse of their first efforts to separate that district from
the Union. After this the movement for statehood pro-

9. Short to Jefferson, Feb. 3; No. 124, March 6; No. 125, June 7;
No. 126, July 1, 1793, Hague and Spain, I, 75–97. Joint despatches of
Carmichael and Short (written by Short but signed by both), April 18,
May 5, June 6, Sept. 29, 1793, printed in *A. S. P., F. R.*, I, 259–278.
The originals are not extant in the State Department, nor is any of
Carmichael's correspondence to the Secretary of State. Copies of missing
joint despatches exist in the Short Papers. "Monotony and ennui seem
to have fixed their reign [here]." Short to T. Pinckney, XXIII, 4119.

ceeded with little danger of frustration. Eastern men
jealous of western progress dared no more to put ob-
stacles in the way. After a year had been consumed by
further Kentucky conventions in arranging with the
Assembly of Virginia the final details of separation, an
enabling act was passed by Congress, and the new state
came into the Union in 1792 under a constitution of
its own making.

The consummation of Kentucky statehood extin-
guished the immediate hopes of the Wilkinson coterie.
The adventurer himself blamed the Spanish order
admitting Kentucky products into Louisiana for the
prostration of the separatist movement. This order,
allowing western settlers to bring their produce down
the river to New Orleans upon payment of 15 per cent
customs duty, and to export it upon payment in addition of the customary provincial 6 per cent export tax,
had provided Kentucky with a tolerable market. The
Governor of Louisiana, up to 1792, also bought on
royal account practically the whole surplus tobacco
crop of Kentucky.[10] Wilkinson from the first had advised against any general admission (outside of favors
to a few pro-Spanish notables like himself) into Louisiana of Kentucky products or any general permission
to Kentucky people to use the river. This was Spain's
chief means of keeping a hold on Kentucky and of
bringing the people of that region to terms. He now
complained to Miró that the general permission to export produce through the Mississippi River on paying
a duty of 15 per cent had brought the consequences
he had feared, because, every motive of discontent

10. Serrano y Sanz, *El Brigadier Jaime Wilkinson*, 43. In 1789 Miró
purchased 235,000 lbs. from Wilkinson alone, "to keep the general
contented." Gayarré, 256.

having thus been removed, the political agitation had subsided, and no longer was there one word said about separation. Nor were the effects produced by this "pernicious" system less fatal in relation to his alternate plan for fostering emigration to Louisiana.[11] Governor Miró agreed with Wilkinson, as his letters to his superiors show, though he tried to persuade him that these privileges would in reality amount to little. Wilkinson's apparent abatement of zeal in the plot, which really had been due to his exposure among patriotic men in Kentucky, provoked Miró's doubts as to his complete usefulness to Spain.[12] Nevertheless, the connection was maintained for the sake of the information which Wilkinson conveyed about the movements on the Kentucky frontier. Miró continued to recommend the payment of a pension, as well as another one, solicited by Sebastian, whom he wished to set to spy on Wilkinson.[13]

Governor Miró was transferred from Louisiana at the close of 1791. The command and administration

11. Gayarré, 277.

12. Serrano y Sanz, *Jaime Wilkinson*, 33.

13. Relevant documents published in Gayarré, 251–300. Amongst the information furnished by Wilkinson was the project of the South Carolina Yazoo Land Company which had purchased from the state of Georgia about 50,000 acres of land in the territory disputed between Spain and the United States, on the east bank of the Mississippi between the Yazoo River and Natchez. Wilkinson tried, in correspondence with the company, to make himself its agent, in order to be able to convey their designs to Miró, and to be go-between of any intrigue which they might be following to secure a Spanish title to the land bought from Georgia, by accepting more or less Spanish protection for their colony. See C. H. Haskins, "The Yazoo Land Companies," *Am. Hist. Assoc. Papers*, V, 400–408, et seq. The Spanish documents dealing with the overtures of the Yazoo Company and their agent, O'Fallon, are published in Serrano y Sanz, *Documentos Históricos de la Florida y la Luisiana*, 382–401, and in his *El Brigadier Jaime Wilkinson*, 23–28, with Spanish map of the South Carolina Company's purchase, and of purchases by other companies.

of the province passed to the Baron de Carondelet, formerly Governor of El Salvador, who held the post at New Orleans for the next six critical years of Spanish-American relations. Carondelet appeared upon the scene only after the first act of the separatist plot had ended. For the next year Wilkinson's correspondence was meager. It dwelt chiefly upon American campaigns against the western Indians and the imminent danger of those nations being crushed. With their defeat he professed to fear that the last bulwark would be gone against a torrent of aggressive western frontiersmen who would sweep into Spain's choicest domains. He warned Carondelet that the sole defense of Louisiana consisted in a political connection with Kentucky, that this was impossible whilst liberal trading privileges continued to palliate demands for the navigation of the Mississippi.[14] Carondelet's first reaction toward Wilkinson was the well-justified one of distrust.[15] He therefore turned to his own plans for improving the military defenses of his province and building up a system of offensive and defensive alliances with the Indian tribes of the Southwest, tribes already bound by conflicting treaties of protection to both Spain and the United States. Of these tribes the Creek was the most important.

After a mission to Georgia to treat with the Creek

14. Carondelet to Floridablanca, Confidential, New Orleans, Feb. 25, 1792. Serrano y Sanz, *Documentos Históricos de la Florida y la Luisiana*, 402.

15. Ibid. For detailed description of military defenses of Louisiana in 1794, see the report written by Carondelet to Godoy (Alcudia), published in English translation in *A. H. R.*, II, 473–506, and (more accurately) by J. A. Robertson, *Louisiana under Spain, France, and the United States*, I, 293–345. For location of Spanish posts in the interior country, particularly in territory claimed by the United States, see Map 3A, p. 68.

Indians in 1789 had failed to win them away from the Spanish alliance, President Washington had succeeded in inducing the half-breed chieftain, Alexander McGillivray, to visit New York. He came with an impressive retinue of chieftains in 1790. There in the presence of the President and the higher officials of state they accepted a treaty of friendship and perpetual peace, in which "the undersigned kings, chiefs and warriors, for themselves and all parts of the Creek nation *within the limits of the United States,* do acknowledge themselves and the said parts of the Creek nation, to be under the protection of the United States of America and of no other sovereign whatsoever." The treaty stipulated a boundary in western Georgia which was to be surveyed in the presence of Creek delegates the following year. For abandoning all claims to land north and east of the agreed line, the tribe accepted an annuity of $1,500. Indian title to the lands thus recognized beyond this line was solemnly guaranteed. The Creek bound themselves to give notice of any design against the United States by any neighboring tribe or person whatsoever. The United States received the right to station four "interpreters" within the Creek country. Separate secret articles, signed by McGillivray and General Knox, made McGillivray the agent of the United States among the Creek, with the rank of brigadier general and a salary of $1,800 a year. Annuities of $100 apiece were also provided for six subchieftains. Secret articles further stated that in case "obstructions" should happen to the commerce of the Creek nation through Spanish territory, either by war or by Spanish prohibitions, it should be lawful for such persons as the President might designate to introduce into and transport through the territories of the United

States $50,000 worth of goods annually free of duties.[16]

The Cherokee in 1791 signed a treaty of peace and friendship, similarly acknowledging the protection of the United States, accepting stipulated guaranteed boundaries and an annuity of $1,500.[17]

We remember that in 1784 the Creek at Pensacola had entered into a treaty almost precisely similar, placing themselves and lands, insofar as they lay within the dominions of the King of Spain, under his protection. It had been the consistent policy of Spain to do this with all the Indians in the disputed area. Under Spanish auspices in 1787 a conference with the Choctaw took place at the Yazoo River to induce that nation to repudiate the treaty of Hopewell, which they had just signed with the United States, and to inculcate them with the obligation not to receive Americans within their domains. Carondelet did his best to get

16. Secret articles of the Creek treaty of Aug. 7, 1790. MS. State Dept. Italics inserted. See A. P. Whitaker, *Spanish-American Frontier*, 138–139.

A. G. Pickett, *History of Alabama*, 407, was the first to reveal this treaty, which is not published in Kappler's standard collection of Indian Treaties, when he came into possession of what apparently was the Indian copy. Panton as the agent of Miró had tried to induce McGillivray, before parting for New York, not to abandon the Spanish alliance: "The fixing of your boundaries, acknowledgment of mutual independence, and closing all manner of cause of future hostility, are all proper objects for a treaty, and no doubt embrace your utmost attention—but in becoming friends with those people you will carefully avoid any engagements that may clash or run contrary to those you have made on this side. Your connexion with the Spanish Government is far more safe and respectable than it can be made by those republican gentry and merits your attention beyond anything they can offer." Panton to McGillivray, Pensacola, June 7, 1789, Archivo Nac. Cuba, Florida Corres., Leg., Expedte., 5, No. 7.

17. In addition they permitted a road to be built through their territory and to allow the navigation by American citizens of the Tennessee River. Kappler, *Indian Treaties*, 24–26. The annuity was raised to $5,000 by a confirmation of the treaty in 1794.

McGillivray to go back on the treaty of New York and to incite the Indians against the United States. He gave him twice as big a pension as he received, as a brigadier general, from the United States. The chieftain's allegiance readily shifted to the higher bidder. "Confronted by the imminent peril of the Georgians invading the Indian lands ceded by the Indians, or at least by McGillivray," Carondelet sent orders to the Spanish commanders at Natchez and Saint Marks to make gifts of arms and ammunition to the Creek. As a result that nation refused to carry out the New York treaty. Hostilities between it and the Georgia settlers broke out anew, despite the remonstrances of the Secretary of War to the "American agent," McGillivray.

In conformity with this plan of reorganizing the military defenses of Louisiana, Miró in 1791 ordered the seizure and occupation of Walnut Hills, the site of present Vicksburg, some sixty miles north of Natchez and one hundred north of the line of 31° north latitude. This was done professedly to anticipate occupation there by the South Carolina Company, which had bought land from Georgia on the bank of the Mississippi south of the Yazoo, without the approbation of the federal government. The following spring Gayoso de Lemos, the talented commandant at Natchez, negotiated, with the assistance of liberal libations of firewater (an unscrupulous means used by both the American agents and the Spanish during this period), a treaty with the Choctaw and Chickasaw by which Spain received possession of an area about Walnut Hills. There he erected and garrisoned Fort Nogales. Louisiana was now guarded by lines of Spanish fortresses, though very thinly garrisoned, on both sides of the Mississippi: on the west by three posts of Arkansas, New Madrid, and

St. Louis; on the east by control of the high points of land, suitable for batteries, as far north as Vicksburg. That there remained one more strategic high point of ground between Nogales and the Ohio, Ecores de Margot, where the present city of Memphis, Tennessee, now stands, was a fact of great concern to the Spanish Governor, who feared that American settlers or possibly the American army might occupy it and be in a position to intercept Spanish river communication with St. Louis.[18]

This strategic point of Nogales now fortified—during the American Civil War it was the great commanding fortress of the Mississippi—Carondelet turned his attention to the erection of a system of Indian alliances as a means of supporting his military defenses. In his efforts to seduce the Creek from the treaty of New York, he had sent an agent, Pedro Olivier by name, into the Creek country to induce them to join in a general confederation with the Cherokee, Choctaw, and Chickasaw, which Carondelet proposed to erect under the protection of the King of Spain. Though McGillivray at first hesitated because Carondelet refused to guarantee Creek territory not included in Spain's dominions, such a general treaty eventually was signed at Nogales on October 28, 1793.

This last treaty, the capstone of Spanish Indian policy in the Southwest, reaffirmed in their entirety the old treaties of 1784, brought the Cherokee for the first time under Spanish protection, and declared an offensive and defensive alliance among the four tribes. No action under this alliance was to be taken without a previous consultation with the Spanish authorities. The Indians

18. For location of Spanish posts in the interior of the Mississippi and Mobile valleys, see Map 3A, p. 68.

agreed to defend Louisiana and both Floridas against all attacks. They invoked the good offices of Spain to secure a settlement of their boundaries with the United States—exactly as Brant's confederation of the northwestern tribes at that very moment was being tutored by Governor Simcoe, of Upper Canada, to seek the mediation of Great Britain[19]—and to terminate the difficulties which had broken out again between the Creek and Cherokee and the United States. Provision was made for the methodical distribution of annual supplies and presents to the several tribes at fixed convenient depots. The treaty tribes agreed to admit Spanish commissioners. Finally, "the several Indian nations are to be considered as one only, under the protection of His Catholic Majesty, the King of Spain and Emperor of the Indies, and His Catholic Majesty assures them his protection in all cases in which they may need it." [20]

To support and control the vacillating Indian tribes of this confederation, a new stronghold, appropriately named Confederación (near Gainesville, Sumter County, Alabama), was planted on the bend of the Tombigbee, far north of the 31° boundary claimed by the United States.[21]

With this new fortified outpost dominating the tribes of the upper Mobile basin, Carondelet hoped further to construct an alliance of the southwestern group of tribes with the northwestern confederation that had

19. *Jay's Treaty,* 130–132.

20. Serrano y Sanz, *España y los Indios Cherokis y Chactas,* 37–77. Text of the treaties of 1792 with the Choctaw and Chickasaw and of 1793 with the confederation are given in his appendix. English translation of the Treaty of 1792 in *A. S. P., F. R.,* I, 280.

21. Carondelet to Alcudia, New Orleans, Nov. 24, 1794, describing the defenses of Louisiana, *A. H. R.,* II, 503.

been successfully opposing, under covert British assistance, the American army operating north of the Ohio.
A combination like this might scour with fire and
tomahawk all the American settlements to the west of
the mountains. Turning that country into a desert
place might compel the United States to make peace
with the Indians and to respect their lands; Louisiana
might yet be put beyond all danger for years to come—
particularly if liberal reinforcements of Spanish garrisons for his already established posts should be forthcoming to Carondelet from other Spanish capitals in
the new world.[22] There was more or less negotiation
going on between the newly formed southwestern confederation of the four treaty tribes and Brant's confederation of the northwestern nations. It is easy to understand that this was a source of lively apprehension to
the United States Government which aimed at all
costs to prevent the calamity of an active alliance between these two native confederations, the one under
British tutelage and secret assistance, the other under
the alliance and supply of England's European ally,
Spain.[23]

Carondelet's policy of weaning away the Creek to
repudiate the treaty of New York and of inciting them
and the Indians generally to war against the United
States, by means of his agents in their territory, of

22. In the winter of 1793–1794 the impetuous Governor of Louisiana
sent a messenger to Detroit with offers of cooperation with English
policy and even action against the American troops then organizing
for Wayne's famous campaign. Canadian Archives, Q, 69–71, 38, 41.

23. "It is of high importance that the Southern Indians should be
prevented from joining the Indians north of the Ohio, and no expedient occurs, so proper to attain such an end, as inducing them to
join our army." Instructions to Leonard Shaw, temporary agent to the
Cherokee, Feb. 17, 1792, *A. S. P., I. A.*, I, 247.

furnishing them with arms and ammunition, and of planting another garrisoned fort in their midst, was thus vitally dangerous to the security of American settlements in the whole West and to the territorial integrity of the nation as constituted by the peace settlement of 1783. For fear of stirring up a war which might sweep over all the back country between Lake Erie and the uncertain Florida boundary and possibly develop into an open conflict with Spain, and even with England, the federal government made great efforts to restrain the Georgians from occupying land ceded by the Creek at New York, and postponed running the boundary line according to the articles of that treaty. When reports came in of the Spanish agent Olivier's presence and activities among the Creek,[24] Jefferson brought the matter to the attention of Viar and Jaudenes.[25] They noncommittally referred it to Madrid. Some months later, nervous over the increasing public indignation at Spanish Indian intrigues, they delivered a note to Jefferson denying that Spain encouraged the Creek to hostilities. With it was enclosed an extract of a letter from Carondelet declaring that the treaty of New York was null and void because contrary to the Creek treaty of 1784 with Spain. "I have engaged the nation to await in peace the result of the negotiations which are under treaty in Madrid," piously wrote Carondelet, "and I hope the United States will take the same measure, and will suspend running the line of

24. For description of Olivier's activities, see the letters of the United States Indian agent for the southwestern tribes, James Seagrove, to the Secretary of War, May 24, 1792; to the President, July 5, 1792, *A. S. P., I. A.,* I, 296–304. For Spanish sources concerning same, see documents quoted in the several works of Serrano y Sanz.

25. Viar and Jaudenes to Jefferson, July 11, 1792, State Dept., Notes, Spain, I.

demarcation in that part, until the conclusion of the negotiation." To this proposition Jefferson agreed.[26]

Needless to say, Washington and his advisers were themselves awaiting anxiously the hoped-for settlement which Carondelet professed to expect from Madrid. But the proofs of his intrigues were too copious to pass by in utter silence. Copies of the exchange of notes with Jaudenes and Viar were sent to Short and Carmichael with instructions to enter into "friendly but serious expostulation" on the conduct of Carondelet and his subordinates, and to propose mutual abstention by both nations from the maintenance of agents among the Indian tribes in the disputed area.[27]

As the months passed by it became apparent in Philadelphia that Spain meant to prolong the negotiations at Madrid indefinitely. It also became increasingly obvious that she intended to continue her intrigues with the Indians in the region thus purposely left unsettled as to sovereign title. In May, 1793 (after news had arrived of the probability of war between Spain and France), Viar and Jaudenes, in official answer to Jefferson's former complaints against the presence of Olivier among the Creek, communicated a copy of the Indian treaty of 1784 at Pensacola, which they cited as justifying that action. A few days later they delivered copies of the treaties of 1792 signed at Nogales with the Chick-

26. He did not fail to point out that for the last year the United States had deferred the marking of the boundary as provided by the treaty of New York. See *A. S. P., F. R.,* I, 139.

27. "Should they [the Spanish Court] absolutely decline it, it would be proper to let them perceive, that, as the right of keeping agents exists on both sides, or on neither, it will rest with us to reciprocate their own measures. We confidently hope that these proceedings are unauthorized on the part of Spain," etc., etc. Oct. 14, 1792, Instructions, I, 199. See also instructions of Nov. 3, 1792, in Jefferson's *Writings,* VI, 129.

asaw and Choctaw.[28] Jefferson acknowledged the communications with the remark that the negotiations then proceeding in Madrid rendered any observations on those treaties unnecessary.[29] In return he received a complaint from the Spanish agents that, in contrast to the peaceful attitude of Governor Carondelet, Governor Blount, of the Southwest Territory, had required from various Indian chiefs a decisive answer "whether they would take up arms against the United States in case that Spain should enter into war with them"; and had distributed to various chieftains medals with the effigy of the President and the legend, *George Washington, President, 1792,* and others with *Friendship and Trade, without End.*[30] "We leave it to the President's sagacious consideration," they added, conveying samples of the medals, "to determine whether in view of these and many other actions (which we reserve for the present) taken by its agents, some with the open authority of the Government and some perhaps without it, the United States could easily vindicate whatever complaints they might formulate against the Governor of New Orleans (which we doubt have any foundation unless in presumption or suspicion) even if the latter should proceed on the ground of reciprocity." They complained that Governor Blount was trying to secure the alliance of the Chickasaw against the Creek and thus get from them a grant of land on which to erect a fort on the Mississippi at Ecores à Margot[31] which

28. Jaudenes and Viar to Jefferson, May 7, and May 12, 1793, State Dept., Notes, Spain, I; Jaudenes and Viar to Alcudia, No. 156, Phila., May 29, 1793, A. H. N., Est. Leg., 3895.

29. Domestic Letters, I, 121.

30. *A. S. P., F. R.,* I, 262.

31. Also called Ecores de Magros, Barrancas de Margot, or Chickasaw Bluffs, at present Memphis, Tenn.

would cut off Spain's communications between New Orleans and the Missouri settlements at New Madrid on the west bank of the Mississippi.[32] "We see with no little feeling that the continuation of peace, good harmony and perfect friendship between our country and the United States is in the future very problematical, unless the United States take more opportune and energetic means than those which for a long time have been adopted in that part of the world." [33]

III

The increasingly hostile tone of the successive notes of Jaudenes and Viar convinced Jefferson that the Spanish commissioners were attempting to pick a quarrel with him at a time when the international situation seemed favorable to them for it.[34] It was to deprive them of that indulgence that he sent the special messenger whose arrival in Spain we have just noted. The courier brought a long memoir to be handed to the Spanish Court describing the Indian situation, justifying the position of the United States, and sharply complaining of the unfriendly tone of the Spanish agents. Were we to understand, asked Jefferson, "that if we

32. At site of the present city of that name in southeast corner of Missouri.

33. Enclosed in Jaudenes and Viar's No. 168, of July 14, 1793, to Alcudia, A. H. N., Est. Leg., 3895.

34. "There is too at this time a lowering disposition perceivable both in England and Spain. The former keeps herself aloof and in a state of incommunication with us, except in the way of demand. The latter has not begun auspiciously with C. and S. at Madrid, and has lately sent 1,500 [sic] men to N. Orleans, and greatly strengthened her upper posts on the Mississippi." Jefferson to Madison, June 2, 1793, Writings, VI, 277. "Spain too is mysterious—nothing promising at Madrid, and contrary symptoms on the Mississippi. Were the combination of kings to have a very successful campaign I should doubt their moderation." To Monroe, June 4, 1792, ibid., VI, 281.

will not fold our arms, and let them [the Indians]
butcher us without resistance, Spain will consider it a
cause of war?" Such was understood from Viar and
Jaudenes. "This is indeed so serious an intimation,
that the President has thought it could no longer be
treated of with subordinate characters, but, that his
sentiments should be conveyed to the government of
Spain itself. . . . If Spain chooses to consider our self
defense against butchery as a cause of war to her, we
must meet her also in war, with regret, but without
fear; and we shall be happier to the last moment, to
repair with her, to the tribunal of peace and reason." [35]
In a separate despatch by the same conveyance to Spain,
Jefferson explained to Carmichael and Short that "a

35. Jefferson to Carmichael and Short, June 30, 1792, *A. S. P., F. R.*,
I, 265. For Cabinet decision of June 20, to this effect, see *Writings*,
VI, 314. Jefferson denied the charge of setting the Chickasaw against
the Creek. His proposition to do so was considered adversely in the
Cabinet. (See *Writings*, VI, 275). He defended American gifts of arms
and ammunition to the Chickasaw because Spain had given the same
to the Creek. He denied any intention to occupy Chickasaw Bluffs; on
the contrary the Government had forbidden the Yazoo companies to
settle the land they claimed there. He justified the practice of giving
medals to the Indian chiefs as one of long standing.

Jaudenes and Viar defended the practice of furnishing arms and
ammunition to the Indians within territory claimed by Spain. See
their note of Dec. 26, 1793, to Jefferson, enclosed in their No. 206,
of March 13, 1794, to Alcudia, A. H. N., Est. Leg., 3895 b.

Jefferson informed the Spanish agents curtly that the President had
decided to treat on the subject of their note directly with the Court of
Madrid: "In doing this, it will be impossible not to manifest the im-
pression which the style, as well as the matter of your communications,
make on the Government of the United States." *Writings*, VI, 344. Then
Gardoqui's young protégés, alarmed at the reception of their note,
tried to submit evidence to show their peaceful intentions. They made
matters worse by delivering to the Secretary of State the draft in poor
English of a proclamation which they proposed that President Washington should sign and issue to the public exonerating them from all
blame in stirring up hostility between the two nations! State Dept.,
Notes, Spain, I.

great object in sending this courier [was] to fix a term
to those uncertainties which have now existed for ten
years, Spain in the meantime advancing her posts into
our country and meditating, as it is believed, to take
our posts. You will be pleased to remain at Madrid until further orders, whatever be the prospect of issue to
your negotiations. If it be unfavorable, you will allege
as the cause of your stay that you expect ulterior instructions." The courier, it was confidently expected,
would be back in Philadelphia by December, 1793,
when Congress convened again.[36] Then, in the lack of
success, the whole Spanish question could be placed
before that body for decision.

The American commissioners plenipotentiary had
been waiting long months in Madrid for such new
orders as the arrival in America of news of the war in
Europe and the new Anglo-Spanish alliance might
inspire. These instructions finally arrived at Madrid, by
the special messenger, one Blake, September 24, 1793.[37]
The commissioners meanwhile had interpreted the new
Anglo-Spanish alliance as having potentially a greater
purview than Europe. Consequently they had refrained
from pushing their demands for the adjustment of the
Mississippi and the boundary issues. To their con-
sternation the new instructions brought by Blake took
no notice of the changed international situation in
Europe. Jefferson's letters showed no evidence that
their Madrid despatches from February to May, 1793,
describing the altered situation, had been received before the courier's departure. On the contrary, Carmichael and Short were now directed to present the

36. July 12, 1793, Instructions, I, 381.
37. Receipt of despatches by Blake was acknowledged in Short and
Carmichael's despatch of Sept. 29. *A. S. P., F. R.*, I, 278.

Indian issue and to use it as a means of pressing a settlement of the larger disputes. This uninviting task lay before them as they interpreted the articles of the Anglo-Spanish alliance (a copy of which Short had adroitly secured the previous month) to mean that a rupture with either ally, for any reason no matter how different from those expressed in the treaty, would be made a common cause by both.[38]

The "friendly but serious expostulations" directed by Jefferson's earlier correspondence, against Olivier's incendiary activities among the Creek, had already been made by the commissioners. Oral assurances by Gardoqui on this point were satisfying. But pressed to give similar assurances in writing to be transmitted to the President, Gardoqui, after much delay, handed them a note full of recriminations against the conduct of the American Indian agent among the southwestern tribes. He stated that the latter had been endeavoring to separate the Creek from their alliance with Spain. Because the agent had fomented hatred and enmity of the Indians against Spain, Spain therefore had a perfect right to keep a representative for herself among her treaty tribes "for the purpose of keeping them in peace." When the boundary was settled all these Indian troubles would also cease, wrote Gardoqui; meanwhile the President could rely on the strictest orders to Spanish agents to avoid every ground of complaint on the part of the United States.

These well-sounding phrases did not stop the murder of Georgian settlers who attempted to occupy the lands ceded by the treaty of New York, nor the furnish-

38. Carmichael and Short to Sec. of State, Aug. 20, Sept. 29, 1793, *A. S. P., F. R.*, I, 277, 278. Short to T. Pinckney, Aug. 23, 1793, Short Papers, XXIV, 4227.

ing to the hostile savages of arms and ammunition for the prosecution of such murder. Corroborative documents descriptive of such atrocities[39] accompanied the newly received memoir from Jefferson which Carmichael and Short now presented to the Spanish Court on October 1, 1793. To make the move as impressive as possible they stressed the arrival of their instructions by a special messenger from America, who was even then waiting impatiently that he might take the Spanish answer to the President before Congress should assemble.

No answer came. In vain the special messenger waited—month after month. Utilizing one transparent excuse after another, Godoy and Gardoqui juggled the two American commissioners back and forth and put off any categorical answer to the President's demand to know if Spain would take the side of the Indians in case of war between them and the United States. All that Carmichael and Short could get from the imperturbable Spaniards was the empty comfort that Spain would not interfere between the United States and such Indians as inhabited its territory. This, of course,

39. "In my last letter, I informed you of the frequent incursions of the Creeks, and the reason I had to apprehend some daring attempts from them. Since that time, they have killed Mr. Ramsay, and a person who had lately arrived from Charleston. This happened the 24th instant. They were very nigh killing Moses Rice the preceding day, notwithstanding he was accompanied by the King Fisher and his wife, and they had formerly been intimate with him. Mr. Ramsay was not above thirty yards from his own house, when he was killed and scalped on the spot. The other person reached the house, but instantly expired. The open and avowed intention of the Creeks, is to kill every white man they meet; and they declare that such is their orders. The great quantity of ammunition given to the Indians by the Spaniards, persuades me that we are indebted to the latter for these visitations." L. D. Shaw, Agent of the United States to the Cherokee Nation, to Governor Blount, Aug. 29, 1792, *A. S. P., F. R.,* I, 284.

meant Spain's definition of the territory of the United States. For his part, Godoy said there would be no delay in permitting a *discussion* of the boundary negotiation.[40]

IV

After observing this contemptuous treatment of the American commissioners and the demands presented by them, it is somewhat surprising to find that a little before the date which we have now reached, that is, in November, 1793, Gardoqui, in conversation with Carmichael and Short, had informed them that the King desired to form with the United States an alliance offensive and defensive, or, if such were not agreeable, defensive. His idea was to purchase the alliance by yielding to the contentions of the United States in regard both to the navigation of the Mississippi and the Florida boundary. With much warmth Gardoqui begged the commissioners to communicate this royal desire to the President, with the proposal that regular ministers plenipotentiary be exchanged by both governments to reside at the respective capitals. The commissioners had no powers to negotiate such a treaty; on the contrary, Jefferson recently had warned them not to guarantee Spanish colonies in America against either internal revolutions or against any foreign power.[41] Carmichael and Short did not even mention this

40. Alcudia to Carmichael and Short, S. Lorenzo, Dec. 18, 1793, *A. S. P., F. R.,* I, 439. See ibid., 328 and 433–442, for description in the commissioners' despatches, of the procrastination of the Spanish negotiators. The joint despatches of Carmichael and Short were accompanied by a copious and prolix correspondence of Short with the Secretary of State. See Hague and Spain, I.

41. Jefferson to the U. S. Commissioners to Spain, March 13, 1793, *Writings,* VI, 203.

overture in their official despatches, a surprising omission in view of the importance of the proposal, if only
from the significance of Spain's willingness to make
such concessions under conditions. In the dark days of
the American Revolution the United States had proposed in vain to Spain to yield all claims to the navigation of the Mississippi to the sea in return for an alliance
with that monarchy. Now Gardoqui was asserting that
the King was prepared to recognize those very claims if
the United States would but ally itself with Spain in
her hour of need. A curious reversal of positions, the
proposal for such an alliance, it is still more interesting
when compared with the articles initialed between Jay
and Gardoqui at New York in 1786, when Jay had
proposed to forbear to use the Mississippi for twenty-
five years in return for an alliance and mutual guaranty
of Spanish and of American territory in North and
South America. Short described this new proposal in
a private letter to Jefferson on November 13, 1793.[42]

42. "In whatever light the United States chuse to consider this overture, they should lose not a moment in sending a minister-plenipotenti-
ary here, for various reasons." The disadvantages of having only a
chargé d'affaires at Madrid lay in the fact that this was the lowest
diplomatic rank at that capital. Such was not flattering to the proud
Spanish Court; moreover, the diplomatic representatives of higher
rank—only the most insignificant states, like the City of Hamburg,
maintained agents of the third rank, i.e., chargés—had prior access to
the Foreign Minister in all ordinary business. As Short graphically
explained in a letter to Thomas Pinckney (Oct. 12, 1793, Short Papers,
XXIV, 4286) and later to the Secretary of State (Despatch No. 129),
Carmichael in his regular business with the Minister, such as spoliation
cases and the interests of American citizens in Spain, labored under
unnecessary inconvenience because of his lowest rank, "the etiquette
established giving him no opportunity of speaking with the Minister
until those of the first and second order have finished their audience,
when he [the Minister] has had his head already saturated with their
communications and is on tip-toe generally with his watch in his hand

In noting Gardoqui's overture, the reader is instantly reminded of Jefferson's former reaction to the announcement by Jaudenes in 1791, that the King was ready to resume a direct negotiation with the United States. On this occasion we recall that the Secretary of State had declared enthusiastically, perhaps too enthusiastically and too hastily, that if Spain would acknowledge the American right to navigate the Mississippi, the United States would be willing to guarantee Spanish sovereignty over the remaining Spanish dominions in North America, as fixed by the treaty. But Jefferson's ardor for guaranteeing Spanish dominions in America had cooled since the Nootka Crisis, "for when we thought we might guarantee Louisiana on their ceding the Floridas [sic] to us, we apprehended it would be seized by Great Britain,[43] who would thus completely encircle us with her colonies and fleets. This danger is now removed by the concert between Great Britain and Spain.[44] And the times will soon enough give independence and consequently free commerce to our neighbors, without our risking the involving ourselves in a war for them." [45]

Before Short's private letter of November 13, 1793, telling of Gardoqui's proposal for alliance could reach its destination, Jefferson had resigned from office; and since the proposal was not mentioned in the commis-

---

to be precisely at the hour assigned with the King or elsewhere. He [Carmichael] experienced the same inconvenience with the latter Minister of that department and must do it with all, from the nature of things established here."

43. I.e., during the Nootka Crisis.

44. This was written before the Anglo-Spanish alliance of May 25, 1793, had been signed.

45. To the commissioners to Spain, March 23, 1793, *Writings*, VI, 206.

sioners' joint despatches,[46] the verbal overture of Gardoqui went absolutely unheeded. There is no doubt
what the answer of Washington in 1794 would have
been to such an overture even if formally made on
paper. Already the principles of the Farewell Address,
advising against entangling alliances with European
nations, were fixed in his mind, as indeed they were
in the mind of every responsible American statesman
of the period. It is quite likely that Gardoqui's verbal
overture in November, 1793, was a maneuver to delay
the American negotiation by transferring it across the
ocean and making it contingent upon the conclusion
of an alliance. Yet it is not impossible that Spain, now
harassed by a European war and consequently unable
to divert troops to defend Louisiana and Florida, was
beginning to think of a policy sincerely adopted a few
months later, that is, of getting from the United States,
in the form of a mutual guaranty of territorial integrity, a self-denying ordinance against future American
expansion on the frontier of those colonies. Certainly
the willingness of Jay in 1786 to sign a treaty guaranteeing Spanish possessions in *both* North and South
America, and Jefferson's impulsive remark to Jaudenes
in 1791 gave some ground for a European not entirely
informed of the instinctive aversion of American statesmen to any European alliance, even the French one,
to believe that such a commitment might be possible.
At any rate, whether possible or impossible, it served
as a pretext for delay, and delay was still, in November,
1793, convenient to Spanish purposes.

46. Their joint despatches from Aug. 1, 1794, on did not leave Madrid
by the special messenger Blake until Jan. 6, 1795. Receipt was acknowledged by Jefferson's successor, Randolph, on April 4, 1795. Short to
Sec. of State, No. 188, Madrid, Jan. 9, 1795, Hague and Spain, I, 432.

Godoy had recently professed a willingness to *discuss* the boundary issue, as a means of putting an end to difficulties concerning the Indians. The commissioners, we have observed, not taking seriously Gardoqui's verbal overture for an alliance, concerning which moreover they had no powers or instructions, had not been eager to undertake such a discussion of the old issues in view of the unfavorable circumstances of the recently-concluded Anglo-Spanish alliance; but under the urge of Jefferson's last instructions, received from the hands of the special courier Blake, they submitted on December 7, 1793, another justificatory memoir on navigation and boundaries.[47]

To this the Duke of Alcudia answered that the subject was now before him, and assured the commissioners that the King, desiring to give the United States the most unequivocal proof of the sincere friendship between the two countries, would have the matter of the boundary examined with the greatest expedition.[48] This meant nothing.

V

Such was the languishing condition of the Spanish-American negotiation as the decisive year 1794 opened. Unduly encouraged by Godoy's offer to *discuss* issues, the commissioners now pressed him for a more definite answer to the last formal statement of their stock-worn arguments which everybody in Madrid considered at this moment so derisible. Again excuses, delay, and no definite answer. After they had waited for about five months, Godoy, to put the negotiations even further

47. Short Papers, XXIV, 4349.
48. Short to Sec. of State, No. 134, Madrid, Dec. 20, 1793, Hague and Spain, I.

out of reach, despatched an instruction to the Spanish agents at Philadelphia to complain that the persons of Carmichael and Short were not of sufficient splendor or rank to be impressive to the King.[49] This step, of course, was hidden from both commissioners. Finally, on September 7, 1794, after nearly a year of waiting for an answer to their original demands as to navigation and boundaries, during which time Carmichael had received a letter of recall and Short had been established at Madrid as regular minister with single powers replacing the joint commission,[50] Godoy calmly in-

49. Alcudia to Jaudenes and Viar, Aranjuez, May 9, 1794, Spanish Legation, Vol. 201; Jaudenes to Randolph, Aug. 16, 1794, Short Papers, XXVI, 4645; State Dept., Notes, Spain.

50. Carmichael had long ceased to be active in the negotiation, because of illness. He had paid no adequate attention to the routine business of the office. Realizing that he was now utterly useless to the United States, Jefferson advised that the President accept a request for recall, which Carmichael, a sick man, and anxious to get home to America, had already made.

Short was really in a most embarrassing position in regard to the incapacity of his colleague, but he refrained from complaint in the numerous official despatches of his own which he deemed it his duty to send to the Secretary of State. In a carefully phrased private letter to Jefferson, Nov. 13, 1793, Short made this restrained comment on Carmichael: "You will see by our joint letters and mine separately the awkward situation in which I have been since my arrival in this country, finding it impossible to advance under our joint commission and not knowing how to retire from hence. I had hoped that the President would have terminated our joint commission one way or the other. It has been from the beginning infinitely disagreeable for various causes and particularly with respect to those to which I have forced myself to be silent, though perhaps my delicacy pushed me further than was consistent with duty. Government must certainly have been ignorant of them, though I cannot conceive how this can have been the case for so long a time." Short Papers, XXIV, 4331. Carmichael's letter of recall is dated May 28, 1794. It arrived in Madrid, Aug. 8, 1794. Short was presented as minister about Sept. 16, 1794. Much time was spent by the Court in deciding the precise status of a minister, as distinct from a minister plenipotentiary. Not until after news of Jay's Treaty

formed Short, to his utter amazement, that some new
propositions, the nature of which the young Duke did
not reveal, had been despatched to the King's representatives at Philadelphia, to be presented to the President. All further negotiation therefore would have to
be suspended until an answer to these propositions
should be received at Madrid.[51]

The negotiations with Spain, begun so enthusiastically by Jefferson in 1791, had now reached a preposterous pass. The President, displeased by the bellicose
expressions and truculent demeanor of the subordinate
agents, Jaudenes and Viar, had refused to deal any
more with Spain through them, and had transferred the
Indian issue to Madrid, where the other questions of
navigation and boundary were under discussion. Meanwhile the wars of the French Revolution had commenced in Europe, and in February, 1793, had involved
England, and then Spain. Godoy and Gardoqui, under
the shelter of the new Anglo-Spanish alliance, had taken
a year to exhaust the ordinary pretexts for procrastination. This having been leisurely done, they now tossed
the whole negotiation—Indians, boundary, navigation,
and anything else—back across the Atlantic to Philadelphia, into the hand of those very agents, themselves
of doubtful diplomatic rank, altogether unaccredited,
of whom the President had complained as being so
distasteful to him, but whom the Spanish Minister for

---

was received in Madrid was Short informed that he would be regarded
as a diplomatic representative of the second class rather than the third.
There is no space to go into the petty objections raised by Godoy on
this point, technicalities in regard to the commissioners' powers, etc.,
for the purpose of delay. Short's despatches for those days are full of
the subject.

51. Short to Sec. of State, No. 169, Madrid, Sept. 16, 1794, Hague and
Spain, I, 297.

Foreign Affairs now described as living up to the nature of their instructions. More than that, Godoy had given a final fillip to the whole farce by complaining to the President that the American commissioners themselves were not of sufficient splendor or rank for the King.

The new propositions for the President, not divulged to Short, consisted of a formal overture for an alliance, an invitation which had already been made verbally to the commissioners by Gardoqui as early as November, 1793. But between November, 1793, and July 7, 1794, when the propositions were finally formulated in writing in Madrid, some epoch-making events had taken place in Europe and America, events which made it desirable for Spain to present such proposals with a far greater degree of earnestness and anxiety than when Gardoqui first had mentioned them to Carmichael and Short.

Before we follow to Philadelphia the propositions for the President and note their strange fate, we shall do well to observe the far-from-smooth course of that interesting product of the French Revolution, the Anglo-Spanish alliance.

CHAPTER 10

Godoy's Propositions for the President and Their Fate

I

England's prime concern in the French war had not been so much the danger of revolutionary principles—though indeed they were a matter of lively dread to Pitt and to Edmund Burke—but the threat to her security and naval primacy caused by the French invasion of the Low Countries and the occupation of the channel ports. Spain's principal anxiety, on the other hand, had been the spectacular danger of infection from republican doctrine, and protection of the Bourbon autocracy with the bulwark which this gave to the holy faith. French sea power was of no danger to Spain. On the contrary, it had been useful in the past and might yet be in the future. After the revolutionary storm had been stilled by the First Coalition and a Bourbon restored to the French throne, Spain would be rather certain again to look to the French fleet, her chief protection against the naval power of Great Britain. The sudden emergency of the French Revolution had brought two ancient enemies together in what seemed to many Spaniards a most unnatural and unholy alliance against a traditional ally. When it touched the vital question of sea power, the anomalous union immediately weakened. This happened within a few weeks after the signature of the alliance, when a joint Anglo-Spanish naval force blockaded Toulon.

The commander of the British fleet, Admiral Hood, addressed to the inhabitants of that French Mediterranean port and naval arsenal on August 23, 1793, a proclamation announcing that he was "to take possession of the city and harbor of Toulon in the name of the King Louis XVII until the re-establishment of peace." He bespoke the confidence of the people of Toulon in the "generosity of a frank and loyal nation." Through the connivance of royalist sentiment the great maritime base and twenty-seven ships-of-the-line were delivered over to the British and Spanish fleets. As promptly the indignant republican authorities of France laid siege to Toulon. The fall of the city to the revolutionary forces was imminent on the 18th of December. Rather than allow the vast naval stores to fall into the hands of the republicans the English set fire to the arsenal and abandoned the unfortunate citizens, except for the few thousands who managed to escape on Spanish and British warships and in small harbor craft, to the bloody vengeance of the Jacobins. The French fleet was not removed from the harbor as it might have been. Nine ships-of-the-line and three frigates were burned under the personal supervision of Captain Sir William Sidney Smith. The remainder, except for three withdrawn by the British, were salvaged by the French republicans, and not many years later served to transport Napoleon's army to Egypt, only to meet their end at the hands of Admiral Nelson in the battle of Aboukir Bay.

The firing of the French fleet, rather than its evacuation, opened the eyes of Spaniards to the real purpose

of English warfare and its incompatibility with the
interests of Spain. "Toulon and all that it contained,"
declared the Spanish Admiral Langara, after the holo-
caust, "was a depot confided to the honor of Spain as
well as that of England. The ruin of the French navy
cannot but be prejudicial to the interests of Spain." [1]
This deed took the heart out of Spanish loyalty to the
British alliance. It was not even necessary to wait for
Lord Howe's decisive crippling of the French navy in
the famous action of the First of June, 1794, to realize
that Spain had been affrighted by the apparition of
the republican ogre into marrying a selfish spouse with
whom she had really nothing in common.

Immediately after Toulon the Spanish Government
began covertly to consider ways and means of breaking
loose from the British alliance. As early as February,
1794, the Spanish Minister at Copenhagen was making
peace overtures to the French Minister at that Court.[2]
The invasion of Spain by French armies helped to
crystallize the peace movement there. After Thermi-
dor it was possible to construe the French Government
as settled down to more conservative principles. In
September, 1794, Godoy resolved on peace negotiations,
opened up a contact with the enemy through a French
officer sent to Barcelona in the interest of prisoners of
war.[3] Spanish terms on this occasion were too exorbi-
tant, but Godoy kept up his démarches, sometimes be-

1. Marc de Germiny, *Les brigandages maritimes de l'Angleterre*,
II, 32–44. This work must be used with great discrimination. See also
A. T. Mahan, *Sea Power and the Wars of the French Revolution*, I,
92–108.

2. Correspondence of Philippe de Grouvelle, Arch. Aff. Étrang.,
Danemark, Vols. 169 and 170.

3. Baumgarten, *Geschichte Spaniens zur Zeit der Französischen
Revolution*, 532–537.

ing engaged simultaneously in several devious and indirect channels of communication with the enemy. One
of these intricate and involved affairs, carried on with
William Short, will presently assume significance for
our narrative.

II

This condition of dissatisfaction with the British alliance and unwilling prosecution of the war was prevailing strongly in Madrid in July, 1794, when another
special courier, this time a Spanish one, arrived from
Philadelphia, with despatches from Jaudenes and Viar,
dated the previous March and April and describing the
crisis in America which had led to Jay's mission to
London as a last means of preserving peace with England. The Spanish agents, knowing nothing of recent
political tendencies in Europe, analyzed the Anglo-
American situation as likely to bring the United States
into either a war or an alliance with England. To them
this meant, simply enough, that the United States
would have to declare war either against France, or
against the allied powers, England and Spain. If against
France, that enemy of Spain and of England would be
completely cut off from all sources of overseas supply,
and British and Spanish naval forces cruising in American waters would be largely released for European duty.
If against Great Britain (and with her, her ally, Spain),
a blockade of American ports by the British navy would
follow. American products would then lose their market
and a civil war between pro-British and pro-French
elements would be fairly sure to follow. Either case,
thought Jaudenes and Viar, would be preferable to
American neutrality; for the loose control which the
federal government maintained over its western citizens

made it more difficult to keep up the defenses of Louisiana when the United States was unperturbed and neutral than when actually an enemy but convulsed by internal turbulence. They begged instructions to cover all contingencies.[4]

The arrival of this news caused an immediate meeting of the Council of State. On July 7, 1794, Godoy read the despatches. He then exposed Spain's position, as he conceived it, modified as it had been recently by the increasing incompatibility of the British alliance. In case of a rapprochement between France and the United States, while the latter should be indisposed toward Spain, no restraint would be placed on expeditions like those which Genêt[5] had attempted to commis-

4. Jaudenes and Viar to Alcudia, No. 213, Phila., March 13, 1794. See also Nos. 214–223, March and April, 1794. All these despatches left Philadelphia by the same courier late in April, 1794. A. H. N., Est. Leg., 3895 *bis*.

5. It is not considered necessary to the purposes of this essay to review the well-known history of the Genêt mission to the United States and the attempts of that French Minister to raise a battalion of dissatisfied western frontiersmen, under the command of American officers holding French commissions, to march from Kentucky and Georgia against the Spanish provinces. It is enough to realize that the Spanish officials were naturally much alarmed. Jefferson appears at first to have tolerated Genêt's intrigues in Kentucky so long as they did not result in actual open recruiting within American territory; but Genêt's impetuous conduct soon destroyed all sympathy, even of Jefferson, with his mission, and led to the demand for his recall. The Spanish agents at Philadelphia complained about Genêt's plots in the West and as a result President Washington issued his proclamation of March 24, 1794, against enlisting American citizens, under color of foreign authority, for hostile expeditions against the territory of a friendly power. This was followed by the more inclusive prohibitions of the neutrality act of June 5, 1794, which for the first time made such action a crime under the American law. Jaudenes and Viar were satisfied that the United States Government was sincere in its efforts to prevent such expeditions. The correspondence of the Spanish governors in Louisiana and Florida is full of anxiety on the subject. See A. G. C.,

sion in the American West for the capture and plunder of the Spanish provinces. In case of a war between the United States and Great Britain, he quoted Article VII of the Anglo-Spanish treaty of May 25, 1793, to show that England might call on Spain to make a common cause with her.[6] He declared that Great Britain was preparing to make war on Spain on some pretext or other, as soon as the French navy should have been safely destroyed and the colonies captured, after which the English would possess themselves similarly of Spain's colonies. He believed that the Council should advise the measures which prudence dictated under these circumstances, that is, to protect the overseas dominions against a British, or a British-American attack—by an alliance between Spain and the United States. To get this aid the King ought to be willing to yield to the American boundary claim, despite its arbitrary nature, as well as to the demand for the free navigation of the Mississippi. Such an alliance ought to be secured before England herself should make a similar one at the expense of Spain. The United States was the power which could either help or damage Spain most in the new world. Godoy proposed that the Governor

Leg., 7235 (L. C. trans.). See also the correspondence of Jaudenes and Viar, A. H. N., Est. Leg., 3895 and 3895 *bis*. For a list of references on the Genêt episode, particularly its western bearings, see *Jay's Treaty*, 146, n. 25.

6. "Art. 7. If one or the other of the two high contracting parties shall be attacked, molested, or inquieted, in any of their States, rights, possessions, or interests, in any time or manner whatsoever, by sea or by land, in consequence, or in hatred, of the articles or stipulations contained in the present treaty, or the measures which shall be taken by the said contracting parties in virtue of this treaty, the other contracting party is obliged to succor and make common cause with him, in the manner which is stipulated by the preceding articles." Translation of the Spanish text by Short, in *A. S. P., F. R.*, I, 277.

of Louisiana be instructed to offer to the United States explanations of the recent alliance of Spain with the Indian confederation of the Southwest, assuring that it was only for the purpose of preventing the Indian nations from undertaking any move against the United States without the knowledge and consent of Spain, and that propositions for an alliance and reciprocal guaranty of territory be made immediately to the President of the United States, through the Spanish agents at Philadelphia.[7]

7. Following are the significant extracts from the minutes of the Council of State for July 7, 1794, as recorded by its secretary:

"If the United States should succeed in reaching a reconciliation with England, His Excellency [Godoy, the Duke of Alcudia] considered our situation in respect to the States even more critical, because according to all the probabilities and facts which were noticeable, England was already acting as if she intended to declare war on us on some pretext or other, as soon as she should have taken possession of the enemy [French] islands and all the commerce of France, and to throw herself on our possessions in America; and after having weakened Spain as she was now doing with France, to establish her sovereignty over all the seas. England being so united today with Holland, the Emperor and Prussia, and Spain not being able to secure, at least for some time, friendship and union with France in case of war with England, we ought to take the precautions which prudence and necessity dictated. One of these was to procure friends, and among them those who could help us most and who as enemies could most harm us. Such precisely were the United States, who if they were with us against England, in addition to insuring our possessions on that continent and depriving the English of the great assistance which they got from those provinces in the war before the last, could enable us to count on them for our own defense, and for offense against the enemy. From all this, it was necessary to anticipate the English and to see how they [the Americans] could be attracted to our friendship without loss of time; that this made it urgent to reply not only to our *encargados* at Philadelphia, but to those of the United States in Madrid, who had been handing in notes in very energetic and even irregular terms about the delay in adjusting the boundary and the navigation of the Mississippi, as well as concerning the restitution of two merchant ships detained at Cadiz, speaking of getting passports for their captains

III

So in a flash did European complications change the
whole face of the Spanish-American dispute. Jefferson

who were going back to their own country to seek the justice which
they had not encountered in Spain. . . . The time had come when the
negotiation could no longer be delayed as had been done up till now,
because of not consenting to the principal point of the free navigation
of the River Mississippi to the sea, which the United States pretend
should be conceded to them. . . . Such being the state of things, and
the Duke being conscious of the paucity of his years and experience
[continue the minutes of the Council] it occurred to him to seek in
those of the Council what it thought was necessary, to weigh and
combine the different matters, points and circumstances of the time
being, that it might recommend to His Majesty what it judged to be
most opportune.

"In corroboration of what the Duke of Alcudia explained, Don
Diego de Gardoqui said that always, and especially since he had resided
as *encargado de negocios* of His Majesty in the United States of America, he had believed that the greatest evil that could happen to Spain
was that that new power should succeed in uniting with England to
work in common accord against this monarchy. . . ."

Gardoqui then read the paper which he had written for Floridablanca
when the negotiation had been resumed with the United States in
1791, recommending a settlement of the navigation question. He
further recapitulated the negotiation which he himself had undertaken in America with Jay, "the same who had now been sent to
England, and who had been here during the war." He recalled the
tentative agreement which he had initialed with Jay for the settlement
of the boundary and the occlusion of the lower Mississippi, and the
failure of Congress to accept the same. He demonstrated the subject on
a map. He emphasized the strong pro-British party in America, particularly in the northern states, which might succeed in dominating the
whole country if Spain did not take advantage of the irritation produced by the recent English spoliations.

"The Count of Campomanes [to continue with the text of the
Council's minutes] then said that not only did it appear to him very
convenient and necessary that Spain in the existing circumstances
should try to hold the United States of America as friends, but also to
grant them some extension of lands as they desired, even though it
should amount to between thirty and fifty leagues, since that was not
of so much importance—Spain holding such extensive countries—
when one saw her exposed to losing all; endeavoring at the time of

had quit office on December 31, 1793, but his patient
waiting for European troubles formidable enough to
embarrass Spain in America now seemed about to re-

the cession to save as much as possible those lands which because of
their situation, configuration or peculiarity of ground and other qualities, would best protect the Spanish part. So far as concerned the
navigation of the Mississippi, although he knew the lack of authority
of England to cede it to the United States, and consequently that the
latter had no right to demand it from Spain, he observed the ardor
which those States had for it, and the efforts which they were making
to get it, which would increase if they secured from England the
protection they had already tried to get from France. Bearing in mind
that the free navigation of a river through the territories of different
princes was no new thing, and was even admitted in many instances
under certain regulations and agreement between the same princes,
and urging the powerful reasons which the Señores Alcudia and
Gardoqui had given for gaining the friendship of the States, he was of
the opinion that the free navigation of the Mississippi might be considered in terms least onerous and most useful to Spain which the
navigation could allow.

"The Duke of Alcudia then said that if it should be possible to form
an alliance with the United States without the risk of England getting
word of such a design to frustrate it, it would be the means of assuring
ourselves entirely of them, and of counting on their assistance for
whatever event; but in order to avoid this risk and to advance as much
as possible the winning of their friendship and preference, they might
be made to understand from now on our good dispositions to grant
them favors as to boundaries and the navigation of the Mississippi, as
long as they would assure us, as should be hoped, a good and sincere
friendship; giving straightway orders to the *encargados de negocios* of
His Majesty to be communicated to the United States, and nominating
on both sides commissioners plenipotentiary to meet on the spot to
fix the boundary line by common agreement. This not only would
destroy any bad feeling caused in the States by the detention of their
two ships and the arrival of their captains with tales of alleged
grievances, but would gain the States on our side. England should be
told that no alliance was being discussed with them [the United States],
that only an adjustment of outstanding issues was under way. As to
the States we should continue to cultivate them carefully in order to
fix them for our friendship and in time secure a real alliance.

"All of this the Council approved and His Majesty resolved that it
should be done immediately." Actas del Supremo Consejo de Estado,
1794, 29–37, A. H. N. Est.

ward his successors. Godoy sent the Spanish messenger back to Philadelphia with instructions to Jaudenes and Viar to convey to the President the King's willingness to settle the boundary question and that of the navigation of the Mississippi on the basis of a Spanish-American alliance.

I believe that little will be risked,[8] [he wrote] in fixing the former [the boundary] according to the claims of the States, as much as may be compatible with our treaties with the Indians, and in granting the latter [the navigation of the Mississippi] with the restrictions which the interest of his [Majesty's] subjects requires; but the King desires that the equivalent (*premio*) of this direct favor (*condescendencia*) be a solid alliance and reciprocal guaranty of our possessions and those of the States in America. To this end His Catholic Majesty desires that the President send a person with full power, which these [American plenipotentiaries in Madrid, Carmichael and Short], who are most addicted to France, do not hold, for a treaty of alliance to be independent of the circumstances and relationships of the [present European] war.

The Spanish agents meanwhile must do all in their power to prevent too close relationships between France and the United States, and, above all, to further an understanding between the United States and Spain before the English could secure a treaty with the same republic prejudicial to the interests of Spain.

Short, who had learned so suddenly from Godoy that

8. A draft for the instructions, in Godoy's handwriting, contains after the word "risked" the clause, "particularly when the Kentuckians are disposed to separate themselves from dependence on Congress and to place themselves under His Majesty's protection." This clause was retained in two further drafts, dated July 25 and 26, but was omitted in the final instruction of July 26, despatched in cipher to Jaudenes and Viar. It is the latter, now in the Departmento de Estado, Papers of the Spanish Legation in the United States, from which the quotation in the above text is taken. The drafts are preserved in A. H. N., Est. Leg., 3895, and 3895 *bis*.

these new Spanish propositions had been sent to the President, remained unaware of their content. Dated at Madrid the 26th of July, 1794, and despatched from thence the 31st of the same month, they were acknowledged by Jaudenes on December 8.[9] This means that they reached the American capital shortly after the Senate of the United States had confirmed the nomination of Thomas Pinckney,[10] regular Minister at London, to serve as envoy extraordinary to Spain for the settlement of the long pending issues. Pinckney's appointment had been decided under much different circumstances in August, 1794, not long after Jaudenes and Viar had made official complaints which vividly contrast with the irenic proposals which they were now directed to present. We recall that Godoy in May, 1794, as a part of his technique of procrastination, had instructed the Spanish agents at Philadelphia to state to the President that his representatives in Madrid, Short and Carmichael, lacked sufficient powers for the objects in view, "that unless the ministers whom the United States should nominate were to be considered by His Majesty in every circumstance as possessing

9. Jaudenes to Alcudia, No. 275, Phila., Dec. 8, 1794, A. H. N., Est. Leg., 3895 *bis*.

The same instructions allowed the appointment of consuls in the United States, as had been previously advised by Jaudenes and Viar, more for the sake of securing reliable intelligence from the west and south as to separatist plots than for commercial usefulness. As a result Viar was appointed consul-general of Spain. Jaudenes thereafter had charge of diplomatic interests.

10. The mission was first offered to Thomas Jefferson, and later to Patrick Henry. Randolph to Jefferson, Aug. 28, 1794, Domestic Letters, VII, 192. Both refused. Senator Pierce Butler of South Carolina served as the confidential informant of Jaudenes and Viar, according to their despatches. He hoped, and they hoped, that he would secure the appointment to Madrid. See Jaudenes to Viar, Nos. 161, 240, 273, A. H. N., Est. Leg., 3895, and 3895 *bis*.

that character, splendor and carriage which corresponds with residence near the royal person and with the gravity of the subjects to be treated," the King could not enter into any treaty. The shortcomings of Carmichael were described by Godoy—with some justice, the student of that individual's character must acknowledge— as "already notorious," the conduct of Short was asserted to be "not very circumspect." [11] This had been written by Godoy at Madrid two months before the disconcerting news about Jay's new mission had arrived there and at a time when it had still been a purpose of the Spanish Court to resort to all possible devices to put off the American negotiation as long as possible.

The Pinckney mission itself—which we shall have occasion to review in detail in Chapter 12—therefore was not the result of the new circumstances produced by the departure of Jay and the shifting international alignment caused by the breaking down of the First Coalition against France. Resolved upon several months before the Anglo-American crisis of 1794, it had been merely another complacent American step of "patience and persuasion," in answer to an artificial complaint by Spain of the kind which only a strong power would make to a contemptibly weak government—befitting language, that of the Spaniard Godoy, for a republic! Secretary Randolph at that time had thought the Spanish negotiations in a state of "complete stagnation." He believed war not unlikely, and sent to Short directions to despatch information about Spain's military

11. Jaudenes to Randolph, Aug. 15, 1794, in Jaudenes' No. 273 to Alcudia of Nov. 30, 1794, A. H. N., Est. Leg., 3895 *bis*. The instructions of Alcudia, on this subject, were dated at Aranjuez, May 9, 1794. Spanish Legation, Vol. 201.

preparations in America and her means of harming the
United States in that quarter.[12] Like the special mission
of John Jay to London, the sending of Thomas Pinckney to Madrid was regarded in the United States as an
impressive diplomatic gesture made as a last attempt to
secure American rights by peaceful means.[13] So far as
any new facts then within the knowledge of the President and his advisers would indicate, we see that there
was in November, 1794, when Pinckney's instructions
were despatched, no more chance of success from an
ostentatious special mission than there had been for
several years past in the tiresome and unfruitful diplomacy of Carmichael and Short.[14] Washington was not
sure that Kentucky meanwhile could be kept from
committing hostilities against Spanish authorities before
the long-delayed Madrid negotiations could be brought
to a successful close. But the Administration was not
prepared to utilize this impatience, as Lafayette and
Montmorin had once advised, for an offensive against
Spain.[15] Pinckney, as we shall see, luckily reached

12. Randolph to Short, Aug. 18, 1794, Instructions, II, 136–153.

13. The appointment of an envoy extraordinary, as an impressive
gesture when all other expedients had been exhausted, came to be a
characteristic device of early American diplomacy.

14. Randolph by now had received Short's letters telling of the un-
even relations between Spain and Great Britain, and of Toulon. The
Secretary was inclined to discount this very considerably, believing
that Spain could not collect confidence enough in the stability of
French councils to be able to desert her ally for the arms of her enemy.
Randolph to Short, Aug. 18, 1794, Instructions, II, 136–153.

15. This reluctance may have been due to some uncertainty about
the situation in Kentucky arising out of the agitation of the Wilkinson
conspirators. I do not believe that at any time the "Spanish" Conspiracy embodied more than a very few men. Those were persons of
secondary importance. The Kentucky people were loyal to the United
States, but easily stirred up to violence against Spain. Washington,
however, was so anxious about the Kentucky situation in the summer

Madrid after the diplomatic scene, unbeknown to the Government of the United States, had been shifted completely. Spain, for reasons of European politics, had suddenly reversed her policy. She then became anxious for a settlement of outstanding issues and for an actual alliance with the United States.

IV

What was the fate of the propositions for the President, which had left Madrid for Philadelphia on July 31, 1794?

Jaudenes[16] received promptly enough the new proposals of alliance which he was instructed to convey to the President. Nevertheless, he did not deliver them immediately. Under the pretext that he was unable to decode with absolute precision the ciphered portions,

---

of 1794, that he sent to that state a special commissioner, Colonel James Innes, brother of Wilkinson's tool, Harry Innes, though not of the same stripe. Innes took with him copies of the whole diplomatic correspondence with Spain, for exhibition to the Governor and to the members of the legislature. The purpose of the mission was to frustrate any plot for separation which might exist, and to prevent the West from forcing the hand of the Government while the last resort to peaceful negotiations was being exhausted. Randolph to James Innes, Aug. 8, 1794; to the Governor of Kentucky, Aug. 15 and 25, 1794, Domestic Letters, VII, 180. Innes made a report to the Secretary of State on the Kentucky situation, but I have not been able to find it in the archives of the State Department or elsewhere. It would be a source of prime importance.

The Innes mission was prompted by petitions to the Congress and the President from the Kentucky Democratic Society, asking to see copies of the Madrid correspondence, and to be assured that every means was being taken by the federal government to secure the navigation of the Mississippi. See E. Merton Coulter, "The Efforts of the West to Open the Navigation of the Mississippi," *Miss. Valley Hist. Rev.*, XI, 381; A. P. Whitaker, "Harry Innes and His Spanish Intrigue, 1794–1795," ibid., XV, 236–248.

16. Jaudenes was now the sole diplomatic agent. Viar had been made consul-general.

he allowed over three months to expire without acting on his unmistakably positive instructions. Meanwhile Randolph had learned from Short's despatches that some new overtures, nature unknown, were to be expected through Jaudenes. Randolph inquired whether they had come. Jaudenes denied having received anything of the kind. Randolph reported this back to Short. Short then learned from Godoy that Jaudenes had already acknowledged receiving the proposals, which had been dated the previous July 26 (1794), but that the President's answer to them had not yet been vouchsafed. Randolph finally got this last information from Short in March, 1795. Still nothing at all had been received by the Department of State from the Spanish diplomatic agent, though it had become now well known that he had received something to deliver. Having now caught Jaudenes unequivocally in a falsehood, the Secretary of State indignantly demanded an explanation. Jaudenes was forced to hand in the long-delayed propositions, which he did on March 25, 1795. As submitted they were worded somewhat differently from Jaudenes' actual instructions dated July 26, 1794. He described them as contingent "insinuations" rather than precise proposals—that was why he had not delivered them sooner, he explained, for he had hoped to receive further explanatory instructions. Because of this variation the long-awaited propositions proved to be so indefinite that they did not alter in the least the existing unsatisfactory character of the Madrid negotiations as understood in the United States.[17] The President could not even reply to such vague overtures,

17. "The points on which I understand it to be the will of the King my master to adjust the pending negotiations with the United States, are, subject to the receipt of further explanatory declarations for which I am waiting. as follows:

since Jaudenes himself had explained them to be subject to further explanatory instructions.

What was the reason for Jaudenes' strange deportment? The pretext of difficulty with deciphering disappears when one examines the translations of the cipher as left in the official papers of the Spanish legation in the United States.[18] The real explanation is that Jaudenes had embarked on a sinuous intrigue for alliance between Whiskey Rebellion insurrectionists of Pennsylvania and the Kentucky separatists, a professed representative of whom had approached him in the

"First. His Majesty will enter into a negotiation with the United States as soon as the latter shall have authorized a person with full powers to proceed to that Court for the purpose.

"I flatter myself that this point is covered (ventilado) by the nomination recently made by the executive power of the United States.

"Second. The King will agree to fix the boundary as favorably to the claims of the United States as may be compatible with his treaties with the Indians.

"Third. His Majesty will agree to grant the navigation of the Mississippi with the restrictions demanded by the interests of his subjects.

"Fourth. The King desires that the equivalent for these favors be a treaty of alliance independent of the circumstances and relationships of the present war, and a reciprocal guaranty of his possessions and those of the United States of America.

"Fifth. His Majesty hopes that the commercial points will equally be regulated on the footing of reciprocity.

"The preceding is what I persuade myself I ought to deduce from the despatch in question [i.e., of July 26, 1794] and what I have received from my superior to the present time, to be the will of the King, and I have the honor to inform you frankly of the same that you may place it before the President of the United States for the light which it may give him in his decisions on these matters." Jaudenes to Randolph, March 25, 1795, enclosed in his No. 286 of April 4, 1795, from Philadelphia. A. H. N., Est. Leg., 3896.

The above paragraph in the text is based on Jaudenes' correspondence between Dec. 8, 1794, and April 4, 1795, in A. H. N., Est. Leg., 3895 bis and 3896; and Domestic Letters, I, 1–91.

18. Spanish Legation, Vol. 207. There are a few uncertainties about certain minor parts of the instructions, but nothing that the student cannot puzzle out easily and clearly.

summer of 1794, not long after he had written home the alarming despatches about the Anglo-American crisis and Jay's mission to England.

Remembering the intrigues of Gardoqui in the West, Jaudenes and Viar during their sojourn in America had kept a watchful eye on Kentucky and had been quick to note any further symptoms of discontent. For some time after the admission of the new state into the Union all seemed quiet there. But early in 1794 they reported conversations representing the "Kentucky Senators" to have stated that if the federal government did not secure the navigation of the Mississippi, Kentucky would do what its interests dictated.[19] An emissary from the Whiskey rebels appeared before Jaudenes in October, 1794. He purported to have also the support of unnamed personalities in Kentucky, who stated that they were bound to secure the navigation of the Mississippi, if not from the federal government then from an understanding either with Great Britain or with Spain. Jaudenes gratified the emissary, who gave his name as M. Mitchell, with one hundred -dollars, and sent him back to his constituents with a promise that if they would declare their independence from the United States, Spain would be glad to treat with them for the navigation of the Mississippi; but that no such negotiation could happen as long as they were under the federal government of the United States, which, he artfully added, had been wilfully blocking all of Spain's attempts for a friendly treaty. Mitchell disappeared. In due time he returned with the memorized text of a destroyed letter from the "secret committee

19. Jaudenes and Viar to Floridablanca, No. 9, July 27, 1791, A. H. N., Est. Leg., 3896; No. 215 and a separate "confidential" of Jaudenes to Alcudia, March 13, 1794, ibid., Leg., 3895 *bis*.

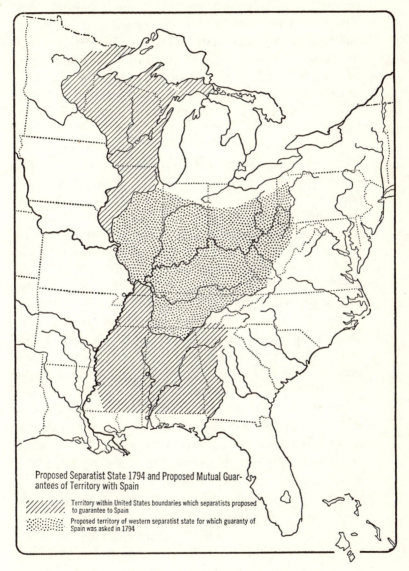

Proposed Separatist State 1794 and Proposed Mutual Guarantees of Territory with Spain

///// Territory within United States boundaries which separatists proposed
       to guarantee to Spain

:::::: Proposed territory of western separatist state for which guaranty of
       Spain was asked in 1794

MAP 4

of correspondence of the West." This he set down on paper. It was a proposal for an offensive and defensive alliance between Spain and a proposed new independent transappalachian state, with a reciprocal guaranty of territory and a treaty of navigation and commerce for the free use of the Mississippi. For the unsigned signatories of the paper Jaudenes was referred to Baron Carondelet. So is our reader, at an appropriate place below.

The boundaries of the new state which Spain was expected to guarantee were roughly defined as "all the territory to the East of the Tennessee River from its confluence with the Ohio upstream to the Alleghany watershed, along the summits of that range of mountains to the source of the Alleghany River, thence in the most direct line which could be drawn to Lake Erie." That, and all the territory north of the Ohio and drained by waters flowing into that river to the east of the Mississippi *and Illinois* rivers, was indicated as the extent of the intended state. In return for thus being guaranteed what was practically the Ohio Basin east of the Illinois and Tennessee rivers, the new statemakers were willing themselves to guarantee to Spain the territory of her Indian allies to the south of the Tennessee according to the terms of the treaties of 1784 and after, as well as the territory "to the north of the River Mississippi joined to the River Illinois." As soon as the independence of the new state was declared, the King of Spain was to furnish it with a river squadron and munitions for ten thousand men. A loan of money would also be necessary.

The conspirators desired a definite answer from Jaudenes by the first of April, 1795. If it was to be in agreement with their proposals, they asked that the

King appoint plenipotentiaries to treat with them at New Madrid as soon as possible.[20]

The stratagem completely captivated Jaudenes. He eagerly begged for instructions to negotiate with these men when their envoy should return for his answer the following April. Only a few weeks after he had sent his despatches relating this intrigue, he received the instructions of July 26, 1794, to present to the President of the United States proposals for an alliance and mutual guaranty of territorial integrity! This would spoil all his plans. Keen over the prospect of dividing the United States and extending Spanish territory to Lake Michigan, he delayed submission of Godoy's propositions until he should have received an answer to his despatches of October 31, 1794, describing this last intrigue. Before he could receive such an answer, and before the first of April when the person Mitchell was to return, he had been compelled by the importunities of Secretary Randolph at last to submit the new Spanish proposal of alliance. The expected emissary of the separatists in fact did not again return to Philadelphia, so far as Jaudenes' despatches inform us.[21] The western conspirators, for this was nothing less than a revival of Wilkinson's old conspiracy, meanwhile had resorted to Governor Carondelet, at New Orleans, as the fountainhead of their expected succor.

20. Jaudenes to Alcudia, No. 250, Oct. 31, 1794, A. H. N., Est. Leg, 3895 *bis,* enclosing the paper mentioned.

21. In July, 1795, Jaudenes sent Argote Villabos, Spanish consul for Virginia and Kentucky, on a secret mission to Kentucky to open up connections with the Kentucky conspirators, and to tell them that Jay's Treaty, recently published, was a violation (in regard to the Mississippi) of Spanish rights and would cause such umbrage in Spain as to defeat any treaty with the federal government of the United States. He was to persuade the westerners to enter into direct negotiations with Spain at Philadelphia. Jaudenes to Alcudia, No. 297, Phila., July 29, 1795, A. H. N., Est. Leg., 3896.

CHAPTER 11

Jay's Treaty and Its Effect

I

Interesting intrigues of Jaudenes with the western separatists, which had led to his delay in delivering Godoy's propositions for the President, did not change the new-born desire of that Spanish Minister for an alliance with the United States in return for recognition of American claims to the navigation of the Mississippi and the boundary line of 31°. The notorious propositions for the President, drafted on July 26, 1794, had been despatched to Jaudenes on the 31st of the same month only after another meeting of the Council of State, in which had occurred a thorough canvass of the whole situation as based on a *précis* of the most recent reports of Governor Carondelet, of Louisiana, including the latter's correspondence with Wilkinson. Nothing therein elucidated had caused any modification in the recently adopted policy of conciliation and alliance with the United States, as decided by the Council so promptly after the arrival in Madrid of news from Jaudenes and Viar of the Anglo-American crisis of March, 1794, and the departure of Jay for London. When it became known in Madrid, in December, 1794, that a treaty had been signed by Jay with Great Britain, the Spanish Court—this means Godoy—became still more confirmed in this policy and genuinely anxious for a treaty of alliance at the cost of conceding the principal American demands. The separate peace of Basle, between Spain and the French Republic, which followed on July 22, 1795, with the resulting end of the Anglo-Spanish alliance and the imagined danger of revenge from Great Britain on a deserting ally, made Godoy even more anxious for the most cordial understanding with the United States, for fear of a combination of that country with Great Britain to the damage of Spanish possessions in America.

The effect of Jay's Treaty and of the Peace of Basle on the long-pending Spanish-American negotiation will be duly recorded, but to put them in the proper setting it is necessary first to set forth the history of a remarkable intrigue by which William Short attempted to make the Franco-Spanish secret peace negotiations dependent upon the recognition by Spain of the rights asserted by the United States.

As we follow the course of this business, to which Carmichael was not privy, we should remember that the latter was at that time absolutely incapacitated physically, that practically the entire labor of the special negotiation had devolved from the first on Short. Carmichael at the time did not have the strength to sign official correspondence, much less to write the despatches to the Secretary of State or the joint notes to the Spanish Government.[1] But until September 5,

---

1. "C. returned here [from Madrid] the day before yesterday, but he had such a nervous trembling of the hand, with which he is much afflicted, like our friend Paradise, that he could not—notwithstanding every effort he made—sign his name to the letter I had written to the Duke to remind him of his delay. Still he persisted in returning last evening to Madrid. I was obliged therefore as he desired, disagreeable as such a step is and in such a case, to imitate his hand and sign it for him." Short to Jefferson, private, S. Lorenzo, Nov. 13, 1793, Short Papers, XXIV, 4331.

1794,[2] he remained the regular chargé of the United States, as well as joint commissioner plenipotentiary, albeit in name only. On that day he took leave of the King, but, unable to set out for the United States, he lingered on in Madrid until his death a few months later. If ever a colleague was justified in undertaking separate and secret negotiations without the privity of his official associate, it was William Short.

From the beginning of his sojourn in Spain Short had been impressed with the unnatural character of the Anglo-Spanish alliance. His letters to the Secretary of State show that he foresaw an eventual collision of interest between the two new allies, and he advised that until some turn of European politics should bring this to pass it would not be expedient to press the American demands of the Mississippi and the Florida frontier. He was quick to appraise the significance of the affair of Toulon, which in fact he had more or less foreseen, but to his amazement the Spanish Court did not appear to him to look upon that as a disaster.[3] As a result he

2. Short to Sec. of State, No. 186, Sept. 4, 1794, Hague and Spain, I, 295.

3. "A foreign minister who had a conference with him [Godoy] yesterday has told me that he seemed far from regretting the loss of the French vessels and arsenals, and even regarded it as a fortunate event for Spain." After allowing for deception on the part of Godoy, Short added: "Should the case be as he states it, the inference would be that this court count on no future contingency to throw their fleet into the same scale with that of France, and therefore put themselves and their foreign possessions at the mercy of Great Britain, a circumstance which it is difficult to suppose a government so enlightened as that of Spain and so jealous of those possessions as they have shown in all instances where we are concerned, and where certainly there was no room either for jealousy or apprehension," would approve. Short to Sec. State, No. 136, Madrid, Jan. 3, 1794, Hague and Spain, I.

was persuaded that Godoy and the King were for steadfastly continuing the war against France, and that the opposition to this came from the rest of the Ministry. Until the year 1795 was well advanced, in fact, Short continued mistakenly to believe that Godoy was opposed to peace.

In casual conversations with Gardoqui, Short had taken care from the first to point out the real meaning for Spanish interests of the British alliance. The Toulon incident, the subsequent British occupation of Corsica, and the increasingly aggressive British attitude in the West Indies, offered admirable occasions for such discourse. He found Gardoqui taking more and more interest in the subject, ultimately expressing himself as against the French war and desirous of peace, even at the cost of breaking the British alliance. He made it evident however that the existence and terms of that alliance required that any separate peace negotiation with France be pursued and concluded with greatest secrecy.

After these confidential conversations had developed sufficiently to produce this expression of opinion from Gardoqui, Short suggested a solution which he advanced as beneficial to the interests of Spain, France, and the United States. First he proposed that Spain quickly come to a settlement with the United States by recognizing its demands as to navigation and boundary. This was to be the indispensable preliminary to a further step. If Spain would do this Short declared that he could immediately return, via Paris, to The Hague, his regular station. His well-known special mission to Madrid having been successfully terminated, his departure from that capital would excite no suspicion. In Paris he promised to place himself at the disposal of the Spanish Ministry as an intermediary in opening up overtures of peace.

I observed to Mr. Gardoqui [recounted Short some months later in first describing this affair to the Secretary of State], that he was to take notice that I was not authorized either by the United States or by France to make this proposition, and that in it I acted absolutely on my own instigation, that I believed, however, that it would be agreeable to them or I would not undertake it, and that that belief resulted from my knowledge of the wishes of our government, and reflexion on the designs and intentions of France, that I would not conceal from him that my leading motive in this business was the interest of the United States, and the service of the Government by which I was employed, and that I conceived these two objects deeply concerned to see peace re-established between France and this Country. . . . It was evident that he listened with great pleasure thereto, and from the first opening of this road to peace showed that if it depended on him alone he would pursue it.

But it did not depend on Gardoqui alone. It was Manuel de Godoy, Duque de la Alcudia, who was supreme in the Council of State. His was the deciding vote, and Short wrongly believed that the young Duke was determined to continue the war, that Gardoqui had little influence over him. "I was sure Mr. Gardoqui spoke his real sentiments to me, but I was far from being sure he would express them to the Duke, and if he did it was by no means certain that they would be adopted by him." Gardoqui maintained to Short that he was working gradually on the Duke to bring him around to their point of view. These conversations went on up until the end of June, 1794, when the Court removed from Aranjuez to Madrid, to remain a few weeks before seeking surcease from the summer heat at the mountain retreat of San Ildefonso on the opposite slopes of the wooded Guadarrama Mountains, overlooking the old city of Segovia and its noble Roman aqueduct. It was just before the departure of the Court from Aranjuez that Short reported to Gardoqui a rumor that was then prevalent in Europe, following the Anglo-American crisis of the spring of 1794, that Jefferson was to be sent to France to tighten the ties between the two republics. This caused Gardoqui to observe that Jefferson's supposedly great influence on the French might be availed of for peace, and to say that he, Gardoqui, would be a friend to any plan of union of the three powers—the United States, Spain, and France—and this notwithstanding the fact that two of them were republics. He repeatedly asked Short to apprise him as soon as this rumor should be confirmed.

So far all of this had been in private conversations. Nothing had been entrusted to paper and the whole affair was regarded as absolutely confidential between the two men, not to be conveyed to any other person. Nothing was heard of Jefferson until after the Court had again moved to San Ildefonso. But meanwhile the Council meeting of the 7th July, 1794, had been held and the decision reached to send the propositions of alliance to the President. This decision was not yet conveyed to Short. Nor did he know that, a few weeks previously, at the very time these interesting conversations had been going on between him and Gardoqui, that Godoy had complained to the President through the Spanish agents at Philadelphia about the conduct and the lack of splendor and rank of the American commissioners, mentioning specifically that Short was "not very circumspect." [4] This may or may not have been

4. Alcudia to Jaudenes and Viar, Aranjuez, May 9, 1794, Spanish Legation, Vol. 201.

known to Gardoqui; according to Short, the other ministers did not know much about what was going on at
the Foreign Office. On July 20, 1794, Short apprised
Gardoqui by letter that Jefferson positively was not
going to Paris. He added: "I feel a full confidence
that whatever could have been done by his presence
there can be done by the other means which I spoke to
you about." [5] This was the first of many secret written communications, couched in less and less noncom-
mittal language, referring to the affair. Short con-
tinually urged Gardoqui to press Godoy. Gardoqui
asserted in his turn that he was leading the Duke on
the right path. On August 30, 1794, Short received
news of his appointment as Minister to the Court of
Madrid, and the termination of the joint commission.[6]
This, of course, made it impossible to carry out his
proposed plan of retiring, as a matter of course, from
Madrid to The Hague by way of Paris after any settlement of the Spanish-American negotiation. But he still
clung to the idea and wrote Gardoqui that it would
be possible for him, under given conditions, to make a
trip to Paris just the same.[7]

Gardoqui professed to be all agreement to Short's
idea. Conferences and letters followed, which show
Short's eagerness to get Godoy also committed to such
an arrangement. Godoy himself had previously sent

5. Short to Gardoqui, Madrid, July 20, 1794, Short Papers, XXVI,
4594.

6. Short to Sec. of State, No. 164, Madrid, Aug. 30, 1794, Hague
and Spain, I, 274.

7. Short in vain delayed presenting his new credentials until Sept. 5,
in the hope that before Carmichael took leave the American negotiation might be terminated, so that Short could leave for Paris and
The Hague before it was announced that he had been appointed
Minister to Spain. Same to same, Nos. 167 and 168, S. Ildefonso, Aug.
25, ibid., 293, 295.

off (July 31, 1794) the propositions to the President, but not until September 7, 1794, did he announce that fact to the American Minister without divulging their nature. This, we recall, had the effect of suspending all formal negotiation on the affairs originally intrusted to the joint commission. When Short, at Gardoqui's request, took up with the Duke the subject of a separate peace with France to be made by the American envoy's secret mediation, but only *after* a satisfactory settlement of the issues pending with the United States, Godoy showed unmistakably by his countenance that he was unwilling to discuss the question. Gardoqui professed great surprise, when Short informed him of this, and explained it by the inexperience and hesitation of a young minister, who had understandable compunctions about breaking the first treaty he had ever set his name to.

Actually, of course, Godoy, like Gardoqui, was awaiting the answer of the President to the propositions of alliance. We have seen how the awkward schemings of Jaudenes with the western separatists caused that agent to postpone presenting these, that finally they were delivered in such a vague and qualified way that they were never answered. Meanwhile the months slipped by, with the American negotiations at a standstill. Winter arrived, with the French armies already invading Spain, but temporarily halted in the northern provinces. On the third of December, 1794, Short wrote the long despatch to the Secretary of State, from which we have just quoted, giving a faithful narration of the whole intrigue to date and what he had hoped to accomplish by it.

I cannot omit observing [he concluded] that the key to the whole of this business is—that the Duke and consequently the King and

Queen have been fully decided against any reconciliation with France, that their will alone is absolute when uncontrolled by circumstances. They found themselves somewhat in this situation after the affair of Irun and the advancing of the French. The alarm in consequence thereof was that both the Duke and Queen were afraid to take anything on themselves during that alarm and for the first time left the other ministers masters in their own departments and at liberty to express their sentiments. This state of things, however, was only of short duration. As soon as the French stopped at Tolosa and the people in these quarters began to rise in mass the alarm subsided so far as to put things nearly on their former footing.[8]

But Gardoqui soon came back to the subject again, proposing that Short secure passports from the French Government allowing the two to take a trip for their health to the waters of Bagnères, in the French Pyrenees, as a means of opening up a secret negotiation with France. On December 21, 1794, in Madrid, Short and Gardoqui had "a full conference on all that had preceded with respect to an attempt toward putting an end to the war between France and Spain—and to which he [Gardoqui] added as usual what he called his favorite idea of forming a close partnership between the three, viz: France, Spain and the United States." By such a partnership Gardoqui explained himself as meaning a "close alliance." Short insisted that as a first step the disputed rights of the United States should be settled; after that had been done, he remarked, he would consider himself authorized to act, without committing the Spanish Court in any way, either to ascertain previously the disposition of France, by means

8. Short to Sec. of State, No. 183, Madrid, Dec. 3, 1794, Hague and Spain, I, 370. The correspondence between Gardoqui and Short is carefully preserved in the Short Papers. See folios (beginning in Vol. XXVI) 4594, 4610, 4616, 4621, 4623, 4639, 4647, 4671, 4673, 4703, 4753, 4762, 4805, 4810.

of the American Minister at Paris, James Monroe, or to endeavor to get the French Government to make overtures to Spain, or to be himself a vehicle for proposals. But first the American issues must be settled, and nothing could be done without the will of the Duke both for a settlement with the United States and a resulting negotiation with France under Short's secret offices.[9] At no time did he commit himself to Gardoqui's idea of a triple alliance, or to any kind of an alliance.

We assume that Gardoqui was here Godoy's mouthpiece. Short to some extent had misread Godoy's actions. The Duke was secretly striving at this time for peace with France, as we have shown in the last chapter, and as we shall show still more in the next. He knew that Short had no powers for alliance, and he was now holding off the American negotiation until he could get an answer from the President to the propositions which had been sent in the hope of forestalling any Anglo-American treaty which might be the result of Jay's mission to England. If a secret peace with France could be accompanied by the erection of a triple offensive and defensive alliance of Spain, France, and the United States, Great Britain might well pause before attempting to execute vengeance on her deserting ally. At the same time all danger of American aggression against Spanish colonial dominions, under shelter of a possible British-American treaty, would have been eliminated.

The Jay negotiation, as we have already pointed out in mentioning the decision of the Spanish Council of State, had assumed primary significance in the Spanish-American negotiations. Short had reflected abundantly

9. Short to Sec. of State, No. 186, Madrid, Sept. 29, 1794, Hague and Spain, I, 412.

on the good that might result for his own situation if a
satisfactory treaty should be signed by Jay in London,
but he was absolutely uninformed by his own Government as to the parallel negotiation then proceeding
in England, despite the fact that it was of utmost importance for him to know it. In vain he had appealed
to Pinckney, the regular minister there, for information,
and to John Trumbull, the secretary of Jay. These
persons hesitated to interfere in Jay's business or to
trust any information to the mails.[10] December 22,
1794, the day after the conference above described
between Gardoqui and Short, an English mail arrived
with a letter from Jay of November 24, 1794, telling
of the signature of a treaty between the United States
and Great Britain, and another from Pinckney, of
November 27, conveying in cipher a digest of the
terms.[11] The Spanish Ambassador in London at the
same time notified Godoy of the settlement of disputes
between the United States and Great Britain, stating
that the British had agreed to evacuate the frontier
posts in eighteen months, and that the treaty also contained articles of advantage to the Americans in matters of commerce and navigation between the United
States and the British West Indian islands.[12] Presumably it arrived in the same mail.

10. Short to Humphreys, Aranjuez, Mar. 21, June 20, 1794; to
Pinckney, Oct. 1, Oct. 15, 1794; to Trumbull, Oct. 23, 1794; to Sec.
of State, Dec. 12, 17, 1794; to Jay, Jan. 7, 1795, Short Papers, XXV–
XXVII.

11. Short to Pinckney, Madrid, Jan. 7, 1795, ibid., XXVII, 4919.

12. That portion of the despatch, dated Nov. 21, 1794, which refers
to this is as follows: "The disputes between this Court and the
United States of America have finally been settled. England will
restore within the time of eighteen months the forts which by virtue
of the last treaty of peace were kept as security for the debts of the
Americans; also regulations of advantage to the latter in commerce

Realizing the significance of this treaty in suggesting to Spain that the United States might now have British support in its demand for the Mississippi and other claims based on the Anglo-American peace treaty of 1783, Short saw that events were beginning to break nicely for the advantage of the United States. He felt that the time had come to clinch the claim to the navigation of the Mississippi, to secure recognition of the boundary contended for by the United States, and, more than that, to break into Spain's commercial monopoly in her colonies of North and South America. Spain, he thought, particularly in case of a separate peace with France, which Short was so assiduously attempting to engineer, would be in a position, after deserting from Great Britain and in face of an imagined Anglo-American rapprochement, to yield almost anything the United States might demand.[13]

II

The special courier Blake at last was about to depart as the news arrived in Madrid of the signature of Jay's Treaty. Carmichael was too ill by now to attempt the journey home to Maryland. Short, who had been exasperated beyond measure by the repeated delays of Blake's departure, due to Carmichael's desire to

and navigation to the English islands are made [se harán tambien arreglos ventajosos a la navegacion y comercio de estos en las Islas Inglesas, etc.]" Del Campo to Alcudia, No. 4, London, Nov. 21, 1794, A. H. N., Est. Leg., 4294.

13. Short to Sec. of State, No. 186, Madrid, Dec. 29, 1794, Hague and Spain, I, 412. News of Jay's Treaty reached Short only a few days after he had written a long letter to Secretary Randolph analyzing Spain's military advantages and disadvantages in case of war with the United States, information for which Randolph had asked on Aug. 18, in anticipation of the failure of the negotiation. Short to Sec. of State, Madrid, No. 185, Dec. 12, 1794, Hague and Spain, I.

keep him for a traveling companion, now himself held
the courier a few more days, in order to be able to
inform the Government of the Spanish reaction to Jay's
Treaty. Without directly seeking a conference with
Gardoqui, which might betray undue eagerness, Short
managed to throw himself in the way of that Minister
in order to give him a chance to continue the subject
of the former conversations in regard to a separate
peace with France and to see how he was affected by
this new American treaty.

> With him [wrote Short in his despatch of December 29, 1794],
> I had only vague and general conversation in the same old way
> but evidently more reserved in respect to pacification with France,
> probably wishing first to see whether this new arrangement with
> England might not have rendered it less safe to communicate to
> me his wishes as to France. On the subject of our treaty he said
> little, pretended it was a fortunate circumstance to have been
> able to have settled such differences in a manner that would avoid
> the misfortune of war, and expressed his satisfaction at it from
> his regard and attachment to the United States. When I observed
> to him how much more fortunate Mr. Jay had been in his mission,
> which was certainly a more difficult and less hopeful one, than
> we had been here, he brought forth a shower of protestations at
> his personal regret at the delay which had taken place here, of
> all his personal efforts to have had the business long ago con-
> cluded, and of his full persuasion that there would not be a
> moment's delay after the President's answer should be received,
> which might be now expected every day, his expressions of friend-
> ship for the United States, and of his desire to see the closest
> ties formed between them and Spain, were if possible warmer
> than ever, but all this of course led to nothing.

Short waited to meet Godoy in his regular audience
with him as Foreign Minister. The younger Spaniard
proved not so hackneyed as Gardoqui in the ways of
dissimulation. He registered mortification and disappointment. Short recalled to him the delay which he

had met in trying to settle affairs between the United States and Spain. The Duke held off. As soon as the answer should arrive from the President, he declared, Spain would hasten to negotiate a treaty, and it would not be a treaty which would stipulate *eighteen years,* as did that of Great Britain, for evacuation of the frontier posts.[14] Short, without divulging the terms of the treaty, corrected Godoy on the item of eighteen years.

The Duke enquired [wrote Short] with seeming anxiety as to the time when the treaty with England would have arrived in America, and comparing the dates was much pleased with the consideration that the propositions made from hence [i.e., the proposals for alliance, of July, 1794], would have been received and decided on long before. He said more than once that if the treaty were to be postponed, as he understood, being completely executed for some time to come, he still had hope that we should make one and fulfill it yet sooner, than that with England would be, as the King did not intend to ask for any further delay as England had done.

The announcement in Spain of an adjustment between the United States and Great Britain achieved by John Jay in London had prompt results in Spanish official conclaves. The very next day after Short's above-described interview with Godoy there occurred an important meeting of the Council of State. Already the British, observing the apathy of their ally in prosecuting the war outside of Spain proper, had been demanding more effective cooperation in naval affairs and specifically assistance in a campaign then under

14. Godoy's conjecture about eighteen years doubtless arose from a misreading of Del Campo's despatch of Nov. 21, 1794, above cited, which stated that the period set for evacuation was eighteen months. Actually Jay's Treaty stipulated June 1, 1796, as the date by which all British troops should be withdrawn from American soil.

way for the suppression of the revolt in the French half
of the island of Santo Domingo. The activity of the
British in that island could not but be prejudicial to
the interests of Spain in the New World. In the Council
Godoy declared that Spain, rather than deliberating on
the means of making with Great Britain joint conquests
in the island of Santo Domingo or elsewhere, as requested by the British, ought to do all in her power to
prevent the British from making them, and to endeavor
to keep her own possessions in order and tranquillity,
immune from the contagion of insurrection. England,
said he, soon would have only Austria left with her in
the Coalition. Deserted on all quarters she would seek
a reconciliation with America. He did not mention the
existence of Jay's Treaty, which must have been in the
thought of the Council, since it was known to both
Godoy and Gardoqui; but he declared that Spain should
endeavor to forestall such a dire event as an Anglo-
American *entente,* by concluding as soon as possible,
as the Council had already agreed in policy, an arrangement with the United States.[15]

Although Godoy had now turned with unusual alacrity to the idea of an American alliance and settlement
accordingly of the Mississippi Question and boundary
issue, he did not lose sight of the intrigues of Carondelet
and Jaudenes with the Kentucky conspirators and the
possibility offered by them as an alternate policy in
case he should be anticipated by the British in winning
the support, even the alliance of the Americans. Splitting off the western settlements from the union of the
United States seemed, particularly at that time, to
afford too good a prospect of success to be abandoned

15. Actos del Supremo Consejo de Estado, Dec. 29, 1794, A. H. N.,
Est.

altogether. In answering, February 15, 1795, the pleas which had come from Jaudenes for powers to deal with the western separatist intrigues, Godoy resorted to fine ambiguity. His Majesty approved, said the Duke, of the means which Jaudenes had taken, through the representative of the western people, to destroy the false ideas which the English were trying to instill to the prejudice of Spain:

> In order to block those ideas and to weaken the influence of the British Government among the inhabitants of Kentucky, His Majesty desires you, in accordance with what I advised you in my letter of July 26 [1794], to continue to assure them of the good faith with which we proceed; and that we may the more confirm them in this concept, you will set up with the greatest secrecy direct negotiations with them, to hold them off until we can settle the question of the important points on which we are now treating with the [United] States. This will serve to keep them devoted to us in case the States do not accept the just propositions which we are making to them.[16]

Similar instructions at the same time went out to Carondelet, who in fact had been responsible, through Wilkinson, for the resurrection of this old plot which dated back to Wilkinson's first visit to New Orleans in 1787.[17]

It is apparent that a primary aim of Spanish policy was now alliance with the United States, with a mutual guaranty of territory, which would act as an estoppel to all further American aggression on adjacent Spanish dominions and which would counteract the menace of

16. Minutes of reply to Jaudenes' No. 250, about Feb. 15, 1795, which is the date of endorsement of receipt of Jaudenes' No. 250. A. H. N., Est. Leg., 3895 *bis*. At the same date, Feb. 15, 1795, arrived despatches from Jaudenes of Oct. 31, 1794, giving copies of Jay's instructions. Ibid.

17. Alcudia to Carondelet, Aranjuez, Feb. 21, 1795, A. H. N., Est. Leg., 3896.

the unknown terms of Jay's Treaty, terms which were
feared by the Spanish to contain an agreement by the
United States and Great Britain to support each other
in maintaining, perhaps by force, the free navigation
of the Mississippi as guaranteed in the treaty of 1783.
That the full terms of Jay's Treaty do not appear to
have been known to Godoy until after the signature of
Pinckney's Treaty, traditionally known as the treaty of
San Lorenzo, on October 27, 1795, is a significant sup-
position in our study of these highly complicated negotiations.[18] It is further apparent that Godoy, now
contemplating a desertion of the British alliance, wished
to support himself as much as possible for encountering
the indignation of Great Britain in the case of a separate
peace between France and Spain. This could be accomplished partially by an alliance with the United
States, purchased, he conceived, by yielding to the
well-known American demands. Such would relieve
Spain from embarrassment in Louisiana and the Floridas. It could be accomplished still more fully if he
could bring the United States into a triple alliance
with Spain and France, to be negotiated simultaneously
and secretly with the proposed French separate peace.
As the separate peace negotiations with France took
more tangible shape during the clandestine conversations which the Duke began to hold through more than
one channel with that republic, the idea of coupling a
Franco-Spanish peace and alliance with such a triple
alliance became more and more attractive.

To return to Short and his covert discussions with
Gardoqui and Godoy. News of Jay's Treaty had been
welcome intelligence for him, who had been reading
the chapters of swiftly changing European history with

18. See note at end of the next chapter.

uncommon appreciation and understanding. He was now the sole minister of the United States in Madrid. Carmichael, recalled, was on his deathbed. He finally died on February 9, 1795.[19]

When every prospect seemed to Short so good for the success of his long-drawn-out negotiation, when Spain was wooing the United States so eagerly and waiting so anxiously for an answer to the long-delayed propositions for the President, when fame and reputation among his countrymen and consequent political preferment seemed in the grasp of the deserving diplomatist, he opened on January 13, 1795, a despatch[20] from Randolph, dated November 9, 1794, stating that Thomas Pinckney was to be despatched on a special mission from London to Madrid, as envoy extraordinary and commissioner plenipotentiary for the settlement of matters of navigation, boundary, and commerce, the very issues which Short, thanks to the recent favorable whirl of the European kaleidoscope, was on the point of settling. This cruel turn of fate was to rob a faithful and able agent of an opportunity which should have been reserved for him in compensation for the months of useless labor and patience and the enduring of indignities and tergiversations which he had experienced at the hands of the Spanish Court.

19. Carmichael died leaving mysterious debts and unexplained usages of United States moneys collected by him from the King of Spain as indemnity to the American capturers of the Dover Cutter, during the Revolutionary War. His last months are described in Short's despatches. In anticipation of returning home, Carmichael had shipped to Cadiz his private effects and papers, and also the public papers of the legation. See Short to Sec. of State, Nos. 191 and 192, Madrid, Feb. 13 and 24, 1795, Despatches, W. Short, Madrid. Neither private nor public papers have been recovered.

20. Short to Messrs. N. & J. Van Staphorst and Hubbard, Madrid, Jan. 14, 1795, Short Papers, XXVIII, 4936.

Short's chagrin and disgust on receiving news of Pinckney's appointment were complete.[21] It seemed the last culminating blow in a career of diplomacy which had met with one hard disappointment after another, ever since he had received the post of chargé at Paris in 1789.[22] When, after Pinckney's arrival, he

21. Short to Sec. of State, No. 186, Madrid, Jan. 16, 1795, Hague and Spain, I.

22. Short's private papers are full of bitter reflections on the ill-deserved treatment he had received as a career diplomatist. Allowing for a certain amount of human feeling on such a matter, the investigator is constrained to have much sympathy for him and to agree that he had an unusually bad run of luck. A typical letter of discouragement is the following:

"Your letter offers me your congratulations upon my appointment here. I can now accept thereon only offers of condolence rather than congratulation. My health suffers too much in this climate to render it supportable to me, and the affairs of the United States at this juncture do not admit of my leaving it. I should probably have remained but a little time at the Hague had I returned there, my determination to return and settle in my country being fixed. The place here is thought more important to the United States at this time and under that consideration alone more agreeable—in all other respects the Hague is preferable—my grade here is the same as at the Hague, but what is worse my salary is the same also, although the expenses are at least double. I am willing to give my time to the public, but I have not a sufficient fortune to give any part of it. I have been long enough in the public service. My inclination and my situation both dispose and decide me to withdraw from it as soon as it can be done with propriety. I shall return to America to enter my own service, and I hope I shall succeed better in that line. I have borne the brunt of public service in Europe. I have had all the thorns—others have gathered the roses. I have received in every instance the compliments of our government for my exertions in their service—the rewards have been given to those who begin, and whilst we talk of equality in America, the fact is that Government have shown greater marks of inequality in the distribution of their diplomatic service than any government in Europe does at present. . . . Our Government is the only one who makes these distinctions. They keep low people of the Canaille like myself in low grades—the first places are given to the high-blooded who commence—their rank, I suppose, is thought sufficient. I have experienced this in two instances.

learned from Randolph that Pinckney's appointment
and his own consequent displacement had been due to
complaints by Godoy that Short had not been "very
circumspect," his indignation knew no bounds. He had
a feverish interview with Godoy, who disavowed any
such statement—a disavowal ludicrous to anyone who
has read Godoy's own despatch of May 9, 1794, to
Jaudenes and Viar—and said Carmichael (now dead)
was the only one he had complained about. In a formal
note for the rather meager satisfaction of Short, the
Duke eventually testified that the American's person
and character had always been most acceptable to His

It shall be my fault if I experience it in a third. . . ." Short to
Messrs. N. and J. Van Staphorst and Hubbard, Madrid, Oct. 1, 1794,
Short Papers, XXVI, 4688. See also same to same, Nov. 12, 1794, in
similar tone, ibid., XXVII, 4770. The two disappointments referred
to were the appointment of Morris as Minister to France in 1792,
instead of Short, who had been chargé there; and the appointment of
Pinckney to the London post at the same time, instead of Short, who
by virtue of more diplomatic experience in a professional career conceived himself to have a better claim to the appointment. Jefferson's
correspondence with Short suggests that Jefferson was using his influence for Short, but that Washington made the appointment without
consulting anyone or announcing his decision to anyone before it
was sent in. The appointment of Short to the place at Madrid was
due to Jefferson.

The above letter of disappointment was written before the final
blow of Pinckney's appointment to supersede Short at Madrid! Concerning that, Short wrote Jefferson, Sept. 2, 1795, after he had learned
that his patron had ceased to have any influence in the State Department at the time of Pinckney's Madrid appointment, unbosoming his
feelings as follows: "I have never been more astonished. This circumstance [i.e., Pinckney's appointment as envoy extraordinary and sole
commissioner plenipotentiary] like every other which has proceeded
from the agents of Government for some time towards me has seemed
formed on purpose to embitter and perplex the rest of my life. I
thank my God that a few weeks more and the curtain will be dropped
forever between them and me. This will not cure the wounds already
received, but it will save me from receiving others." Short Papers,
XXIX, 5271.

Majesty.[23] Godoy actually had the nerve to state orally that although Pinckney's physiognomy was pleasing, he had just as lief negotiate with Short! But the damage to Short had already been done. To his great credit he curbed his indignation, venting it only in caustic and cynical letters to his friends. The appointment of Pinckney was the cause of Short's resigning from the diplomatic service, but again to his great credit he remained at Madrid to cooperate with Pinckney and placed his services loyally at the new plenipotentiary's elbow during the negotiations which are to be related in the next chapter. Meanwhile, pending Pinckney's long-delayed arrival in Madrid, Short's diplomacy with Gardoqui and Godoy continued.

III

Randolph's letter of November 9, 1794, to Short, apprising him of Pinckney's appointment as envoy extraordinary, had stated: "You will not however abstain from pursuing the negotiation until Mr. Pinckney arrives, and even then your cooperation will be requested. Before this time you must have received a separate power, which has been long ago forwarded. It is not the intention of the President to deviate from the instructions formerly given as to the limits, navigation of the Mississippi and commerce." [24] Relying on this instruction, Short, in his disappointment at having been superseded at such an auspicious moment, pursued with renewed energy the affair of presenting his good offices for a secret peace negotiation with France

23. Short to Sec. of State, No. 205, Madrid, July 29, 1795, Despatches, W. Short, Madrid, 80.

24. Instructions, II, 223. The single power had been sent July 12, 1794.

at the price of a previous acknowledgment by Spain of
the long-standing American demands against her. In
informing Godoy of Pinckney's appointment, he mentioned in proper language that he himself continued to
be empowered to settle the outstanding issues with
Spain and placed himself at Godoy's disposal in case
that minister might not care to await Pinckney's arrival.[25] The Duke, who had no wish to acknowledge
the American contentions except in return for a treaty
of alliance, and who assumed that Pinckney probably
had the powers for an alliance which Short lacked, did
not warm up to the idea of thus negotiating with Short
on the American issues, but he proved quite eager to
pursue the affair of a secret peace with France by
means of Short's personal good offices. Short still refused, as before, to undertake any such step without
first having secured a settlement of the Mississippi
Question and the boundary.[26] To elude this condition
precedent, Godoy now for the first time told Short the
nature of the much-mentioned propositions for the
President, despatched to the United States the previous
July; they had empowered, said he, the Spanish agents
at Philadelphia to settle these issues in a treaty satisfactory to the United States. Still Short refused to be
beguiled. Until he knew authentically that these issues
had been settled he would take no step in any mediation service. He offered to go ahead if Godoy would
but make authentic "simple declaration" that Spain recognized the American right to navigate the Mississippi
to the sea, and accepted 31° as the northern boundary

25. Short to Alcudia, Madrid, Jan. 17, 1795. Short Papers, XXVIII,
4946.

26. Short to Sec. of State, Nos. 193 and 194, Aranjuez, March 3
and March 13, 1795. Hague and Spain, II, 7, 15.

of West Florida. Godoy parried this, by explaining that Great Britain would immediately suspect something, and the French negotiation, which it was necessary to conduct with the greatest secrecy, might thereby be frustrated. Short was now sure that Spain wanted an alliance, but he divined rightly that the United States by policy had no intention to commit itself to any such proposition. "The alliance is a point this Court has, under present circumstances, really at heart," he reported to the Secretary of State, "and to obtain it would be willing, I conceive, to pay a high price on other points. *As far as I can judge, however, the United States will be unwilling to entangle themselves with European politics by connexions of this kind.*"[27]

With no precise information from his Government[28] on its attitude toward an alliance, and certainly without powers on the subject, Short had discerned, intuitively and accurately, the polestar of Washington's foreign policy. The answer of the Secretary of State to this despatch did not reach Short until long after he had left Spain. Too late to be of guidance to him, it is interesting as an emphatic confirmation of Short's own sentiments and another illustration of what was in Washington's mind when he was outlining the points for his famous Farewell Address. "You intimate in your letter of March 3," wrote Timothy Pickering, Ran-

27. Ibid., No. 193, italics inserted.
28. His copious and prolix despatches, faithfully representing every detail of his business and his political environment, elicited no such complete correspondence from the Secretaries of State. His despatches are one long lament of his embarrassing lack of information. Frequently he had to rely on Spanish officials for information about happenings in his own country, not to mention events in other countries. See, for example, Short to Pinckney, S. Ildefonso, Sept. 12, and Oct. 12, 1793, Short Papers, XXIV, 4236, 4286; and to Sec. of State, No. 183, Dec. 3, 1794, Hague and Spain, I, 369.

dolph's successor, "that Spain wants an alliance with us; but rightly conclude that the United States will on no consideration which Spain can offer, entangle themselves with European politics by connections of this kind." [29] Not even for the free navigation of the great Father of Waters, which meant so much economically and politically to the new union of the United States.

It was well that Short not only dodged all proffer of alliance, but that he refused to accept Godoy's assurances that the Spanish agents at Philadelphia were settling the American issues. They held no such powers as the Duke had asserted. Indeed they had no accredited diplomatic appointment of any kind. In presenting the propositions for the President—a business which he bungled so badly—Jaudenes, who had now succeeded as sole agent at Philadelphia, had been instructed merely to deliver the propositions and to say that if an American plenipotentiary should be equipped with proper powers Spain would agree to such a treaty and alliance.

Short's confidence in Godoy and Gardoqui was badly shaken again when he found that Gardoqui, during the secret conversations in regard to a French peace, had been communicating behind Short's back with James Monroe, American Minister in Paris, for Monroe's intervention as a peacemaker in the hope of not having to pay that American the diplomatic price which Short had insisted on charging for his proposed secret good offices. Monroe, after discussing the subject with the French Committee of Public Safety, and emphasizing the desirability of accompanying any peace negotiation with Spain by insisting upon the settlement by Spain of the American issues, replied to Gardoqui, upon the advice

29. Aug. 31, 1795, rec'd Feb. 23, 1796, via Monroe, when Short was in France. Short Papers, XXIX, 5269.

of the Committee, stating that he had best make his applications direct to the Committee.[30] Monroe promptly apprised Short all about it.[31]

It was soon apparent to Short that Godoy thought Pinckney had been despatched to Spain as envoy extraordinary as a direct result of the President's having received from Jaudenes the propositions for alliance, as Short himself doubtless also supposed, and that therefore the Spanish Minister would await Pinckney's arrival before signing any treaty with the United States. Such a conclusion on the part of Godoy would have been entirely natural, but it was mistaken; Pinckney, as we have seen, had been ordered to replace Short because Godoy —then anxious only to delay matters—had complained of the lack of character, rank, and personal qualities of both Carmichael and Short, and his instructions had been despatched to him long before the propositions were delivered by Jaudenes to Randolph on March 25, 1795.

All the while that Godoy was thus talking with Short it was evident that he had plenty of channels of communication with France;[32] the American Minister at Madrid was not at all indispensable for such peace negotiations, as he eventually came to realize. To expect Spain to pay such a high price to the United States for secret peace services with France, unless it should be expected thereby to seal the American alliance, or even the triple alliance that Godoy now desired, was unreasonable. In May, persuaded that Spain was already engaged in peace conversations with France, following the sep-

30. *Writings of Monroe*, II, 7–31.

31. Short to Sec. of State, No. 193, Aranjuez, March 3, 1795, Despatches, W. Short, Madrid, II, 12.

32. Short to Sec. of State, No. 193, Aranjuez, March 3, 1795. Hague and Spain, I.

arate peace between France and Prussia, Short agreed, without insisting on any prior settlement between Spain and the United States, to transmit to Monroe at Paris the expression of Spain's desire to treat for peace. He did this because he felt that Pinckney, long overdue, would presently be in Madrid with full instructions, before any answer could arrive from Monroe or before any such negotiation through the American Minister at Paris could gain headway; and that it would not be expedient to antagonize Spain's newly-discovered friendly attitude by refusing at least to forward such expressions to France. This he did, but the overtures thus made to Monroe resulted in nothing.[33] Monroe conferred with Pinckney, then in Paris on his way to Spain. Pinckney knew but did not reveal to Monroe the terms of Jay's Treaty, except for the misleading sentence: "Nothing in this treaty contained shall, however, be construed or operate contrary to former and existing public treaties with other sovereigns or States." This was not enough to reassure France, when transmitted to the French Government by Monroe. Pinckney and Monroe agreed that the negotiation of Jay's Treaty had so alienated France as to make it most unwise for the United States now to intervene in this delicate matter of Franco-Spanish peace negotiations.[34] Spain's peace with France was made eventually through other and more direct channels.

If we do not take into consideration his eagerness at last to win a great diplomatic triumph personally, after years of humiliation, discouragement, and disillusion-

33. Short to Sec. of State, No. 197, Aranjuez, May 7, 1795, Despatches, W. Short, Madrid, 7. Hague and Spain, II, 24.

34. See *Writings of Monroe*, II, 277–288; also Beverley Bond, *The Monroe Mission to France, 1794–1796*, 23–27; and "Monroe's Efforts to Secure Free Navigation of the Mississippi," *Miss. Hist. Soc. Proc.*, IX, 260.

ment, we cannot understand how a man of Short's un-usual perspicacity could have expected success for his ingenious project, particularly when he himself was convinced that the United States would never and should never buy an acknowledgment of its rights from Spain by agreeing to an entangling European alliance. Yet it was transparently clear that only on some such basis was Gardoqui or Godoy willing to listen to such a proposal as that conceived by the eager and disappointed diplo-matist, William Short.

We must now turn to Thomas Pinckney to observe how he arrived in Madrid at the psychological moment, so opportune for gathering the laurels which might well have gone to the capable Short, but which by luck were to fall upon the brow of the elegant South Caro-linian, who, through no fault of his own, crowded an able and faithful public servant off the stage of public notice into the total obscurity of a history unrecorded until now. Pinckney, as Short acknowledged two years later, after the affair was finished, was "a well-inten-tioned man." [35]

35. To Jefferson, Dec. 26, 1797, Short Papers, XXX, 5416.

CHAPTER 12

Pinckney's Treaty

I

If the real purpose of Godoy in asking for the re-placement of Carmichael and Short at the Court of Madrid had been, as he professed, to secure an American representative of greater rank and splendor to reside near the King, it would seem that no citizen of the United States was qualified to fill such demands with more éclat and satisfaction than Thomas Pinckney, of South Carolina, "judicious, affable and solid man," so the Spanish agents in Philadelphia had described him in 1792 when he set out for London to become United States Minister at the Court of St. James's.[1]

Born in 1750 to a name celebrated in the earliest annals of that colony and state, he had been taken as a child to England where his father went in 1753 to become colonial agent. There the boy passed the next nineteen years. Educated at first at Westminster School, where he made the acquaintance of English youths of high social standing, some of whom were to be of value to him in his later public life, he studied afterwards at Oxford, and in France, where he pursued a year of military study and presumably acquired the elements of a language which was one day to be useful in his unex-pected career as a diplomatist. In the Inner Temple, in

1. "Juicioso, afable, y de solidez." Jaudenes and Viar to Florida-blanca, Phila., May 11, 1792, A. H. N., Est. Leg., 3894.

London, he completed his professional training for the law.

The English boyhood and education of Pinckney made him none the less an ardent patriot upon his return to America in 1772. When the Revolution broke out he volunteered in the South Carolina militia and played a virile and honorable part in the history of that war, from which he emerged as a major in the Continental Army, after having been made a prisoner, as he lay, dangerously wounded, on the battlefield of Camden. He served with credit as governor of his native state during the turbulent years 1787 and 1788. A younger son, he married happily a woman of wealth, to which competence he added the fruits of his own profession and the profits of plantation management. In the social strata of southern life no family held greater prestige than the wealthy planter Pinckneys, and none has transmitted it to more worthy, representative, or honorable descendants.[2]

In 1791, after having refused an appointment as federal judge, Thomas Pinckney accepted the post of minister to Great Britain, for which court he set out the following spring. The appointment was due to Washington's own unadvised choice of the South Carolinian as a distinguished and representative southerner; personally the President's acquaintance with him had no experience to recommend him. Aside from William Short there were at that time few available men who had a diplomatic career behind them—Jefferson was now Secretary of State, John Adams Vice President, and John Jay Chief Justice. As Minister to the Court of St. James's, Pinckney served in a distinguished if not a highly important capacity. During that time he han-

2. For Pinckney's early life, see C. C. Pinckney, *Thomas Pinckney.*

dled no great issue, because the more important business was being dealt with directly by the Secretary of
State and the British Minister at Philadelphia, George
Hammond, always remembering in this connection that
Alexander Hamilton's informal and intimate contact
with the British Government was the determining factor
in Anglo-American affairs during Washington's Administration.[3] To Pinckney in London was left the work of
protesting against the impressment of American seamen
and, if possible, securing their release, and the routine
business of the day, including the presenting of notes
by Jefferson combating the British arbitrary orders-in-
council of 1793 and 1794. To his confessed chagrin,
Pinckney was temporarily set aside when John Jay was
sent by the Federalist leaders as envoy extraordinary
and minister plenipotentiary to London. To his great
credit, the South Carolinian stood loyally at his post
as regular minister and assisted Jay to the extent required of him, and wrote to the Secretary of State
commending Jay's negotiation under difficult circumstances of a treaty which might be opposed by some, but
which was preferable to war, and about the best that
could be had. The same conduct, though not the same
opinion, under similar but personally more aggravating
circumstances, added to a long chapter of disappointments, was exhibited by William Short when Pinckney
arrived in Spain as envoy extraordinary and sole commissioner plenipotentiary to take from his hands a
negotiation which then seemed to be on the threshold
of a spectacular success.[4] Pinckney construed the ap-

3. *Jay's Treaty*, 63–108.
4. Pinckney wrote to the Secretary of State from London, June 23,
1794: "With respect to this gentleman's [Jay's] mission, as it personally concerns me, if I were to say I had no unpleasant feelings on the
occasion I should not be sincere; but the sincerity with which I

pointment as envoy extraordinary to Spain as a just compensation for his judicious and meritorious conduct in
London during the Jay negotiations.

make this declaration will, I trust, entitle me to credit, when I add,
that I am convinced of the expediency of adopting any honorable
measures, which may tend to avert the calamities of war, or by its
failure cement our union at home; that I consider Mr. Jay's appointment, from the solemnity of the mission, supported by his established
reputation, diplomatic experience and general talents, as the most
probable method of effecting this purpose; and that I am sensible of
the delicacy respecting myself with which this measure has been
carried into execution. Under these circumstances, it will be scarce
necessary for me to say further, that I will cheerfully embrace every
opportunity of promoting the objects of Mr. Jay's mission and of
rendering his residence here agreeable." Despatches, Great Britain,
IV, 289.

For Pinckney's approval of Jay's negotiation and treaty, see Pinckney to Sec. of State, Sept. 15, and Nov. 16, 1794, Despatches, Great
Britain, IV. In stating, Nov. 16, that Jay's Treaty was about the best
that could be had Pinckney declared that Jay "has communicated
freely with me on this subject during his negotiations, and I have
witnessed the great difficulties which have occurred in several of the
articles." After Jay's Treaty had been published in America and the
vials of public wrath opened against it, Pinckney wrote to Jefferson,
Feb. 26, 1796, that while Jay had advised with him throughout the
negotiation, he himself had not been present at any of the conferences
with Lord Grenville and could not share the merits or demerits of
the treaty. Ibid., III. See also my "The London Mission of Thomas
Pinckney," A. H. R., XXVIII, 244.

Short, while not persuaded of the expediency of adopting the
method of sending an envoy extraordinary to Madrid, nevertheless
wrote in similar vein to the Secretary of State: "I am too nearly and
deeply interested in the measure which you do me the honor to
announce to me as intended by the President, to allow myself the
liberty of expressing any sentiment respecting it. I have no right to
desire or expect that out of any personal consideration to my feelings
a special envoy should not be sent here, as it is deemed conducive to
the public interests. I should not only be unworthy of public confidence, but unworthy also of being a citizen of the United States if I
could for a moment put my feelings, whatever they may be, in the
balance against considerations of that kind. How much soever I may
regret therefore the peculiar circumstances which contrast my situation under this measure with that of any other known to me, it will

If Pinckney's educational training and nineteen years' residence in England, before the sterner years of the American Revolution, had not produced an original or highly pleasing literary style nor the intellectual alacrity or energy of a Jefferson or a Madison, it had developed a cogency of reasoning and some perspicuity of argument and had endowed him with an appreciation of literary merit and a devotion to the classical culture which the best English minds of that day had been so content to indulge. Contact with the European world, too, had served to polish the natural urbanity, social balance and dignity which were the patrimony of his name. A Federalist in political sympathy and follower of the domestic policy of Alexander Hamilton, he nevertheless was not on the "inside" of that leader's pro-British foreign policy. A southerner, he was staunch on the question of the Mississippi; there is no reason to believe he felt less vigorously on the navigation of the river than did his cousin Charles, who made the famous speech in Congress in 1786 against Jay's proposed cloture of that waterway.

Cultured man of the world and respected veteran of the Revolution and citizen that he was, Thomas Pinckney was not one of the half-dozen great leaders in the United States of his time, any more for example than was James Monroe. It is nothing to his discredit not to place him in that immortal little group. A man of

in no degree diminish my earnest wishes for the success of Mr. Pinckney's mission (which you will see from my late letters is already insured) nor my best efforts to serve him, in whatever he may think it necessary."

Despite his statement that he would not express any sentiments as to his own predicament, Short did so abundantly in the rest of the letter. See Short to Sec. of State, No. 189, Madrid, Jan. 16, 1795, Short Papers, XXVIII, 4940.

parts, good judgment, elegant person, of impressive
personality if of somewhat impressionable character, he
moved easily and nobly through a distinguished life,
doing well the tasks he was called on to perform, making no great mistake and encountering no measurable
public misfortune. Comparing the despatches of the
two men, the student is inclined to believe that the less
distinguished and more humble, certainly the more unfortunate "career" diplomatist, William Short, equaled
Pinckney in ability if not in urbanity and poise, and
that he had a closer grip on the complicated European
diplomacy of the French Revolution. For if Pinckney
had understood the international situation as thoroughly
as Short, he would have lost not one moment in setting
out for Madrid immediately he was notified of his
appointment.

Actually Pinckney did not leave London until late
in the spring of 1795. This was because John Jay,
himself waiting in London for spring and a less tem-
pestuous passage to America and hoping meanwhile to
receive his treaty back ratified by the Senate, so that
he himself could bring home the exchanged ratifications, advised Pinckney not to set out for Madrid until
the treaty had been ratified. "In my opinion, Mr.
Pinckney should defer a certain Business," he wrote
ponderously to the Secretary of State, "until the treaty
is ratified:—it will afford him strong ground for strong
measures:—I think this Government would rather promote than mar the Business alluded to:—indeed I am
convinced of it, from a Variety of considerations." [5]

5. Postscript to Jay's despatch of Jan. 7, 1795, Despatches, John
Jay, England.

Randolph's interpretation of this is interesting: "I presume it is
too late to give such an instruction, even if it were advisable; and
Mr. Jay probably calculated on an earlier decision on the treaty than

If the treaty had been ratified and its full terms known in Spain when Pinckney arrived there, as Jay had desired, it is doubtful whether he could have achieved such a successful ending of his Spanish mission. Fortunately for Pinckney, and fortunately for the United States, the packet-boat that bore Jay's Treaty was delayed in winter storms and did not reach America until after the expiration of the session of Congress which Jay had counted on for its ratification. Pinckney's full powers and credentials did not reach London until February 23, 1795. Without waiting any longer for the return of the treaty, Jay left England April 12, 1795.[6] Pinckney delayed a few weeks until he learned that the treaty would not be considered for several months, until a special session of the Senate could be called to pass upon it. He then left promptly for Madrid, via the Netherlands and France, about May 15.[7]

As to the chief purpose of his mission, Pinckney received no additional instructions. He was merely referred by Randolph to Jefferson's statements and arguments originally presented to Carmichael and Short,

---

will in fact take place. I own, that from Mr. Short's communications, Mr. Jay's ideas appear well-founded. But to arrest Mr. Pinckney's progress for the reason given by Mr. Jay, would be interpreted into a stratagem for obtaining the votes of those, who are interested in the Mississippi, for the ratification of the treaty. Without a doubt Mr. Pinckney, whose intercourse with Mr. Jay has been unreserved, is impressed with his sentiments; and will probably find an occasion of keeping off the business, until it is ripened by ratification. Indeed the delays of the Spanish Court and the communications with Mr. Short will consume some time, before the negociation commences seriously." Randolph to Washington, Phila., April 24, 1795, Domestic Letters, VIII, 152.

6. *A. S. P., F. R.,* I, 519.

7. Pinckney to Sec. of State, London, Feb. 2, Feb. 23, April 3, 1795, Despatches, Great Britain, IV, 338; to Short, London, May 10, 1795, rec'd June 23, 1795, Short Papers, XXIX, 5124.

as well as a résumé of Jay's old discussions with Gardoqui in 1785–1789. Some observations by Randolph on the reasons for Pinckney's nomination are, nevertheless, interesting.

The negotiation was entrusted to Pinckney, instead of Short, Randolph explained, as a result of the complaints made through Jaudenes by the Spanish Minister concerning Carmichael and Short. Even though it was well understood that all this was a subterfuge for procrastination on the part of the Spanish Government, the Secretary stated:

Peace and harmony with all nations being the supreme policy of the United States, it was thought best to cast upon Spain the odium of the miscarriage of the negotiation, if at length it should miscarry. We therefore condescend for this moment to yield to the subtleties of procrastination; not only presuming that there may be due some attention to the professions of friendship on the part of Spain [but], that the controversy ought to be brought to a conclusion.

Referring to the late "violence" of the Kentuckians, who had as good a reason as any people ever had to cause them to look upon the Mississippi "as a right to be derived from God," Randolph asserted that hitherto the Government had been able to restrain them from such enterprises as that of Genêt for the invasion of Louisiana, only by the promise of securing by peaceful negotiation the navigation of the river. If that navigation were to be refused, the United States should know of it:

but should this be the case you will not give any ground to the Spanish Minister to suppose that hostility is our alternative. If we break off in ill humor we in some degree lose the choice of peace or war. If we show no symptom of ill temper, we are not debarred from resorting to any expedient which we approve. It is not impossible, too, that in the settlement of peace with

France, some opportunity of pressing the Mississippi may be presented, if we should be disappointed now. If any hint of this sort should be capable of improvement, you will doubtless communicate your ideas to our minister at Paris. Our reputation with the French Government is on a strong footing.

It is of immense importance for us to know, if it can be ascertained, whether Great Britain is under no engagement to Spain to support her in the retention of the Mississippi?

The Spanish Court have greatly deceived themselves, by an opinion, that the whole union are not cordial in their intention to secure the Mississippi to Kentucky. Some parts of it indeed may differ upon the political effect, but I cannot suffer my mind to yield a moment to the belief, that any man will be base enough to sacrifice so important a right.

Your station in London will serve as one among many reasons, for repelling the arts of procrastination.[8]

These observations, it should be recalled, were written before it was known certainly that Jay's Treaty would be signed with Great Britain, while the Anglo-Spanish alliance was still presumed to be in vigor, when the only intimation of any possibility for a settlement with Spain came from Short's letter of the summer of 1794 indicating the success of the French armies in northern Spain; when the policy of the Administration, at least in regard to Spain, was still the Jeffersonian one of "patience and persuasion," of waiting for some confidently anticipated chapter of accidents which would present a favorable moment for pressing the claims of the United States. It was before France had been alienated by the negotiation of Jay's Treaty. What that chapter of accidents would really be, or that it would happen so very soon, was known to no one in America when Pinckney was appointed in November, 1794.

Pinckney's full-power designated him "envoy extraordinary and sole commissioner plenipotentiary," with

8. Randolph to Pinckney, Nov. 28, 1794, Instructions, II, 245.

powers to negotiate and sign, for submission to the
President for ratification by and with the advice and
consent of the Senate, a treaty or treaties "concerning
the navigation of the River Mississippi and such other
matters relative to the confines and territories of the
United States and His Catholic Majesty, and the intercourse to be had thereon," and also "of and concerning
the general commerce between the United States and
the kingdoms and dominions of His Catholic Majesty."
A second and separate full-power authorized him as
"envoy extraordinary," but not as "sole commissioner
plenipotentiary," similarly to negotiate and settle American spoliation claims against Spain.[9] Thus from the
moment of presentation to the Spanish Court, Pinckney
completely superseded Short in regard to the issues of
the Mississippi, boundary and commerce, but not necessarily in regard to spoliations, though as a matter of
fact Short did not handle these, either, after Pinckney's
arrival, except in an advisory capacity, in which function he served Pinckney on all the several issues.

II

Mentioning here the subjects of commerce and spoliations makes it desirable very briefly to describe these
two questions, while we are waiting for Pinckney to
make the long carriage journey from Calais to Madrid.

Spanish municipal regulations placed American commerce on a most-favored-nation basis, without any treaty
guaranty. American consuls had been appointed at
Cadiz, Alicante, and Malaga, but like all foreign consuls
in Spain they were not allowed to exercise any judicial

9. Ibid., I, 533.

functions.[10] In the United States Spanish consuls at New York, Philadelphia, and Charleston enjoyed privileges similar to those of other European nations. All Spanish colonial ports in America, as we have observed, notably Havana and New Orleans, were closed to American as well as to all other foreign ships after the war of independence. The waning prosperity of New Orleans, particularly after the European war had destroyed all trade with France in 1793, and the necessity of securing proper goods to supply the Indian trade, as well as the scarcity of Spanish bottoms after 1793, caused the proclamation of an ordinance of June 9 of that year, opening a free trade for the ports of New Orleans, Pensacola, and St. Augustine with foreign countries in foreign ships, which must first touch for license at designated ports in Spain. Except for the trade in negroes which was made free of duty, all goods exported to foreign countries were required to pay a duty of six per cent and all imports into Louisiana from elsewhere than

10. ". . . the consuls of the United States are here on the same footing with those of the other powers, none of whom are allowed to exercise jurisdiction, and this is a point which it would be impossible to obtain. In the consular convention with France in 1769 it was refused. This government makes a distinction in the privileges of consuls, who are subjects of Spain and those who are not so. . . . In the present situation of things it will probably be found best not to multiply subjects by attempting a consular convention." Short to Sec. of State, No. 185, Madrid, Dec. 12, 1795, Hague and Spain, I, 406. Short changed his mind about this, after the European situation had become more advantageous for the United States, and on May 7, 1795, advocated, in addition to an attempt to get trading privileges in Spanish American ports, the negotiation of a consular convention. Pickering, after receiving this, instructed Pinckney, Sept. 3, 1795, to secure a consular convention modeled on Article XVI of Jay's Treaty, if this should be possible without hazard to the general negotiation. Before this instruction arrived, Pinckney had signed his treaty providing for residence of consuls on a most-favored-nation basis.

Spain fifteen per cent tariff. This trade was restricted to such nations as had treaties of commerce with Spain. That alone excluded American ships, but the necessity of first touching at a Spanish peninsular port would have excluded them in practice,[11] even had there been at that time a treaty of commerce between Spain and the United States.

Even before the war the necessities of certain of the Spanish provinces, Louisiana and Cuba especially, had caused licenses to be issued, through the Spanish diplomatic agents at Philadelphia, for the importation into Spanish West Indian ports, and New Orleans and St. Augustine, of flour and provisions from the United States. After the beginning of the war between Spain and France these emergencies became more frequent. Even American ships were allowed to carry cargoes of foodstuffs to Havana and New Orleans and Santo Domingo. Jaudenes caused quite a scandal by his trafficking in such licenses for his own profit.[12] Officially Spain did not care to acknowledge these emergency leaks in her exclusive colonial navigation system, and Gardoqui affirmed to Short, at the very moment when American flour was being received in Havana, that it would never be admitted there.[13]

11. Text of the ordinance in *A. S. P., F. R.*, I, 273.

12. For reports of such shipments, see Jaudenes and Viar to Alcudia, Nos. 173, 174, 197, 251, July 14, Sept. 20, 1793, A. H. N., Est. Leg., 3895; Oct. 31, 1793, ibid., 3895 *bis*. For Jaudenes' trafficking in licenses, see Pickering to Short, Aug. 31, 1795, Short Papers, XXIX, 5269, which states that Jaudenes was selling licenses for flour at one to two dollars a barrel, and was estimated as making $50,000 a year. See Short to Sec. of State, No. 209, S. Ildefonso, Aug. 28, 1795, Despatches, W. Short, Madrid, 109, for expressions of dissatisfaction by Godoy on this point. See also Pinckney to Short, Paris, Dec. 21, 1795, Short Papers, XXX, 4364.

13. "You will know that our flour is admitted at the Havannah, but what you will not suspect is that this was done at the very

Trade between the United States and Spain proper was most one-sided. By far the greatest part was in American bottoms, which took to the peninsula principally foodstuffs, notably flour, wheat, corn, rye, fish, and salt meat; and lumber;[14] and brought home partly Spanish and partly other European goods purchased at Lisbon and Atlantic ports as far north as the Baltic. After war broke out in 1793 between Spain and England on the one hand, and France, American neutral carriage at least to the northern ports, safe from the Algerines, prospered greatly. American vessels trading to Cadiz from ports other than Spanish colonies far outnumbered those of any other flag, including that of Spain but excepting that of Great Britain.[15] This was before the truce between Algiers and Portugal, engineered by British diplomacy in 1793, let loose those corsairs into the Atlantic and crippled American commerce to southern Spanish ports. Exports from the United States to Spain rose from roughly one-fifteenth of the American total in the year 1790, the first for which there is any statement, to about one-eleventh of the total of the year 1792; in the war year 1793 they were approximately one-eighth of all exports from the United States.[16] Imports from Spain into the United States constituted only a very small fraction of the total American imports, not more than one or two per cent.[17] The one-sidedness of this trade had not es-

moment that Mr. De G. gave his word it would never be done and that he had taken measures against any such step." Short to Humphreys, March 4, 1794, Short Papers, XXV, 4444. See also Short to Sec. of State, No. 141, Madrid, Feb. 13, 1794, Hague and Spain, I, 175.

14. *A. S. P., Commerce and Navigation,* I. See index for comparative statements of commodities exported.

15. *A. S. P., F. R.,* I, 445.

16. For figures, see *A. S. P., Com. & Navig.,* I, 146, 300, 317.

17. Ibid., 200.

caped the attention of the Spanish agents at Philadelphia, who advocated discrimination against American
commerce in Spanish ports as a means of putting pres-
sure on the United States to alter its discrimination
in tariff and tonnage duties in favor of American ships
and in other issues,[18] and in 1792 a royal decree imposed certain discriminating tariff charges on the importation of various goods into Spain from continental
America in foreign vessels, thus imitating the principle
of the American acts of 1789 and 1790.[19]

Jefferson's instructions to Carmichael and Short on
the subject of commerce had looked to the desirable
consummation of reciprocal commercial privileges of
nationals for each party in *all* the dominions of the
other; but, realizing that Spain was "not ripe for an
equal exchange on that basis," had marked out the
principle that citizens of the United States and subjects of the King of Spain should have at least most-
favored-nation privileges in the dominions of each country. Really, though Jefferson had not been made aware
of it, most-favored-nation privileges in Spain were more
valuable to foreigners, thanks to the special privileges
which incautious Spanish ministers had allowed to be
written into treaties with Great Britain, than the rights
enjoyed by Spanish nationals.[20] He also instructed Car-

18. The discrimination in tonnage and tariff duties granted to
American ships by the tariff and tonnage acts of 1789 and 1790
affected Spanish as well as all foreign ships. Jaudenes to Floridablanca,
Confidential No. 1, Phila., Aug. 27, 1791; Jaudenes and Viar to
Floridablanca, Phila., Nov. 6, 1791, A. H. N., Est. Leg., 3894.

19. Voted that "on the following articles proceeding from continental
America in foreign ships be charged the following: 16 *reales vellon*
per 100 lbs. of salt fish; 20 *reales* per 100 lbs. of salt meat; 20 *reales*
per 100 lbs. of rice; 7 *reales* per *fanega* of wheat; 12 *reales* per 100
lbs. of flour; 5 *reales* per *fanega* of maize." Actas del Supremo Consejo
de Estado, June 18, 1792, A. H. N., Est.

20. Ante.

michael and Short to strive for some free ports for American shipping in the Spanish West Indies, like those already existing since 1784 in the French West Indies; and to secure a treaty of commerce based in general on those in force between the United States and France, the Netherlands, Sweden, and Prussia,[21] all of which were based on the famous original model draft for such treaties drawn up by a committee of the Continental Congress in 1776.[22]

Because of failure to make any headway upon the larger questions of the Mississippi and the boundary, as well as the Indian issue which was involved with the latter, Carmichael and Short never got to any serious discussion of commercial matters. Unlike Anglo-American relations of the same period, commerce cannot be said to have been a vital issue in Spanish-American diplomacy, though American navigators looked enviously at the closed ports in the Caribbean and South America; never after 1786 was a majority of the states or of Congress willing to exchange the navigation of the Mississippi for a favorable commercial treaty with Spain. A treaty of commerce was a desirable but not an indispensable item to be included in any general settlement with Spain such as Pinckney had now set out to achieve.

The matter of spoliations had assumed by 1795 greater importance than the question of commerce itself.

During the war of the American Revolution, Spain had given adherence to the Armed Neutrality of 1780, by which enemy property on neutral ships was free from capture, with the exception of contraband of war. The Anglo-Spanish alliance of May 15, 1793, over-

---

21. *Writings*, V, 476–481.
22. See E. C. Burnett, "American Negotiations for Commercial Treaties, 1776–1786," *A. H. R.*, XVI, 579–587.

turned these principles. Article V was similar in content to articles in the treaties negotiated between Great Britain and the several members of the First Coalition and also with the old armed neutral of 1780, Russia. It stipulated that the two crowns should take "all measures in their power to injure the commerce of France and to oblige her by this means to make a fair peace," and Article VI agreed that they would use all their efforts to prevent neutral powers from giving, "by virtue of their neutrality, any protection, direct or indirect, to French commerce or French property, either on the seas or in the ports of France." Spain thus forswore the principles of the Armed Neutrality and accepted for the time being the British system, by which enemy property on neutral ships was subject to capture. Great Britain, it will be remembered, by orders-in-council of June 8 and November 6, 1793, and January 8, 1794, put into effect the principle of stopping all neutral ships bound for French ports with provisions, providing for the pre-emption at appraised values of such cargoes, with indemnity to the ship for demurrage. Great Britain also applied the Rule of 1756, in the last two of these same orders.[23] All this was contrary to the provisions of the treaties of the United States defining neutral rights. By the Spanish *ordenanza de corso* of May 1, 1794, it was announced that Spain would follow the same practice toward neutral shipping as observed by her enemies.[24]

23. The order-in-council of Nov. 6, 1793 (superseded by that of Jan. 8, 1794) had gone beyond the Rule of 1756 in that it prohibited all commerce between the United States and the French West Indies, which commerce had been largely open before the war. For discussion of the orders, see *Jay's Treaty*, 154–158.

24. See Pinckney to the Prince of the Peace, San Ildefonso, Sept. 20, 1795, referring to but not giving the text of the ordinance. *A. S. P.,*

The precise procedure of Spanish admiralty officials toward American neutral ships is rather difficult to determine. There seems to have been comparatively little trouble from spoliations during 1793, though three seizures during that year gave rise to lively protests on the part of the United States and added to the issues already existing between that republic and Spain, the one of neutral rights. The *Betsy,* an American merchant ship, left Delaware Bay, August 18, 1793, bound for "the West Indies," presumably the French West Indies, with a cargo of foodstuffs. Six days later she was captured by the Spanish ship *Infanta,* Captain Merino, and brought into the port of Coruña, September 30. The conduct of the Spanish captain was most irregular in his treatment of the ship's papers and the personal property of the crew, some of whom were placed in irons and fed throughout the long voyage with meager and unwholesome rations; and the American captain was deprived of decent food and forced "to drink only water for forty-two days," while Merino had plenty else to drink and slaughtered and ate the livestock found on the *Betsy.* Both vessel and cargo—American property—were condemned without affording the American captain any use of his own ship's papers or any chance of defense. The sentence itself was not even conveyed to him until six months after it had been pronounced. Godoy, appealed to by Carmichael (who as regular chargé d'affaires had under his office, before his recall, all matters not specifically charged to the joint commission), refused to interfere. Nor did Short later meet with any success in his importunities con-

---

F. R., I, 539. See also Pinckney's proposed article on spoliations, in Appendix III of this volume.

cerning this ship. The case lay under appeal to the *junta suprema,* when Pinckney arrived.[25]

Two other American merchantmen, the *Rooksby* and *Greenway,* were brought into Cadiz in 1793 by a Spanish frigate, which had made the captures before the Anglo-Spanish alliance had been signed. The cargoes were condemned on the ground that they were French property. That they were such seems to have been admitted tacitly by Short, in his representations concerning the cases. The Spanish authorities then offered to return the vessels, after long delay pending judgment had rendered them unseaworthy, and after they had been abandoned long since by their crews. Short declined to receive the vessels in such condition and insisted on damages for the owners for losses thus sustained and for diversion from their destined route. Godoy then offered to have the vessels reconditioned and returned, without mentioning damages for demurrage. Short demanded further indemnity for this, too. He also refused to admit the justice of taking French property from American decks, excepting contraband of war, particularly in this instance, where the ships had been seized before the adoption of the Anglo-Spanish treaty of May 25, 1793; and "even admitting that they [Spain] were to be bound by the convention between Spain and England, yet it cannot be expected that that convention should bind and direct the conduct of their citizens until it were known to them—and these vessels were seized before the convention was communicated, of course before the American owners of the vessels could know that Spain had changed their rule of con-

25. *Re* the *Betsy,* Short Papers, XXVII, 4926. (Do not confuse with four other *Betsies* in these spoliations.)

duct on board of neutral vessels." [26] Even the arbitrary British system, Short pointed out, offered damages for delay to the neutral carrier, in case of confiscation of enemy property found on it.[27]

These three cases at Coruña and Cadiz remained for a long time the only spoliations cases encountered in Spain, except for the cargo, French property, of one American ship detained at Santander at the opening of the war. But in October, 1794, the Spanish Government issued an order directing that all vessels destined to the ports of the province of Guipuzcoa, then occupied by the French, be stopped and detained as if destined to the ports of France. As a result Spanish privateers brought into Bilbao a "considerable number" of American vessels alleged to be so destined, though some of them claimed to have been really destined to Bilbao itself. Short in protesting these cases attacked the principle of seizing enemy property, except contraband, on neutral ships, and tried to convince Godoy that it was not in Spain's interest to follow the British practice. This was in April, 1795, after Spanish policy had changed so abruptly toward the United States and when Godoy was maneuvering for a secret peace with France and an accompanying alliance, to include if possible the United States. The Duke now (April 6, 1795) verbally promised Short to observe toward the United States in the future the same principles followed by France—that is, neutral rights as defined in the Franco-American treaty of 1778, but he expressed the hope that Short would not ask him to com-

26. Short to Sec. of State, No. 174, Madrid, Oct. 17, 1794, Hague and Spain, I, 331.

27. Short to Sec. of State, No. 177, Madrid, Nov. 1, 1794, ibid. See also *A. S. P., F. R.*, I, 540.

mit this assurance to writing, "as he wished to avoid all suspicions of deviating from the convention with England." [28] As a result all the vessels detained at Bilbao were eventually released, and secret orders were given toward the end of the month to the Minister of Marine to observe Article XXIII of the Franco-American treaty (right of neutrals to trade between port and port of the enemy in goods not contraband, and recognition of the principle of free-ships-free-goods) but not Article XXIV, the article which limited contraband to warlike instruments only, excluding foodstuffs and naval stores.[29] The vigilant and indefatigable Short then set about drawing up a claim for damages for the detention of the Bilbao spoliations.[30]

The above cases concerned American ships brought into Spanish European ports. Numerous others arose in the West Indies, though few in comparison with British spoliations in those seas; this was because Spain's cruisers and privateers were far less numerous than those of her ally, and her prize courts less reckless in their decisions. Moreover, spoliations on Spanish ships by French privateers illegally fitted out in American ports in 1793 acted as a set-off as well as a potential means of restraint against the activity of Spanish armed vessels toward American neutral bottoms. Early in 1794 a memorial by Spanish owners of privateers was made to the General of the Marine at Havana, complaining that, of forty vessels under American

28. Short to Sec. of State, No. 197, Aranjuez, May 7, 1795, Hague and Spain, II. See also Pinckney to Consul Obrien, S. Ildefonso, Aug. 2, 1795, Pinckney Papers, Spain, 90–103.

29. Alcudia to Jaudenes, S. Ildefonso, Aug. 25, 1795, Spanish Legation, Vol. 202.

30. Short to Sec. of State, Nos. 197, 198, May 7, 1795, Despatches, W. Short, Madrid, 24.

colors brought into the harbor of Santiago de Cuba by their privateers, and loaded with the produce of French West Indian colonies, such as coffee, sugar, molasses, indigo, and cotton, not one had been declared a legal prize, although it was said the connection between the French and the Americans was well known and the deceit of the latter in the courts of law notorious.[31] Submitting this statement to Randolph, Jaudenes and Viar proposed that all American ships leaving ports of the United States be equipped with certificates counter-signed by an official Spanish agent, stating that their cargoes were owned by American citizens. Randolph refused to agree to this, for it would have implied that American ships had no right to carry enemy property not contraband; and he referred the Spanish representatives to his letter of May 1, 1794, to the British Minister, as setting forth the American principles of neutral rights. This was a repudiation of the principles of the British orders-in-council of June 8 and November 6, 1793, the so-called "provision orders," and a denial that foodstuffs could be considered contraband, even to the qualified extent of pre-emption by the captor at appraised values.[32]

In a statement sent to Short, April 4, 1794, was a list of nine spoliations by Spain to date, not including the *Betsy* but including the *Rooksby* and *Greenway*; presumably seven of these were West Indian cases.[33] In May of that same year Jaudenes and Viar delivered to Randolph a list of five Spanish merchantmen alleged to have been captured by French privateers illegally fitted

31. Viar and Jaudenes to Sec. of State, May 6, 1794, State Dept., Notes, Spain, I.
32. *A. S. P., F. R.*, I, 451.
33. Randolph to Short, April 14, 1794, Instructions, II, 342.

out in the United States and proscribed by the Government thereof.[34]

As a result of the spoliation cases in American waters, and reports of the *Rooksby, Greenway,* and *Betsy* in Spain, Short was instructed, July 31, 1794, to secure some basis of compensation in general rules and principles of law and then to get a commission appointed to assess the actual damages.[35] Short's success in obtaining from Godoy an acceptance of the principles of the French-American treaty of 1778 has been noted. Such was the status of the spoliation question when Pinckney arrived in Spain.[36]

34. Domestic Letters, VII, 308. For correspondence between Randolph and Jaudenes and Viar, relating to certificates and neutral rights, see Spain, Notes, I and IA, in State Dept., and Domestic Letters, VI, VII, VIII.

35. Instructions, II, 125.

36. On Aug. 4, 1794, Jaudenes and Viar asked Godoy the following questions concerning the policy of Spain:

1. In the case of American vessels loaded with French property, should the ship as well as the cargo be confiscated? Should freight be paid?

2. In case of an American boat detained with American property aboard, should freight be paid?

Answers to these questions were desired in order to cooperate with Spanish naval commanders operating in American waters. In reply, Oct. 24, 1794, Godoy sent copies of Articles 5, 8, and 18 of the *Ordenanza* of July 1, 1779, prescribing rules for the conduct of privateers. Article XVII states that: "Vessels which present in good faith their registers and manifests of cargo, shall be allowed to navigate freely, even though bound for an enemy port not blockaded, as long as they do not have anything suspicious about them [como en ellos no haya cosa sospechosa] and are not carrying contraband articles, in which must be included all foodstuffs of whatever kind going to any enemy place blockaded by sea or land." This was qualified by Godoy's covering letter which said that particular cases must be considered by themselves, because if a fixed rule were adopted much injustice might be done. A. H. N., Est. Leg., 3895 *bis.* These rules of 1779 were almost as liberal as those of the Armed Neutrality, but in 1793-1795, according to the actual conduct of the Spanish marine, they were superseded by the principles of the Anglo-Spanish alliance.

III

If Godoy had known the full, precise terms of Jay's Treaty during negotiations with Pinckney, we suggest, it would have injured rather than helped American interests; because that Minister imagined there was something in the treaty tantamount to alliance, dangerous to Spanish interests in America, whereas actually it contained nothing so portentous. Luckily Pinckney's delay in London did not damage his chances in Madrid, for one reason because notwithstanding Jay's and Pinckney's desires, the full terms of Jay's Treaty do not appear to have been known in Madrid until after Pinckney had concluded his business there and departed from Spain,[37] and for another reason because, through no foresight of his own, the long wait in London caused him to arrive in Madrid, June 28, 1795, at the proper phychological moment.

The situation at that date could not have been more favorable for the success of his mission. Prussia and the Netherlands had already left the Coalition against France. French armies in increased strength were pressing through the Pyrenees into the heart of Spain. Godoy was now anxiously and directly negotiating, through several separate channels, with the French, and the terms of peace were rapidly assuming shape. His proposal at Basle for an alliance with France was not fulfilled in these negotiations, though it was to be consummated, to the devastating ruin of Spain, a few months later. On July 22, 1795, the Peace of Basle was signed secretly in Switzerland, but the courier bearing the document did not reach the Spanish capital

37. See note at end of this chapter.

until the third of August. It was ratified in Paris on
July 29.[38]

Pinckney misread the international puzzle. It seemed
desirable to him to conclude his negotiation before
Spain should have signed a peace with France, thus
relieving her of an embarrassing war and allowing her
to turn her energies more freely to her overseas interests. He did not at first realize that Godoy's main
anxiety was what England would do to Spain for deserting the Anglo-Spanish alliance. He did not then
divine the Duke's distress at the negotiation of Jay's
Treaty, the unknown terms of which had been interpreted by the Spanish Court as a union of interests
between the United States and Great Britain in North
America which might be turned against Spain, once
she should desert the British alliance and antagonize
the United States by again refusing to treat on the
Mississippi Question and the boundary.

38. For the Peace of Basle of July 22, 1795, see Lavisse, *Histoire
de France contemporaine*, II, 266, where reference is made to the
monographs used by Sorel; R. Guyot, *Le Directoire et la paix de
l'Europe*, 106; Hermann Baumgarten, *Geschichte Spaniens zur Zeit
der Französischen Revolution*, 532–573; José Gomez de Arteche, "La
mision del Marques de Iranda en 1795," published in his *Nieblas de
la historia patria* (Madrid, 1876), 69–128. This last describes a second
(or possibly it was a third) peace negotiation which Alcudia was trying
to carry on with France at the same time as Iriarte's negotiations with
Barthélemy at Basle. This illuminating contribution is based on the
family correspondence of Iranda.

The Gardoqui-Short intrigue described in the last chapter was only
one of Godoy's attempted channels of communication with France.
One of Short's servants departing for his home in France carried a
passport and open letters for Monroe. Monroe replied with open
letters direct for Short, with enclosures of inconsequential messages
from French friends for Gardoqui. This indicated to Godoy that the
road was clear through the enemy lines if he wished to convey a
message, at least so Short concluded. See *Writings of Monroe*, II, 206,
et passim; Short to Sec. of State, No. 193, March 3, 1795, Despatches,
W. Short, Madrid, II, 7.

At Madrid Pinckney learned that the Court was still sojourning at Aranjuez, where the royal family customarily lived during the spring months. Thither he repaired, only to find royalty on the point of departure for Madrid. He could get little further than an introduction to Godoy, and a review of the negotiations with Short, who introduced him to the Foreign Minister. Both Americans then followed the Court back to the capital. Here the monarchs remained only ten days before moving again to the summer residence at San Ildefonso. The French Revolution and its wars, the rise and fall of coalitions, the making and breaking of alliances, the fate of overseas dominions, the invasion of Spain itself, nothing could stop the regular seasonal movements of the royal persons seeking the climatic advantages of the several royal *sitios*. During the ten days' confused stop at Madrid Pinckney did manage to be presented to the King and to have two conferences with Godoy.

In these first discussions it was evident that Godoy, whose negotiations with France were not then terminated, still clung to his plan of confronting Great Britain, simultaneously with his separate peace with France, with a triple alliance of Spain, France, and the United States. He made it plain to both Pinckney and Short, who was also present, that he wished to establish such a triple alliance and make it simultaneously with the separate peace then being negotiated with France.[39] He told Pinckney, as he had told Short pre-

39. "He received the answer from Mr. Short, which he had previously given him, with great propriety, on former occasions, of a nature somewhat similar, which is, in substance, that a generous and friendly conduct would ensure to both parties all the benefits of an alliance, and that the first object was to establish our rights on just principles, when objects of mutual convenience and accommodation might with propriety be resorted to." *A. S. P., F. R.,* I, 535.

viously so many times, that he could come to no conclusion on the principal points of the American negotiation until he should have received an answer to the propositions for alliance which he had sent to the President the previous July—a year ago—those same propositions which already have assumed such significance in our narrative. To Pinckney this indicated: "that they are still anxious for further delay, which is to them equivalent to a cession of our rights, so long as we shall acquiesce therein, they being in possession of the object in controversy." Through Short's despatches, he had meanwhile received notice from Randolph of the ultimate delivery of the famous propositions, with an exact copy of them as delivered by Jaudenes.[40] It will be remembered that Jaudenes had taken it upon himself, when at length forced by Randolph to deliver the propositions, to qualify them as subject to further elucidation and clarification, contingent upon his receipt of further instructions, that for this reason it had been impossible for the President to consider them as a direct and unequivocal proposal to which an answer could be given.[41] Pinckney was therefore ably to reply to Godoy that, as late as March, 1795, "Mr. Jaudenes

40. "Thus you see how completely our government is tantalized by the Spanish ministry. Indeed, after a treatment which degrades them and insults us; which cuts up by the roots every title to confidence; moderation would be grossly misplaced. . . . P. S. . . . The hints of propositions in Mr. Jaudenes's letter convince me that the Spanish government feel a want of our guarantee; but their evasions, the depressions of their temper at one moment and exstacy at another, as events smile or frown, prove that they are governed by a species of political cowardice, which dares not face their own affairs, which deceives itself by merely postponing the evil day, and which will grant nothing upon principles of liberal policy." Randolph to Short, Phila., April 5, 1795, rec'd May 26, 1795, Short Papers, XXVIII, 5062.

41. Ante, p. 212.

did not conceive himself authorized to make any direct propositions to the President, notwithstanding he had received the instructions to which the Duke alluded, and therefore that it was in vain to wait for an answer to the propositions, which, without further instructions, could not be brought forward in a mode through which any answer could be given to them."

Godoy could not believe that Jaudenes had not presented the propositions, and said that he was awaiting daily an answer thereto. Pinckney then sent to the Duke, July 10, a copy of the propositions as delivered by Jaudenes, April 4, 1795, to Randolph. At this moment the Court moved to San Ildefonso and the negotiation again was interrupted. Meanwhile couriers were galloping across France, rushing to Madrid the secret treaty of Basle, just signed on the 22nd of July. The French treaty had been concluded without the desired alliance. Godoy's only immediate chance of bolstering his position in the face of England was by a dual alliance with the United States, or, failing that, a treaty of friendship.

Randolph's despatch to Short, enclosing the propositions as qualified by Jaudenes, had not stated what the answer of the President would have been had the proposal been made in an unequivocal and straightforward manner—one supposes because the policy of the United States seemed so obvious that no comment was necessary. But, we remember, previous instructions by Jefferson to Carmichael and Short had forbidden them to engage in any guaranty of Spanish possessions in America, either against foreign nations or against domestic rebellion, and had warned them not to purchase what belonged to the United States by right.[42] Pinckney

42. Ante, p. 190.

therefore felt justified in taking steps effectually to
put an end to Godoy's expectations for an alliance and
mutual guaranty of territorial integrity. In the first
conference at San Ildefonso he told the Duke emphat-
ically that he was not authorized to insert in any treaty
a guaranty of Spanish possessions in America.[43]

With this declaration the Duke appeared much mortified,
conceiving, as was natural, that the proposals, though informally
made, had been considered and rejected by our Government. I
then proceeded to state how ready the United States were to
enter into every other friendly stipulation, and urged the arguments that occurred to me for an immediate settlement of the
points in controversy; the result was that he promised to proceed
with me in our negotiations concerning the limits, etc., without
the guarantee. I urged the fixing a day to proceed to the business,
which he said was impossible, as he wished some further information. This, however, not immediately taking place, I requested,
in three or four days, another conference, in which he still urged
that he was not prepared, but said that he would very shortly
enter into the business; and, from his conversation, I collected
that he had really been looking into the subject.

Now the great news was publicly known. On August
3 a copy of the secret treaty with France arrived at
Court. It was immediately ratified and sent back to
Paris. Four days later the end of the French war was
announced in Madrid. In the streets of the city sedate
old men embraced each other with joy. The populace

43. "This administration proposed to our government by their
chargé d'affaires in Philadelphia a close alliance and mutual guarantee
of our territorys in America. Our Secretary of State sent these proposals to Mr. Short, but without any instructions either to him or to
me on the subject. I have declined acceding to the proposal and the
minister has proceeded to treat with me on the subject of the Mississippi
and limits in which he promises we shall meet with little difficulty.
At his desire I have proposed to him the project of a treaty on these
subjects and commerce but nothing definite is yet done." Pinckney
to Monroe, Aug. 28, 1795, Pinckney Papers, Spain, 127.

was delirious with happiness.[44] Godoy received from a grateful, supine monarch the title of Principe de la Paz. But it was necessary to face the English.[45]

Godoy hastened to prepare the Spanish Ambassador at London to encounter the protests of that Government. The motives for continuing the war no longer existed, he explained; no advantages had come to Spain since hostilities had been declared; the country had been overwhelmed with disasters; the King must now look to the welfare of his own subjects.[46] Standing

44. Short to Sec. of State, No. 206, Madrid, Aug. 9, 1795, Despatches, W. Short, Madrid, 96.

45. "The court had received the first copy of this treaty by the messenger who arrived here some days ago from Basle and was re-despatched immediately with the ratification. The intention of the Minister was not to let this get into public until the ratifications should have been exchanged and the treaty thus ratified received here. [Actually, the treaty had already been ratified by France, on the 29th of July.] He has been disappointed in the manner above mentioned [i.e., announcement of the treaty by the French General, Moncey, to the Spanish commanding officer on the enemy's lines]. The secret of the real place and manner of the negotiations has been hitherto conducted by him with a good deal of address. As he knew many eyes were upon him, he seems to have adopted a plan of directing their view to several places at the same time in order to *dépayser*— accordingly not only Iriarte, but d'Iranda, Ocaris, and a secret or supposed agent at Paris for some time divided the attention of the Arguses [sic] placed here to watch the Duke—they have been completely blinded by him and certainly far from expecting this event at present. The most unequivocal proof of this surprize exists here." Short to Pinckney, Madrid, Aug. 10, 1794, Short Papers, XXIX, 5339.

"I should have liked to have been a witness yesterday morning of the audience of the English Ambassador, and am very sorry you passed it over [i.e., Pinckney's letter of August 9, to which Short was replying, did not mention this]. I think there must have been a good deal of embarrassment on both sides." Same to same, same date, ibid., 5241. For Godoy's elaborate dissimulation in regard to the negotiation of the secret peace of Basle, see Baumgarten, *Geschichte Spaniens*, I, 74.

46. Godoy to Del Campo, S. Ildefonso, Aug. 5, 1795, A. G. C., Leg., 8150 (L. C. trans.).

before the imagined vengeance of Great Britain, Godoy hastened to clinch the friendship of the United States.

The day following the public announcement of the peace, Godoy told Pinckney that their business would be settled speedily to their joint satisfaction, since His Majesty was determined to sacrifice something of what he considered his right, in order to testify his good will to the United States. At a meeting of the Council of State of August 14, 1795, it was decided to proceed with the United States on the basis of conceding the right of navigation of the Mississippi and yielding the boundary of 31°, and this without an accompanying alliance or mutual guaranty of territory. "His Majesty would have left in those and other parts of America," said Godoy, "possessions, peoples and rights of great importance and sufficient for our commerce and navigation." [47]

The nervous Prince of the Peace was cowering before the anticipated vengeance of a deserted ally which already had contracted with the United States a mysterious treaty that had all the earmarks of a definite understanding which might be used against Spain in America, possibly to force open the navigation of the Mississippi and to wrest away her vast and vacant provinces north of Mexico.[48] "Everything is to be

47. Actas del Supremo Consejo de Estado, Aug. 14, 1795, A. H. N., Est.

48. Godoy in his *Memoirs* (II, 2, of the English edition of 1836), adduces the activity of the English fur-traders on the upper Missouri as one of the reasons which made him fear the British menace in Louisiana. This was the subject of considerable discussion in the Council, at which reports on the subject were read, but not until several months after the signature of the treaty with the United States. See Actas del Supremo Consejo de Estado, May 27, 1796. For brief sketch of early Spanish activity on the upper Missouri and rivalry with British traders in that region, see F. J. Teggart in *Am. Hist. Assoc. Ann. Rept., 1908*, I, 183; and A. P. Nasatir in *Miss. Vall. Hist. Rev.*, XVI (1929–1930), 359–382, 507–528.

feared," the Spanish Ambassador at London reported September 18, after noting England's reaction to the Peace of Basle and her great preparations for launching a campaign in America.[49] This confirmed Godoy's own fears. Far more than at any previous time it appeared to him necessary for the sake of Spain's overseas possessions, stripped bare by the recent European war of effective military defense, to conciliate the American republic. More troops than ever would be needed at home after the peace, he had some time previously prophesied to the Council, in order to defend the peninsula itself and to insure protection against possible risings of Spanish radicals.[50] The costly reinforcements for which Carondelet had been pleading for the defense of Louisiana and the Floridas could not be spared.[51]

Pinckney now began to see the light. "My present opinion is, that the new position of Spain with respect to England will induce them to come to a decision with us," he wrote to Randolph.

The Prince of the Peace actively and earnestly began to negotiate. With the Mississippi Question and the boundary conceded by Spain, the biggest difficulties had disappeared. Pinckney pressed Godoy at first for a treaty of commerce with reciprocal rights of nationals in all the domains of each party. It was soon evident that Spain would make no concessions here; by virtue of her existing treaties, to open up her colonial ports to the United States would be to open them up *ipso facto* to all European nations who enjoyed most-fa-

49. A. G. C., Est. Leg., 8150 (L. C. trans.).

50. Actas del Supremo Consejo de Estado, Dec. 29, 1794, A. H. N., Est.

51. In 1795, in addition to his other huge estimates, Carondelet wanted $200,000 for Kentucky alone, and $100,000 a year for Indians, to say nothing of heavy increases of military expenses. Serrano y Sanz, *El Brigadier Jaime Wilkinson*, 73–75.

vored-nation privileges. Pinckney therefore forbore to push this point further. The two principal issues which remained were the adjustment of spoliations and the arrangement of the article for fixing the free navigation of the Mississippi. We have seen that Pinckney had instructions to get an agreement on principles for reparation for spoliations and then to set up a mixed commission to adjudicate them. Concerning the navigation question, his instructions, like those of his predecessors, cautioned him to avoid, if possible, accepting the navigation of the Mississippi as a *grant* from Spain rather than an acknowledgment of a right, and to procure the cession of a port or at least a landing place in Spanish territory near the mouth of the river for transshipment of goods from river boats to ocean-going vessels.

On the question of the spoliations Pinckney, taking advantage of the fact that Godoy in his verbal concessions to Short had accepted the definition of neutral rights in the Franco-American treaty of 1778, urged the Prince to accept the principles of the Armed Neutrality of 1780 as the basis of assessing damages to American neutral shipping by Spanish armed vessels. Godoy absolutely refused to do this or even to admit that his declaration to Short had any retroactive force applying to spoliations occurring before the date of that declaration, April 6, 1795. On this point he would not yield. This was not settled until the final conference of the two men preceding signature of the treaty. On the Mississippi Question Pinckney held out for a right of deposit at the mouth of the river and tried to write the whole navigation article in such a way as to imply a recognition of American right. On August 15 Pinckney presented the sketch of a proposed treaty of friendship, commerce, and navigation, with a separate article on the navigation of the Mississippi, which it is desirable to quote, in its English translation from the French:

That the navigation of the Mississippi be recognized as free to both nations, and all facilities for its use [*pour la rendre utile*] be mutually accorded.

Godoy asked for a full-length draft of a treaty. Negotiations on the details of the draft consumed the next four weeks. On September 18 Godoy returned a counterdraft, which left out the articles of commerce, omitted mention of a deposit, and rejected Pinckney's wording of the navigation article. In return Pinckney let go the commercial articles, at first proposing that the matter of a treaty of commerce be left to be drafted later by a mixed commission, each government enjoying, reciprocally, most-favored-nation privileges meanwhile.[52] Eventually he relinquished even this, but he insisted on the right of deposit, and objected strenuously to Godoy's wording of the navigation article.[53] He said:

The words *solo et exclusivamente* (alone and exclusively) should be omitted, for Spain could scarcely confide in the good faith of the United States, nor in this convention, which she is about to conclude with them, if they agreed to an article which would be an infraction of another treaty, previously made. Now, by the treaty of peace between the United States and Great Britain,

52. For Pinckney's Sketch and his proposed articles, see Appendix III at end of this volume.

53. I have not been able to locate Pinckney's full draft, nor Godoy's counterdraft, either in Spain, in the U. S. State Department, in the Pinckney Papers, or in the Short Papers. Pinckney's "Sketch," and proposed articles are given hereafter in Appendix III. Pinckney's comments on Godoy's draft, but not Godoy's draft itself, are printed in *A. S. P., F. R.*, I.

concluded in 1783, it is stipulated that the navigation of the
River Mississippi shall continue free to the subjects of Great
Britain and the citizens of the United States. It appears that the
following provision would have all the desired effect: "It is
nevertheless agreed, that nothing contained in this article shall
be construed or interpreted, to communicate the right of navigating this river, to other nations or persons, than to the subjects
of His Catholic Majesty and the citizens of the United States."

It is highly important to notice that this qualification,
desired by Pinckney to remove a contravention of the
Mississippi article of the treaty of peace between the
United States and Great Britain of 1783, was not written into the final treaty with Spain.

In reply to Godoy's neglect to include an article providing for the right of deposit, Pinckney, demanding
such a stipulation, argued that the United States was
entitled to more than that; he asked for an outright
cession of a plot of ground on the lower river. He
maintained that the right to the navigation of the Mis-
sissisppi had now been accepted as incontestably proven.
Without a right to land and transship goods within
Spanish territory at the mouth of the river, the acknowledged right, he asserted, would be "illusory, without utility, and without effect." If the port of deposit
were granted, he intimated, his Government would
not press its perfectly good claim for large damages
already sustained by the twelve years' interruption of
that navigation right.

Godoy sent Pinckney a brief note October 7, assuming that, as a result of their discussions, the treaty
was closed, and asked that it be signed forthwith.
Pinckney refused to sign without securing what he
termed "one of the principal objects of his mission,"
the right of deposit, and he suggested some other small
revisions in the articles of the treaty draft which had

been already accepted by both in principle. It was at this time, too, that he made a last attempt to get Godoy to accept the principles of the Franco-American treaty of 1778, or the Armed Neutrality of 1780, as the rules for adjudication of spoliation cases. As to the right of deposit, Pinckney had offered to accept, pending a future agreement on the place of such a depot, that citizens of the United States should have the right of depositing their goods, free of duty charge, in the New Orleans customs house, to which the owners of the deposited goods were to have a key, with another key for the proper Spanish official. Godoy offered to allow this, without granting a key for the American owners of the deposited goods. The question of deposit and the rules for adjudication of spoliation still remained the only issues which prevented the completion of the negotiation. Godoy refused any cession of a place of deposit, or even to mention the matter of deposit in the main body of the treaty. His furthest concession was to promise to propose to His Majesty that, in a separate convention, the United States be given a facility of deposit at New Orleans pending further arrangements.[54] Pinckney refused this. Godoy answered, October 20, that he could not vary in the least what he had already said concerning the deposit, observing that His Majesty would look into the means by which the navigation of the Mississippi could increase the commerce of his subjects and of the citizens of the United States. Pinckney still refused to budge.

Short had been called by Pinckney to San Ildefonso from Madrid, for consultation on points brought up in the draft projects. In October, the Court moved

54. Pinckney to Short, San Lorenzo, Oct. 11, 1795, Short Papers, XXX, 5307.

to San Lorenzo, its autumnal residence, and Short retired to Madrid, close at hand, where he was kept informed by Pinckney of the progress of the negotiation. Short now advised Pinckney to take some vigorous and decisive step on the question of deposit, which would reveal the real intentions of the Spanish Government.[55] Pinckney decided to do this and to make the right of deposit a *sine qua non*. On October 24, 1795, he therefore asked for his passports, on the assumption that the negotiation had failed. It was no bluff. His correspondence with Short shows he was determined to leave if they had been handed to him.[56] He resolved to stake everything to get the right of deposit. It was a bold and daring move, and successful. Godoy capitulated. Another conference was held the next day at which an agreement was reached. Pinckney accepted a mixed commission, without prior agreement on rules of international law, for adjudication of the spoliations. Godoy on his side consented to the principle of *permitting* the *privilege* of deposit for three years at New Orleans with the liberty of continuing it at the expiration of that period, if another equal establishment

55. "I observe the minister's promise as to the depot at N. Orleans. I have no doubt he would come into it notwithstanding his manner of holding off, and you will recollect I expressed this opinion at the Cruz de Malta. I have no doubt either that if such a view of the whole subject could be pressed upon him, and such alternatives could be presented to him as might be done by our Government, that he might be brought further in the line we wish him to walk in. I should prefer therefore infinitely the idea you mentioned of getting the ultimatum of this Court and sending it forward to our Government, letting this Government have no hope at the same time from anything the Envoy of the United States should say or do, that the views of the United States were within that ultimatum, so as to leave them free to extend their views as far as they should judge convenient or proper. This Government will certainly give as little as they can. . . ." Short to Pinckney, Madrid, Oct. 13, 1795, Short Papers, XXX, 5312.

56. Pinckney to Short, Oct. 23, 1795, ibid., 5334.

should not be granted elsewhere on the river upon the expiration of that period.[57]

The treaty was signed on October 27, 1795, at San Lorenzo, the village which nestles at the foot of the southern slopes of the Guadarramas, where the cathedral and palace of the Escorial rise against the somber background of the mountains and stand gloomy guard over the tombs of the Kings of Spain. A mighty ruler of empire built it. Could the great Philip II, seated there by his palace on his chair of stone and gazing as was his wont of a summer evening out across the baked and sterile plains to the distant spires of his capital— could that powerful monarch, ruling in three continents, with his galleons ranging seven seas, ever have imagined that at this very place one day an upstart court adventurer, rising by his amorous intrigues with a Queen of Spain over the ruin of able ministers, would sign such a fateful treaty? That proud King slept mercifully on in the still depths of the royal sepulchre beneath the heavy pile of the Escorial. A new state, also undreamed of by him, had arisen across the Atlantic. Thanks to Europe's convulsions it was able to declare and secure its independence and to achieve its territorial integrity

---

57. "You were right in your conjecture, my dear Sir; the negotiation has been again brought forward and is newly determined—the two points on which we before divided were the facilities of navigation and the spoliations. On the first we have agreed upon N. Orleans for 3 years paying only storage, but this permission to be continued unless an equal establishment is assigned elsewhere on the Mississippi. The principle of the British treaty for reference to Commissioners is agreed upon for the spoliations. We only wait for the wording of this article to be agreed on all points. It gives much concern to be apprised that this arrangement will not be approved by you. I can only say that a sense of duty on mature reflexion has induced me to accede to these terms;—if I have erred it has been clearly with my eyes open. . . ." Pinckney to Short, San Lorenzo, Oct. 25, 1795, Short Papers, XXX, 5339.

—more than that, to take that first step in a career of expansion which was to witness, in our own times, the extinction of the last American vestige of that vast colonial empire over which the son of the Emperor Charles V once held sway.

A few days before Pinckney had brought the negotiation to a head by asking for his passports, that is on October 19, he was informed by the Spanish Government of the occupation of Barrancas de Margot (Chickasaw Bluffs, present Memphis, Tenn.) by a Spanish detachment following a rumor that American settlers had designed to occupy Muscle Shoals on the Tennessee.[58] After the treaty was signed Godoy delivered a note to the American envoy stating that this place, "comprehended within our ancient limits," had been occupied at the order of the Governor of Natchez, after having heard of the intention of inhabitants of Kentucky and neighboring states to occupy Muscle Shoals, and that as a consequence of the new treaty of friendship, limits, and navigation having now been signed, orders had been sent out to the Governor of Natchez to suspend all hostilities, in case any should have occurred between him and the citizens of the United States, "leaving matters in the situation in which they may be on the receipt of the order until the ratification of the treaty." Further, the Governors of the two Floridas (Louisiana was not mentioned) had been enjoined to maintain the most complete harmony with the commanders of the troops of the United States on their frontiers; and it was hoped that the President of the United States would expedite the issue of similar orders on his part.[59]

58. Same to same, Oct. 19, 1795, ibid., 5324.
59. Where not otherwise indicated by footnotes, this narrative on Pinckney's negotiations in Spain follows his printed despatches in

Pinckney, his mules and carriage waiting for him at Madrid, and his pockets full of Spanish concessions, proceeded immediately and triumphantly to London. Soon afterwards he resigned his regular post there and returned home to take his chances, on the strength of his newly acquired prestige, in the presidential campaign of 1796. The disappointed Short, with difficulty nursing his bitterness to himself, accompanied Pinckney on the long ride as far as Paris.[60] He had now resigned from the service forever. Thus ended the history, so far as the foreign service is concerned, of our first "career diplomatist." [61] The maladroit Jaudenes was recalled by Godoy. We hear no more of him in the annals of Spanish diplomacy. As his successor in what was hoped to be a time of better days between the two governments, there went out to Philadelphia as regular minister of Spain to the United States, the Marques de Casa Yrujo, who during the next eleven years was to play so important a role in Spanish-American affairs.[62]

A. S. P., F. R., I, 538–549. The files of the State Department contain little else than what is printed, and nothing of significance not contained in *A. S. P., F. R.,* I. Some additional material, from the Pinckney Papers, has been cited.

60. Pinckney's secretary, Charles Rutledge, son of the Chief Justice of South Carolina, was left at Madrid as *locum tenens.* David Humphreys, former Minister at Lisbon, was transferred to Madrid, in 1796.

61. During the last months of Jefferson's Administration as President, Short was nominated as United States Minister to Russia. The Senate rejected his nomination. Through no demerit of his own, the unlucky Short had fallen victim to the anti-administration opposition in the last weeks of Jefferson's term of office, when objection to the obnoxious embargo was rising so high. See Professor Charles E. Hill's study of James Madison as Secretary of State in the Knopf series, *The American Secretaries of State and Their Diplomacy,* Vol. III.

62. He had been a secretary in the Spanish embassy at London in 1786; in the Netherlands, 1789; in the Foreign Office at Madrid, 1789–1793; and secretary of the embassy in London, 1793–1795.

These latter conferences between Pinckney and Godoy, on the question of spoliations and the matter of deposit, consumed about five weeks. There seems at this time to have been no studied effort on Godoy's part to delay the negotiation. The difficult points were settled with reasonable celerity, considering the normal methods of Spanish diplomacy and the journeyings of the Spanish Court, which made three distinct and separate moves during Pinckney's brief sojourn in Spain. But the investigator, in following the negotiation as it is preserved in the sources which have come down to us, cannot help but feel a sense of almost dramatic suspense. What if the actual text of Jay's Treaty had arrived in Spain before Pinckney signed with Godoy! What if Godoy, before setting his name to a document which marks the initial disaster in a career which was to be full of great mistakes, had discovered that after all the articles of Jay's Treaty were not so formidable as he had imagined! Would he then have been alarmed at the conception of an Anglo-American understanding and a possible military combination directed at Louisiana and the Floridas? Would he have made the enormous concessions which he made? If Jay's Treaty had been known *in its full text* in Spain would Pinckney's triumph have been possible?

NOTE

This study assumes that the *full* text of Jay's Treaty was not known by the Spanish Government until after the treaty of San Lorenzo was signed on October 27, 1795.

Professor Arthur P. Whitaker has disputed this assumption most learnedly in several publications: *The Spanish-American Frontier, 1763–1795* (Boston, 1927); "New Light on the Treaty of San Lorenzo; An Essay in Historical Criticism," *Miss. Vall. Hist. Rev.*, XV (March, 1929), 435–454;

"Godoy's Knowledge of Jay's Treaty," *A. H. R.*, XXXV (July, 1930), 804–810. In the following comments I have profited by some of his corrections without being fully convinced by his evidence and arguments.

In a controversy which arose over the inconsistency of the maritime articles of Pinckney's Treaty with those of Jay's Treaty, Casa Yrujo, the Spanish Minister at Philadelphia, complained that after signing the treaty of 1795 with the United States the Spanish Government had been surprised to read Jay's Treaty with England with its contrary maritime articles. Timothy Pickering, then (May 17, 1797) Secretary of State, argued as follows with Yrujo: "That [treaty] with Great Britain was concluded on the 19th day of November, 1794; and that with Spain on the 27th of October, 1795. Further, the treaty with Great Britain was published in Philadelphia on the first day of July, 1795; almost four months before the treaty with His Catholic Majesty was concluded; and nearly ten months before it received its ratification, at which time (Spain and the United States being then at peace with the World) it does not appear that His Catholic Majesty found the smallest difficulty in giving his final sanction to his treaty with the United States, on account of their prior treaty with Great Britain. Moreover, Mr. Thomas Pinckney, who negotiated the treaty with Spain, being privy to the whole negotiation with Great Britain, and perfectly acquainted with every article of the British treaty, it is hardly to be doubted, that he communicated to the Prince of Peace [*sic*] every information concerning it which had any relation to his negotiation with Spain." (*A. S. P., F. R.*, II, 16). The implication here is that the Prince of the Peace must have learned from Pinckney of such terms of Jay's Treaty as concerned the Spanish negotiation. Exactly what terms did and exactly what terms did not so concern the Spanish negotiation is not vouchsafed by Pickering. There is nothing in Pinckney's correspondence with the State Department to suggest that he apprised the Prince of any of the terms of the British

treaty; but in the Pinckney Papers in the South Carolina
Historical Society is a copy of a letter from Pinckney to
Godoy, dated September 25, 1795 (after it became known
that Jay's Treaty had been ratified in America), conveying
the following extract from Jay's Treaty: "Nothing in this
treaty contained shall however be construed to operate
contrary to any former or existing treaty." This is the true
sense but not the precise language of the corresponding sentence in Jay's Treaty. It is apparently all that Pinckney
divulged, so far as his official correspondence reveals. Dr.
Whitaker has published an autographed letter of Pinckney,
written September 26, 1795, from San Ildefonso to William
Short, which found its way (apparently intercepted) into
the Archives of the Indies in Seville, in which Pinckney
said, "I . . . return herewith the American newspapers and
request you to lend me the other set. Mr. Jay's Treaty I
find has made impressions here very unfavorable to our
negotiations." He thinks this means that "the Spanish
Court has seen the text of Jay's Treaty." It may indeed suggest that very strongly, but it is also susceptible of different
meanings, one of which might be that the Spanish Court
knew about the treaty but not necessarily its text.

Secretary of State Pickering made a more categorical
statement on January 22, 1798, in a report transmitted by
President Adams to Congress on the delays in the execution
of the treaty. "What I supposed probable [on May 17, 1797].
. . . I am now authorized to assert [italics inserted] . . .
that when the treaty between the United States and Spain
was negotiated by Mr. Pinckney with the Prince of Peace,
the latter was furnished with an entire copy of the treaty
of amity, commerce and navigation between Great Britain
and the United States: consequently it is, to the last degree,
preposterous for the Spanish government now to complain
that the treaty with Great Britain rejected the principle
'free ships made free goods' or that it extends the list of
contraband, with a perfect knowledge of the articles of
the British treaty, on these points, if the Spanish govern-

ment had any objections to make, this was the time. . . .
The same observations will apply to the question governing
the navigation of the Mississippi." (*A. S. P., F. R.,* II, 83).
This last statement of Pickering, to Congress, is the strongest
evidence we have that Godoy had seen the text of Jay's
Treaty before he signed with Pinckney, but note its studied
language: "I am authorized to assert." Presumably it was
Thomas Pinckney who authorized him to assert, because
Pinckney was then a member of Congress in Philadelphia
and had spoken in the House of Representatives only three
days previously. Pinckney could have "authorized" Pickering "to assert" this to Congress all he wanted to, but that
did not mean it was strictly true; in other words, Pickering's
assertion may have been a finesse; he never made such a
direct assertion to the Spanish Government.

When first I began this study it appeared to me certain
that Godoy must have known the text of Jay's Treaty. The
treaty was published in Philadelphia on July 1 and known
to Monroe in Paris about August 15, 1795 (*Writings of Monroe,* II, 339). Pinckney had an American newspaper with the
text, in September (Pinckney Papers). But the despatches
of the Foreign Office in Madrid from London and Paris
which are endorsed before October 27, 1795, do not contain copies of the treaty. For fear I had overlooked something while personally examining the archives in Madrid,
before publishing the first printing of this book in 1926 I
asked Dr. Whitaker to inspect the London and Paris despatches for evidence on this question, during the course
of his researches in Spain. He informed me that he found
no evidence that the text of the treaty reached the Spanish
Government before it decided to yield the two principal
points (boundary and Mississippi navigation) to the United
States. (See *A. H. R.,* XXXII, 675.) He was also good enough
to have copied for me the two despatches from the Spanish
embassy at London which mentioned Jay's Treaty. One of
these was the despatch of Del Campo, of November 21, 1794,
mentioned above, p. 228, which told very little, except to

mention evacuation of frontier posts and arrangements for West Indian-commerce. The other was that of Del Campo's successor, Las Casas, of December 22, 1795, following the exchange of ratifications of the British-American treaty. He sent a copy which had just been printed in London, and commented: "Basically and fundamentally the stipulations of the general treaty of peace of 1783 now establish for both parties in articles III and IV, of which I enclose a copy, the free use of the Mississippi. And although it ought to be supposed that communication to the Court of Spain and the consent thereof had preceded this (in the case of England because of the intimate alliance in which she was then living with her [Spain], and in the case of the Americans by consequence of their reiterated professions exclusively to the King our master), it is to be noted that no such circumstance is mentioned in any part of the treaty. I send a copy in English, having none in French. In all the American provinces [states] every article has been much discussed. Here it has been kept secret, it being all the while imagined that it would not be carried into effect because of the resistance of the Americans to its ratification." On the margin is the comment, presumably of Godoy: "February 26, 1796; The King has already taken precautions with respect to the perfidious treaties of the English." (A. H. N., Est. Leg., 4231).

It is significant, though not conclusive, that in the Spanish declaration of war on England, October 7, 1796, it was stated as one of the causes of the war (in addition to the British naval activity in the Mediterranean and Caribbean in 1793 and 1794) that: "The English Ministry evinced equal bad faith by keeping a profound silence respecting its negotiations with other powers, namely, the treaty concluded on the 19th November 1794 with the United States of America, without any regard or consideration for my well-known rights."

The Spanish despatches from Paris, when resumed after the re-establishment of diplomatic relations, do not mention the treaty, although Monroe had received Philadelphia newspapers containing the text by the middle of August, 1795. In France, however, protest was postponed until after the actual ratification of that document, and the voting of the required appropriations by the House. There must have been American newspapers at that time in France containing the text. The re-establishment of good communications between France and Spain, however, did not occur immediately after the exchange of ratifications of the peace of Basle. Iriarte, negotiator of the peace of Basle, was appointed ambassador at Paris, but died too soon to take his post. His successor did not establish himself until April, 1796. (R. Guyot, *Le Directoire et la paix de l'Europe,* 233; and F. P. Renaut, *La Question de la Louisiane,* 18.)

Randolph gave to Jaudenes a copy of Article III, the Mississippi article, on July 1, the day after Senator Mason gave to the public the text of the treaty. Jaudenes promptly sent a printed copy of the full treaty to Godoy, July 2. Date of receipt of this despatch is not endorsed. The next batch of despatches of Jaudenes, sending another copy and elaborating on the significance of the treaty, which batch was dated July 29, did not arrive in Madrid until December, if we are to go by endorsements. Godoy did not answer any of these despatches until December. In the first printing of this book, I said that I assumed, without being able to prove it *absolutely,* that the July 2 despatch did not get to Madrid until after October 27.

That the treaty had been ratified by the United States Senate was known in Madrid, in September, by accounts from London, but its full text does not appear to have been known. The September number of the *Mercurio de España,* printed under its London news an announcement of the ratification of the pact by the United States, and the text of Article XII, the excised article. The *Gazeta de Madrid* for October 20, 1795, under a London dateline of September 5, also mentioned this news of ratification as having been received from America. Without mentioning the text of the treaty it declared that the treaty had stirred up a great deal of opposition, and that: "In Charleston a great number of citizens assembled to determine whether the said treaty was prejudicial to the honor of the United States, dangerous to its existence, or destructive to its commerce, manufactures, navigation and agriculture. It was the general opinion that the treaty was equivalent to a humble recognition of dependence of the United States on the King of Great Britain, and an abandonment of rights and privileges which could not in the future be enjoyed except by the grace and consent of the King." All this evidence convinced me that Godoy still lacked precise information of the full terms of Jay's Treaty when he signed the one with Pinckney. Further, it seemed inconceivable that he could have made such a surrender had he known that the Anglo-American treaty was so harmless or that he could have accepted, had he the text of Jay's Treaty before him, such a one-sided spoliations article (see note 7, Chapter 13). Why then did the King of Spain exchange ratifications of the treaty, April 25, 1796, having in the meantime received the text of Jay's Treaty? To argue that he had already pledged to it perhaps may not be impressive. France in 1796 was drifting into difficulties with the United States as a result of Jay's Treaty. It would not have been politic for Spain, as France's prospective ally, to tempt a war with the United States, at a time when she was likely to have an English one on her hands soon; in that case Louisiana would have possibly been lost to Great Britain. The execution of the ratified treaty was deferred, as we shall see in the following chapter, but this very reason just mentioned was responsible for Spain's finally executing the treaty in 1798.

Dr. Whitaker has concluded that Godoy in fact did possess the text of Jay's Treaty when he signed with Pinckney. In his *Spanish-American Frontier, 1763–1795* (p. 206) he states positively that "Godoy had a copy of it [Jay's Treaty] in his possession a full month before he signed with Pinckney." In "New Light on the Treaty of San Lorenzo; an Essay in Historical Criticism," *Miss. Vall. Hist. Rev.*, XV, 435–454, he argues plausibly that "in all human probability" a

Philadelphia newspaper of July 1, 1795, containing a full text of Jay's Treaty was in Godoy's hands before he signed the treaty with Pinckney, among other reasons because, as he shows, nineteen out of twenty Spanish despatches (of those endorsed with date of receival or perusal—numerous other despatches were not so endorsed) during 1793–1795 got through from Philadelphia to Madrid in less than sixteen weeks, which was the time elapsed between July 2, 1795, when Jaudenes despatched the printed Jay's Treaty to Godoy, and October 27, when Pinckney and Godoy signed their treaty. This however does not conclusively prove that this particular unendorsed despatch of July 2, 1795, with its enclosure, the printed Jay's Treaty, reached Madrid before October 27. Dr. Whitaker shows that one of those twenty despatches, and that one sent in this very same month of July, 1795, took more than sixteen weeks. Others, impossible to trace (because not endorsed), may also have taken more time. In a note in *A. H. R.,* XXXV, 804–810, on "Godoy's Knowledge of the Terms of Jay's Treaty," Dr. Whitaker introduces two previously unexploited documents from Spanish archives to prove his point. One is a memoir, drawn up by a subordinate in the Spanish foreign office, which states explicitly that at the time of the negotiation with Pinckney the Spanish Government knew that Jay's Treaty had been concluded but "was ignorant of the content of its articles." On this memoir Godoy autographed instructions for a note to be directed to the French Ambassador at Madrid detailing Spain's grievances against the United States in order that France and Spain might protest together. The other document is the actual note, drawn off at Godoy's direction from the memoir, to the French Ambassador, of December 15, 1796, in Madrid, which declares that when His Majesty concluded the treaty with the United States he knew of Jay's Treaty and that Pinckney's Treaty was so framed as to frustrate Article III [the Mississippi navigation article] of that treaty. This note said (according to a French translation which Dr. Whitaker

found in the French archives): "When His Majesty concluded his treaty with the United States on October 27,
1795, he already knew that they had signed with the English
on November 19, 1794, and the difficulties which opposed
its ratification. In order to prevent the effect of Article 3
of the said treaty of 1794 in which the English assured themselves the liberty to navigate the Mississippi that they had
contracted in the one of 1783, His Majesty agreed in Article
4 of that of 1795. . . ." This by no means stultifies, as Dr.
Whitaker believes, the evidence of the memoir from which
it was drawn off; rather it supports my argument that the
full text of the treaty was not known. Dr. Whitaker regards
the memoir, at first blush such conclusive evidence that the
Spanish Government did not know the text of Jay's Treaty,
to be under analysis merely a "useful fiction,"—just as I
suspect Pickering's statement of May 17, 1797, cited at the
beginning of this note, to be a finesse.

The interested reader should not fail to consult Dr. Whitaker's arguments in detail. With due respect and admiration
for this scholar's accomplished erudition, I do not believe
that he has proven unquestionably that Godoy had available the full text of Jay's Treaty when he signed with
Pinckney.

It is unlikely, though not impossible, that indisputable
evidence may be turned up in the future to prove that
Godoy did know the full terms of the treaty. In that case
it would appear surprising to me that he should have signed
such articles with Pinckney, but it might still be explained
that, even though knowing that Jay's Treaty (provided it
had no secret articles) was not an alliance with Great Britain
or anything approaching such, it nevertheless in Godoy's
mind cleared up the issues between the two English-speaking
countries and prepared the way for a possible and dreaded
Anglo-American combination against Spain and Spanish
colonies—to secure for the United States New Orleans, and
the navigation of the Mississippi which was recognized in
Jay's Treaty, and for Great Britain, possibly, the province

of Louisiana and the recovery of the Floridas. In this connection it should be borne in mind that from 1797 to 1800
relations between the United States and Great Britain were
very close; and that Alexander Hamilton was plotting with
Miranda, apparently with the support of Pitt, for the revolution and possible conquest of South America in case of
war between the United States and·France which might
involve France's new ally, Spain.

CHAPTER 13

Conclusion

It is unlikely that any treaty ever agreed to by the United States, aside from that of peace and independence, has been accepted with more general satisfaction and approval by the country than that of San Lorenzo. Since we have spent so much time and space in explaining the history of the negotiations which led to this treaty, we are justified in a somewhat detailed analysis of its articles,[1] and comment thereon.

After the declaration of amity in Article I, it is stipulated in Article II that the southern boundary of the United States "shall be designated by a line beginning on the River Mississippi at the Northernmost part of the thirty first degree of latitude North of the Equator, which from thence shall be drawn due East to the middle of the River Apalachicola or Catahouche, thence along the middle thereof to its junction with the Flint, thence straight to the head of St. Mary's River, and thence down the middle thereof to the Atlantic Ocean." All garrisons and troops of either party within the territory of the other should be evacuated within six months or sooner after the ratification of the treaty, they being permitted to take with them all their "goods and effects." This stipulation coincided exactly with the contention of the United States for the boundary line of the Anglo-American treaty of 1783. It must

1. For official English and Spanish text of the treaty, see Appendix V to this volume.

be regarded as a great Spanish concession, for the claim of Spain to territory south of the line of the Yazoo was stronger than that of the United States. It was a complete recognition of one of the principal American issues.

The joint survey of this line, to be undertaken within six months of the ratification by surveyors to meet at Natchez, and to be escorted if desired by joint military detachments of equal strength, was provided for by Article III.

The Mississippi navigation article (Article IV), which was phrased only after much study and labor, must be quoted entire:

It is likewise agreed that the Western boundary of the United States which separates them from the Spanish Colony of Louissiana, is in the middle of the channel or bed of the River Mississippi from the Northern boundary of the said States to the completion of the thirty first degree of latitude North of the Equator; and his Catholic Majesty has likewise agreed that the navigation of the said River in its whole breadth from its source to the Occean shall be free only to his Subjects, and the Citizens of the United States, unless he should extend this privilege to the Subjects of other Powers by special convention.

Was this a recognition of right or a grant by the King of Spain to the United States? The language in itself is fairly clear as stipulating a restricted grant. We have observed how Pinckney strove in vain to insert another formula devised to reserve the contention of the United States to a right to navigation of the river. He was not able to insist upon the sentence which he had proposed: "It is nevertheless agreed, that nothing contained in this article shall be construed or interpreted, to communicate the right of navigating this river to other nations or persons, than to the subjects of His Catholic Majesty, and to the citizens of the

United States." This would not have denied the claim by other nations or persons to the navigation of the river by virtue of other treaties or circumstances, merely denying such right to flow from the treaty of San Lorenzo. That Pinckney tried to get such a qualification and failed, that he subsequently accepted the article above quoted, is sufficient evidence to the impartial investigator that he gave up a claim to a right and accepted a grant. Timothy Pickering, Secretary of State, made a weak argument in 1797, that the use of the words "His Catholic Majesty has likewise agreed," without repetition of the words, "The United States *and* His Catholic Majesty," as agreeing together, made Spain the *sole party* to the *excluding clause;*[2] but though Pinckney may possibly have comforted himself with mental reservations when accepting this phraseology, it is not impressive. The article as accepted was a direct stultification, as Godoy later correctly argued, of the American argument on which the claim to the navigation of the Mississippi was originally founded, and a contravention of Article VIII of the Treaty of Peace, which had stipulated that the "navigation of the River Mississippi, from its source to the ocean, shall *forever*[3] remain free and open to the subjects of Great Britain and the citizens of the United States"; and of Article III in Jay's Treaty, which repeated the stipulation with the additional provision that all ports and places on the eastern side of the river, to whichsoever party belonging, could be freely resorted to by both parties. To enforce the provision of Pinckney's Treaty, the last signed, and presumably therefore the governing one, would have placed an estoppel on the Missis-

2. *A. S. P., F. R.,* II, 16.
3. Italics inserted.

sippi article of Jay's Treaty. Pinckney knew that well
enough. He had been privy to all the details of Jay's
Treaty. He even showed Godoy the sentence of Jay's
Treaty saying that nothing in it should be construed or
operate contrary to any former or existing treaty. It
was not open dealing. But then Godoy himself was not
noted for open dealing, as the previous chapters of this
volume must have shown.

Jay when in London had not succeeded in putting
into his treaty an article which he had drafted obligat-
ing each party not to make political connections with
the Indians dwelling within the territories of the other;
and to restrain its Indians from hostilities against the
other, and to make common cause, in case of the other
party's being engaged in hostilities with its own Indians, 'to the extent of prohibiting and preventing any
supplies of ammunition or arms from being given or
sold even by Indian traders to such belligerent tribe
or tribes or to any individuals therein.[4] Pinckney succeeded in putting a somewhat similar article (V) into
his treaty, with even stronger provisions: both Spain
and the United States agreed "to restrain by force all
hostilities on the part of the Indian Nations living
within their boundaries: so that Spain will not suffer
her Indians to attack Citizens of the United States, nor
the Indians inhabiting their territory; nor will the
United States permit these last mentioned Indians to
commence hostilities against the Subjects of His Catholic Majesty, or his Indians, in any manner whatever."
This latter provision assumed great significance in subsequent Florida history.

Articles VI, VII, VIII, IX, X, and XI contained the
conventional provisions for protection of vessels of the

4. *Jay's Treaty*, 288.

one party in the territorial waters of the other; protection against embargo or detention for public or private purposes of ships of one party within the jurisdiction of the other; against seizure for debts or crimes without due process of law (an article which assumed importance a century later in the Cuban insurrection); protection of vessels of the one party forced to take refuge in the ports of the other; restoration of property of citizens or subjects of the one party taken by the other party from pirates; mutual assistance to shipwrecked vessels and mariners; disposition of estates of citizens or subjects of one party in the domains of the other. Article XII provided for official descriptive sea-letters and certificates establishing identity of ship and cargo in case of war in which one party should be neutral, the other belligerent. Article XIII, taken from the treaty of 1785 between the United States and Prussia, stipulated that in case of war between the two parties, merchants of one residing within the jurisdiction of the other should be allowed one year in which to collect and transport, inviolate, their merchandise. Article XIV, modeled on all the earlier American treaties, forbade subjects or citizens of the one party to take out privateering commissions from any prince or state with which the other party should be at war.

One of the most interesting portions of the treaty was that containing the articles on neutral rights—Articles XV, XVI, XVII, XVIII. They adopted the principles of the Armed Neutrality, which were mainly also those of the previous treaties of the United States, excepting that just signed with Great Britain which while not relinquishing the principles in theory nevertheless acquiesced for the duration of the war in the British contrary practice. Pinckney, fully cognizant of the articles of Jay's Treaty and their heavy concessions on these points, now put into the Spanish treaty articles conformable to the old creed: free ships make free goods; neutral ships may trade freely from port to port of the enemy, except in contraband of war or to a really blockaded or besieged enemy port—a repudiation of the British Rule of 1756; and a carefully stipulated list of contraband strictly limited to enumerated warlike implements. The contraband article studiously and elaborately listed non-contraband, including as such especially naval stores and provisions, and all else not mentioned in the enumerated list of contraband. Article XVIII restricted the right of search of neutral ships by belligerent cruisers to small boarding parties and provided that the neutral ship should be equipped with sea-letters and certificates, a form for which was declared to be annexed to the treaty.[5]

These were traditionally American articles going back to the model treaty plan of the Continental Congress, the "plan of 1776" and the elaborations on it in the treaties with France (1778), the Netherlands (1782), Sweden (1783), and Prussia (1785), and so inconsistently and purposely omitted from Jay's Treaty of 1794 with Great Britain.

"Consuls shall be reciprocally established with the privileges and powers which those of the most favored Nations enjoy in the Ports where their consuls reside,

5. The forms of ships' passports were conspicuously omitted from both the signed and ratified texts of the treaty. Each government then issued a form of its own; but in 1797 Secretary Pickering and the Marques de Casa Yrujo agreed on forms for the ships of each nation, respectively. A copy of the American form exists in the archives of the Department of State; and one of the Spanish forms is printed in *Colleción de los tratados de paz, alianza, comercio, etc.* (Madrid, 1801), III, 429–431. I am indebted to Mr. Hunter Miller, former Treaty Editor of the Department of State, for this information.

or are permitted to be." So said Article XIX *in toto.*
This shut out American consuls from Spain's colonial
dominions. As to commerce, it was left out except for
the provision in the first paragraph of Article XXII
which provided that the two parties "will in future
give to their mutual commerce all the extension and
favor which the advantage of both Countries may
require." This not only excluded citizens of the United
States along with the subjects of all other countries
from Spain's American colonies, but did not even provide for the most-favored-nation commercial privileges
which were a feature of all other American treaties.
American commerce thus remained at the mercy of any
sudden change in Spanish municipal law; so, reciprocally, did Spanish commerce with the United States.
Because of the one-sidedness of the trade this article
was of greater advantage to Spain than to the United
States. This was one of the reasons why William Short
did not approve of the treaty. Another was because no
entrance for American trade into any of the Spanish
colonies was granted—which Short believed could have
been secured; and still another objection which he had
was that no specific rules for adjudication were laid
down to govern the mixed commission for judgment
on spoliations by Spanish ships of war on American
neutral shipping. By Article XXI this mixed commission, set up according to the machinery for such
established by Jay's Treaty, was to decide "according
to the merits of the several cases, and to justice, equity,
and the laws of Nations." [6] Unlike the rule of the British-
American treaty spoliation mixed commission, cases
brought before this tribunal did not require to have
exhausted the ordinary course of judicial proceedings.

6. See Appendix IV to this volume.

This was a distinct advantage for the United States. If Godoy was negligent in overlooking this point, he was even more careless in not detecting a perfectly good opportunity to place before the same mixed commission the spoliations on Spanish vessels in 1793 by French privateers illegally fitted out in American harbors. Pinckney could hardly have refused to make such an article reciprocal.[7]

The second sentence of Article XXII covered the entrepôt provision. When the compromise concerning this was reached at the eleventh hour of the final negotiation Pinckney wrote Short that "we have agreed upon N. Orleans for 3 years paying only storage, but this permission to be continued unless an equal establishment is assigned elsewhere on the Mississippi." As actually worded this part of the article read:

His' Catholic Majesty will permit the Citizens of the United States for the space of three years from this time to deposit their merchandize and effects in the Port of New Orleans and to export them from thence without paying any other duty than a fair price for the hire of the stores, and his Majesty promises either to continue this permission if he finds during that time that it is not prejudicial to the interests of Spain, or if he should not agree to continue it there, he will assign to them on another part of the banks of the Mississippi an equivalent establishment.

Did the terms of this sentence reserve the right to the King of Spain to revoke the entrepôt *altogether* at the expiration of three years, if he found during those three years it had been prejudicial to the interests of Spain? The reader may see for himself, by consulting the original English and Spanish texts of the treaty,

7. That Godoy permitted these points to escape him is another very strong argument to show that he could not have known the text of Jay's Treaty.

in Appendix V of this volume, that it was somewhat ambiguous on this point.

Finally, the last article (XXIII), concerning ratifications, should be noticed. Pinckney's powers authorized him to sign and to send the treaty to the United States for ratification by the President by and with the advice and consent of the Senate. This article textually ignored the Senate:

The present treaty shall not be in force untill ratified by the contracting Parties, and the ratifications shall be exchanged in six months, or sooner if possible.

A treaty such as this encountered no opposition in the Senate! It was immediately and unanimously ratified, as soon as submitted, and returned forthwith to Spain, where ratifications were exchanged, April 25, 1796, barely within the allowed six months.

The treaty was not so promptly executed. The history of the long, unpleasant, and highly involved chapter of bickerings over its execution must be told very briefly. The delay was due principally to two things: Governor Carondelet's pursuit of the Wilkinson intrigue; and the incompatibility of the terms of Jay's British treaty with those of Pinckney's Spanish one, together with the realization in Spain that after all the terms of Jay's Treaty were on the whole comparatively innocuous, so far as that monarchy was concerned.

When it became known in Louisiana that direct negotiations on the Mississippi and boundary questions had been resumed at Madrid, Carondelet was influenced, largely by Gayoso de Lemos, to take up again Wilkinson's project. That Spanish vassal and American officer had accepted from President Washington a commission as lieutenant colonel, from which he soon advanced to brigadier general and second in command of the army of the United States, then operating against the western Indians. He was, early in 1792, apprised that the King of Spain at length had formally decided in favor of his pension of $2,000 a year, long since solicited, considerable arrears of which already had accumulated.[8] After the French war and American popular sympathy for it became evident, Carondelet realizing the fluctuating allegiance of the Indians and the precarious military defenses of the frontier—at the most he could muster no more than 2,800 men for the defense of Louisiana and the Floridas, half of these raw militia and half-breed hunters[9]—turned with increasing eagerness to Wilkinson and his fellow plotters. The latter had proved his usefulness to his paymasters by sending information of George Rogers Clark's project for an attack in 1793–1794, with French backing, of Kentucky riflemen on New Orleans.[10] Incidentally he sent in a bill for $8,640, in addition to his pension arrears, for expenses incurred in frustrating Clark's project. A copious secret ciphered correspondence quickly developed with Wilkinson, at United States

8. Gayoso de Lemos to Floridablanca, Jan. 7, 1792, Serrano y Sanz, *El Brigadier Jaime Wilkinson*, 37. See ibid., 42, for Gayoso's memorandum on "The Political Status of Louisiana," July 5, 1792, printed in English in J. A. Robertson's *Louisiana under Spain, France, and the United States*, I, 269. See account rendered by Brigadier General James Wilkinson, U.S.A., to Spain, entitled "Quenta de W.," in requesting payment for his services as a Spanish vassal and pensioner in stirring up sedition in the American West. A. H. N., Est. Leg., 3886. A photograph of this document is opposite p. 348 of the first edition (1926) of this work.

9. Carondelet and Gayoso de Lemos to Las Casas, New Orleans, Oct. 20, 1793, in Las Casas's compendious report of Nov. 21, 1793, A. G. C., Est. Leg., 7235. (L. C. trans.)

10. See ante, p. 117.

army headquarters, and with his coterie in Kentucky.[11]

In the transmission of this note the Spanish fort at Nogales where Gayoso de Lemos commanded proved a valuable listening-post for Kentucky, as well as an advanced defense for Louisiana. Wilkinson now advised the cultivation of Kentucky "notables," through heavy subventions to be distributed through his own fingers, and the promise of Spanish gunboats, arms, and ammunition to assist the independence of that state. Carondelet approved the huge estimates. They included $200,000 for bribes, 20 field pieces, 10,000 stand of arms, and two Spanish regiments to garrison the upper river forts of Spain. The Governor requested his Court forthwith to sanction this expenditure.[12] To his disappointment the grants were not made. They must have caused amazement at Madrid. The annual expenses of the government of Louisiana were already ten times the annual revenue,[13] and Carondelet was

11. Las Casas (Governor-General of Cuba and Louisiana) to Del Campo de Alange (Minister for War), Nos. 398, 415, 444, 452, 453, 454, 1793–1794. These voluminous documents contain copious enclosures relating to the Kentucky intrigue in 1793–1794 and to Spanish efforts to counteract Genêt's projects. A. G. C., Est. Leg., 7235. (L. C. trans.)

12. See A. H. N., Est. Leg., 3886, and Actas de la Suprema Junta de Estado, May 2, July 25, Aug. 1, 1794, A. H. N., Est.

13. According to Gayarré, p. 371, the expenses in 1795 were $864,126, and customs income $57,506. In 1790 the revenue from all sources was $66,163. Miró, Carondelet, and Gayoso in vain requested free trade with European countries and American ports as a means of reviving the drooping prosperity of the province. All that they could secure was the ordinance of June 9, 1793, allowing Spanish subjects of Louisiana to trade freely with all friendly nations who had treaties of commerce with Spain, through the ports of New Orleans, Pensacola, and St. Augustine, and providing they first stopped at a designated port in Spain to secure license. The commerce of Louisiana did not revive until after the discovery of profitable sugar-making in 1794. How much the removal of restrictions on trade to Europe contributed to this is still to be determined.

asking for other big sums for necessary fortifications and for annuities for the Indians. Godoy and his associates did not for a moment think of diverting such masses of money to a profitless province, any more than they approved the repeated recommendations of Louisiana governors for resurrecting the prosperity of the colony through the opening of unrestricted trade with Europe and America.

Carondelet's new projects for Kentucky were carefully considered by the Council of State, as we have noted in a previous chapter, on July 25, 1794. At this meeting extracts from Wilkinson's letters were read. They did not alter the decision to propose alliance to the United States. Godoy allowed the Governor of Louisiana to continue to cultivate Wilkinson and his friends while the President's answer to the new proposals (of July 26, 1794) was pending. As we have seen, this remained pending much longer than expected. During that time, 1794–1795, Carondelet zealously pursued his intrigues. Upon Wilkinson's advice, he occupied Chickasaw Bluffs,[14] the next high spot of ground above Nogales, 255 miles up the river, as the crow flies from Natchez, and 355 miles north of 31°. Here as an outpost for Nogales, the new fort was erected from which a helping hand might be reached out to Kentucky insurrectionists. In the winter of 1795–1796, Benjamin Sebastian was attracted by way of Nogales and Natchez down the river to New Orleans,[15] bringing with him

14. Chickasaw Bluffs had been variously denominated Écores à Margot, and Barrancas de Margot. The fort was called San Fernando de las Barrancas. It was located near the present site of Memphis. See Carondelet to Alcudia, July 1, 1795, Serrano y Sanz, op. cit., 95.

15. For secret ciphered correspondence between Carondelet and Wilkinson, in July, 1795, arranging for this negotiation, and promises by Carondelet to negotiate a satisfactory treaty in "less than a month,"

a paper purporting to give full powers from leading notables of Kentucky who had in secret convention at the house of George Nicholas resolved on a treaty with Spain. The credential was signed by George Nicholas, Harry Innes, William Murray, and by Sebastian himself.

These too are the signatories of the unsigned letter of the "secret committee of correspondence of the west," who had also been in contact with Jaudenes during the Whiskey Rebellion. Sebastian was actually at New Orleans with his "full power" in January, 1796. Carondelet was then anxiously waiting for instructions to permit him to sign a treaty with them.[16] Before his requests could be answered he received, in February, 1796, a copy of the treaty signed with Pinckney. With it were orders to suspend all activities at the new post. Even this treaty did not completely destroy his hope of seducing Kentucky. Sebastian thought that if it could be shown in Kentucky that the Atlantic states had any undue advantage in the treaty, his friends would still go ahead with their movement for independence. Carondelet persuaded him to wait at New Orleans until news should arrive as to the attitude of Kentucky toward the treaty, meanwhile "to agree between us on the means of achieving the desired end while circumstances are preparing for it." [17]

Sebastian lingered a while at New Orleans, but in

---

see Papeles de Cuba, Leg., 2374. (See Perez's *Guide*.) At my request Dr. A. P. Whitaker kindly had this correspondence photographed for me.

16. Carondelet to Alcudia, Nos. 67 and 69, Jan. 9 and 30, 1796, ibid., 74. The enclosures referred to but not included in No. 67, may be found in A. H. N., Est. Leg., 3886, including Wilkinson's financial account rendered by himself, Jan. 1, 1796.

17. Carondelet's No. 73 to the Prince of the Peace, Feb. 10, 1796, A. H. N., Est. Leg., 3886.

the spring departed for Kentucky via Philadelphia. With him went a special agent of Carondelet. This was one Thomas Power, whose business it was to proceed to the Ohio country to deliver ten thousand dollars to Wilkinson and to stir up any discoverable sentiment for revolt. He appealed to that treacherous personality now to step forward and become the "Washington of the West." Power had authority from Carondelet to state that Spain did not intend to carry out the terms of the treaty. The mission proved unprofitable, except to Wilkinson.[18]

Godoy allowed Carondelet to continue this intrigue.[19] It was unsuccessful: first, because Wilkinson and his followers never represented the overwhelming sentiment of Kentucky loyalty to the Union; and secondly, because the text of the treaty of 1795 secured for the men of the western waters everything they could desire.

We have noted that Pinckney's Treaty and Jay's Treaty conflicted in regard to maritime principles. In 1796 Spain resumed her traditional diplomacy and became, fatally, the ally of France—now under the less delirious rule of the Directory—and the enemy of Great Britain. Though the published text of Jay's Treaty did not reveal the dreaded Anglo-American understanding or alliance which Godoy had feared, it was highly repugnant to the liberal maritime principles which the United States had pledged itself, both before and after signing that instrument, to observe in its dealing with France and Spain respectively.[20] Spain

18. Gayarré, 355–366.

19. Godoy's instructions of (precise date unknown), 1796, in answer to Carondelet's despatches of Jan. 9 and 30, and Feb. 10, 1796. A. H. N., Est. Leg., 3886.

20. With France by the treaty of 1778, with Spain by the treaty of 1795.

also felt rightfully concerned at the third (Mississippi) article of Jay's Treaty. That had stated that the river should "according to the treaty of peace be entirely open to both parties." Pinckney's Treaty contained an agreement by the King of Spain to open the river only to citizens of the United States and subjects of the King of Spain. Which treaty should be supreme on this subject? Spanish diplomatists might flatter themselves that the later treaty had undone the earlier, just as Jay's Treaty in some respects was alleged to have undone the earlier Franco-American treaty of 1778. Subsequent to the Spanish treaty, however, the United States ratified, in 1796, an additional article to Jay's Treaty. This contained the provision "that no stipulations in any treaty subsequently [to Jay's Treaty] concluded by either of the contracting parties, with any other state or nation, or with any Indian tribe, can be understood to derogate in any manner, from the rights of free intercourse and commerce, secured by the aforesaid third article." The purpose of this explanatory article had been to remove an inconsistency between Jay's Treaty and the Treaty of Greenville of August 3, 1795, with the northwestern Indians. This purpose could have been achieved perfectly without the inclusive phrase "any other state or nation." Spain had quite proper reason for protesting, as she did, this additional article. She had equally good reason, and her ally France even more,[21] to object to the maritime

21. The principles of Jay's Treaty repudiating free ships free goods and the old definition of contraband, etc., applied only to the duration of the war in which Great Britain was *then* engaged, namely the war with France which did not end until 1801. Spain had since made peace with her former enemy France, and thus temporarily withdrawn from that war. Therefore while Spain remained in a brief interim of neutrality, in which Pinckney's Treaty was signed, it did not technically

provisions of Jay's Treaty.[22]

A period of several years' disagreeable dispute over the execution of the treaty was the result of these conflicts of obligations on the part of the United States. American officers appeared promptly at Natchez to arrange for the details of evacuation and joint survey of the boundary. In the spring of 1797 strategic reasons impelled the Spanish officials to evacuate their garrison at Chickasaw Bluffs, after razing the works which had been erected there. The guns, munitions, and most of the troops were taken up the river to St. Louis, on the western side. Fort Confederación on the Tombigbee was also relinquished at the same time, its garrison being moved down the river to Fort St. Stephens, at tidewater about ninety miles above Mobile, and still north of the recently agreed boundary line of the United States.[23] Numerous good excuses were found to delay further the evacuation of the remaining posts on the east side of the Mississippi, Nogales and Natchez, while

conflict with Jay's Treaty, the maritime provisions of which did not govern relations between the United States and Spain. But Spain soon became engaged in the same old war in which England was a belligerent against France, though now as an ally of France. In this war the English prize courts governed themselves by the provisions of Jay's Treaty. By Jay's Treaty British cruisers could take Spanish property from neutral American decks, while Pinckney's Treaty denied analogous rights to a belligerent Spain.

22. For notes passed between Secretary Pickering and Yrujo on this, see State Dept., Notes, Spain, Vol. 1A. See also *A. S. P., F. R.*, II, 68, 69, 98, where a few of the most essential notes are printed. Yrujo's energetic notes were so distasteful to Pickering that President Adams requested his recall by Spain. But Yrujo cultivated the good graces of the Jeffersonians and the Spanish Government managed to delay his recall until after the election of 1800, when it became unnecessary. For Yrujo's despatches, 1796–1800, see A. H. N., Est. Leg., 3896 *bis*, 3897.

23. For Spanish correspondence relating to this, see confidential despatches of Morales, Intendant at New Orleans, to Department

the protests against alleged American violation of the treaty were being presented at Philadelphia by the new minister, Yrujo. The Blount intrigue in Tennessee in 1797, by which British agents conceived the possibility of duplicating, with more success, Genêt's old project of recruiting western frontiersmen to attack Spanish provinces—for Great Britain was now the enemy of Spain and France—presented a valid reason for holding the river posts as necessary defenses against a British invasion from Canada across American soil by *force majeure,* with or without the assistance of lawless American western citizens.[24]

Despite dissatisfaction with the hastily concluded treaty of 1795 and good excuses for refusing to execute it, Spain was induced to do so by circumstances of a European nature. In 1797 relations between the United States and France as a consequence of Jay's Treaty became so strained as to make war likely. France now proposed to Spain joint diplomatic protests to the

of Finance, Dec. 31, 1796-May 4, 1797, containing despatches and enclosures explaining evacuation of the upper points and cessation of the movement at Nogales and Natchez, because of the Blount affair and fear of a British attack from Canada. This is in the *expediente* entitled "Correspondence of Spanish Governors and Officials in Louisiana relating to the Disputed Boundary 1789-1799," A. H. N., Est. Leg., 3902. See also, for American correspondence, *Seventh Annual Report* of the Director of the Department of Archives of the State of Mississippi, and *Journal* of Andrew Ellicott, the United States official surveyor. For account of Sir William Dunbar, official Spanish surveyor, see *Publications of Miss. Hist. Soc.,* III, 185–207.

24. We recall that at the time of the Nootka Crisis of 1790, the deliberations of Washington's Cabinet show that the United States would not have attempted by force to prevent a passage of British troops from Canada across American soil against Louisiana in case of war between Great Britain and Spain. For documents relating to the Blount affair, published by Prof. F. J. Turner, see *A. H. R.,* X, 574.

United States against Jay's Treaty.[25] Before this could
be done, diplomatic relations between the two republics
had been ruptured. The Prince of the Peace feared
that Spain might become involved, as France's new
ally, in a war with the United States. In such a conflict Spain had Louisiana and perhaps more to lose,
France nothing in America.[26] This was the reason for
Spain's ultimate, full execution of the treaty of 1795.

Again the wars of Europe had come to the aid of the
United States. A royal order for the evacuation of the
forts north of the new American boundary was issued
September 22, 1797. Nogales, Natchez, and St. Stephens
were given up in 1798.[27] A fine irony of fate caused
them to be delivered to subalterns of Brigadier General
James Wilkinson, at the time commander of the army
of the United States! The joint survey of the boundary
was commenced. Scarcely had it been completed, in
1800, before Louisiana was secretly ceded by Spain to
France, and that chapter of American expansion which
led to the Louisiana Purchase, a chapter made so familiar and so vivid to readers of American history by the
genius and the pen of the late Henry Adams, had
already begun. It was to end with the Florida purchase,

25. See endorsements on Yrujo's despatch No. 4, of Sept. 8, 1796,
and documents associated with No. 4, relating to French proposals for
joint diplomatic action, A. H. N., Est. Leg., 3896 *bis*.

26. Prince of the Peace to Yrujo, Jan. 27, Aug. 14, Dec. 31, 1796,
Spanish Legation, Vol. 205.

27. For details of the final evacuation, see Serrano y Sanz, op. cit.,
76-77; *Seventh Annual Report* of Director of Archives of Mississippi,
and *Journal* of Andrew Ellicott. A great deal of attention has been
devoted to the history of these years of border bickering and delay in
the execution of the treaty. See B. A. Hinsdale, "Establishment of the
First Southern Boundary of the United States," *Am. Hist. Assoc., Ann.
Rept., 1893*, 331–365; F. R. Riley, "Spanish Policy in Mississippi after
the Treaty of San Lorenzo," *ibid., 1897*, 177–182; I. J. Cox, *West
Florida Controversy*.

the carrying of the boundary between the United States
and Spain to the Pacific Ocean, and presently thereafter by the disappearance forever, in the contempo-
raneous revolutions of the South American colonies, of
the sovereignty of Spain from the American continents.
Those revolutions, let it be noted, were themselves the
result of the Napoleonic wars which followed the French
Revolution, and which were so profoundly consequen-
tial in American diplomatic history. The procession
of events which resulted in all this history is bound up
inseparably with the European balance of power and the
wars of the French Revolution.

Thomas Jefferson's reliance on the quarrels of Europe
to solve the predicaments of American diplomacy had
justified itself after all. The treaty to which Thomas
Pinckney succeeded in affixing Godoy's signature at a
psychological moment was one of the greatest successes
in American diplomacy. From it flowed almost im-
measurable consequences for the future territorial expansion of the United States. Issues arising over this
document led to the negotiations which brought, at
the profit of European imbroglios imperfectly understood across the Atlantic, the extension of American
territory to the Gulf of Mexico and to the Pacific
Ocean. If it had not been for the right of deposit and
the necessity of protecting it, it is extremely unlikely
that President Jefferson's diplomatists in 1803 would
have been suing at the Court of Napoleon for the purchase of the island of New Orleans at the very time
when larger issues, unbeknownst to Jefferson, constrained that despot to sell all of Louisiana. What then
would have been the destiny of that great region? A
second Canada? [28]

28. For some highly stimulating conjectures on this, see Channing,
Hist. U. S., IV, 334.

Spanish historians condemn Godoy and the treaty as the beginning of the end of Spain's vast colonial empire in America. So it was. It was due to no particular merit or deserved victory of American diplomacy. Godoy capitulated, perhaps unnecessarily, to circumstances in Europe which argued to him the necessity above all of protecting Spain at home, of sacrificing a small portion of expansive overseas dominions and rights for the better security of the remainder. That it would have been wiser for Spain under Godoy's guidance to have maintained after 1795 her neutrality in the great European cataclysm which ended by destroying her empire, does not concern us here. The French Revolution had engulfed Europe in a series of mighty conflicts which already had impelled Great Britain, in order to keep her much needed navy nearer home and to preserve her best customer at a time when money was needed to finance a great war, to sign Jay's Treaty with the United States. Godoy, fearful of the dominance of England after the destruction of French seapower, possibly of Anglo-American cooperation, and threatened by the invasion of French armies, signed a separate peace with France. The youthful Prince of the Peace allowed himself to be overawed by the anticipated wrath of a disappointed ally. Here his nervous imagination ran away with him. When Spain deserted the alliance England did not declare war. At a time when his other allies were dropping away from him Pitt had enough to confront the French problem without adding to his difficulties. But Godoy feared England. Jay's Treaty, with the subsequent failure at the Basle negotiations to secure a French alliance and even the hoped-for triple alliance with the United States, convinced the Prince that it was indispensably necessary to sign with Pinckney in order that British wrath should not be strengthened by an American alliance which would snatch away from Spain her American colonies then and there. This was Godoy's first mistake. The next, and the greatest, the colossal mistake of all Spanish diplomacy, was his renewal of the French alliance in the secret treaty of San Ildefonso of the following year. Without that Spain might still have had peace with Great Britain and stood aside, at least for several years, perhaps altogether, from the raging whirlpool of Europe soon to be stirred to its depths by the sword of the conquering Corsican.

Appendixes

Bibliographical Note

The following notes are intended to give to the reader a description of the source material used for the preparation of this volume without encumbering it with an unnecessary enumeration of the numerous monographic publications and standard general historical works which have been used and to which reference is made in footnotes. The literature of American history is now so easily known through the several bibliographical manuals on the subject that the student may easily consult for himself the existing secondary material on nearly any topic by turning to the appropriate pages of J. N. Larned's *Literature of American History*, and its supplement (Boston, 1902), for material printed before 1902; and, for material printed since that time, to Miss Grace Griffin's annual *Writings on American History*, to S. F. Bemis and Grace Griffin, *Guide to the Diplomatic History of the United States, 1775–1921* (Washington, 1935, reprinted Gloucester, Mass., 1959), and to Oscar Handlin and others, *Harvard Guide to American History* (Cambridge, Mass., 1954). For Spanish bibliography see B. Sanchez Alonso, *Fuentes de la historia española* (Madrid, 1919), and Miguel Gomez del Campillo, *Relaciones diplomaticas entre España y los Estados Unidos, segun los documentos del Archivo Nacional*, 2 vols. (Madrid, 1944–1946). In connection with bibliographical aids, which have to such an extent reduced the labor of the investigator, one should mention several of the valuable archival guides which have been prepared by the Department of Historical Research of the Carnegie Institution of Washington: W. R. Shepherd, *Guide to the*

Materials for the History of the United States in Spanish Archives (Washington, 1907); R. R. Hill, *Descriptive Catalogue of the Documents relating to the History of the United States in the Papeles Procedentes de Cuba deposited in the Archivo General at Seville* (Washington, 1916); J. A. Robertson, *List of Documents in Spanish Archives relating to the History of the United States, which have been printed or of which Transcripts have been preserved in American Libraries* (Washington, 1910); C. H. Van Tyne and W. G. Leland, *Guide to the Archives of the United States in Washington* (2nd ed., Washington, 1907); A. C. McLaughlin, *The Diplomatic Archives of the Department of State* (Washington, 1904); L. M. Pérez, *Guide to the Materials for American History in Cuban Archives* (Washington, 1907). Mention should also be made in this place of J. C. Fitzpatrick's *Handbook of Manuscripts in the Library of Congress* (Washington, 1918 et seq.); and of the introductory note by J. A. Robertson in C. M. Brevard's *History of Florida* (Deland, Fla., 1924–1925).

The American Revolution and Spanish policy, the subject of a great part of the first chapter, has been covered in the works of Corwin, Phillips, Doniol, and Yela (see note at end of Chapter 1), and more recently in S. F. Bemis, *The Diplomacy of the American Revolution* (New York, 1935, 1937; Bloomington, Indiana, 1957).

The sources for the diplomatic history of the United States Government during the period 1783–1789 are almost completely printed, as is evident by comparison with the manuscript originals in the Papers of the Continental Congress in the Library of Congress, in *Diplomatic Correspondence of the United States, 1783–1789*, which appeared in three editions—the first, used for this book, in 7 vols. (Washington, F. P. Blair, 1833–1834); the second in 7 vols. (Washington, Blair and Rives, 1837); and the third in 3 vols. (Washington, Blair and Rives, 1855). The minutes but not the debates of the Continental Congress are recorded in *Secret Journals of Congress*, 4 vols. (Boston, T. B. Wait,

1820–1821). The new edition of the *Journals of the Continental Congress*, edited by Ford, Hunt, Fitzpatrick, and Hill, is now complete in 34 vols. (Washington, 1904–1937). The debates of the Continental Congress are reflected in the contemporary letters of members of Congress then in attendance. These have been collected, insofar as extant, by Dr. E. C. Burnett of the Department of Historical Research of the Carnegie Institution, which has published them, with his meticulous editing, as one of the Institution's publications: *Letters of Members of the Continental Congress*, 8 vols. (Washington, 1921–1936). Dr. Burnett kindly placed at my disposal a mass of unpublished letters for the period 1783–1789, some of which throw considerable light on Spanish-American affairs in Congress.

The printed sources for the diplomatic history of the United States Government, 1789–1800, are less copious. *American State Papers, Foreign Relations*, Vols. I and II (Washington, 1832), contain the joint despatches of Carmichael and Short, some of their despatches which are not now extant in the State Department. Short's 215 individual despatches from Spain to the Secretary of State, some of which are from 5,000 to 10,000 words in length, are mostly unprinted, and are now preserved in the archives of the Department of State (Despatches, Hague and Spain, I and II). Even more instructive are the private papers of William Short, fifty-five folio volumes of MSS now in the Manuscripts Division of the Library of Congress. They contain not only letterpress copies of Short's official correspondence, but also private letters of great significance, as well as a prolix correspondence with other United States diplomatic agents at European capitals, including some of the joint Carmichael and Short despatches which have not been preserved elsewhere. The first thirty volumes are those which concern Short's career before 1797. The diplomatic papers of Thomas Pinckney are now preserved in letterpress copies in the South Carolina Historical Society's collection at Charleston, in five folio MS volumes. These include copies of the originals in the State Department, with additional supplementary material of considerable importance for understanding Pinckney's mission in Spain. The State Department series of Instructions contains a full file of those to Carmichael, Short, and Pinckney, mostly unprinted. So are the Notes which passed between the Spanish Legation at Philadelphia and the Department of State, except that these are not so completely preserved. Of the missing Notes, however, I have read duplicates in the Spanish archives at Madrid. Most of David Humphreys' despatches from Lisbon and Madrid are printed in F. L. Humphreys' *Life and Times of David Humphreys* (New York, 1917). Some of the unprinted Humphreys material in the State Department is nevertheless of significance. *American State Papers, Indian Affairs,* Vol. I (Washington, 1832), has a vast amount of material on the relations of the United States and Spain with the southwestern Indians. For commercial relations with Spain see *American State Papers, Commerce and Navigation,* Vol. I (Washington, 1832).

The writings of Washington, Jefferson, Madison, Monroe, Hamilton, and other contemporary American statesmen and personalities are obviously of great value. These have been published in well-known editions, but the most complete collections of the originals are available in the Library of Congress.

Much source material relating to Wilkinson and the "Spanish" Conspiracy has been published piecemeal in the *American Historical Review* and elsewhere (see Grace Griffin's *Writings on American History*). Charles Gayarré's *History of Louisiana*, Vol. III, *Spanish Domination* (3d ed., New Orleans, 1885) is still an important and useful work, printing many documents of which transcripts were secured by him from Spanish archives.

The Spanish sources for diplomatic relations with the United States are rich in the extreme. I have done little more than to cover the main series of diplomatic correspondence of the Spanish Foreign Office with and pertaining to the United States. This is replete with communications to and from other departments of the government, and with *expedientes,* or *dossiers,* coming up from the colonial correspondence in the form of *précis* or summaries of colonial matters. This material is now contained in the Archivo Histórico Nacional (see Gómez del Campillo, *Relaciones Diplomáticas* . . .) and also in the archives of the Departmento de Estado (Papers of the Spanish Legation at Washington). The latter collection contains full pages of instructions to as well as despatches from the Spanish agents in Philadelphia (after 1790) and Washington (after 1800), but for the period after 1800 there are many volumes so badly mildewed as to be completely destroyed. The documents in the Archivo Histórico Nacional contain complete collections of despatches from the Spanish diplomatic agents in the United States and in European capitals, but do not contain instructions except in the form of drafts and of ministerial marginalia. The despatches in the Archivo Histórico Nacional are cited in my text by section (*sección*) and bundle (*legajo*) number. Most of them are from the Sección de Estado (Est.).

The Gardoqui Despatches in six folio MS volumes of transcripts in the Durrett Collection of the University of Chicago Library, cover the period of Gardoqui's mission to the United States, 1784–1789. These transcripts were made from the originals which formerly were stored in the Archivo Central at Alcalá de Henares, but which now repose in the Archivo Histórico Nacional at Madrid. The transcripts were copied without method, arrangement, or index and because of this they are very difficult to use. For their provenance see Justin Winsor, *Narrative and Critical History of America,* VIII, 459, which states that the transcripts were at that time (1869) in the possession of Col. John M. Brown, of Kentucky. The latter was the grandson of John Brown, Gardoqui's confidant, and delegate of Virginia to Congress. Only the less incriminating portions of the Gardoqui Despatches relating to John Brown are used by Col. John M. Brown in his exculpatory endeavors for his grandfather (*Political Beginnings of Kentucky*, Louisville, 1889). Small portions of Gardoqui's instructions are printed in Manuel Conrotte's *Intervención de España en la independencia de los Estados Unidos* (Madrid, 1920) and in Manuel Serrano y Sanz's *Documentos Históricos de la Florida y la Luisiana* (Madrid, 1912). After the present study was prepared the Library of Congress had most of the Spanish diplomatic correspondence with the United States photocopied.

The most valuable of all Spanish sources for my study were the minutes of the Spanish Council of State, variously denominated as Actas de la Suprema Junta de Estado and Actas del Supremo Consejo de Estado. They cover the period 1788 to 1799, and contain not only the minutes of the Council of State, the best possible source as to Spanish policy, but also frequent comprehensive summaries of colonial and diplomatic documents digested for the consideration of the Council (and incidentally for the historian) by the several departments represented by their Ministers in the Council.

The Despatches of the Spanish Governors of Louisiana, 1766–1791, is the title of a photographic collection of these despatches, now existing in ten facsimiles in as many different libraries in the United States, including the Library of Congress. The value of these is much diminished because of the fact that they do not go beyond the year 1792 and do not contain the important enclosures which they cover. The Library of Congress has many thousands of typed transcripts of Spanish diplomatic correspondence dealing with the American Revolution, taken from the Archivo General Central at Simancas, but according to no revealed method. There are also many transcripts on Spanish colonial affairs, from the Archives of the Indies at Seville, which are mostly in the same condition. Where they have been used citation has been made to original archive and to transcript.

J. A. Robertson's *Louisiana under Spain, France, and the*

United States, 1785–1807 (Cleveland, 1911) contains select documents relating to the period and subject indicated by the title, with valuable notes.

Dr. Waldo G. Leland, of the Department of Historical Research of the Carnegie Institution of Washington, kindly supplied me with a digest of the correspondence of the French Ministers in Madrid, 1783 to 1793, with their Foreign Office. This was made from the series Correspondance Politique in the Archives des Affaires Étrangères, Paris. It proved of value for some matters of American diplomacy, and is appropriately cited in my footnotes.

Many helpful monographs and works of more general scope may be found indicated in the bibliographical manuals. These are cited in footnotes whenever found useful, but particular mention should be made of T. M. Green's *The Spanish Conspiracy* (Cincinnati, 1891), the shrewd deductions of which have been abundantly substantiated by archival revelations. The brochures of Manuel Serrano y Sanz, *El Brigadier Jaime Wilkinson* (Madrid, 1915) and *España y los Indios Cherokis y Chactas* (Seville, 1916) print representative documents, but the former is by no means a thorough study of Wilkinson, a definitive biography of whom would be of great service to American as well as to Spanish history. Wilkinson's own memoirs are of course of no value for truth in regard to the "Spanish" Conspiracy.

What has been said of Wilkinson's memoirs applies also to those of Godoy—thoroughly unreliable except when supported by independent corroborative evidence.

G. L. Rives's excellent article on "Spain and the United States in 1795," *A.H.R.*, IV, 62–67, shows an appreciation for the significance of European events to explain American diplomacy but had no access to European archives. B. A. Hinsdale's "Establishment of the First Southern Boundary of the United States," *Am. Hist. Assoc., Ann. Repts., 1893*, 331–365, covers the disputes arising over execution of the treaty of 1795, but, like Rives, had access only to American archives. I. J. Cox, *West Florida Controversy, 1793–1813*

(Baltimore, 1918), incidentally interprets that dispute with the assistance of some Spanish material.

The French monographs by F. P. Renaut, *La question de la Louisiane, 1796–1806* (Paris, 1918) and *Le Pacte de Famille et l'Amérique; la politique franco-espagnole de 1760–1792* (Paris, 1922), show evidence of work in French archives but are not reliable in all details, particularly as to American history, and are not adequately documented.

Most important of the various studies of Spain's colonial frontier in North America are the volumes of Arthur Preston Whitaker: *The Spanish-American Frontier, 1783–1795; The Western Movement and the Spanish Retreat in the Mississippi Valley* (Boston and New York, 1927), and *The Mississippi Question, 1795–1803; A Study in Trade, Politics, and Diplomacy* (New York and London, 1934).

The Financial Debt of the United States to Spain and Its Payment; Loans and Subsidies

The precise facts concerning money and supplies furnished by the Spanish Royal Government to the United States during the American Revolution have been shrouded in obscurity. The money and supplies furnished before 1779 consisted entirely of secret subsidies. The royal government held no receipts for loans other than those given by John Jay for comparatively small sums received during his sojourn in Madrid in 1781–1782. It would be unreasonable to suppose it to have been the policy of Spain to loan money to the American insurrectionists on definite terms, even after Spain entered the war against Great Britain in 1779, because it was the fixed policy of Spain not to recognize the independence of the United States, and any arrangement for payment of loans would have looked forward to the establishment of American independence, without which of course the loans would never have been paid. Jay arrived in Spain in 1780 to negotiate a loan and a treaty of alliance. He was not successful in either and was not recognized by the King, as we have already seen in the foregoing study. While he was there Robert Morris, Superintendent of Finances, having exhausted all other expedients of raising money during the war, resorted to his notorious and desperate device of writing drafts on American diplomatic agents in France and Spain, in the hope that by the time the drafts were presented, loans from these countries would have been obtained. The total of moneys advanced to Jay by the Spanish Government for this purpose was reported

to the Governor of Rhode Island, January 4, 1783, by
Robert R. Livingston, Secretary for Foreign Affairs, as
$150,000.[1] Jay gave receipts for the amounts received by
him, but only after much importunity on the part of the
Spanish Ministers.[2] There is evident no stipulated promise
to pay.

In 1790 Alexander Hamilton, Secretary of the Treasury
under President Washington, began his program of paying
off the debts of the United States at home and abroad.
Within two years the credit of the United States at the
world money market at Amsterdam rose from the worst in
the world to the best. In the case of the debt to France
there were definite obligations indicating the loans, with
rate of interest, and a fixed schedule of payments on principal, beginning in 1785, according to the terms of the
funding agreements with that power in 1782 and 1783,
which had been ratified by Congress. Under Hamilton's
administration of the treasury the United States succeeded
in borrowing money from private bankers at Amsterdam
with which it proceeded to take up the arrears due on the
French debt since 1785, together with accumulated interest,
and thenceforth continued regularly to meet payments on
principal and interest as fixed by the schedule of payments
of the funding agreements.[3] In the case of Spain there had
been no such agreements. They would in fact have implied
a recognition of American independence.

Through the courtesy of the State Department, Hamilton
in 1792 directed Carmichael, United States chargé at
Madrid, to apprise the Spanish Government of the desire
of the United States to pay any debts it owed to Spain and

1. Wharton, VI, 195. Livingston stated: "I have reason to believe that
no money has since then been obtained on account of the United States
in Spain."

2. Expediente on "aids (*socorros*) given to the Americans," A. H. N.,
Est. Leg., 3884, Expediente 4.

3. A. Aulard, "La dette Américaine envers la France," *Revue de
Paris*, 15 mai, 1 juin, 1925.

to inquire what amount was owed. Carmichael could get no reply more definite than a promise to consult records and submit a statement as promptly as possible, which statement was never forthcoming.[4] From the records in the Treasury Department Hamilton calculated that the United States owed to Spain $174,011, with interest at five per cent from date of loan.[5] The agent of the United States who

4. Carmichael to Aranda, Madrid, Sept. 19, Nov. 2, 1792; Gardoqui to Aranda, Nov. 2 (two letters), 1792; Aranda to Carmichael, Nov. 5, 1792; Aranda to Gardoqui, Nov. 7, 1792, A. H. N., Est. Leg., 3889 *bis*, Expedte. 1.

5. Through the courtesy of the Honorable the Secretary of the Treasury of the United States, I was permitted in February, 1926, to make an inspection of the archives of the Department in an effort to locate material bearing on this subject. With the assistance of the appropriate attachés of the Department, I was unable to find anything on the Spanish debt, aside from the statements referred to hereafter. The notation of $174,011 as owed to Spain and paid in full, Aug. 21, 1793, with total interest, to Dec. 31, 1792, of $99,007.89, is recorded in *American State Papers, Financial Affairs*, I, 672 (same item repeated elsewhere in ibid.). This is followed in Rafael A. Bayley's *The National Loans of the United States* (1881) and W. F. DeKnight, *History of the Currency of the Country and of the Loans of the United States* (1900), both of them official government publications.

Below is reproduced in print a letter of Joseph Nourse, Register of the Treasury, to Alexander Hamilton, Secretary of the Treasury, Oct. 9, 1792, setting forth the status of the United States debt to Spain. ("Estimates and Statements, 1791 and 1792," Old Loan Office, Treasury Department, Washington):

"Treasury Dept., Registers Office
9 Octo: 1792.

Sir,

I have the Honor to enclose certifyd Copies from the Treasury Books of an Act depending betwixt His mo. Catholic Majesty and the United States, for monies recd. on Loan.* I have the Honor to be

Sir

Your mo: ob: hb: Servt.

Hon: Alexr. Hamilton, Esq:
Secy. of the Treasury

* I canot find that this Loan has been recognized on the Journals of Congress in a like manner with the French and Dutch Loans. It is

transacted the Dutch bankers' loans for payment of arrears
on the French debt was William Short, then Minister of

founded on a settlement made by the late com. for settling the foreign
accts.—entitled Loans from the Court of Spain. This money was paid
to the Hon: James Gardoqui and has been regularly accounted for
by him, having been expended in the purchasing of cloathing, and
in the payt. of Bills of Exc. drawn by order of Congress. The principal
sum recd. was 174,011 drs.

Dr. His mo. Catholic Majesty in a/c with the united States Cr.

By the following Sums paid to the Hon: James Gardoqui of Madrid
viz:

1781 January 1. For so much recd. of the Court	. .17,892
Feb: 28	do.	32,000
April 28	do.	9,036
May 9	do.	14,000
June 22	do.	12,000
Aug: 18	do.	12,000
Dec: 23	do.	51,083
1782 March 21	do.	26,000

174,011

By Int. on 17,892 dollars from January 1781 to 31 decr. 1792
            is 12 Years at 5%   10,735.20
do. on 32,000 do. from 28 Feby. 1781 to do.
            is 11.10.3 at do........ 18,946.67
do. on 9,036 do. from 28 April 1781 to do.
            is 11.8.3............ 5,274.76
do. on 14,000 do. from 9 May 1781 to do.
            is 11.7.22............ 8,151.09
do. on 12,000 do. from 22 June 1781 to do.
            is 11.6.9............ 6,915.
do. on 12,000 do. from 18 August 1781 to
            do. is 11.4.13......... 6,821.66
do. on 51,083 do. from 23 decr. 1781 to do.
            is 11.0.8............28,152.40
do. on 26,000 do. from 21 March 1782 to
            do. is 10.9.10.........14,011.11

99,007.89

Treasury Dept.   99,007.89
    Registers Office 9th. Octo: 1792.

                                          Dolls.   273,018.89

                                                         cts.

the United States at The Hague, who, without any experience in such matters, performed that rather complicated
business in a highly creditable way. Short was also em-

The principal sum received was..................Drs.	174,011.
To which add Interest thereon to the 31 Dec. 1792........	99,007.89
Total Amt. of Principal & Int. a. of Statement.........	273,018.89

Altho' there is no Recognition of this Debt on the Journals of Congress, by a Copy of the original Contract or otherwise, yet in all the
Estimates made by the late Government the annual appropriations
have been made for the payment of its Int. and in the various Reports
from Committees of Congress it has been notic'd as an Existing Claim
due from the United States,—

There is an Acct. opened in the Treasury Books under the Title of
Don Carlos Dildephonso Rico Hombre D'Espagne a copy of which I
inclose. This I have understood from Mr. Lee is to be received as a
Gratuity and not as a Loan

I have the Honor to be

Sir with Real Respect

Your mo: ob: & mo: hb: Serv.

J. N."

This does not agree with Livingston's statement of 1783 that the
loans from Spain were $150,000 and that this was all used for making
up debts. The investigator can do no more than lay out these documents. How much of the $174,011 was used for drafts and how much
for clothing cannot be told, but Jay's correspondence suggests that all
the money received by him, total not indicated by him, was used for
drafts (see Wharton, IV and V, and index). I have been unable to
reconcile the two totals of $150,000 and $174,011.

A search in the Treasury Archives, which are by no means complete,
has failed to reveal the account of "Don Carlos Dildephonso, Rico
Hombre d'Espagne," who by the title was apparently the King. But
the total of subsidies granted to Arthur Lee is enumerated by Conrotte, op. cit., 293-295, and has been included in the reckonings made
in this appendix.

Reverting to the papers of the Continental Congress (accounts of the
Register's Office, Vol. 142, 12, 14, II, 1782-1783) I find an account
certified by Joseph Nourse, of which the following is a literal and
verbatim reproduction:

powered by Hamilton to pay off the Spanish debt of $174,011 with interest, with funds out of these Dutch loans. This he was enabled to do conveniently during his sojourn in Spain, in 1793. The total amount paid by Short to Spain was:

$174,011.00 principal.
94,022.62 interest since March 21, 1782

$268,033.62

This does not agree with the total of the obligation as described in the letter to Hamilton from the Register of the Treasury, of October 9, 1792, as above shown, although it apparently includes interest carried until final payment of the whole debt on August 23, 1793. The small discrepancy, however, arises from profits on exchange operations.[6] Short records that Carmichael (who had been Jay's secretary in Madrid in 1781–1782, and as we have observed had remained there ever since as American diplomatic representative until his recall in 1794, a few months before his death in that city) told him that this sum represented what Jay had acknowledged as having received from the Spanish

"Dr.	Loans and Grants from the		Cr.
	Royal Treasury of Spain to the		
	U. States		
		Livres	Dollars
	By Arthur Lee, Esq. as per No. 1, received Thro' the hands of Gardoqui and Son	375,000	
	By John Jay to the Debit of his account		150,000"

It is to be noted that this is denominated "Loans and Grants." We cannot from this say which was considered a loan and which a grant, but Hamilton's liquidation and Short's correspondence show that the monies secured by Jay were regarded by him as a loan.

6. *A. S. P., Finance*, I.

Government during the Revolution. Short, in his letters to Gardoqui tendering payments on this, assumes that this was in payment of the money advanced to Jay.[7]

When the payment of the $174,011 with interest to 1793 was completed Short requested from Gardoqui, Minister of Finance at the time, an acquittal in full for all financial obligations on the part of the United States toward Spain. Gardoqui gave receipts for the $174,011 and accumulated interest, but despite repeated solicitations he evaded giving receipt for payment in full of all sums owed to Spain. He averred to Short that the United States owed "much more" than that. Short asked what for. Gardoqui could not say, though he himself had been, during the Revolution, the principal instrument through whom money and supplies are said to have passed.[8] At that time he and his assistants were ransacking the Spanish archives—which seem to have been no better on this point than those of the United States today—for evidences and title of American debt,[9] for Godoy had wished to make use of them to the best interests of Spain as a diplomatic equivalent in the general negotiations then on foot with the United States in Madrid.[10] No further titles were ever discovered in Spain. Hence nothing could be presented. Without them the United States could not be persuaded of the existence of further debt, and there the matter ended.

Between 1785 and 1795 Spanish diplomatic agents in the

7. The correspondence of Short with Hamilton and with Gardoqui on this subject is very voluminous and is to be found scattered through Volumes XXIII to XXX inclusive of the Short Papers. The letters *from* Hamilton are nòt preserved, in most instances, even in this remarkably complete collection. I have not been able to find them in the U. S. Treasury Archives. Short recapitulated the matter in several letters to Hamilton, notably those of Oct. 17, 1793, March 7, June 9, June 29, July 30, 1794 (in Vols. XXV, XXVI, Short Papers). See also Short to Gardoqui, Sept. 12, 1795, ibid., XXX, 5281.

8. Gardoqui to Alcudia, July 21, 1794, A. H. N., Est. Leg., 3889 *bis*, Expedte. 1.

9. Ibid.

10. [Alcudia] to Gardoqui, July 13, 1794. Ibid.

United States occasionally tried to make use of an alleged substantial debt of the United States to Spain in the diplomatic negotiations of those years. Gardoqui, we remember, offered the cancellation of this debt, the amount of which he did not stipulate, as one of the inducements to Congress for the acceptance of a treaty which would relinquish claims to the navigation of the Mississippi. Jaudenes and Viar in a recriminating note to the Secretary of State, April 23, 1794, incidentally referred to the debt of $1,640,071.62 which the United States owed Spain. Randolph referred this letter to the Secretary of the Treasury. As a result some exchanges of letters between Oliver Wolcott, Hamilton's successor, and Jaudenes followed in April, 1795, which developed the fact that Jaudenes and Viar had no basis for their figures. At the same time Jaudenes acknowledged that $74,087 had been paid to him in satisfaction of the money advanced to Oliver Pollock, at New Orleans. Jaudenes referred the whole matter to the negotiations then proceeding on that subject between Gardoqui and Carmichael and Short in Madrid. Acting upon further instructions from his government Short, in a note to the Prince of the Peace (Godoy) September 13, 1795, requested information as to these alleged debts mentioned by Jaudenes and Viar, and in Wolcott's letter of May 13, 1795, to Jaudenes and Viar. He repeated the request October 17, 1795,[11] but no further statement was forthcoming Short left Madrid in November, 1795, without any final acquittal in full.[12] These two sums, the $174,011, with interest to August 21, 1793, totaling $268,-033.62, paid by Short in Madrid; and the $74,087 paid by the Secretary of the Treasury to Jaudenes and Viar in 1794 (there is no explanation of whether interest had accrued on this) constitute all that was ever paid by the United States to Spain, which was not able to present evidences of any more debt, despite the many formal requests for such. It is

11. A. H. N., Est. Leg., 3889 *bis,* Expedte. 1.

12. Short to Oliver Wolcott, Secretary of the Treasury, Oct. 29, 1795, Short Papers, XXX, 5344. See also ibid., 5322a, 5328.

therefore to be presumed, in absence of title, that there had been no further loans than those paid by Hamilton, who had begun payment of foreign debts unsolicited and somewhat to the surprise, at least in the case of France,[13] of the creditor governments, and who would have been perfectly ready to pay any valid debt. A million or two dollars more or less on the sum of foreign debts would have made no difference to him in 1792. His main purpose was to restore American credit by making the first overtures to pay any just debt. I repeat that the policy of Spain during the Revolution, of avoiding recognition of American independence at that time, would have made her very wary of entering into any contract with the insurrectionary authorities. There is not any evidence that I have found to indicate that Spain even presented any title to the debts which Hamilton acknowledged of his own initiative and paid.

In the Archivo Histórico Nacional at Madrid, Sección de Estado, is an *expediente* containing Gardoqui's list of subsidies furnished in money and supply to the United States, 1776 to 1779, that is, before Spain entered the war against Great Britain. Including in this the 1,000,000 livres granted, as is well known, secretly by Charles III to Louis XVI in 1776 for support of the American insurrectionists,[14] the total of subsidies furnished by Spain in those years amounted to 7,944,906 *reales* 16 *maravedis vellon,* or $397,-230, not including in addition 30,000 army coats. The Governor of Louisiana also furnished in 1778 a total of $66,961 to Captain Willing and Oliver Pollock. This was eventually paid for, to the amount of $74,087, by Hamilton to Jaudenes. I cannot account for the $7,126 surplus paid on account of Pollock. A guess is that Willing's account may have been considered a subsidy, and that Pollock's may have been treated as a loan with interest. It is not stated in the Spanish list how much went to Willing and how

13. Aulard, op. cit.
14. Doniol, I, 485.

much to Pollock. The Governor of Havana also accepted a draft of $14,424 on Congress, endorsing it to Miralles, to whom it was paid. This is not included in my estimation of Spanish loans and subsidies.

Since Spain held no obligations of the United States, and for good reasons of her own, above set forth, had not desired to take them, it is not possible, strictly speaking, to call any of the financial assistance thus rendered anything but a subsidy. But since the United States Government out of its own initiative decided to consider parts of it as a loan and to repay this with interest, we may estimate as loans the sums which were paid back (not including interest thereon) and as subsidies the sums which were not repaid. We then have a total of $214,098 loans and $397,230 subsidies. It might be interesting to compare this with France's loans to the United States during the American Revolution of $6,171,000 (34,000,000 livres), and subsidies of $1,996,500 (11,000,000 livres).[15]

15. See contract of February 23, 1783, between France and the United States, Malloy, *Treaties* (1910 ed.), I, 487; *Dip. Corres.*, I, 402–405.

Pinckney's Sketches of a Treaty and Drafts of Proposed Articles

On August 15, 1795, Pinckney presented to Godoy what he referred to as "the sketches of treaties." Godoy asked for a full-length draft,[1] which Pinckney prepared and submitted August 28.[2] Godoy then made up a counterdraft, to which Pinckney replied in detail. A copy of Pinckney's comments on Godoy's counterdraft, but not of the counterdraft itself, is printed in *A. S. P., F. R.*, I, 545. Neither the original of Pinckney's comments, nor of Godoy's counterdraft, nor of Pinckney's full-length draft, exists in the State Department, nor in the Pinckney Papers in the South Carolina Historical Society. The Pinckney Papers do, however, contain the "Sketches" proposed by Pinckney on August 15. These are produced below as "A." At a considerably later date in the negotiations, Pinckney proposed two articles, one on spoliations, and one on the entrepôt, to be included in the final treaty. These were both rejected by Godoy. They are endorsed by Pinckney under date of October 2, 1795, and are reproduced below as "B." At the same time (at least it is endorsed with the same date) he presented to Godoy a separate article, in regard to future commercial negotiations, which article Godoy also rejected. It is reproduced below as "C." The several pieces below

1. Pinckney to Monroe, S. Ildefonso, Aug. 15, 1795, Pinckney Papers, Spain, 124.
2. Pinckney to Monroe, August 28, 1795, ibid. Pinckney to Duke of Alcudia, Aug. 29, 1795, *A. S. P., F. R.*, I, 538.

printed, "A," "B," and "C," are all from the Pinckney
Papers.

A. *"Esquisse du Projet d'un traité d'amitié, de commerce et de navigation."* [3]
"Article de paix et d'Amitié.

"Articles pour assurer aux sujets et citoyens de deux
pays reciproquement les droits, les privileges at Exemptions des nations les plus favorisées, pour ce qui regarde le
commerce et la navigation.

"Article pour la protection des Vaisseaux et autres effets
de chaque nation se trouvans dans l'etendue de la Jurisdiction de l'autre, par mer et par Terre.

"Articles usuels sur les naufrages et sur les vaisseaux
pris par les pirates.

"que les biens et les proprietés que les habitans de
chaque nation peuvent avoir dans le territoire des autres
leur seront assuré.

"Qu'ils seront admis reciproquement de poursuivre dans
les tribunaux, leurs droits contre les habitans du pays.
Qu'ils peuvent disposer par Testament ou autrement de
leurs Biens, et que leurs heritiers pourront succeder ab
intestat.

"Les Consuls seront reciproquement rêçus.

"Que dans le cas ou l'un des parties contractans soit en
guerre, il observera vis a vis de l'autre, étant neutre une
conduite fondée sur les principes de la neutralité armée,
laquelle les deux nations ont ci-devant adopté—avec les
articles sur la contrabande de Guerre et autres necessaires
pour donner a ces principes leurs Effets.

"Que les batimens des États Unis de l'Amerique seront
admis dans les Colonies Espagnoles avec les productions des

3. This is not dated, but is filed among papers bearing date of
August, 1795. Pinckney's letter of Aug. 15, 1795, cited in note 1, above,
establishes the date. The French here quoted is Pinckney's own.

dits Etats et seront permis de prendre en retour les productions des dites Colonies sans que ces batimens et productions payent plus de droit que s'ils appartinoient aux
Espagnols et que pareillement, les batimens et productions
des dites Colonies ne payeront dans les ports des Etats
Unis plus de droit que s'ils appartinoient aux citoyens des
Etats Unis."

"Projet

De communiquer mutuellement aux habitans de l'Empire Espagnol at des territoires des États Unis les droits
civiles des Natifs.

"Je parle de droit civile comme distinct du droit politique et je veux dire que les habitans de chaque nation
seroient munis dans le territoire de l'autre, de la protection
de toutes les Exemptions autant pour leurs personnes que
pour leurs biens, que possedent les natifs du Pays, mais
qu'ils n'auroient pas le droit de se meler au Gouverne-
ment, de jouir de charges publiques ni d'aucun privilege
qui regarde l'état politique du pays.

"En considerant ce projet il faut se garder d'envisager
les Etats Unis sous le meme point de vue que les nations
Européannes, vu [sic] que ces dernieres ne peuvent pas etre
les Rivales de l'Espagne ni dans la production de leurs territoires qui sont pour la plupart differens, ni dans les manufactures, vu que les Etats Unis n'en ont point mais qu'ils
offrent un vaste marché aux manufactures Espagnols.

"Cet article pourroit etre limité dans sa duration. Si
l'Espagne a quelque idée de lier ses fortunes avec celle
[sic] des Etats Unis, en Amerique, je ne vois point de
moyen plus sur.

"Que la navigation du Mississippi soit reconnue libre
aux deux Nations, et toutes les facilités pour la rendre
utile accordées mutuellement, Que la limite meridionale
soit reconnue par l'Espagne telle qu'elle fut determinée
par la proclamation du Roi d'Angleterre de 1763 et le
traité de paix entre lui et les États Unis."

B. *Draft of Two Articles Proposed for Treaty.*

ARTICLE I

"Sa Majesté Catholique et les États-Unis de l'Amerique
étant convenus d'un traité de limites et de navigation
lequel a été signé ce jour-ci par leurs Plenipotentiaires
respectifs par le dernier article duquel Sa Majesté declare
que 'des de luego a consequencia de lo estipulado en el
articulo IV tratará S. M. Catolica de facilitar a los
Cuidadanos de los Estados Unidos los medios de disfrutar
la Navegacion del Rio Misisipi cuya libertad se ha pactado
en el expresado Articulo IV' et vu qu'il seroit d'un grand
inconvenient aux citoyens des dits États d'attendre justqu'a
la terminaison des negociations, ulterieures sans les facilités
necessaires pour leur rendre utile la navigation de la Riviere
Mississipi, Sa Majesté est convenu que jusqu'a ce que des
arrangemens pour leur faciliter la navegition de cette
Riviere dont il est question dans le dit article seront faits,
les citoyens des dits Etats Unis auront la liberté de porter
a la Nouvelle Orleans leurs denrées et marchandises dans
leurs batimens arrivans ou de la mer ou de leurs terres sur
la dite Riviere et de les y deposer dans des magasins
auxquels il y aura deux serrures et deux Clefs dont l'officier
de la douane de Sa Majesté tiendra l'une et le proprietaire
l'autre, et ils pourront egalement emporter leurs effets des
dits magasins quand bon il leur semblera sans payer aucun
droit de douane ou autre quelconque excepté le louage
ordinaire et raisonable des dits magasins."

ARTICLE II

"Mr. P's proposal to the Prince upon the subject of
Spoliation—2d. Octr., 1795." [The proposed article here
follows:]

"Sa Majesté Catholique ayant par son 'ordenanza de
corso' en date du 1 Mai [*sic*] autorisé ses batimens de
guerre et corsaires d'amener dans les port de ses domaines
les batimens neutres qui se trouveroient chargés des mar-

chandises appartenantes a ses ennemis et de les y detenir jusqu'a ce qu'il paroitroit [*sic*] que la nation ennemie a laquelle ces marchandises appartiendroient ne refusoit pas mais au contraire qu'elle permettoit la meme privilege: observant la conduite qu'elle aye tenue et tiendra envers l'Espagne, laquelle exigeoit un traitement reciproqué de sa part (*'considerando la conducta que hayan tenido y tanger* [sic] *con nosotros la qual exige un trato reciproco de nuestra parte'*) Et vu qu'il subsiste un traité entre les Etats Unis de l'Amerique et la France par lequel la conduite des deux nations doit etre reglée pendant que l'une des deux soit en guerre et que de plus il paroit que les François ont observé les stipulations de ce traité pour ce qui concerne l'Espagne pendant la guerre qui vient de se terminer, Sa Majesté Catholique, en vue de ce qui est dessus a convenu [*sic*] avec les dits Etats Unis de l'Amerique que tous les batimens appartenants aux citoyens des dits Etats que auront été amené dans les ports Espagnols tant en Europe que dans les domaines de l'Espagne dans les autres parties du Monde, seront jugés selon les stipulations contenues dans le dit traité, et qu'il y aura deux commissaires nommés de la part de chaque nation immediatement aprés la ratification de cette convention qui determineront si selon le dit traité il y aura lieu a des indemnités et qui dans ce cas fixeront la somme qui doit etre resitituée, laquelle Sa Majesté Catholique fera payer sans delai aux parties lesées et s'il arrivoit des cas dans lesquels les dits commissaires ne seroient pas d'accord, ils choisiront de commun accord (s'il le peut, ou sinon par sort) un cinquieme commissaire et la pluralité de voix de ces cinq determinera la question finalement et sans appel."

Endorsed; "Spoliations, 2d. Octr., 1795."

C. *Article Proposed by Mr. Pinckney*

(This document is indorsed "Octr. 2d., 1795. Presented by Mr. P: but rejected.")

"Les deux hautes parties contractantes procederont sans delai a nommer des Commissaires pour arranger un traité de Commerce sur le fondement de la reciprocité et de la convenance, mutuelle, et en attendant, aussitot que l'échange des ratifications de cette convention sera faits chacune des deux parties contractantes jouira dans les domaines de l'autre de touts les droits, privileges et exemptions dont joui [*sic*] ou jouira la nation la plus favorisée, en se soumettant aux mêmes conditions et accordant les mêmes compensations."

Execution of the Spoliations Article (XXI) of the Treaty of 1795 [1]

All the papers of the mixed claims commission that adjudicated the spoliation claims as provided by Article XXI of Pinckney's Treaty have not been found. Mr. Justice John Bassett Moore has utilized all that are known, in his account of the Spanish spoliations in the second volume of his *History and Digest of the International Arbitrations to Which the United States Has Been a Party* (Washington, 1898), pp. 991–1005, amplified in his *International Adjudications*, V (New York, 1933), 1–99. They consist of a volume in the archives of the Department of State of copies of the awards made by the commission, each award containing a statement of the case, and an *expediente* of documents in the Archivo Histórico Nacional (Est., Leg., 3892), relating to payment of the awards. The United States commissioner was Matthew Clarkson, the Spanish commissioner was Josef Ignacio de Viar, then consul-general of Spain in the United States, with headquarters at Philadelphia; they chose as third commissioner Samuel Breck of that city. They sat at Philadelphia from 1797 to 1799 and made 40 awards, aggregating $325,550.07½.

The commission made allowances of damages arising from detention and incidents connected therewith, for plunder and other irregular conduct of the captors, etc., but the texts of the awards do not reveal fully what rules of inter-

[1]. This appendix is based on the account of the spoliations commission in J. B. Moore's *International Adjudications*, Vol. V (New York, 1933).

national law were followed: i.e., whether the commissioners accepted the principle free ships free goods, or whether they defined contraband or blockade. Since the third commissioner was a citizen of the United States, one may guess that they may have followed the American interpretations of neutral rights as laid down in the famous Plan of 1776, the Franco-American Treaty of Amity and Commerce, 1778, and Pinckney's Treaty itself of 1795 under which the commission was set up.

Official Text of the Treaty of 1795 Between the United States and Spain

The text below, in parallel columns, English and Spanish, reproduces the original MS copy of the treaty now in the custody of the State Department of the United States. It is set up from a photostat of the treaty and shows incidentally the carelessness as to punctuation and spelling which characterized official documents of greatest importance. Miller's Treaties, II, 318-338 obviously follows the same original, and where there would be differences between his print and mine, I have corrected mine by his authentic rendition.

His Catholic Majesty and the United States of America desiring to consolidate on a permanent basis the Friendship and good correspondence which happily prevails between the two Parties, have determined to establish by a convention several points, the settlement whereof will be productive of general advantage and reciprocal utility to both Nations.

With this intention His Catholic Majesty has appointed the most excellent Lord Don Manuel de Godoy and Alvarez de Faria, Rios, Sanchez Zarzosa, Prince de la Paz Duke de la Alcudia Lord of the Soto de Roma and of the State of Albalá: Grandee of Spain of the first class: Perpetual Regi-

Deseando S. M. Catolica y los Estados Unidos de America consolidar de un modo permanente la buena correspondencia y amistad que felizmente reyna entre ambas Partes, han resuelto fixar por medio de un Convenio varios puntos de cuyo arreglo resultará un beneficio general, y una utilidad reciproca â los dos Paises.

Con esta mira han nombrado S. M. Catolica al Excelentisimo Sor. Dn. Manuel de Godoy, y Alvarez de Faria, Rios, Sanchez Zarzosa, Principe de la Paz, Duque de la Alcudia: Señor del Soto de Roma, y del Estado de Albalá: Grande de España de primera clase: Regidor perpetuo de la Ciudad de

dor of the Citty of Santiago: Knight of the illustrious Order of the Golden Fleece, and Great Cross of the Royal and distinguished Spanish Order of Charles the III. Commander of Valencia del Ventoso, Rivera, and Aceuchal in that of Santiago: Knight and Great Cross of the religious order of St. John: Counsellor of State: First Secretary of State and Despacho: Secretary to the Queen: Superintendant General of the Posts and High Ways: Protector of the Royal Academy of the Noble Arts, and of the Royal Societies of natural history, Botany, Chemistry, and Astronomy: Gentleman of the King's Chamber in employment: Captain General of his Armies: Inspector and Major of the Royal Corps of Body Guards etc. etc. etc. and the President of the United States with the advice and consent of their Senate, has appointed Thomas Pinckney a Citizen of the United States, and their Envoy Extraordinary to his Catholic Majesty. And the said Plenipotentiaries have agreed upon and concluded the following Articles.

Santiago: Caballero de la insigne Orden del Toyson de Oro: Gran Cruz de la Real y distinguida Orden Española de Carlos III. Comendador de Valencia del ventoso, Rivera, y Aceuchal en la de Santiago: Cabellero Gran Cruz de la Religion de Sn. Juan: Consegero de Estado: primer Secretario de Estado y del Despacho: Secretario de la Reyna Nra. Sra. Superintendente general de Correos y Caminos: Protector de la Rl. Academia de las Nobles Artes, y de los Rles. Gabinete de Historia natural, Jardin Botanico, Laboratorios Chîmico, y Observatorio Astronomico: Gentilhombre de Camara con exercicio: Capitan General de los Reales Exercitos: Inspector y Sargento Mayor del Rl. Cuerpo de Guardias de Corps, etc. etc. etc. y el Presidente de los Estados Unidos con el consentimiento y aprobacion del Senado à Dn. Tomas Pinckney Cuidadano de los mismos Estados y su Enviado Extraordinario cerca de S. M. Catolica y Ambos Plenipotentiarios han ajustado y firmado los Articulos siguientes.

Art. I.

There shall be a firm and inviolable Peace and sincere Friendship between His Catholic Majesty his successors and subjects, and the United States and their Citizens without exception of persons or places.

Art. I.

Habrá una Paz solida ê inviolable y una amistad sincera entre S. M. Catolica sus succesores y subditos, y los Estados Unidos y sus Ciudadanos, sin excepcion de personas ò lugares.

Art. II.

To prevent all disputes on the subject of the boundaries which separate the territories of the two High contracting Parties, it is hereby declared and agreed as follows: to wit: The Southern boundary of the United States which divides their territory from the Spanish Colonies of East and West Florida, shall be designated by a line beginning on the River Mississippi at the Northernmost part of the thirty first degree of latitude North of the Equator, which from thence shall be drawn due East to the middle of the River Apalachicola or Catahouche, thence along the middle thereof to its junction with the Flint, thence straight to the head of St. Mary's River, and thence down the middle there of to the Atlantic Occean. And it is agreed that if there should be any troops, Garrisons or settlements of either Party in the territory of the other according to the above mentioned boundaries, they shall be withdrawn from the said territory within the term of six months after the ratification of this treaty or sooner if it be possible and that they shall be permitted to take with them all the goods and effects which they possess.

Art. III.

In order to carry the preceding Article into effect one Commis-

Art. II.

Para evitar toda disputa en punto â los limites que separan los territorios de las dos Altas Partes Contratantes, se han convenido, y declarado en el presente articulo lo siguiente: â saber. Que el Limite Meridional de los Estados Unidos que sepára su territorio de el de las Colonias Españolas de la Florida Occidental y de la Florida Oriental se demarcará por una linea que empieze en el Rio Misisipi en la parte mas septentrional del grado treinta y uno al Norte de Equador, y qe. desde alli siga en derechura al Este hasta el medio del Rio Apalachicola ô Catahouche, desde alli por la mitad de este Rio hasta su union con el Flint, de alli en derechura hasta el nacimiento del Rio Sta. Maria, y de alli baxando por el medio de este Rio hasta el Occeano Atlantico. Y se han convenido las dos Potencias en que si hubiese tropa, Guarniciones, ô Establecimientos de la una de las dos Partes en el territorio de la otra segun los limites que se acaban de mencionar, se retirarán de dicho territorio en el termino de seis meses despues de la ratificacion de este Tratádo, ô antes si fuese posible, y que se les permitirá llevar consigo todos los bienes y efectos qe. posean.

Art. III.

Para la execucion del articulo antecedente se nombrarán por ca-

sioner and one Surveyor shall be appointed by each of the contracting Parties who shall meet at the Natchez on the left side of the River Mississippi before the expiration of six months from the ratification of this convention, and they shall proceed to run and mark this boundary according to the stipulations of the said Article. They shall make Plats and keep journals of their proceedings which shall be considered as part of this convention, and shall have the same force as if they were inserted therein. And if on any account it should be found necessary that the said Commissioners and Surveyors should be accompanied by Guards, they shall be furnished in equal proportions by the Commanding Officer of his Majesty's troops in the two Floridas, and the Commanding Officer of the troops of the United States in their Southwestern territory, who shall act by common consent and amicably, as well with respect to this point as to the furnishing of provisions and instruments and making every other arrangement which may be necessary or useful for the execution of this article.

da una de las dos Altas Partes contratantes un Comisario y un Geometra qe. se juntarán en Natchez en la orilla izquierda del Misisipi antes de expirar el termino de seis meses despues de la ratificacion de la convencion presente, y procederán à la demarcacion de estos limites conforme à lo estipulado en el articulo anterior. Levantarán planos, y formarán Diarios de sus operaciones que se reputarán como parte de este Tratado, y tendran la misma fuerza que si estubieran insertas en el. Y si por qualquier motivo se creyese necesario que los dichos Comisarios y Geometras fuesen acompañados con Guardias, se les darán en numero igual por el General que mande las tropas de S. M. en las dos Floridas, y el Comandante de las tropas de los Estados Unidos en su territorio del Sudoeste, que obrarán de acuerdo y amistosamente asi en este punto, como en el de apronto de viveres ê instrumentos, y en tomar qualesquiera otras disposiciones necesarias para la execucion de este articulo.

Art. IV.

It is likewise agreed that the Western boundary of the United States which separates them from the Spanish Colony of Louissiana, is in the middle of the channel or bed of the River Mississippi from the Northern boundary of the said States to the completion

Art. IV.

Se han convenido igualmente que el Limite Occidental del territorio de los Estados Unidos qe. los separa de la Colonia Española de la Luisiana, está en medio del Canal ô Madre del Rio Misisipi, desde el limite septentrional de dichos Estados has-

of the thirty first degree of latitude North of the Equator; and his Catholic Majesty has likewise agreed that the navigation of the said River in its whole breadth from its source to the Occean shall be free only to his Subjects, and the Citizens of the United States, unless he should extend this privilege to the Subjects of other Powers by special convention.

Art. V.

The two High contracting Parties shall by all the means in their power maintain peace and harmony among the several Indian Nations who inhabit the country adjacent to the lines and Rivers which by the preceding Articles form the boundaries of the two Floridas; and the beter to obtain this effect both Parties oblige themselves expressly to restrain by force all hostilities on the part of the Indian Nations living within their boundaries: so that Spain will not suffer her Indians to attack the Citizens of the United States, nor the Indians inhabiting their territory; nor will the United States permit these last mentioned Indians to commence hostilities against the Subjects of his Catholic Majesty, or his Indians in any manner whatever.

And whereas several treaties of Friendship exist between the two contracting Parties and the said Nations of Indians, it is hereby agreed that in future no treaty of alliance or other whatever

ta el complemento de los trienta y un grados de latitud al Notre del Equador; y S. M. Catolica ha convenido igualmente en que la navegacion de dicho Rio en toda su extension desde su orilla hasta el Occeano, será libre solo à sus Subditos, y á Ciudadanos de los Estados Unidos, â menos que por algun tratado particular haga extensiva esta libertad à subditos de otras Potencias.

Art. V.

Las dos Altas Partes contratantes procurarán por todos los medios posibles mantener la paz, y buena armonía entre las diversas Naciones de Indios que habitan los terrenos adyacentes â las lineas y Rios que en los articulos anteriores forman los limites de las dos Floridas; y para conseguir mejor este fin se obligan expresamente ambas Potencias à reprimir con la fuerza todo genero de hostilidades de parte de las Naciones Indias que habitan dentro de la linea de sus respectivos limites: de modo que ni la España permitirá que sus Indios ataquen â los qe. vivan en el territorio de los Estados Unidos ô â sus ciudadanos; ni los Estados qe. los suyos hostilizen â los Subditos de S. M. Catolica ô â sus Indios de manera alguna.

Exîstiendo varios tratados de amistad entre las expresadas Naciones y las dos Potencias, se ha convenido en no hacer en lo venidero alianza alguna ô tratado (excepto los de Paz) con las Na-

(except treaties of Peace) shall be made by either Party with the Indians living within the boundary of the other; but both Parties will endeavour to make the advantages of the Indian trade common and mutualy beneficial to their respective Subjects and Citizens observing in all things the most complete reciprocity: so that both Parties may obtain the advantages arising from a good understanding with the said Nations, without being subject to the expence which they have hitherto occasioned.

ciones de Indios que habitan dentro de los limites de la otra parte; aunque procurarán hacer comun su comercio en beneficio amplio de los Subditos y Ciudadanos respectivos, guardandose en todo la reciprocidad mas completa: de suerte qe. sin los dispendios que han causado hasta ahora dichas Naciones á las dos Partes contratantes consigan ambas todas las ventajas qe. debe producir la armonía con ellas.

Art. VI.

Each Party shall endeavour by all means in their power to protect and defend all Vessels and other effects belonging to the Citizens or Subjects of the other, which shall be within the extent of their jurisdiction by sea or by land, and shall use all their efforts to recover and cause to be restored to the right owners their Vessels and effects which may have been taken from them within the extent of their said jurisdiction whether they are at war or not with the Power whose Subjects have taken possession of the said effects.

Art. VI.

Cada una de las dos Partes contratantes procurará por todos los medios posibles protexer y defender todos los Buques y qualesquiera otros efectos pertencientes â los Subditos y Ciudadanos de la otra que se hallen en la extencion de su jurisdiccion por Mar ô por Tierra; y empleará todos su esfuerzos para recobrar y hacer restituir â los Propietarios lexitimos los Buques y Efectos que se les hayan quitado en la extension de dicha jurisdiccion estén ô no en guerra con la Potencia cuyos subditos hayan interceptado dichos Efectos.

Art. VII.

And it is agreed that the Subjects or Citizens of each of the contracting Parties, their Vessels, or effects shall not be liable to any embargo or detention on the part of the other for any military expedition or other public or

Art. VII.

Se ha convenido que los Ciudadanos y Subditos de una de las Partes contratantes, sus Buques, ô efectos no podran sugetarse â ningun embargo ô detencion de parte de la otra, â causa de alguna expedicion mili-

private porpose whatever; and in all cases of seizure, detention, or arrest for debts contracted or offences committed by any Citizen or Subject of the one Party within the jurisdiction of the other, the same shall be made and prosecuted by order and authority of law only, and according to the regular course of proceedings usual in such cases. The Citizens and Subjects of both Parties shall be allowed to employ such Advocates, Sollicitors, Notaries, Agents, and Factors, as they may judje proper in all their affairs and in all their trials at law in which they may be concerned before the tribunals of the other Party, and such Agents shall have free access to be present at the proceedings in such causes, and at the taking of all examinations and evidence which may be exhibited in the said trials.

Art. VIII.

In case the Subjects and inhabitants of either Party with their shipping whether public and of war or private and of merchants be forced through stress of weather, pursuit of Pirates, or Enemis, or any other urgent necessity for seeking of shelter and harbor to retreat and enter into any of the Rivers, Bays, Roads, or Ports belonging to the other Party, they shall be received and treated with all humanity, and enjoy all favor, protection and help, and they shall be permitted to refresh and provide themselves at reasonable

tar, uso publico, ô particular de qualquiera que sea; y en los casos de aprehension, detencion, ô arresto bien sea por deudas contrahidas û ofensas cometidas por algun Ciudadano ô Subdito de una de las Partes contratantes en la jurisdiccion de la otra, se procederá unicamente por orden y autoridad de la Justicia, y segun los tramites ordinarios seguidos en semejantes casos. Se permitira à los Ciudadanos y Subditos de ambas Partes emplear los Abogados, Procuradores, Notarios, Agentes, ô Factores que juzguen mas à proposito en todos sus asuntos y en todos los Pleytos qe. podrán tener en los Tribunales de la otra Parte, â los quales se permitirá igualmente el tener libre acceso en las causas, y estar presentes â todo exâmen y testimonios que podran ocurrir en los Pleytos.

Art. VIII.

Quando los Subditos y habitantes de la una de las dos Partes contratantes con sus Buques bien sean publicos y de guerra, bien particulares ô mercantiles se viesen obligados por una tempestad, por escapar de Piratas ô de Enemigos, ô por qualquiera otra necesidad urgente â buscar refugio y abrigo en alguno de los Rios, Bahias, Radas, ô Puertos de una de las dos Partes, serán recibidos, y tratados con humanidad, y gozaran de todo fabor, proteccion y socorro, y les será licito proveerse de refrescos, viveres y demas cosas necesarias para su sustento, para

rates with victuals and all things needful for the sustenance of their persons or reparation of their Ships, and prosecution of their voyage; and they shall no ways be hindered from returning out of the said Ports, or Roads, but may remove and depart when and whither they please without any let or hindrance.

componer los Buques, y continuar su viage, todo mediante un precio equitativo; y no se les detendrá ô impedirá de modo alguno el salir de dichos Puertos ô Radas, antes bien podran retirarse y partir como y quando les pareciere sin ningun obstaculo ô impedimento.

Art. IX.

All Ships and merchandize of what nature soever which shall be rescued out of the hands of any Pirates or Robbers on the high seas shall be brought into some Port of either State and shall be delivered to the custody of the Officers of that Port in order to be taken care of and restored entire to the true proprietor as soon as due and sufficient proof shall be made concerning the property there of.

Art. IX.

Todos los Buques y mercaderias de qualqiera naturaleza que sean que se hubiesen quitado à algunos Piratas en Altas Mar, y se traxesen à algun Puerto de una de las dos Potencias, se entregarán alli â los Oficiales ô Empleados en dicho Puerto â fin de que los guarden y restituyan integramente â su verdadero propietario luego que hiciese constar debida y plenamente que era su legitima propiedad.

Art. X.

When any Vessel of either Party shall be wrecked, foundered, or otherwise damaged on the coasts or within the dominion of the other, their respective Subjects or Citizens shall receive as well for themselves as for their Vessels and effects the same assistence which would be due to the inhabitants of the Country where the damage happens, and shall pay the same charges and dues only as the said inhabitants would be subject to pay in a like case: and if the operations of repair should require that the whole or any part of the cargo

Art. X.

En el caso de que Buque perteneciente à una de las dos Partes contratantes naufragase, varase, ô sufriese alguna avería en las Costas ô en los dominios de la otra, se socorrerá â los Subditos ô Ciudadanos respectivos, asi â sus personas, como a sus Buques y efectos, del mismo modo que se haría con los habitantes del Pais donde suceda la desgracia, y pagaran solo las mismas cargas y derechos qe. se hubieran exîgido de dichos habitantes en semejante caso. y si fuese necesario para componer el Buque qe. se descargue el cargamento en todo

be unladen they shall pay no duties, charges, or fees on the part which they shall relade and carry away.

ô en parte, no pagarán impuesto alguno, carga, o derecho de lo que se buelva â embarcar para ser exportado.

Art. XI.

Art. XI.

The Citizens and Subjects of each Party shall have power to dispose of their personal goods within the jurisdiction of the other by testament, donation, or otherwise; and their representatives being Subjects or Citizens of the other Party shall succeed to their said personal goods, whether by testament or ab intestato and they may take possession thereof either by themselves or others acting for them, and dispose of the same at their will paying such dues only as the inhabitants of the Country wherein the said goods are shall be subject to pay in like cases, and in case of the absence of the representatives, such care shall be taken of the said goods as would be taken of the goods of a native in like case, until the lawful owner may take measures for receiving them. And if question shall arise among several claimants to which of them the said goods belong the same shall be decided finally by the laws and Judges of the Land wherein said goods are. And where on the death of any person holding real estate within the territories of the one Party, such real estate would by the laws of the Land descend on a Citizen or Subject of the other were he not dis-

Los Ciudadanos ô Subditos de una de las dos Partes contratantes, tendran en los Estados de la otra la libertad de disponer de sus bienes personales bien sea por testamento, donacion, û otra manera, y si sus herederos fuesen Subditos ô Ciudadanos de la otra Parte contratante, sucederán en sus bienes ya sea en virtud de testamento ô ab intestato y podran tomar posesion bien en persona ô por medio de otros que hagan sus veces, y disponer como les pareciere sin pagar mas derechos que aquellos qe. deben pagar en semejante caso los habitantes del Pais donde se verificase la herencia. Y si estubiesen ausentes los herederos se cuydará de los bienes que les hubiesen tocado, del mismo modo que se hubiera hecho en semejante ocasion con los bienes de los naturales del Pais, hasta que el legitimo Proprietario haya aprobado las disposiciones para recoger la herencia. Si se suscitasen disputas entre diferentes competidores que tengan derecho â la herencia, seran determinadas en ultima instancia segun las leyes y por los Jueces del Pais en que vacase la herencia. Y si por la muerte de alguna persona que poseyese bienes raizes sobre el territorio de una de las Partes contratantes, estos bienes

qualified by being an alien, such
subject shall be allowed a reasonable time to sell the same and to
withdraw the proceeds without
molestation, and exempt from all
rights of detraction on the part of
the Government of the respective
states.

raizes llegasen à pasar segun las
leyes del Pais à un Subdito ô
Ciudadano de la otra Parte, y
este por su calidad de extrangero
fuese inhabil para poseerlos, ob-
tendra un termino conveniente
para venderlos y recoger su pro-
ducto, sin obstaculo, exento de
todo derecho de retencion de
parte del Gobierno de los Estados
respectivos.

Art. XII.

The merchant Ships of either of
the Parties which shall be making
into a Port belonging to the
enemy of the other Party and
concerning whose voyage and the
species of goods on board her
there shall be just grounds of
suspicion shall be obliged to
exhibit as well as upon the high
seas as in the Ports and havens
not only her passports but likewise certificates expressly shew-
ing that her goods are not of the
number of those which have been
prohibited as contraband.

Art. XII.

A los Buques mercantes de las
dos Partes qe. fuesen destinados
à Puertos perteneciences â una Potencia enemiga de una de las dos,
cuyo viage y naturaleza del cargamento diese justas sospechas, se
les obligará à presentar bien sea
en alta Mar bien en los Puertos
y Cabos no solo sus pasaportes
sino tambien los certificados que
probarán expresamente que su
cargamento no es de la especie
de los que están prohibidos como
de contrabando.

Art. XIII.

For the beter promoting of
commerce on both sides, it is
agreed that if a war shall break
out between the said two Nations
one year after the proclamation
of war shall be allowed to the
merchants in the Cities and
Towns where they shall live for
collecting and transporting their
goods and merchandizes, and if
anything be taken from them, or
any injury be done them within
that term by either Party, or the
People or Subjects of either, full

Art. XIII.

A fin de faborecer el comercio
de ambas Partes se ha convenido
que en el caso de romperse la
guerra entre las dos Naciones,
se concedera el termino de un
año depues de su declaracion à
los Comerciantes en las Villas
y Ciudades que habitan, para
juntar y transportar sus mercaderias, y si se les quitase alguna parte de ellas ô hiciese
algun daño durante el tiempo
prescrito arriba por una de las
dos Potentias, sus Pueblos ô

satisfaction shall be made for the same by the Government.

Subditos, se les dará en este punto entera satisfaccion por el Gobierno.

Art. XIV.

No subject of his Catholic Majesty shall apply for or take any commission or letters of marque for arming any Ship or Ships to act as Privateers against the said United States or against the Citizens, People or inhabitants of the said United States, or against the property of any of the inhabitants of any of them, from any Prince or State with which the said United States shall be at war.

Nor shall any Citizen, Subject or inhabitant of the said United States apply for or take any commission or letters of marque for arming any Ship or Ships to act as Privateers against the subjects of His Catholic Majesty or the property of any of them from any Prince or State with which the said King shall be at war. And if any person of either Nation shall take such commissions or letters of marque he shall be punished as a Pirate.

Art. XIV.

Ningun Subdito de S. M. Catolica tomará en cargo ô patente para armar Buque ô Buques qe. obren como Corsarios contra dichos Estados Unidos, ô contra los Ciudadanos, Pueblos, y habitantes de los mismos, ô contra su proprieded ô la de los habitantes de alguno de ellos de qualquier Principe que sea con quien estubieren en guerra los Estados Unidos.

Ygualmente ningun Ciudadano ô habitante de dichos Estados Unidos pedirá ô acceptará encargo ô patente para armar algun Buque ô Buques con el fin de perseguir los Subditos de S. M. Catolica, ô apoderarse de su propiedad, de qualquier Principe ô Estado que sea con quien estubiese en guerra S. M. Catolica. Y si algun individuo de una ô de otra Nacion tomase semejantes encargos ô patentes sera castigado como Pirata.

Art. XV.

It shall be lawful for all and singular the Subjects of the Catholic Mayesty, and the Citizens People, and inhabitants of the said United States to sail with their Ships with all manner of liberty and security, no distinction being made who are the proprietors of the merchandizes laden thereon from any Port to

Art. XV.

Se permitirá à todos y â cada uno de los Subditos de S. M. Catolica; y â los Ciudadanos Pueblos y habitantes de dichos Estados qe. puedan navegar con sus Embarcaciones con toda libertad y seguirdad, sin que haya la menor excepcion por este respeto aunque los propietarios de las mercaderias cargadas en las referidas

the Places of those who now are or hereafter shall be at enmity with his Catholic Majesty or the United States. It shall be likewise lawful for the Subjects and inhabitants aforesaid to sail with the Ship and merchandizes aforementioned, and to trade with the same liberty and security from the Places, Ports, and Havens of those who are Enemies of both or either Party without any opposition or disturbance whatsoever, not only directly from the Places of the Enemy aforementioned to neutral Places but also from one Place belonging to an enemy to another Place belonging to an Enemy, whether they be under the jurisdiction of the same Prince or under several; and it is hereby stipulated that Free Ships shall also give freedom to goods, and that everything shall be deemed free and exempt which shall be found on board the Ships belonging to the Subjects of either of the contracting Parties although the whole lading or any part thereof should appartain to the Enemies of either; contraband goods being always excepted. It is also agreed that the same liberty be extended to persons who are on board a free Ship, so that, although they be Enemies to either Party they shall not be made Prisoners or taken out of that free Ship unless they are Soldiers and in actual service of the Enemies.

embarcaciones vengan del Puerto que quieran y las traygan destinadas à qualquiera Plaza de una Potencia actualmente enemiga ô qe. lo sea despues asi de S. M. Catolica como de los Estados Unidos. Se permitirá igualmente à los Subditos y habitantes mencionados navegar con sus Buques y mercaderias, y frequëntar con igual libertad y seguridad las Plazas y Puertos de las Potencias enemigas de las Partes contratantes ô de una de ellas sin oposicion û obstaculo, y de comerciar no solo desde los puertos del dicho enemigo à un Puerto neutro directamente, sino tambien desde uno enemigo â otro tal bien se encuentre bajo su jurisdicion ô bajo la de muchos; y se estipula tambien por el presente tratado que los Buques libres asegurarán igualmente la libertad de las mercaderias, y que se juzgaran libres todos los efectos que se hallasen â bordo de los Buques que perteneciesen â los Subditos de una de las Partes contratantes, aun quando el cargamto. por entero ô parte de el fuese de los enemigos de una de las dos; bien entendido sin embargo qe. el contrabando se exceptua siempre. Se ha convenido asimismo que la propria libertad gozarán los sugetos que pudiesen encontrase â bordo del Buque libre aun quando fuesen enemigos de una de las dos Partes contratantes, y por lo tanto no se les podra hacer Prisioneros ni separarlos de dichos Buques, à menos qe. no tengan la qualidad

de Militares, y esto hallandose en aquella sazon empleados en el servicio del enemigo.

Art. XVI.

This liberty of navigation and commerce shall extend to all kinds of merchandizes excepting those only which are distinguished by the name of contraband; and under this name of contraband or prohibited goods shall be comprehended arms, great guns, bombs, with the fusees, and other things belonging to them, cannon ball, gunpowder, match, pikes, swords, lances, speards, halberds, mortars, petards, granades, salpetre, muskets, musketball bucklers, helmets, breast plates, coats of mail, and the like kind of arms proper for arming soldiers, musket rests, belts, horses with their furniture and all other warlike instruments whatever. These merchandizes which follows shall not be reckoned among contraband or prohibited goods; that is to say, all sorts of cloths and all other manufactures woven of any wool, flax, silk, cotton, or any other materials whatever, all kinds of wearing aparel together with all species whereof they are used to be made, gold and silver as well coined as uncoined, tin, iron, latton, copper, brass, coals, as also wheat, barley, oats and any other kind of corn and pulse: tobacco and likewise all manner of spices, salted and smoked flesh, salted fish, cheese and butter, beer, oils, wines, sugars, and all sorts of salts, and in general all provisions

Art. XVI.

Esta libertad de navegacion y de comerico debe extenderse â toda especie de mercaderias, exceptuando solo las que se comprehenden bajo el nombre de contrabando ô de mercaderias prohibidas: quales son las armas, cañones, bombas con sus mechas y demas cosas pertenecientes â lo mismo: balas, polvera, mechas, picas espadas, lanzas, dardos, alabardas, morteros, petardos, granadas, salitre, fusiles, balas escudos, casquetes, corazas, cotas de malla y otras armas de esta especie propîas para armar â los Soldados. Portamosquetes, bandoleras, Caballos, con sus armas y otros instrumentos de guerra sean los que fueren. Pero los generos y mercaderias que se nombrarán ahora, no se comprehenderán entre los de contrabando ô cosas prohibidas: â saber, toda especie de paños y qualesquiera otras telas de lana, lino, Seda, algodon, û otras qualesquiera materias, toda especie de vestidos con las telas de que se acostumbran hacer, el oro y la plata labrada en moneda ô no, el estaño yerro, laton, cobre, bronce, carbon, del mismo modo que la cevada, el trigo, la avena, y qualesquiera otro genero de legumbres: el tabaco y toda la especieria, carne salada y ahumada, pescado salado, queso y manteca, cerveza, aceytes, vinos, azucar y toda especie de sal, y

which serve for the sustenance of life. Furthermore all kinds of cotton, hemp, flax, tar, pitch, ropes, cables, sails, sail cloths, anchors, and any parts of anchors, also ships masts, planks, wood of all kind, and all other things proper either for building or repairing ships, and all other goods whatever which have not been worked into the form of any instrument prepared for war by land or by sea, shall not be reputed contraband, much less such as have been already wrought and made up for any other use: all which shall be wholy reckoned among free goods, as likewise all other merchandizes and things which are not comprehended and particularly mentioned in the foregoing enumeration of contraband goods: so that they may be transported and carried in the freest manner by the subjects of both parties, even to Places belonging to an Enemy, such towns or Places being only excepted as are at that time besieged, blocked up, or invested. And except the cases in which any Ship of war or Squadron shall in consequence of storms or other accidents at sea be under the necessity of taking the cargo of any trading Vessel or Vessels, in which case they may stop the said Vessel or Vessels and furnish themselves with necessaries, giving a receipt in order that the Power to whom the said ship of war belongs may pay for the articles so taken according to the price thereof at the Port to which they may ap-

en general todo genero de provisiones que sirven para el sustento de la vida. Ademas toda especie de algodon cañamo, lino, alquitran, pez, cuerdas, cables, velas, telas para velas, ancoras, y partes de que se componen, mastiles, tablas, maderas de todas especies, y qualesquiera otras cosas que sirvan para la construccion y reparacion de los Buques, y otras qualesquiera materias que no tienen la forma de un instrumento preparado para le guerra por tierra ô por mar no seran reputadas de contrabando, y menos las que estan ya preparadas para otros usos. Todas las cosas que se acaban de nombrar deben ser comprehendidas entre las mercaderias libres, lo mismo que todas las demas mercaderias y efectos que no estan comprehendidos y nombrados expresamente en la eneumaracion de los generos de contrabando: de manera que podran ser transportados y conducidos con la mayor libertad por los Subditos de las dos Partes contratantes, á las Plazas enemigas, exceptuando sin embargo las qe. se hallasen en la actualidad sitiadas, bloqueadas, ô embestidas. Y los casos en que algun Buque de Guerra, ô Esquadra que por efecto de avería û otras causas se halle en necesidad de tomar los efectos que conduzca el Buque ô Buques de comercio, pues en tal caso podra detenerlos para aprovisionarse y dar un recibo para que la Potencia cuyo sea el Buque que tome los efectos, los pague segun el valor que

pear to have been destined by the Ship's papers: and the two contracting Parties engage that the Vessels shall not be detained longer than may be absolutely necessary for their said Ships to supply themselves with necessaries: that they will immediately pay the value of the receipts: and indemnify the proprietor for all losses which he may have sustained in consequence of such transaction.

tendrian en el Puerto adonde se dirigiese el propietario segun lo expresen sus cartas de navegacion: obligandose las dos Partes contratantes â no detener los Buques mas de lo que sea absolutamente necesario para aprovisionarse, pagar inmediatamente los recibos, y â indemnizar todos los daños qe. sufra el propietario â consequencia de semejante suceso.

Art. XVII.

To the end that all manner of dissentions and quarels may be avoided and prevented on one side and the other, it is agreed that in case either of the Parties hereto should be engaged in a war, the ships and Vessels belonging to the Subjects or People of the other Party must be furnished with sea letters or passports expressing the name, property, and bulk of the Ship, as also the name and place of habitation of the master or commander of the said Ship, that it may appear thereby that the Ship really and truly belongs to the Subjects of one of the Parties; which passport shall be made out and granted according to the form annexed to this Treaty. They shall likewise be recalled every year, that is, if the ship happens to return home within the space of a year. It is likewise agreed that such ships being laden, are to be provided not only with passports as above mentioned, but also with certificates containing

Art. XVII.

A fin de evitar entre ambas Partes toda especie de disputas y quejas, se ha convenido qe. en el caso de que una de las dos Potencias se hallase empeñada en una guerra, los Buques y Bastimentos pertenecientes à los Subditos ô Pueblos de la otra, deberan llevar consigo patentes de Mar ô pasaportes que expresen el nombre, la propiedad, y el porte del Buque, como tambien el nombre y morada de su dueño y Comandante de dicho Buque, para que de este modo conste que pertenece real y verdaderamente â los Subditos de una de las dos Partes contratantes; y que dichos pasaportes deberan expedirse segun el modelo adjunto al presente tratado. Todos los años deberán renovarse estos pasaportes en el caso de que el Buque buelva â su Pais en el espacio de un año. Igualmente se ha convenido en que los Buques mencionados arriba si estubiesen cargados, deberán llevar no solo los pasaportes sino tambien certificados que contengan el pormenor

the several particulars of the cargo, the place whence the ship sailed, that so it may be known whether any forbidden or contraband goods be on board the same; which certificates shall be made out by the Officers of the place whence the ship sailed in the accustomed form; and if any one shall think it fit or adviseable to express in the said certificates the person to whom the goods on board belong he may freely do so; without which requisites they may be sent to one of the Ports of the other contracting Party and adjudged by the competent tribunal according to what is above set forth, that all the circumstances of this omission having been well examined, they shall be adjudged to be legal prizes, unless they shall give legal satisfaction of their property by testimony entirely equivalent.

del cargamento, el lugar de donde ha salido el Buque, y la declaracion de las mercaderias de contrabando qe. pudiesen hallarse âbordo; cuyos certificados deberán expedirse en la forma acostumbrada por los Oficiales empleados en el Lugar de donde el Navio se hiciese â la vela; y si se juzgase util y prudente expresar en dichos pasaportes la persona propietaria de las mercaderias se podra hacer libremente: sin cuyos requisitos sera conducido à uno de los Puertos de la Potencia respectiva y juzgado por el tribunal competente con arregelo â lo arriba dicho, para que exâminadas bien las circunstancias de su falta sea condenado por de buena presa si no satisfaciese legalmente con los testimonios equivalentes en un todo.

Art. XVIII.

If the Ships of the said subjects, People or inhabitants of either of the Parties shall be met with either sailing along the Coasts on the high Seas by any Ship of war of the other or by any Privateer, the said Ship of war or Privateer for the avoiding of any disorder shall remain out of cannon shot, and may send their boats aboard the merchant Ship which they shall so meet with, and may enter her to number of two or three men only to whom the master or Commander of such ship or vessel shall exhibit his passports con-

Art. XVIII.

Quando un Buque perteneciente â los dichos Subditos, Pueblos, y habitantes de una de las dos Partes fuese encontrado navegando â lo largo de la Costa ô en plena Mar por un Buque de Guerra de la otra, ô por un corsario, dicho Buque de guerra ô corsario â fin de evitar todo desorden se mantendrá fuera del tiro de cañon, y podra enviar su Chalupa â bordo del Buque mercante, hacer entrar en el dos ô tres hombres â los quales enseñará el Patron, ô Comandante del Buque sus pasaportes y demas

cerning the property of the ship made out according to the form inserted in this present Treaty: and the ship when she shall have shewed such passport shall be free and at liberty to pursue her voyage, so as it shall not be lawful to molest or give her chace in any manner or force her to quit her intended course.

Art. XIX.

Consuls shall be reciprocally established with the privileges and powers which those of the most favoured Nations enjoy in the Ports where their consuls reside, or are permitted to be.

Art. XX.

It is also agreed that the inhabitants of the territories of each Party shall respectively have free access to the Courts of Justice of the other, and they shall be permitted to prosecute suits for the recovery of their properties, the payment of their debts, and for obtaining satisfaction for the damages which they may have sustained, whether the persons whom they may sue be subjects or Citizens of the Country in which they may be found, or any other persons whatsoever who may have taken refuge therein; and the proceedings and sentences of the said Court shall be the same as if the contending parties had been subjects or Citizens of the said Country.

documentos que deberan ser conformes â lo prevenido en el presente tratado, y probará la propiedad del Buque: y despues de haber exhibido semejante pasaporte, y documentos, se les dejará seguir libremente su viage sin que les sea licito el molestarles ni procurar de modo alguno darle caza û obligarle à dejar el rumbo qe. seguía.

Art. XIX.

Se establecerán Consules reciprocamente con los privilegios y facultades que gozaren los de las Naciones mas faborecidas en los Puertos donde los tubieren estas ô les sea licito el tenerlos.

Art. XX.

Se ha convenido igualmente que los habitantes de los territorios de una y otra Parte respectivanente seran admitidos en los tribunales de Justicia de la otra Parte, y les sera permitido el entablar sus Pleytos para el recobro de sus propiedades, pago de sus deudas, y satisfaccion de los daños que hubieren recibido bien sean las personas contra las quales se quejasen Subditos ô Ciudadanos del Pais en el que se hallen, ô bien sean qualesquiera otros sugetos que se hayan refugiado alli; y los Pleytos y sentencias de dichos tribunales seran las mismas que hubieran sido en el caso de que las Partes litigantes fueren Subditos ô Ciudadanos del mismo Pais.

Art. XXI.

In order to terminate all differences on account of the losses sustained by the Citizens of the United States in consequence of their vessels and cargoes having been taken by the Subjects of his Catholic Majesty during the late war between Spain and France, it is agreed that all such cases shall be referred to the final decision of Commissioners to be appointed in the following manner. His Catholic Majesty shall name one Commissioner, and the President of the United States by and with the advice and consent of their Senate shall appoint another, and the said two Commissioners shall agree on the choice of a third, or if they cannot agree so they shall each propose one person, and of the two names so proposed one shall be drawn by lot in the presence of the two original Commissioners, and the person whose name shall be so drawn shall be the third Commissioner, and the three Commissioners so appointed shall be sworn impartially to examine and decide the claims in question according to the merits of the several cases, and to justice, equity, and the laws of Nations. The said Commissioners shall meet and sit at Philadelphia and in the case of the death, sickness, or necessary absence of any such commissioner his place shall be supplied in the same manner as he was first appointed, and the new Commissioner shall take the same oaths, and do the same

Art. XXI.

A fin de concluir todas las disensiones sobre las perdidas que los Ciudadanos de los Estados Unidos hayan sufrido en sus Buques y cargamentos apresados por los vasallos de S. M. Catolica durante la guerra que se acaba de finalizar entre España y Francia se ha convenido que todos estos casos se determinarán finalmte. por Comisarios que se nombrarán de esta mamera. S. M. Catolica nombrará uno, y el Presidente de los Estados Unidos otro con consentimiento y aprobacion del Senado, y estos dos Comisarios nombrarán un tercero de comun acuerdo: pero si no pudiesen acordase cada uno nombrará una persona, y sus dos nombres puestos en suerte se sacarán en presencia de los dos Comisarios, resultando por tercero aquel cuyo nombre hubiese salido el primero. Nombrados asi estos tres Comisarios, jurarán que exâminarán y decidorán con imparcialidad las quejas de que se trata segun el merito de la diferencia de los casos, y segun dicten la justicia, equidad, y derecho de gentes. Dichos Comisarios se juntarán y tendran sus sesiones en Filadelfia, y en caso de muerte, enfermedad, ô ausencia precisa se reemplazará su plaza de la misma manera que se eligió, y el nuevo Comisario hará igual juramento y exercerá iguales funciones. En el termino de diez y ocho meses contados desde el dia en que se junten, admitirán todas las quejas y reclamaciones autorizadas

duties. They shall receive all complaints and applications, authorized by this article during eighteen months from the day on which they shall assemble. They shall have power to examine all such persons as come before them on oath or affirmation touching the complaints in question, and also to receive in evidence all written testimony authenticated in such manner as they shall think proper to require or admit. The award of the said Commissioners or any two of them shall be final and conclusive both as to the justice of the claim and the amount of the sum to be paid to the claimants; and his Catholic Majesty undertakes to cause the same to be paid in specie without deduction, at such times and Places and under such conditions as shall be awarded by the said Commissioners.

por este articulo. Asimismo tendran autoridad para exâminar baxo la sancion del juramento â todas las personas que ocurran ante ellos sobre puntos relativos â dichas quejas, y recibirán como evidente todo testimonio escrito que de tal manera sea autentico que ellos lo juzguen digno de pedirle ô admitirle. La decision de dichos Comisarios ô de dos de ellos sera final y concluyente tanto por lo qe. toca â la justicia de la queja como por lo que monte la suma que se deba satisfacer â los demandantes, y S. M. Catolica se obliga â hacer las pagar en especie sin rebaxa, y en las epocas lugares, y baxo las condicones que se decidan por los Comisarios.

Art. XXII.

The two high contracting Parties hopping that the good correspondence and friendship which happily reigns between them will be further increased by this Treaty, and that it will contribute to augment their prosperity and opulence, will in future give to their mutual commerce all the extension and favor which the advantage of both Countries may require; and in consequence of the stipulations contained in the IV. Article his Catholic Majesty will permit the Citizens of the United States for the space of

Art. XXII.

Esperando las dos Altas partes contratantes que la buena correspondencia y amistad que reyna actualmente entre si se estrechará mas y mas con el presente tratado, y que contribuirá à aumentar su prosperidad y opulencia, consederán reciprocamente en lo succesivo al comercio todas las ampliaciones ô fabores que exigiese la utilidad de los dos Paises; y desde luego à consequencia de lo estipulado en el articulo IV. permitirá S. M. Catolica por espacio de tres años a los Ciudadanos de los Estados Unidos que deposi-

three years from this time to deposit their merchandize and effects in the Port of New Orleans and to export them from thence without paying any other duty than a fair price for the hire of the stores, and his Majesty promises either to continue this permission if he finds during that time that it is not prejudicial to the interests of Spain, or if he should not agree to continue it there, he will assign to them on another part of the banks of the Mississippi an equivalent establishment.

Art. XXIII.

The present Treaty shall not be in force untill ratified by the Contracting Parties, and the ratifications shall be exchanged in six months from this time, or sooner if possible.

In witness whereof We the underwritten Plenipotentiaries of His Catholic Majesty and of the United States of America have signed this present treaty of Friendship, Limits and Navigation and have thereunto affixed our seals respectively.

Done at San Lorenzo el Real this seven and twenty day of October one thousand seven hundred and ninety-five.

ten sus mercaderias y efectos en el Puerto de Nueva Orleans, y que las extraigan sin pagar mas derechos qe. un precio justo por el alquiler de los Almacenes ofreciendo S. M. continuar en termino de esta gracia si se experimentase durante aquel tiempo que no es perjudicial á los intereses de la España, ó si no conviniese su continuacion en aquel Puerto proporcionará en otra parte de las orillas del Rio Misisipi un igual establecimiento.

Art. XXIII.

El presente tratado no tendrá efecto hasta que las Partes contratantes le hayan ratificado, y las ratificaciones se cambiarán en el termino de seis meses, ó antes si fuese posible contando desde este dia.

En fe de lo qual Nosotros los infraescritos Plenipotenciarios de S. M. Catolica y de los Estados Unidos de America hemos firmado en virtud de nuestros plenos poderes este tratado de Amistad, Limites, y Navegacion, y le hemos puesto nuestros sellos respectivos.

Hecho en San Lorenzo el Real à veinte y siete de Octubre de mil setecientos noventa y cinco.

| SEAL | THOMAS PINCKNEY. |

| SEAL | EL PRINCIPE DE LA PAZ. |

| SEAL | THOMAS PINCKNEY. |

| SEAL | EL PRINCIPE DE LA PAZ. |

Index

Abbreviations, key to, xv.

Adams, Henry, historian, 311.

Alcudia, Duke of, see Godoy.

Alliance, proposed between Spain and U. S. during American Revolution, 27–8; proposed by Gardoqui to Jay (1786), 77–81; Anglo-Spanish, 169, 187, 196, 198–204; proposed by Gardoqui (1793), 190; by Godoy, 195–7, 203–7, 267–93; proposed triple alliance, between U. S., Spain and France, 227–69; proposed by Kentucky separatists to Spain, 214–7; by Tennessee separatists, 140–1; France and Spain, 314.

Anse à la Graisse, (New Madrid), Spanish fortified post, 123.

Apalachicola River, 6, 63, 104.

Aranda, Count de, Spanish ambassador at Paris, introduces Arthur Lee to Spanish Ministry, 10; advises Spanish recognition of independence of the U. S. and alliance with same, 12–13; discusses boundaries with Jay at Paris, 30–4; American overture to, 59; political ruin of, for Godoy's advancement, 170.

Arkansas, Spanish fortified post at, 83.

Armed Neutrality of 1780, principles of, 259–60, 298.

Barbary States, 82, 257.

Barrancas de Margot, see Ecores à Margot.

Basle, Treaty of, between France and Spain, 219; signed, 267–8; announced in Madrid, 272–3.

Bermuda Islands, Dickinson's proposal to obtain with Spanish aid, 21.

Blake, U.S. courier, 187, 229.

Blount, William, project to attack Louisiana, 310.

Boundaries, of Louisiana and the Floridas, 1–6, 20–1, 29–35, 41–5, 63, 71–2, 79–87, 102–5, 294–5, 311–12; proposed mutual guaranty of boundaries by Spain and U. S., 78; U. S.-Spanish boundary settled, 294–7; surveyed, 311.

Bowles, William Augustus, British adventurer among Creek Indians, 141n.

Brown, John, member of Continental Congress from Kentucky District of Va., and one of Wilkinson's coterie, 115; intrigue with Gardoqui, 132–7; his specious explanation of failure of Kentucky statehood (1788), 133; hopefully harbors project of separating Kentucky, 144.

Buell's Map, 65n.

Butler, Senator Pierce, Gardoqui's informant, desires appointment as U. S. envoy to Spain, 208n.

Campeche wood-cutting rights, 37.

Canada, proposal to get Spain to assist U. S. to obtain, 20–1.

Canary Islands, 78.

Carmichael, William, U. S. chargé

in Spain, and joint commissioner plenipotentiary, arrives in
Spain with Jay (1780), 24;
Humphreys brings instructions
to, 152, 155; appointed joint
commissioner, 161; early career,
166–7; paucity of official correspondence, 167; death in Madrid, 219–20, 235; as agent in
paying U. S. debt to Spain,
326–7.

Carmichael and Short (see also
separately) joint mission to
Spain, 161–96; lack of splendor
and carriage complained of by
Godoy, 195, 208–9.

Carolina, early boundaries, 5, 19.

Carondelet, Baron de, Spanish
Governor of New Orleans, appointed, 175; at first mistrusts
Wilkinson, 175; Indian policy,
175; furnishes munitions to
Creek, 178; occupies Walnut
Hills, 178; Indian alliances negotiated by, 179–80; occupies
Confederación, 180; incites Indians against U. S., 181–2; relations with Western separatists,
217, 232–3; reports read in Spanish Council of State, 218; negotiations with Wilkinson and Sebastian at New Orleans, 302–7.

Charles III of Spain, 1, 38, 73.

Chattahoochee River, 6, 30.

Cherokee Indians, U. S. treaty
(Hopewell) with, 50, 52; U. S.
treaty of 1791 with, 177; renewed difficulties with U. S.,
179–80.

Chickasaw Bluffs, see Ecores à
Margot.

Chickasaw Indians, U. S. treaty
(Hopewell) with, 50–1; Spanish
treaty with, 54, 178–9.

Chocktaw Indians, U. S. treaty
(Hopewell) with, 50; Spanish
treaty with, 54.

Clark, George Rogers, leads raid
on Spanish storekeeper, 117;
project of invasion of Louisiana,
303.

Confederación, Spanish fortified
post on Tombigbee, 180, 309.

Congress, Continental, attitude on
Mississippi navigation, 16–22,
81–90, 144–7; and Indians, 47–8;
in session at N. Y., 66; and
Jay's proposed Spanish treaty,
81–90; and Kentucky, 132.

Constitution of U. S., adopted,
147; effect on foreign relations,
158.

Contraband, defined in Pinckney's
Treaty, 299.

Corwin, Professor E. S., cited, 15.

Creek Indians, abortive treaties
with Georgia, 48–53; Spanish
treaties with, 54; Spanish munitions furnished to, 56–7; U. S.
treaty (of N. Y.) with, 176; hostilities with Georgians, 178; with
U. S., 180; weaned away by
Carondelet, 181–5.

Cumberland settlements and Spanish intrigue, 137–42.

Deane, Silas, U. S. commissioner
at Paris, 10.

Demarcation Bulls of Pope Alexander VI, 4, 154.

Deposit, right of, see Entrepôt.

Dickinson, John, member of Continental Congress, proposals re
Spanish negotiation, 21.

Dunn, Isaac, agent of Wilkinson
sent to New Orleans, 130, 144.

East Florida, 5–6, 30.

Ecores à Margot, Spanish fortified post established near present Memphis, Tenn., 184, 282.

Entrepôt (right of deposit), Jefferson constructs U. S. right to, 152; Pinckney's negotiation for, 278–80; ambiguous article thereon, in Pinckney's Treaty, 301.

Euphrasia (Euphrasee) River, 65, 104.

Family Compact, 2, 12, 14.

Flint River, 64, 294.

Florida, see also Boundaries, 1–6, 13, 16, 37, 38, 39, 101, 293.

Floridablanca, Count of, Spanish Minister, policy toward American Revolution, 9, 12–14; early career, 11; explains Jay's departure from Spain, 29; conferences and correspondence with Lafayette, 71n; instructions to Gardoqui, 62, 72, 79n, 103, 107–8, 126–7; advises Gardoqui to treat with western separatists (James White), 128; policy of attracting inhabitants of western U. S. to La., 129; opinion on suggested exchange of Gibraltar for Florida, 160; invites American negotiation at Madrid, 163; ruined to make way for Godoy, 170.

France, policy towards La. (1763), 1–5; and American Revolution, 13; policy toward Spain and U. S. in peace negotiations (1782), 31–4, 35n; declaration of war against Great Britain, 151; invasion of Spain, 225; peace with Spain, 267–8; effect of Jay's Treaty on, 243; proposes joint diplomatic action with Spain against U. S., 310.

Franklin, Benjamin, at Paris (1782), 10, 29.

Franklin, abortive "state" of, 137–43.

Free ships, free goods, 299.

French Revolution, 150, 156, 163–4, 168, 198, 313.

Galvez, Bernardo de, Captain-General of Louisiana and Cuba, instructions to Gardoqui re boundary, 62–5.

Galvez, Josef de, Spanish Minister of the Indies, Miralles to, 16; instructions to Gardoqui, 62.

Gardoqui, Diego de, Spanish diplomat and Minister, arrives at Philadelphia, 55; early career, 60–2; negotiations with Jay in U. S., 60–108; appraisal of Jay and Mrs. Jay, 62; instructions to, 62–6; fear of western separatism, 92; agrees with Jay on Mississippi formula, 93; entertains members of Congress, 99–100; Jay represents his views to Congress, 100–1; ceases to negotiate with Jay or Congress, 102; comments on proposed neutral Indian buffer state, 106; instructed to conspire with western separatists, 138; and James White, 92, 108, 126, 137–40; and John Sevier, 139–43; and James Robertson, 139–43; leaves U. S., 147; opinion on American note (1791), 157–9; Minister of Finance in Godoy's Government, 171; negotiations with Carmichael and Short, 171–2, 188–91; proposes alliance again (1793), 190–4; secret conferences with Short, 221–9, 241; proposes to visit Bagnères with Short, 226; opinion to Short on Jay's Treaty, 230; on Louisiana trade, 256; and U. S. debt to Spain, 331–4.

Gayoso de Lemos, Spanish commander at Nogales, 178, 302–6.

Genêt, Edmond, his mission to U. S. (1793), 202n, 310.

Georgia, early boundaries, 5–6; separate negotiations with Creek Indians, 48; Indian murders in, 188.

Gérard, Conrad Alexandre, French minister to U. S., 17, 18, 20.

Gibraltar, 13, 14, 37, 159.

Godoy, Manuel de, Spanish Minister, rise of, 170–1; willingness to *discuss* matters with Carmichael and Short, 194; transfers negotiations to U. S., 194–7; his propositions of alliance for the President, 198–217; reaction to Jay's mission to England, 202–4; proposes to Council an alliance with U. S., 203–7; Short's peace intrigues dependent upon approval of, 222; efforts for separate peace with France, 200, 219, 234; conference with Short re Jay's Treaty, 230–1; instructions to Jaudenes re Kentucky separatists and Whiskey rebels, 232–3; does not know full text of Jay's Treaty, 234, 284–93; policy of alliance with U. S., 234; communicates with France, 242; negotiations with Pinckney, 267–93; negotiates separate peace with France, 267–73; allows Carondelet to continue Wilkinson intrigue, 305; gives order to execute treaty with U. S., 311; failure of his foreign policy,

313–14; and U. S. financial debt to Spain, 331–2.

Grasse, Comte de, French naval commander, defeated by Rodney, 37.

Great Britain, policy towards La., 1–6; and Spanish diplomacy in the American Revolution, 8–9; colonial policy in Mississippi Valley, 6, 39–40; alliance with Spain (1793), 169, 187, 196; concern in French war, 198.

Green, Gen. Thomas, writes letter extolling lawless acts of G. R. Clark, 117.

Grimaldi, Marquis de, Spanish Minister, 8, 10.

Hamilton, Alexander, ability as statesman, vii; urges joint Anglo-American attack on Louisiana to open up Mississippi, 158; informal and intimate relations with British Government, 247; pays off U. S. Revolutionary debts to France and Spain, 326–34.

Henry, Patrick, declines Spanish mission, 208n.

Hiawassee (Euphrasia) River, 65, 104.

Honduras, 71.

Hood, Admiral, and Toulon incident, 199.

Hopewell, Indian treaties there, with U. S., 50, 177.

Humphreys, David, takes instructions to Carmichael, 152.

Iberville River, as boundary, 2, 3, 6.

Illinois, 16.

Indians, British policy, 6; Rayneval's memoir on boundaries for,

31–4; Southwestern Indians (see Creek, Chickasaw, Choctaw, Cherokee), 40, 46–58, 175–82; proposed Indian neutral barrier state in Southwest, 104–5; article in Pinckney's Treaty, 297.

Innes, Harry, Wilkinson's fellow-conspirator, 113, 115, 144, 156, 211n.

Innes, Col. James, sent to Kentucky by Washington, 211n.

Jackasses, presented to Washington, 96.

Jamaica, 38.

Jaudenes, Josef de, Spanish agent in U. S. (see also Viar), informs Jefferson of Spain's desire to renew negotiations, 160; Jefferson's expostulations to, 182, 183, 185–6; hostile tone, 185; opinion on Anglo-American crisis (1794), 201–2; acknowledges receipt of Godoy's propositions for the President, 208; delays submitting them, 211–17, 270–1; intrigues with separatists, 213–17, 232–3; trafficking in export licenses, 256; asks instructions re Spanish maritime policy, 266n; recalled, 283; in negotiation re U. S. debt to Spain, 332.

Jay, John, President of Continental Congress and interviews with Miralles, 16; instructions of Congress to, re Spanish negotiation, 22; sketch of his career and character, 22–4; negotiations in Spain (1780–1782), 24–9; negotiations with Aranda in Paris, 30–4; suggests to British that they repossess the Floridas, 39; Gardoqui's appraisal of, 62; presented with Spanish stallion,

73; reports to Congress on Mississippi navigation recommending cloture for 25 years, 84–7; urges action by Congress, 100–2; agrees with Gardoqui on Mississippi formula, 93; reports again to Congress, modifying views on Mississippi navigation, 145–7; mission to England, 201, 214, 227–8; delays Pinckney in London, 250.

Jay, Mrs. (Sara Livingston), marriage, 23–4; decisive influence on her husband, 62; cultivated by Gardoqui, 72; Gardoqui acts gallant to, in the King's interest, 75.

Jay's Treaty, effect of on Spanish-American diplomacy, viii, 227–9, 234, 243, 267, 284n, 296–7, 299, 300, 302, 307–14.

Jefferson, Thomas, trust in Europe's distress for America's advantage, 150–3; Secretary of State, 149; instructions to Carmichael, 153; to Short, 153–4; to Carmichael and Short, 186–7; sounds France on Mississippi Question, 155; begins Spanish negotiation, 155–62; and Indians, 182–8; offers at first to guarantee Spain's territory, 160–1; warns against guaranty of Spain's territory, 190, 271; quits Department of State, 205–6; declines Spanish mission, 208n; rumored mission to Europe, 223; reliance on Europe's quarrels justified, 312.

Kentucky's pioneer settlements, 46, 76, 82, 92; separatists, 109–18, 129–37, 172–4, 210, 213–17, 303–7; conventions, 111–17, 131; pe-

368

INDEX

titions to Congress, 132, 136;
statehood, 173.

Knox, Henry, Secretary of War,
negotiations with McGillivray,
176.

Lafayette, Marquis de, conversations and correspondence with
Floridablanca, 71n; good offices
invoked by Jefferson, 155.

Langara, Spanish Admiral, opinion on Toulon incident, 200.

Lee, Arthur, mission to Spain, 10;
and Spanish subsidies, 329n.

Lee, Henry, member of Continental Congress and informant of
Gardoqui, 92; receives "loan"
of $5,000 from Gardoqui, 94;
Gardoqui uses in attempt to influence Washington, 99.

Lee, Richard Henry, President of
Continental Congress, friend of
Gardoqui, 95.

Livingston, Robert R., on Spanish
loan, 326.

Louis XV of France, 1–3.

Louis XVI of France, 7, 156, 163.

Louisiana, ceded by France to
Spain, 1–4; Miralles reports on,
16–17; possibility of British possession discussed, 40; ordinance
of June 9, 1793, regulating trade
of, 255; cession to France, 311.
See also Mississippi Navigation
question, Mississippi trade,
Boundaries, Kentucky separatists, Wilkinson.

Luisa, Queen, 170.

Luzerne, Comte de, French minister to U. S., 21.

Madison, James, letters cited on
Mississippi navigation question,

87n, 90n; advocates Kentucky
statehood, 133n.

Marshall, John, application to by
Wilkinson, 118.

Marshall, T. M. exposes Spanish
conspiracy to Washington, 136.

McGillivray, Alexander, importunities to Spain, 54–6; dissatisfaction at meagerness of Spanish
munitions furnished the Creek,
57; correspondence with James
Robertson, 140–2; accepts U. S.
pension and military commission, 176; accepts twice as big
a pension from Spain, 178.

Miró, Esteban, Spanish Governor
of New Orleans, anxiety re Indian allegiance, 57–8; interviews
with Wilkinson, 119–24; correspondence with Wilkinson, 134–
5, 173–4; with Robertson, 140–2,
143; transferred from Louisiana,
174.

Mississippi Navigation Question,
origin of, 2–7; Miralles reports
on, 15–16; Congress debates
question of instruction on, 18–
22; Jay's contingent offer to recognize Spain's exclusive rights
to, 26–7; offer withdrawn by
Jay, 28–9; in treaty of peace
with Great Britain (1783), 34–5;
Spanish arguments, 43–4; U. S.
claim to, analysed, 44–6; Jay-
Gardoqui negotiations on (1785–
1786), 71–3; effect of western settlement on, 73–4, 76; Jay's proposal to Congress to forbear use
of, 85; Congress debate on proposed treaty for forbearing use
of, 85–90; Jay-Gardoqui formula
for, 93; Gardoqui works on Va.
and N. C. delegates to relinquish claims to, 94; Washing-

ton and, 96–100; Floridablanca's proposed articles for, 103–5, 107; Spanish trade regulations for, 127–31; effect on Ky., 115, 116, 126, 136; N. C. and, 144–5; Jay's report to Congress (1788), 145–7; resolutions of Congress affirming U. S. claim (1788), 147; Short requests Godoy to declare it open, 239; Pinckney's proposed article for, 277; article in Pinckney's Treaty recognizing U. S. demand, 295–6; incompatibility of this article with Article III of Jay's Treaty, 296.

Mississippi trade, 131.

Mitchell, M., agent of separatists, 214, 217.

Mitchell's Map of North America, used by Jay and Aranda, 30, 34n.

Monroe, James, Jay reveals his project to, 84; smells a plot of Jay's supporters, 90; correspondence with Gardoqui from Paris, 241–3.

Montmorin, Comte de, French Minister of Foreign Affairs, agrees to transmit U. S. note to Spain, and advises U. S. to take Mississippi navigation, 155–7.

Morris, Gouverneur, opinion on Mississippi navigation, 18.

Morris, Robert, and bills on Spain, 325.

Muscle Shoals, Spanish fear U. S. occupation of, 282.

Muter, George, brief connection with Wilkinson, 115.

Nashville, Tenn., settled, 138.

Natchez, District and post of, 6, 309, 311.

Navarro, Martin de, Spanish Intendent at New Orleans, treats with Wilkinson, 119; endorses Miró's advice re Wilkinson, 124; memoir on defenses of La., 128.

Newfoundland fisheries, in diplomacy of American Revolution, 13, 18, 21.

New Madrid, Spanish post at, 123.

Nogales, Spanish fortified post near present Vicksburg, occupied, 178; a listening post for Kentucky, 304; given up, 311.

Nootka Crisis, effect on Spanish-American diplomacy, 151-2, 154, 156.

North Carolina, and western settlements, 137–45.

Ohio River, in suggested U. S. boundary, 31; extension of Spanish claims to, 63, 64; Washington's plans to connect with Virginia rivers, 97, 98; as boundary of proposed neutral Indian buffer state, 104; proposed boundary of western separatist state, 216.

Olivier, Pedro, Spanish agent among the Creek, 179, 182, 183.

Ordenanza de corso, regulates Spanish treatment of neutrals, 260.

Ordinance of June 8, 1793, re Louisiana trade, 255.

Panton, William, British trader licensed by Spain to trade with Indians, 56–7.

Panton, Leslie and Co., trading company, 56.

Pelzer, Louis, cited, 131.

Philadelphia Federal Convention, 88, 90, 95.

Philip II of Spain, 281.

Pickering, Timothy, Secretary of

State, says U. S. is against European entanglements, 240–1; arguments with Yrujo on navigation article of Pinckney's Treaty, 285–7, 309n.

Pinckney, Charles, speech in Congress opposing Jay's proposed forbearance article, 87.

Pinckney, Thomas, reasons for his mission to Spain, 209–10; news of proposed mission received by Short, 235; physiognomy pleases Godoy, 238; early career, 245-50; delay in leaving London, 250–1; instructions, 251–4; arrival in Madrid, 267; negotiations with Godoy, 267–84; and navigation article, 295–6; sketches of a treaty and drafts of proposed articles, 335–40.

Pinckney's Treaty, see San Lorenzo.

Pitt, William, ultimatum to Spain, 151, 154.

Pollock, Oliver, U. S. agent at Havana during Revolution, 332, 333, 334.

Portugal, 8.

Posts, on northwestern frontier held by British, 78.

Potomac navigation, 95, 97, 99.

Power, Thomas, carries pension to Wilkinson, 307.

Principe de la Paz, see Godoy.

Proclamation of 1763, adjusting colonial boundaries, 5-6.

Propositions for the President (see also Godoy), sent to U. S. by Godoy, 196–7; delivery postponed by Jaudenes, 211–17; delivered, 217, 271.

Randolph, Edmund, Secretary of State, conceives Spanish negotiation in complete stagnation, 209; and Jaudenes's delay in submitting Godoy's propositions, 212; apprises Short of Pinckney's mission, 235, 237.

Rayneval, French diplomatist, proposes western boundaries for U.S., 31–4, 103, 104.

Rendon, Spanish observer in U. S., 46.

Revolution, American, 7, 191.

Robertson, James, leader of Cumberland settlements, intrigue with Gardoqui and Miró, 140–3.

Rodney, British admiral, defeats De Grasse, 37.

Rumsey's discovery of mechanical device for pushing boats upstream, 98.

San Lorenzo, treaty of, 234, 281, 294–314; literal reproduction of State Department text, 343–62.

St. Mary's River, as boundary of Florida, 6, 19, 40.

St. Stephens, Spanish fortified post on lower Mobile, 309, 311.

Santo Domingo, 232.

Sebastian, Benjamin, and Spanish conspiracy, 115, 144; at New Orleans, 305–7.

Secret committee of correspondence, of western separatists, 214, 216.

Sevier, James, sent to Gardoqui, 140.

Sevier, John, leader of "state" of Franklin, intrigues with Gardoqui, 137–43.

Short, William, appointed joint commissioner plenipotentiary to Spain, 161–2; early career, 164–5; arrival Madrid, 168; reports Gardoqui's suggestion of alliance, 191; secret conferences with Gardoqui and Godoy, 219–29, 234–8; unaware of nature of Godoy's propositions for the President, 207–8; reports reaction of Spain to Jay's Treaty, 230; receives news of Pinckney's appointment, 235–8; believes U. S. unwilling to entangle itself in Europe, 240; crowded off stage, 244; protests Spanish spoliations, 266; advises Pinckney to take a strong step, 280; disappointed, he leaves Spain, 283; disapproves of Pinckney's treaty, 300; agent in paying off U. S. Revolutionary debt, 328–31.

Smith, Capt. Sir Sidney, burns French royalist fleet at Toulon, 199.

Spain, policy toward La. (1763–1783), 1–5, 119, 173; in American Revolution, 8–14; financial assistance to U. S., 10, 83, 103, 325–34; danger to, of American political ideals, 38–9; Indian policy, 53–5; 175–85; trade with U. S., 58–9, 83, 173–4, 300; proposed mediation between U. S. and Great Britain, 78; alliance with U. S. proposed, 77–80, 190–7; proposed mutual guaranty of territory with U. S., 83–4; maximum and minimum boundary claims, 67–70; proposed treaty with, 107–8; policy in American West, 126–48; and French Revolution, 156; invaded by France, 225; policy of alliance with U. S., 233; and neutral rights, 259–60, 298–9; spoliations by, 261–6, 341–2.

"Spanish" Conspiracy, 109–25. See also Wilkinson, White, Jaudenes, Gardoqui, Mitchell, H. Innes, Sevier, Robertson.

Spanish Council of State, deliberations, 103, 129, 202–4.

Spoliations, 261–6, 341–2.

Steuben, General von, proposal to Spain, 118.

Tennessee, pioneer settlers in, 46, 109, 137–8; separatists, 137–44; organized as state, 142.

Toulon, French royalist fleet destroyed by British, 199, 220.

Trade, Mississippi River, 130–1; Spain and U. S., 58–9, 83, 254–9, 300; Louisiana, 255.

Treaty of Paris (1763), 1–6; of Utrecht (1713), 5; of alliance, U. S. and France (1778), 9; of Aranjuez (1779), 14; of peace, (1783), 37–41; Indian treaties, with Spain and U. S., 46–58, 175–85; provisional treaty with U. S. proposed by Floridablanca, 103, 107; Anglo-Spanish (1793), 169, 187, 196; of Basle (1795), 219; of San Ildefonso (1796), 314. See also Jay's Treaty; San Lorenzo, treaty of.

Trumbull, John, 228.

United States, Spain's service in expansion of, 39; policy with Southwestern Indians, 46–53; trade with Spain, 58, 83, 254–8; and proposed Spanish mediation with Great Britain, 78; and proposed mutual guaranty of territory with Spain (1795), 78; and treaty with Spain (1795), 245–81.

Vergennes, Comte de, and Franco-American alliance, 9; requests

Congress to formulate peace terms, 18; conference with Aranda re U. S. western boundary, 31–5; and claims of U. S. and Spain, 35n.

Viar, Josef de, Spanish agent in U. S. and associate of Jaudenes, 160, 182, 183, 185–6, 208, 266n, 332, 341. See also Jaudenes.

Villiers, Capt. Baltazar de, Spanish officer takes possession of east bank of Mississippi, 64, 83.

Virginia, lack of government in Ky., 111; acts of Jan. 6, 1786, and Jan. 10, 1787, re Ky., 114, 131; change in U. S. Government annuls act of Va., 135.

Wallace, Caleb, supporter of Wilkinson, 144.

Walnut Hills, see Nogales.

Washington, George, agrees with Jay on Mississippi navigation, 89; letter to Henry Lee quoted by Gardoqui, 92; letters from Henry Lee on navigation, 95; gift of jackass to by King of Spain, 96; efforts to unite eastern and western rivers, 96–100; assurances, 128; Spanish conspiracy disclosed to, 136; takes up issue with Spain, 147; dreads British encirclement, 152; increased power of his Administration, 158; letter to Henry Lee, 159; Indian medals with his effigy, 184; and entangling alliances, 193; not sure of Kentucky, 210.

Washington's Farewell Address, 193, 240.

West, the settlement of after the Revolution, 46–7, 109–10; population of, 73, 85.

West Florida, 5–6, 40, 45, 63, 93, 104.

Whiskey Rebels, combination with western separatists, 214–17.

Whitaker, Dr. Arthur P., acknowledgments to, ix, 56n, 141n, 143n, 284–93.

White, James, tool of Gardoqui, confidential information to Gardoqui, 92; changes Spanish policy, 92, 108; idea of separating West from Union, 126; Floridablanca's instructions to Gardoqui re White, 127–8; schemes with Gardoqui re separation of Tennessee and Franklin, 137–42; petty trafficking, 142.

Wilkinson, James, early career, 110–12; in Kentucky conventions, 113–16; plot to separate Kentucky, 113–37, 143; plans to descend Mississippi, 118; at New Orleans, 121–5; memorial, 122–5, 129; trade with Kentucky, 130–1, 173–4; writes to Miró, 134; and Spanish pension, 144, 302–3; and Kentucky statehood, 173; continued correspondence with Miró, 173; with Carondelet, 175; plot resurrected, 233, 302–7; bill to Spain for services rendered, 303; southwestern posts delivered to, 311.

Willing, Capt., Spanish financial assistance to, 333.

Wouves d'Argès, La. colonization scheme, 127–30.

Yazoo River, as boundary, 6, 41, 104–7, 177, 178.

Yela Utrilla, Spanish historian, cited, 35n.

Yrujo, Marques de Casa, Spanish minister to U. S., 283, 309n.